THE GOD CONNECTION

the GOD Connection

BASIL GALA, PhD

Torchflame Books
Vista, CA

Copyright © 2024 by Dr. Basil Gala

All Rights Reserved. No part of this publication may be reproduced, stored in or introduced into a retrieval system, or transmitted in any form or by any means (electronic, mechanical, photocopied, recorded of otherwise), except as permitted under Section 107 or 108 of the 1976 International Copyright Act, without the prior written permission of both the copyright owner and the publisher of this book, except by a reviewer who wishes to quote brief passages in connection with a review written for insertion in a magazine, newspaper, broadcast, website, blog or other outlet. For information, address Top Reads Publishing Subsidiary Rights Department, 1035 E. Vista Way, Suite 205, Vista, CA 92084, USA.

ISBN: 978-1-61153-361-3 (paperback)

ISBN: 978-1-61153-364-4 (ebook)

Library of Congress Control Number: 2024914948

The God Connection is published by: Torchflame Books, an imprint of Top Reads Publishing, LLC, USA

For information about special discounts for bulk purchases, please direct emails to: publisher@torchflamebooks.com

Cover design: Jori Hanna

Book interior layout: Jori Hanna

Printed in the United States of America

To the memory of my beloved parents, Elias and Georgia Galanoudes, who gave to their three children all they had of material possessions and unconditional love.

CONTENTS

Introduction	xiii
Preface	xv

1. IS GOD REAL OR AN ILLUSION?   1
   1. The Notion of God: Opium or Elixir?   2
   2. Can You Contact the Cosmic Mind?   6
   3. Nietzsche: Antichrist or Prophet?   10
   4. William James: God Madness?   12
   5. Bertrand Russell: A Paradox of Faith   13
   6. Voltaire: God's Joker   15
   7. Freudian Slips   16
   8. Whitehead: There is a God Process   17
   9. The Socratic Way: Finding God with Questions   18
   10. Confucius Avoided Religious Confusion   21
   11. Spinoza Spinning a Logical God   22
   12. American Gurus Preached on the Self   24
   13. Dewey: Tools of Religion   25

2. SPIRITS ARE IDEAS   27
   1. How Was the Idea of Spirit Born?   28
   2. Our Souls are Personality Patterns   32
   3. Do Animals and Plants Have Spirits?   35
   4. Are Ghosts and Goblins Real?   38
   5. Do Spirit Media Tell Us the Truth?   41
   6. Do Dreams Bring Us Messages?   43
   7. Are Angels Creatures of Light?   47
   8. Do Out-of-Body Travels Actually Happen?   50
   9. Was Plato's World of Ideas an Illusion?   53
   10. Do Genes and Environment Determine Our Lives?   57

3. PROPHETS: MESSENGERS FROM GOD OR LUNATICS?   60
   1. What Is God According to the Prophets?   61
   2. How Do We Recognize God?   62
   3. Shall We Revive the Ancient Greco-Roman Gods?   65

4. Visions of Death from Gilgamesh, Zoroaster and the Egyptians	69
5. Moses: Fountainhead of Three Major Faiths	70
6. Does Christianity Lead the Way?	73
7. Is Islam the Message in Arabic?	76
8. The Buddha Guides Us to Nirvana	80
9. Laotse Shows the Way, or Tao	83
10. Zen Teaches Whimsical Enlightenment	86
11. The Mormon Tablets Are Sources of Discipline	90
4. GURUS, SAINTS, AND PATRIARCHS: ARE THEY CONDUITS TO GOD?	**93**
1. Teacher and Guru: Ladders to Heaven?	93
2. How to Be a Good Master or Disciple	96
3. Saints and Swamis Salvage Our Souls	99
4. How to Apprentice to a Sorcerer	102
5. Do Oracles and Prophesies Tell the Future?	105
6. Holy Men and Apostles Light Our Path	108
7. Popes and Patriarchs Guide the Faithful	111
8. Music, Mathematics, and Mysticism May Make Meaning out of God.	114
9. Four Great Christian Mystics Lead Us to the Light	117
10. God and His Sons Bring Salvation	121
5. THE FRUITS OF BLIND FAITH ARE ROTTEN	**125**
1. Bad Religion May Serve God Too	126
2. Insanity and Religiosity Often Go Together	129
3. The Cults Will Be with Us Always	132
4. Crusades, Holocausts, and Gulags Continue Today	135
5. Heretics: To Save Their Souls, Burn Their Bodies	139
6. Drug Heavens are for the Unwary	142
7. What Good Comes from Evil?	146
8. Evil: Is It Dysfunction or Possession?	149
9. Witchcraft and Human Sacrifices Appease Satan	152
10. Satan in Hell Watches Under Us	155
6. MEDITATION: GATEWAY TO HEAVEN?	**158**
1. States of Consciousness: A Stairway to God	158
2. Spirit Channels are Information Valves	161
3. The Faith Switch Turns the Light On	164
4. Is Your Soul Immortal?	167
5. A Cosmic Computer Saves All Events of Your Life	170

6. Judgment Day is Coming	172
7. Heaven, Hell, and Purgatory Are Ajar for Us	175
8. The Relaxation Response: A Road to Recreation	178
9. Meditation, Contemplation, and Hypnosis Work	181
10. God and Satan: Servers in the Spiritual Internet	184
7. GOD LIKES SEX	**188**
1. Yin and Yang Gave Birth to the Universe	189
2. The Earth Mother Makes the World Bearable	192
3. Why the Madonna and Virgin Birth Inspire Us	195
4. Most People Go the Way of All Flesh	198
5. Do Fasting and Chastity Purify Our Spirits?	201
6. Romance Can Bring You Closer to God	204
7. Zen Sex is Pure Love	207
8. Who Are the Dark-Eyed Virgins of Paradise?	210
9. Open Polygamy and Polyandry for All the People	214
10. Does the Soul Enter the Body at Conception?	217
8. CAN WE HAVE MORALITY WITHOUT RELIGION?	**220**
1. Social Consciousness Builds Morality	221
2. Is God Merciful and Compassionate?	224
3. Purity of Soul Is Our Armor against Satan	227
4. Widows and Orphans Need Looking After	230
5. The Poor In Spirit Point to Humility As a Path	233
6. Peacemakers Are Children of God	236
7. Thou Shalt Not Steal; Thou Shalt Not Lie	240
8. Heal the Sick and Injured	242
9. Good Works Pave the Way to Heaven	245
10. Listen and Pray to the Lord of Love	248
9. HOW TO EXPLORE YOUR SUBCONSCIOUS MIND	**252**
1. Delve with Freud into the Subconscious	253
2. Let Us Revisit the Relaxation Response	256
3. Hypnotic Trances Can Lead to Greatness or Gloom	259
4. How to Be Enthusiastic Like a Gifted Genius	262
5. Cross over the Razor's Edge Without Getting Cut	265
6. How to Reach Deeper Levels of Meditation	268
7. Use Different Types of Meditation to Advantage	271
8. Follow the Drug Path at Your Peril.	274
9. How to Survive and Thrive on the Forbidden Planet	277
10. Coming Home to God	280

10. FINDING YOUR COSMIC CONNECTION	284
1. An Evolving God and Heaven Watch over Us	285
2. This Oscillating Universe Gave Rise to God	288
3. Travel in the Fourth Dimension	291
4. Going beyond Space and Time	294
5. Linking up with Infinite Intelligence	297
6. Mysticism and Reason Can Work Together	300
7. God Follows the Non-Interference Principle	303
8. We Are Spiritual Senders and Receivers	305
9. Does God Need Us Humans?	308
10. Let Us Recapture Our God Connection	311

ADDITIONAL ESSAYS

1. LIFE AFTER DEATH	317
2. LEVER AND LOGIC: MASTERING THE UNIVERSE	323
3. DOES THE LAW OF CONSERVATION OF INFORMATION HAVE IMPLICATIONS FOR IMMORTALITY?	327
In Search of Meaning	327
4. CAN SCIENCE BE A GUIDE TO MORALS?	331
5. GOD IS THE GREAT INVESTOR (AND WARREN BUFFET IS HIS PROPHET)	336
6. ON CHARITY AND RUTHLESSNESS	341
7. HOW TO BE AN ANGEL	345
8. ON QUALITY	352
9. MIND OVER MATTER	358
10. BLESSED BE THE STRESSED	363
11. THE PRICE OF MASTERY	365
Moderate versus Great Effort	366
Finding our limits	367
Training for growth	368
Changing behavior	371
The cause of stress illness	372
The feedback loop for growth	372
Solitude and isolation	374
Acute stress, chronic stress	375
Healing from chronic stress	377
Struggle and Transformation	379
12. ON DEATH AND DENIAL	382

13. PRAXIS: THE ART OF VIRTUOUS ACTION	389
14. LIFE: IS IT A PHYSICAL SYSTEM, OR IS IT MORE?	402
15. IS CONTEMPLATION THE ULTIMATE ACTIVITY OF A HUMAN?	407
16. IS CONSCIOUSNESS AN ILLUSION?	412
17. DEFEATING DEATH	418
18. ON NON-REDUCTIVE PHYSICALISM	432
19. THE FIFTH FORCE	437
Why Call Life a Force?	437
Is Life Beyond Our Understanding?	440
How We Feel Life	441
The Zoticon Particle	442
Death and Transfiguration	443
Life is an Organizing Force	444
Love and Hatred	445
20. WHAT TO DO ABOUT GAIA?	447
21. THE UNIVERSE OF PERFECTION	451
Afterword	457
Bibliography	465
About the Author	469
Index	471

INTRODUCTION

The God Connection is a philosophical treatment of both good and unsavory aspects of religion written for the educated layman. It is written in simple and direct language and embodies scientific insights as well as inspirational passages.

This book points out to you the evils of corrupt religious practices, while it instructs you in sound mystical experiments. *The God Connection* is a personal adventure into spiritual thought and meditation, complemented with scholarly research of the histories and achievements of great religious movements worldwide.

PREFACE

Dear Reader or Browser,

You are probably wondering now whether this book is a polemic against your religion, a deviant view of God, therefore a heresy, or an apology, which justifies faith and tradition as seen today. Perhaps you have picked up this unpretentious volume at a bookstore and are skeptical about its sticker price; it should be stacked with the dusty volumes at $2 for two, you think.

You may also be wondering whether you will be offended or preached to until you have dozed off. I hope to do neither, but you may catch me lecturing, which is what I did for many years to glassy eyed students at the University. I am now approaching ninety-two and retired from that line of work, thank God.

This is a philosophical volume on religion, quirkier and more personal than most such treatments of God. My version of the Truth includes some technical and scientific sprinklings of computer science, which was my discipline for the PhD that I hold from the University of Southern California.

I was born and raised in Greece near Athens and attended high school at Athens College, a Greek American preparatory institution that is attended by many of the Greek elite and many scholarship students like me. I was baptized and indoctrinated in the state church as a Greek Orthodox Christian. The Greek Orthodox Church, which was established by St. Paul, Saul of Tarsus, just a few years after Christ's crucifixion, is like Roman Catholicism from which it split several centuries later in the Schism.

Greek Orthodoxy follows a very strict religious discipline. The Madonna is worshipped with ardor as the mother of God and the source of Divine Compassion. My mother was on very intimate terms with Madonna; she used to pray to her nightly, calling her mother of mothers. As a child I attended liturgy every Sunday and sang with the Church choir. On weekdays I ran after every passing black-robed, bearded, ponytailed priest with a top hat to kiss his hand and get his blessing.

My dad, a bank manager, was a free thinker and agnostic. He died seventeen days after celebrating his one hundred years of age. The nearness of death had not stimulated any sense of faith. He lived with me in his last year when his main interest was his next meal. Then food started tasting bad to him, and he died of malnutrition. I lost my mother in 1997 to dementia and finally congestive heart failure at age ninety-two. When Mom and Dad argued, usually over money that she overspent, she called him an infidel. I do not recall Dad ever saying bad things against religion, and in all his lengthy life he had never done anything unethical; rather he had gone out of his way many times to help others. He had been Christian in practice without the dogma.

As for myself, I went along with the prevailing faith, unquestioning. My first exposure to atheism came from my brother, two years my senior, when I was about thirteen years old. We slept in the same bedroom, and there was a period when he kept me up half the night with his talk of religion and his doubts about what the priests taught us in church and school.

Later, in high school, it was the custom for the science students to bait the priest in the class for religious catechism which was mandatory every semester. These fellows were bright, well read, and vicious. They could quote readily from Nietzsche, Russell, Lenin, and other atheists.

Every Church teaching was held up, in their view, to the bright light of reason and the class roared with laughter as the poor priest squirmed and wiggled desperately trying to get his point across. Finally, he would get so exasperated, he would declare, "This is how it is; you have to answer correctly in your tests, or I will fail you." I believed this and answered properly and got an A.

Thus, I graduated with honors and left for the United States to study engineering. With a free ticket on SS *Homeland*, tourist class, I stood on the deck and waved to my family on the dock. My poor little mother, dressed in the traditional black dress of the middle-aged Greek women, was in a torrent of tears but I did not care. I was going to America to become learned, rich, and famous. For a year I attended engineering school in Raleigh, NC, then dropped out to become a traveler, occasional worker at a variety of trades, and a would-be writer for the next six years.

These were adventurous years for me, with frightful difficulties and privations mixed in with occasional happiness. I remember the beginning of this odyssey in a rented room in Chicago. I was working as a bus boy. One Sunday afternoon in the summer of 1954, after a short nap, I experienced a feeling of complete peace, tranquility, and joy. Also, the certainty that no matter what trials and suffering lay ahead for me, I would be all right in the end, and I would eventually succeed in life and be happy.

Five years later, in 1959, I had an intense religious experience; it was very confusing and erratic. I thought I had connected with God and gained vast insights about the Universe and Nature. One of my numerous visions was of planes crashing into skyscrapers, with red flashing flames. It did not seem so serious a matter. I was in the minds of the pilots, firmly believing that this whole show was unreal in a world of illusion and the real world was beyond. I decided that my experiences were not on firm mental ground. I picked up an old volume on college algebra and started sharpening my logical tools again.

I reunited with my mother and brother who had by then also immigrated to the United States, and with their help I was soon back in engineering school. I did well and received my first degree quickly. I devoted myself to rational thinking and for many years looked upon intuition and faith as things to be avoided.

Upon retirement as a university professor, I was financially independent, and I returned to my old love for the humanities and writing. I began a few books such as *The Anatomy of War, Machine Intelligence, True Manhood,* and other subjects that have interested me, which may yet see the light of day. But I settled on God as a philosophical subject because God has got to be the most fundamental of all issues.

What could be more basic than religion to a human being? Religion attempts to answer the questions "Who am I or what am I? What am I doing on this earth? Where am I going? How should I behave to do the right things? What is the meaning of Life?" For many years, I had sought the answers to these questions in scientific studies of evolution, animal and human behavior, history, physics, and cosmology. The clues were there but not any answers. Science does not supply any ethical guidance; it is impartial to good or evil. It is a tool, like a knife, which you can use to carve your food or your enemy.

My questions were the most intimate and fundamental of all. What is the origin of the self, the destiny of the cosmos, and the relationship of self to Nature and human society? What should be my principles of living, my relationship to leaders and prophets, my parents and ancestors? What is my connection to this entity people call God? Philosophy attempts to explore these questions in an impartial and rational manner. It is different from religion because it does not dictate the ultimate Truth. Some philosophers tend to be dogmatic, but in doing so they violate the spirit of philosophy. A philosopher should be a cool-headed observer and thinker. He or she must consider and sometimes accept opinions other than his or her own and even opinions opposed to his or her own. This is also science, but science is not speculative and tends to be strictly rational. Philosophy is allowed to be more intuitive. Philosophy should not create Gods or spirits and should not be involved in rituals and ceremonies. The offerings of philosophy do not require faith, but only reason and good sense. Emotions are felt by the sound philosopher but are not allowed to cloud the clarity of his or her thought.

Preface

Gradually this time, without emotional turbulence, I had a new awakening. Many fears I had held since I was a boy went away. Aging, illness, accident, and death itself ceased to be worries for me. I took care of my safety out of love of life and not fear of death. I now have an inner peace and tranquility that stays with me amid disasters; people remark about my calmness. I find pleasure and fulfillment in doing simple tasks. I have enjoyed looking after my aged parents, my young daughters, and other relatives that can use my help. I invariably sleep well, and if awakened, I quickly return to sleep. I have been a happy man for many years now, and each birthday that comes to me makes me happier. I cannot claim complete illumination, but I feel I am approaching it steadily.

I feel that I am reaching for the light. I am not sure exactly what that means, but I'll share my feelings and thoughts with you in this book on the philosophy of religion. This is not a dispassionate analysis only but also a personal quest. I am a member of the Unitarian Universalist Fellowship in my community. Its ten basic beliefs are such that I can accept without violating my sense of reason. I also attend the Greek Orthodox Church on special holidays and festivals. I want to have faith because I can see what wonderful things faith can do in changing people and the world for the better. At the same time, I am opposed to religious dogma and the sentiment "You are not of my Faith! You are an infidel who will burn in Hell for all eternity!" I see much evil, insanity, or plain idiocy in some religious groups. A prime example is Osama bin Laden's al Qaeda. And I find the scenes of television evangelists and their faithful to be the most hilarious comedy works around.

This is where I come from. What follows are my best offerings to you, dear reader, from a man who has never stopped searching and thinking about the basic questions of existence, and who will not cease to do so until death.

1
IS GOD REAL OR AN ILLUSION?

My father, named Elias, after the Hebrew prophet, was born to Greek Orthodox parents living in Kiutahia, Turkey, in 1899. He followed the faith of his people until he grew up to become a tall, thin, young man with a high forehead and eyeglasses, a young *logios*, intellectual and literary. He read Plato, Aristotle, Nietsche, Schopenhaur, and Bergson, published stories and articles in Smyrna magazines, and along the way, lost faith in what the priests taught. Elias remained dryly kind, compassionate, and charitable all his life but stood aside in the practice of religion. He declared himself an agnostic, non-believer.

"Infidel!" my mother Georgia called him when she was mad at him. She was born and raised in Sampsous, Turkey, of Greek parents, and was short, plump, and ebullient. She was a devout Greek Orthodox like her mother before her.

My parents were living in my house in San Diego, California, when death came to them. They had argued and scolded each other for seventy years. At ninety-two, Georgia suffered a massive heart attack and was gone in two months. To the end, she praised God and fought for her life. I would take her for rides in the San Diego countryside, and she would look up at the pale blue sky, the setting sun, the greenish-brown hills, and galloping ocean, sigh deeply and say, "Oh God, you've created everything with infinite wisdom."

Elias remained detached from God and grew increasingly isolated as his friends died and family scattered. In the end, he lost interest in his favorite books, classical music, and food. He died two years after Georgia, in complete indifference and perfect health, refusing steadfastly all nourishment. "I'm tired. I want to sleep," he kept saying to me. He was one hundred years and seventeen days old. It was one in the morning, and I was away from home. My daughter, Elizabeth, went to check on him because she heard a strange sound from his room. She took his hand, and he opened his eyes, looked at her without saying a word, and stopped breathing.

1. The Notion of God: Opium or Elixir?

Are you an infidel? You may come across ideas in this volume to change your mind and consider spiritual values. Are you a true and unquestioning believer? Be prepared to open up to doubt and thoughts other than what you've known all your life. You exist now, and you experience love, hate, sunrise, and sunset. But where did you come from, and where are you going at the end of your life? Like my father, perhaps you believe you go out like a puff of smoke to be extinguished forever, or like my mother, your faith tells you there's an afterlife for you with God. Both outcomes are true, and what occurs at death depends on how you think while you are alive. Think of God and you go to God.

But does God exist? Great philosophers, Plato, Aquinas, Spinoza, Descartes, Leibniz, and many others have given us proofs of God's existence, but other equally great thinkers, Voltaire, Russell, Freud, and Nietzsche refuted these proofs. God does not exist as rocks and rills, animals and plants, planets and stars do. Otherwise, smart and learned people, scientists, would generally agree about God's existence as they do about natural phenomena; they don't. God is an idea, existing in our minds and hearts, and properly we should ask, is God a useful idea or a harmful one? The answer is that we may use God and related concepts of judgment, Heaven, and Hell, for good or foul ends, as we may use atomic energy to light our cities or destroy them.

God is the spiritual light of the world, and people have thought about God, death, and the afterlife for a very long time indeed. Over a hundred thousand years ago, even the subhuman Neanderthals buried their dead with tools and other objects for use in the next world. Every nation, every people, every tribe has a god or gods and numerous deities, saints, holy, evil spirits and other ethereal beings to worship or fear. Are all such entities products of superstition and nonsense or real and important? My life, experiences, studies, and thoughts reveal to me God, Heaven, holy spirits, and saints can be useful ideas—but handle with care. Yes, there is a god such that you can accept though you may be well-educated, smart, rational, and a free thinker. God and the moral code are ideas we have brought out to the universe from our hearts and minds to rule over lesser notions.

Communism was such a lesser notion. Is religion the opium of the people, as communists taught? The Communist Party banned God in the Soviet Union and set up the State and Stalin for all comrades to worship. Once Stalin mocked the Pope of Rome, "How many army divisions do you have?"[1] Now the Orthodox and Catholic Churches are shepherding the people again, and Protestants raise missions in Eastern Europe. Religion persists. Faith in God is common for most people in all cultures on Earth, but can we accept anything as true just because most people have believed it for a long time everywhere? Most people have always had erroneous beliefs. The vast majority among us don't possess sharp enough intellects to dig deep for truth and distinguish it from enticing falsehood. "They have eyes and see not, and they have ears and hear not,"[2] said Jesus, a distinguished teacher of the Western World. Insanity is also common everywhere on Earth; it's the price we pay for our complex brains. Do we ever accept insane

---

1. Winston S. Churchill, *The Second World War, Vol. 1: The Gathering Storm* (Boston: Houghton Mifflin, 1948), 105.
2. Ezekiel 12:2 (New International Version).

ramblings as true and proper thoughts? Yes, if the person we respect most, our leader, has overpowering charisma.

The leader appears almost supernatural. He seems connected with the Supreme Being. The connection sometimes leads him to madness and destruction. Have you read about the Reverend Jim Jones in Guyana, David Koresh in Waco, Texas, and Shoko Asahara, leader of Aum Shinri Kyo, in Tokyo? Many charismatic leaders lead their flocks and others to the slaughterhouse. Adolph Hitler, though not a declared prophet, had much in common with Mohammed and Moses. So did Alexander the Great, who thought he was God, and Napoleon the Great, who believed in his destiny and infallibility until he rode to Waterloo.

Disaster has been much of our human experience with the supernatural. Today, all over the world, the faithful are often bigoted. Every dedicated member of a particular church or temple thinks he has the connection to the true God. The believer is certain whatever a suitably draped priest, minister, or imam teaches is the correct moral code of behavior. Religion's teachings are not theories that can be disputed with impunity, as theories are treated in science. If you are Christian, Jesus was the true Son of God and the Light of Faith. If you believe in the Buddha, you are a pagan and a proper target for conversion. There is only one Allah for Muslims; Christians and Jews are infidels, although the Quran calls them People of the Book. Are you Irish Christian Catholic in Belfast? If so, you are despised by Irish Christian Protestants across the street. If you're an Arab Muslim Shiite, you can count on the hatred of Arab Muslim Sunnis. In the subcontinent of Asia, you divide people into India and Pakistan, fight wars, and assemble nuclear warheads because one side calls God "Allah" and the other "Krishna."

Yet if we examine all the major religions, below the superficial differences of cultural origin, we find the same essential premises, even the same basic methods of practicing faith. In describing the Quran, Mohammed defined it as simply the message of God in the Arabic language. The basic message: an entity or being operates in nature, unleashing creative or destructive forces, forming the world. This Great

Spirit is connected to us in our innermost minds, and in the material world of nature. When we are being truly creative in our works and we actualize our dreams, we project a force into the universe, uniting the spiritual world inside with the physical world outside. Approach this God inside you with caution, humility, and respect. Give God devoted service and adoration because true believers are rewarded and bad people are punished in this or the next life on Judgment Day.

For you, Jesus may sit in judgment of the dead, but in all faiths, people revere prophets, holy persons, and saints, gifted and trained in contacting the Great Spirit. Supposedly, prophets impart divine messages to the rest of us. Holy persons and saints are angels in the flesh. Moses was such a man, and he was close like a friend to Jehovah. The Old Testament includes passages where Moses admonishes God, with due respect, pointing out to Him how He should treat His people. Moses was very persuasive. Some centuries later, Jesus of Nazareth declared himself to be the Messiah—in Hebrew, the Son of Man: God in the flesh. God was in him and he was in God, being one with Him in spirit due to a very strong link between them. However, in moments of trial, he obeyed God's will, praying for compassion like the rest of us.

Prayer is one path to God, but in all religions, divinity is approached by means of the subconscious mind. The devotee perhaps fasts, remains passive, quiet, and is silent in a natural setting or temple. The holy man prays, meditates, chants in a repetitive manner the same words over and over, and enters a trance. A change in consciousness occurs. The brain waves change to the slower alpha or theta rhythms and inspiration is received. In this state of mind, prophecy gushes forth. "Come with me," wrote Walt Whitman, "and I will teach you the secret of all religions. You will not have to know God secondhand."[3]

Was Whitman a true or false prophet? Just as all societies have quacks, shysters, crooked cops, confidence men, and dirty politicians, they also have false priests. But even though much of religion, stained often with blood, is rough and dirty, in need of cleaning, cutting, and

---

3. Walt Whitman, *Leaves of Grass*, ed. Sculley Bradley and Harold W. Blodgett (New York: W.W. Norton & Company, 1980), 123.

polishing, what remains in our lives is the purest diamond of value and meaning. Religion is at the very core of our being. It embodies the moral code, which has no scientific or any other objective basis. Yes, religion can be good or bad, but somewhere in the wide spectrum of beliefs, I see luminous Hope: God, the Great Idea, lives and loves us.

Still, faith is not enough. We need proper guidance and understanding to arrive at our desired destination at death's door. We need a foundation for critical religious reasoning, a methodology for investigating matters of faith, for accepting or rejecting religious notions, whatever their source: a discourse on the method of religion, such as conceived for science by René Descartes and Francis Bacon in the seventeenth century. You and I, and other free thinkers, have a conflict coming on, looming larger each year, with oily barbarians and nuclear despots. It's imperative we prepare well our minds and spirits, as humanity floats ahead in the twenty-first century, to preserve the Earth and civilization and put out the fires of Armageddon before they spread.

Religion begins in the mind. Let us begin there also.

2. Can You Contact the Cosmic Mind?

Mind is the source of everything. Sure, knowledge comes from personal experience; every other bit of information garnered from others may only bolster or shrink our personal beliefs. I talk to you and I seem human, but am I? I may be only a computer program with some intelligence. Alan Turing, one of the founders of computer science in the late thirties, imagined the making of an intelligent program. The Turing Test of intelligence is one where judges type questions on a terminal for a computer program to answer. If the program leads the judges to think it is intelligent, then it is. The Loebner Prize, an annual competition that ran from 1990 to 2019, offered a high prize of $100,000 to the designer of a program the judges couldn't distinguish from a real human in a Turing Test. Smaller awards were given for the most human-like programs, but the $100,000 prize was never claimed.

Descartes wrote: "I think; therefore, I am."[4] But what is mind? Humans have many minds, perhaps legion, but we'll discuss four: the conscious verbal, the conscious silent and creative, the subconscious, and the cosmic mind of unlimited power. I can connect with the Cosmic Mind because I have experienced contact with it, and you can too. The next step is realizing this God within your mind.

But before you realize God, you have to contend with the four or more minds in your head. Residing in ten billion neurons and innumerable connecting fibers in furious electrical activity, your minds may not be in harmony with each other. They may bicker, fight, and sometimes come to blows one against another, causing you grief and making your life a mess.

First, most widely accepted and recognized, is your ordinary verbal awareness: your consciously logical mind. The organ for this mind is the left brain and the speech center. Words segment and categorize reality. Verbal terms both define and limit. Their use simultaneously empowers and restricts conscious thinking. Feelings, emotions, and sensations normally associated with this state of awareness participate in decision-making and focusing attention to the external world. This is the province of the pragmatic and analytical reasoning that does most of your routine work. Your survival depends on it. Don't put this mind to rest while driving, flying a plane, or operating a harvester.

Your second mind, in the non-verbal right hemisphere of your brain, is the creative and artistic mind. It's conscious also, but silent. Silent thinking is not restricted by language. It doesn't classify impressions and doesn't break them down into their component parts. This mind is not a surgeon, but a sculptor. Feelings, emotions, and sensations are associated with this mind also, but they're focused on the gestalt or the whole of experience rather than on parts of it.

Both the verbal and silent minds communicate through an information channel with a vast area of functioning: your third, subconscious mind. Your subconscious mind is more than 95 percent of the

---

4. Descartes, *Meditations on First Philosophy*, trans. John Cottingham (Cambridge: Cambridge University Press, 1986), 17.

total, and those who can harness its powers wield a vast superiority over the rest of humankind. It's the third mind. It has a complicated structure and carries out many functions. Clearly, the automatic operations of our bodies are controlled by it: breathing, heartbeat, reflex responses, endocrine gland secretions, the parasympathetic system, and responses to fear, anger, and other strong emotions. In emergencies, such as combat, accidents, and environmental threats, it carries out the necessary actions for a chance at survival. These are basic, primitive, animal functions. Yet some of the highest creative tasks are also performed subconsciously. Great scientific, artistic, and religious breakthroughs are conceived in the subconscious and often revealed in dreams.

When Sigmund Freud and others explored the subconscious and wrote about it, they were often ridiculed. They were psychiatrists and their concern was with mental illness caused by emotional trauma buried in the subconscious. To them, the subconscious was a source of trouble, not a cornucopia of ideas and powers. Today it seems incredible that anyone can doubt the existence of the artistic mind or the subconscious. We can observe these minds functioning in ourselves and in others easily, as we can observe the curvature of the Earth from a high mountain. The loci of these minds in the brain can be seen in CAT scans, surgeries, and probing. Consider bicycle riding, driving a car, or doing any task well learned and automatic. Most of our skilled, professional, daily work is done at the subconscious level, allowing the conscious mind to focus, select material, decide on what to do next, allow for new information, and to open the channels of communication to other minds and the environment.

Our subconscious mind, a powerful central processing unit, is programmed by our conscious mind or by others through verbal, visual, auditory, or olfactory signals. We now know how influential television and other media can be in shaping our subconscious attitudes and opinions and even in galvanizing us into action. Parents, friends, teachers, politicians, and religious leaders all can put us in a hypnotic and receptive state and program our subconscious mind, even when we are unaware—especially then—of their influence. Subliminal persuasion is effective because you're drugged and don't know it; then you buy the product.

The fourth mind is vast and largely unexplored by humans. It's cosmic, universal, and supra-conscious. It's infinite intelligence. Freud didn't find it and called it a great illusion. He was not looking for it in the right places. Is the Cosmic Mind part of your own mind, or is it elsewhere, yet you can tap and use it? Is it established through a connection with God? Many great men and women have felt so and have attributed their achievements in science, music, poetry, literature, or religion to inspiration from God, rather than to their own powers. Homer, Mozart, Descartes, Shelley, Tolstoy, Shakespeare, and many other creative persons believed in their Muse.

Today many people are turning to a belief in God or at least the spiritual world: some in the traditional ways of our religions, but others in new or foreign ways. The new practices include Transcendental Meditation, crystals, pyramids, flying saucers, aliens, and other omens. I'm reminded of the many prophetic tools of the past: animal guts, birds, bones, teacups, and hand palms. You may think this stuff is absurd, and I am inclined to agree with you. But let's remember what's important in these practices: not the props, but the person using them.

The way to the Cosmic Mind is via the subconscious, and you can reach it with meditation—an altered consciousness after you have achieved mental tranquility and put out the chatter of trite thoughts, sensations, feelings, and emotions. This universal mind is perhaps the collective of all sentient beings, on Earth and elsewhere, including the spirits of the dead and of others not yet born. What is our individual mind, after all, but the collective function of about ten billion neurons?

How can we know that this fourth mind exists? Many bright and well-informed people argue against it. Yet we infer the existence of the Cosmic Mind from cases like those of Mozart, Mendelssohn, Homer, Saint-Saëns, Shakespeare, and many other geniuses. Some say Homer and Shakespeare did not exist as individuals because no individual could have produced such great works; actually, many poets wrote under the same name. But a group of people does not produce a masterpiece. This is an individual creation, although congenial companions may stimulate the creator. The cosmic connection is with an individual soul and self, not with a committee, as Ayn Rand told us in *The Fountainhead*. If information is produced that we cannot attribute to environment or heredity, what can be the source?

In some individuals, there sometimes arises a sense of the Divine, the source of ideals and moral principles. Such notions don't spring from our animal evolution, from nature with tooth and claw, but from our future as a species or a cosmic source very far away, but also very close. The exact mechanism responsible for the transfer of this spiritual energy is not clear to science. EEG waves have been suggested, but these are very weak and quickly disperse. Interference from other transmitters quickly overwhelms them. Brain waves, not yet detected, emitted at a special frequency may be the medium of spiritual talk.

Such a frequency occurs in the vibrations and palpitations of love, visiting every human bosom, including yours, I'm sure. Love is an inner experience that cannot be explained rationally. God is also an innermost experience, not a thing to be observed outside of you, and you connect with God when you contact the Cosmic Mind inside your own self. With love, your emotional link to other people and things, you change your narrow self to the Universal Self, and you become one with them—and with the mind of God. Such was the experience of many philosophers who broached the ideas of God and the Cosmic Mind. Philosophy, literally love of wisdom, is the search for meanings. The search has given birth to religion, science, and the arts. Almost every major philosopher has embraced religion and ethics, but some philosophers have attacked religion and common morality. Now, as a way of introducing you to my ideas, I will assay a few atheists, then some agnostics, and finally some believers.

3. Nietzsche: Antichrist or Prophet?

A dedicated romantic who studied ancient Greek literature and art, Friedrich Nietzsche, 1844-1900, German Swiss, was a professor of classical literature at the University of Basil, Switzerland. Today he's best known for a pseudo-prophetic work, *Thus Spake Zarathustra*, the life and sayings of Zarathustra, or Zoroaster. In *Zarathustra,* Nietzsche created a messiah for our times, a fiery personality, a prophet plunging himself into an obscure spiritual adventure. Much of this epic poem is a diatribe against the Christian God and Judeo-Christian ethics of meekness and compassion for the weak and unfortunate. With this work and others along the same lines, the philosopher thoroughly aroused the animosity of the religious establishment. Nietzsche became the Antichrist. But he was not just an enemy of Christianity. In *Zarathustra* and other books, Nietzsche offered us the ideal of the superman: a superior species of man who embodies our best virtues and strengths, who seeks life fulfillment in this world rather than in the Hereafter.

In other major works, such as *The Will to Power, Beyond Good and Evil,* and *Ecce Homo,* this philosopher pursues a shocking, almost insane, ethical course. Among other sins, he displays a pathological animosity and contempt for women. Nietzsche, sick from syphilis, died insane at age fifty-six. Yet, his writings have had great influence because they helped liberate Western thinkers from the limiting doctrines of Christianity.

Liberation from Christian thinking led other Western philosophers to consider atheism, agnosticism, and Eastern mysticism as alternatives to established doctrine. Nietzsche influenced the Nazi ideologists, who set up their own ideal of a superior race: Aryan Germans. Hitler's *Mein Kampf* praised *The Will to Power.* With brutal force, Hitler and his followers achieved many stunning successes for a decade until they finally destroyed themselves and Germany. Never underestimate the power of a bad idea.

Ideas, good or faulty, affect young people most critically. When I was in Athens College preparatory school in Greece, each year (along with ancient Greek and Latin), we had a course on religion mandated by the government. It was Orthodox Christian dogma and practice taught by a priest in civilian clothes. Our class was divided into a classical section, filled by those destined for the liberal arts, and a science section for those, such as myself, planning careers in science and technology. Science attracted the best and brightest students then. We were well-read and arrogant. We argued with the priest in religion class constantly and delighted in tearing down the basic tenets of the Christian faith using arguments from Nietzsche's works. The little priest fought valiantly for the Orthodox Faith and Church, but he was outwitted and outnumbered. He squirmed in his seat, and at last he would burst out, "This is how it is. Get it down right in your exams or fail the course." We got it down right to get a high grade, but among ourselves, we admired Nietzsche for his pride and passion. He had been a rebel against the prevalent Christian doctrine in Europe as we were. The man with the lean, high forehead, big, drooping mustache, and fierce eyes was our hero. He had preached against weakness and conformity.

Nietzsche castigated Christians for their love of humility and their concern for the weak, sick, and poor; he praised great and noble actions and the growth of a superior race of men, preaching a new religion for the strong in body and intellect. In our youthful arrogance, we fancied ourselves as noble, superior, and brilliantly intellectual, and we fell for Nietzsche's faulty ethics. Yet, Nietzsche's works were sources of mental challenge and freedom for us in our youth. We drew courage from his passionate writings to look at age-long doctrines and say, "Nonsense!" Then we could go on from there to our own thinking about the world and moral behavior.

4. William James: God Madness?

More respectful than Nietzsche's criticism of Christianity, in *Zarathustra*, but just as penetrating, was William James's *Varieties of Religious Experience*. William James, 1842-1910, Harvard psychologist and philosopher, wrote a detached and objective volume on religion. His book includes many written accounts and case histories of mystical experiences among Christians. James offered as examples George Fox, founder of the Quaker movement, and Joseph Smith of the Mormons. He recognizes both Fox and Smith as geniuses, imbued with "exalted emotional sensibilities, authority and influence."[5] Some of James's stories, however, deal with cases of weird religious behavior because of mental dysfunction and illness. Extreme preoccupation with God, sin, Heaven, and Hell can lead an unstable person to mental illness.

William James's book was an authoritative work on religion as practiced in the West. He was neither an atheist nor a passionate Christian. He tried to be objective, to have an open mind regarding religious experience. James wrote that those with psychic experiences firmly believe we inhabit an invisible spiritual sphere from which help can come in times of need; our souls are mysteriously one with a larger Soul whose instruments we are.

On the other hand, the case histories he described of people possessed by the Spirit often reveal schizophrenia, manic depression, and paranoia. It's hard to come away from reading *Varieties of Religious Experience* without feeling some skepticism about religion. And yet, something important and meaningful happens in such religious experiences as James described. Most people are conventional believers who follow patterns of faith handed to them by others, patterns established by custom and retained by habit. But a few rare persons go to a source deep inside the mind and make their own discoveries, upsetting the established dogmas and the officials who administer churches. These are the mystics who carve spiritual pathways, create new myths and illusions, burn at the stake, die on the cross, give rise to legends, and set up cults, which sometimes end up becoming major religions.

5. Bertrand Russell: A Paradox of Faith

William James dared to describe religious behaviors like psychological case histories. Bertrand Russell, a mathematician and philosopher, opened up the subject of God to logical scrutiny. In a collection of essays entitled *Why I am not a Christian and Other Essays on Religion and Related Subjects,* he shocked his generation with his personal discovery

---

5. William James, *The Varieties of Religious Experience: A Study in Human Nature*, ed. Matthew Bradley (Oxford: Oxford University Press, 2012), 31.

of atheism. Incidentally, he followed that up with another shocker, *Marriage and Morals*, advocating in the nineteen thirties that unmarried couples live together while in college. This cost him a job at City College, New York, at a time when he needed the salary. Russell dealt with Christianity and Christian ethics, not with hostility, like Nietzsche, but with contempt. He also expressed sadness that, unfortunately, this religious dogma was beneath his intellectual height, although he admired its moral teachings. His moral character sprouted as a paradox because he hopped from faith to atheism and back to belief in humanism.

Russell was a liberal, though descended from British nobility. (He acquired the title of Earl after the death of his elder brother.) In his entertaining *Autobiography of Bertrand Russell*, he wrote of his early upbringing as a dutiful Christian by a deeply religious aunt and uncle, his parents having passed away when he was a child. That was a somber faith steeped in the guilt of original sin and the hope of salvation. Russell, a brilliant young man, liberated himself from this dogmatic burden with the help of agnostics such as Voltaire, Marx, and Freud—and the discovery of sex. His intellectual stance towards faith closely parallels Freud's in *The Future of an Illusion*. Religion is not bad; it's mistaken and will be swept away as civilization and science advance.

In spite of his stance on religion, Russell's popular books, from *A History of Western Philosophy* to *The Conquest of Happiness*, won him many readers and money. *Principia Mathematica*, an important early work, had, by his own admission, burned him out for other serious projects. Unless you indulge in symbolic logic, you will not find this book readable. But you will love Bertrand Russell's crystal clarity of thought and subtle wit in his popular books and essays. His writing prowess finally won him the Nobel Prize for literature at an advanced age. And he won recognition for solving an important logical enigma, now known as Russell's paradox.

He was a paradox too, being a moralist, but an atheist too. At eighty-nine years of age, Russell was still fighting for peace and sanity—and being jailed for civil disobedience. He was a true Christian in spirit if not in thought, indulging himself with mystical sentiments in his essay

"A True Man's Faith" while scoffing at mysticism and extolling reason in "Mysticism and Logic." Russell denied God while being securely connected to the Word.

6. Voltaire: God's Joker

Voltaire, 1694-1778, was a rascally philosopher with a long, sharp nose often stuck into the inflated egos of French nobles and churchmen. He lived and wrote his pamphlets and stories fomenting rebellion before the American and French revolutions. Poking fun at the political and religious rulers of France got him jailed twice and finally exiled for twenty years. He's best known for *Candide*, with the unflappable Dr. Pangloss, a caricature of the German philosopher Leibniz. "All is for the best,"[6] Pangloss would declare after pirates captured him and his student Candide. Then the pirates sold them into slavery, and they were tortured. "Divine Providence will provide,"[7] Pangloss would say, glossing over every misfortune and atrocity that fell on the woman Candide loved. Voltaire laughed in this way at religious stupidities.

Voltaire tied many atrocities to the kings and cardinals who ruled people's lives with leaden hands in France and the rest of Europe. On occasion, the princes of the Church and those of the State would feud, as in *The Three Musketeers* of Alexandre Dumas, but normally, they cooperated in suppressing all dissent.

Democracy, however, born in ancient Greece and forgotten for a thousand years, flowered again in America with the 1776 revolution against the king of England. In France, democracy for the masses meant freedom from hunger. "Give us bread!" was their cry, but for intellectuals like Voltaire, democracy meant freedom to think and speak openly without fear of punishment. It was a time when the poor and powerless were allied with free thinkers, students, and intellectuals. King Louis XVI and Marie Antoinette dropped their heads in the guillotine, and the people were free. After a brief period of parliamen-

---

6. Voltaire, *Candide*, trans. Theo Cuffe (Oxford: Oxford University Press, 2008), 5.
7. Voltaire, *Candide*, 5.

tary rule, anarchy and terror came to France and rebellion against the yoke of religion. High-ranking churchmen were usually the second sons of titled men and members of the nobility. So the common people attacked the Church as well as the nobles. People chased liberal ideas with abandon until from the ranks of the military rose Napoleon Bonaparte to defend the Republic at first, later to force a new order and a bloody empire. Voltaire rightly mocked such arrogant pretenders to authority as Napoleon.

Voltaire also laughed heartily at the religious idiocies of his time. Moreover, he fostered liberal ideas and humanism in his day. He judged much of the prevailing religious thinking as nothing but superstition, the stupidities of the masses exploited by their rulers. Voltaire's weapons against the establishment were wit, ridicule, and reason. In his writings, he mined the comic views of life, death, and the divine. With delight, he punctured the claims to wisdom by his contemporary philosophers, such as romantic Rousseau and equable Leibniz. He wrote of Rousseau's penchant for a return to the natural state. Rousseau would have him walk on all fours, but due to advancing age, he was unable to comply. Voltaire was brilliant and often arrogant but kept his mental balance with wit and humor.

7. Freudian Slips

Sigmund Freud, 1856-1939, is known as the father of psychoanalysis. As a medical doctor and psychiatrist, Freud delved into the recesses of the subconscious mind using hypnosis to treat his patients. Many of them suffered from hysteria, a ready diagnosis for frustrated women in those days when men ignored their sexual needs, their intellect, and their aspirations. Freud was also an intellectual, a philosopher, and an atheist. He viewed the subconscious mind as a cauldron of psychoses and the idea of God as simply the product of sick minds. In his book *The Future of an Illusion*, he predicts, with the progress of science, the demise of religion and such mass hallucinations. A century has gone by since his book came out, during which science has made huge advances, but faith in God remains prevalent.

In Freud's view, religion answers some universal needs of mankind: the need for certainty in a chaotic world, the hope of protection from life's vicissitudes, the promise of everlasting life in the face of death's inevitability, and moral guidance in the bewildering passage through the social labyrinth. God is simply an inflated father figure, idealized into an entity of immense power, wisdom, compassion, and authority. The procreator of the believer's family is thus transformed into the creator of the universe, the lawgiver, and the administrator of reward and punishment at the end of life, if not before.

To his credit, though, Freud was the originator of good ideas regarding the subconscious mind. Id, superego, and libido have entered mainstream language in psychological fiction of stories, novels, and plays. Such concepts were impressions of the soul from clinical practice and were tinged by the negative aspects of mental illness. Yet Freud was much admired by many of his contemporaries and other practitioners in psychoanalytic arts, attaining the rank of a cult figure clothed in the prestige of medical science.

Much of what Freud taught in his medical research, psychiatrists have abandoned in their practice. And psychoactive drugs have largely replaced hypnotherapy and psychotherapy, which required many years on a pricey couch. In spite of some shrinkage, however, Freud remains a towering figure among serious investigators of the human spirit, mainly because of the philosophical and psychological interest he stimulated in the subconscious mind.

Yet Freud slips on religion; faith in the supernatural continues to blossom, and today we know natural healing can provide much comfort to disturbed souls. The priest smiles at Freud's id and libido, blessing men, women, and children with peace after confession, enabling them to face the tumult in their lives without couch and Prozac.

8. Whitehead: There is a God Process

Alfred North Whitehead, 1861-1947, an English mathematician and philosopher of science who taught at Cambridge, England, for twenty-five years and at Cambridge, Massachusetts, for thirteen years, was Bertrand Russell's collaborator on the monumental *Principia Mathematica*. The son of an Anglican clergyman, an atheist he was not. But to Whitehead, God is an evolving process in the universe, not a constant and static entity as in the Christian dogma.

Whitehead believed that God is the source of what is of value in the universe, but not the Creator of the material world. He wrote, "God is the poet of the world, with tender patience leading it by his vision of truth, beauty, and goodness."[8]

God, evolving with us, leaves us free to choose between good and evil and moves us by persuasion only. This view of God appears in his books *Religion in the Making*, *Science and the Modern World*, and *Process and Reality*. Today, Whitehead is considered the father of process theology, in which God is process: not changeless and omnipotent but a growing and evolving entity like all living things, opposing the ever-increasing thermodynamic chaos of the universe.

9. The Socratic Way: Finding God with Questions

Socrates based his method on asking probing questions in searching for truth and virtue. Socrates (470-399 BC) was one of the main pillars of Western civilization and many of his contemporaries thought him to be "the wisest, most just and best of men."[9] In 399 BC, he was convicted for preaching against the Greek gods, corrupting the morals of Athenian youth, and punished with death. He could have escaped and gone into exile with the help of his wealthy students, but he chose to uphold the laws of his country and die in jail. According to Plato, his disciple and scribe, Socrates resigned his life by calmly drinking a cup of poison hemlock handed to him by his executioner while continuing a dialogue with friends and students until he became too numb and weak to sit up and talk. He left a legacy of his method: asking probing

---

8. Alfred North Whitehead, *Process and Reality: An Essay in Cosmology*, rev. ed., ed. David Ray Griffin and Donald W. Sherburne (New York: Free Press, 1978), 346.
9. Plato, *Apology*, trans. Benjamin Jowett (New York: Dover Publications, 2002), 21a-22e.

questions to find truth, honor, and God. Having found God, Socrates extolled a just Heaven and the immortality of the human spirit.

The talk that Socrates enjoyed to the end was about duty, the value of the soul, and immortality in a world beyond ours. Socrates, an ugly but impressive lion of a man, as shown in a statue by Lysippus, was never formally educated and worked as a stonemason until he inherited some money from his father. Thereafter, he devoted himself to raising a family with Xanthippe and teaching philosophy. Like Buddha, Jesus, and Mohammed, Socrates did not put his teachings into writing, and we know of them from Plato's works. Socrates' students and disciples were scions of the Athenian elite, as was Plato, the founder of the Academy in Athens, which remained a center of learning for hundreds of years until Christians came to power with Emperor Constantine.

Plato wrote the dialogues of Socrates, *Euthyphro*, *Apology*, *Crito*, and *Phaedo*, having to do with the trial, imprisonment, and execution of Socrates, mainly to expound his mentor's ideas about the meaning of life and death. Socrates was never satisfied with stock answers in the quest for wisdom. He went about the agora of Athens, posing sharp questions to all with a claim to certain knowledge and thus deflating egos. He made enemies. In the evenings, he gathered his disciples in one of their homes and spent the night drinking watered wine and having philosophical talks. He was poor and lived in a small cottage with his wife and children, but he did not charge his wealthy students money, just wine, for their lessons.

Socrates often told his students God spoke to him. He called God his demon, meaning a spirit, not something evil. His friends often caught him in a frozen trance. He would sit without movement for hours. It could have happened on his way to an important occasion, which he completely forgot, or to a meeting with friends who missed him. When questioned about this strange behavior, he would say God had been talking to him, and he had to sit down and listen to what God had to say.

In Plato's *Phaedo*, Socrates asserts his belief in God and the immortality of the soul with complete assurance. He argues his case in detail. Since everything in nature is cyclical, if death follows life, then life must follow death. The soul, not being perishable, survives death and returns to a new body or joins the gods in Heaven. The soul is rewarded by God for doing the right things in life and enters a better world on its next pilgrimage to Earth.

Socrates describes God's Heaven, the ideal world, as he saw it in a dream. Everything in Heaven is well-ordered, bright, tranquil, and perfect in the magnificent company of the gods and other immortal spirits. In this life we sometimes see shadows of this ideal world, like those on cave walls. We look at the outside, the material world, with our senses, but we look at the spiritual world through an inner eye.

Socrates offers this lecture on the ideal world while in jail. His students urge him to let them bribe the guards so he can escape. He responds that he cannot violate the laws of his country. These laws protected and nourished him for seventy years, and he will not disobey them at the end of his life. He says, "I ought to be careful that I did not lose the eye of my soul."[10]

This eye we all possess allows us, should we choose to use it, to look at Heaven "through a glass darkly."[11] What Socrates sees is a world of material objects and energies, but beyond these, spiritual forces or principles, attributes, ideals, and harmonies—like the harmony continuing to exist even after the lyre that gave it sound has been destroyed. Such is the nature of the soul: it lives on after the body has decomposed. The soul goes to a higher earth, free of disease, suffering, and death, where the righteous exist forever in peace and joy. The wicked are punished in Hell and are then sent back to Earth to live in animal bodies until they prove themselves worthy of human form once again.

To support his ideas on God, Heaven, and the soul's immortality, Socrates says, "I believe in the authority of one who shall be nameless."[12] He continues with a vision: The Earth is round, vast, and a hollow place. We look up from the earth to the heavens as fish look at the surface of the water. A better place exists in the heavens for people

---

10. Plato, *Phaedo*, trans. G.M.A. Grube (Indianapolis: Hackett Publishing Company, 2002), 99c-100a.
11. 1 Corinthians 13:12 (King James Version).
12. Plato, *Phaedo*, trans. Benjamin Jowett (Oxford: Clarendon Press, 1892), 108d-109b.

these all other consequences by means of logic, such as in Euclid's geometry. He also wrote political treatises and sided with the losing party in Holland. Thus, he was put in jail. Given his delicate constitution, he became chronically ill with tuberculosis and died shortly after his release from prison.

Before dying, however, Spinoza had developed a following among some bright people. He was offered the chair of philosophy at the University of Heidelberg but refused the job to keep his moral independence. He influenced and was influenced by the famous French mathematician and philosopher René Descartes, thirty-eight years older, one of the founders of modern science. Spinoza also influenced Leibniz, the great German philosopher. They knew each other personally, although Leibniz denied this friendship to protect himself from dogmatic Christians.

Everyone who got to know Spinoza closely loved this gentle little man with the giant intellect. Spinoza never married, like nine out of ten great philosophers. He spent his days spinning his yarns of divine logic, culminating in his epic volume *Ethics*. It's a huge structure of definitions, lemmas, propositions, theorems, and corollaries, but not like any mathematics you were taught in school. It drove away all but the most dedicated scholars of religious philosophy. And yet, there are many gems of thought in this and Spinoza's other works that shine like pure diamonds.

Spinoza begins from Plato's thought of the Ideal World, which is Heaven, and proceeds to establish its validity on the basis of pure reason. God is simply a collection of attributes having to do with virtue. His existence can be proven. Individual souls are aspects of the Divine Being. Any person can look within and find God. We're all capable of communion with our Creator. Finite things are defined by their boundaries, but God has to be outside of space and time—infinite. We partake of that infinity when we merely acknowledge our connection to Him. He wrote, "The mind's highest good is knowledge of God."[19]

---

19. Benedictus de Spinoza, *Ethics*, trans. George Eliot, ed. Clare Carlisle (Princeton: Princeton University Press, 2020).

Spinoza's concept of God, however, is not only logical but also includes emotional content. The Spirit that descends to us is a blend of exalted feelings as well as information. The passions have self-preservation as a goal, and pleasure itself is good, but the wise man's self-seeking is different from the common egoist's: the wise man doesn't feel separate from others or the world. A man is in bondage if he's an unwilling part of the whole but is free through the understanding of himself and his passions. Love of God is a union of thought and emotion, and this love must hold the chief place in the mind.

12. American Gurus Preached on the Self

Emerson, Thoreau, and Whitman: This triad of American writers had much in common. During the turbulent Civil War, they knew and influenced each other. All three were intuitive thinkers who admired Asian philosophy at a time when the West thought Asia had little of value to offer. They preached self-reliance, self-realization, and revelation through our inner selves.

Ralph Waldo Emerson was born first and lived longest (1803-1882). He was the prophet of self-reliance. "Trust your own self" was his motto. You may judge his writing as obscure, but his message was unmistakable. Have faith: rely on yourself and divine guidance. Be confident, and you will achieve your just goals. Emerson was the first man of any importance to recognize the genius of Walt Whitman, who is regarded by most literary critics as the greatest American poet.

Walt Whitman (1819-1892) was born on Long Island, and his father was a farmer and carpenter. Whitman worked as a journalist and later in life subsisted on meager sales of his *Leaves of Grass,* which Emerson praised. During the Civil War, he worked as a war correspondent and nurse. He was probably bisexual and never married, living with his mentally retarded brother.

Whitman spent many happy days wandering along the beaches of Long Island—Paumanok, as he called it by its Indian name—

composing his immortal poems. "I loaf and invite my soul,"[20] he wrote. Whitman was a mystic and as close to the Source as anyone ever was. "Come and stay with me," he wrote, "and I will show you the source of all religions."[21] In *Song of Myself*, he wrote, "And I know the spirit of God is the brother of my own."[22]

Whitman's spiritual brother was Henry David Thoreau (1817-1862), who wrote *Walden* and was a naturalist, essayist, and poet. Like Emerson, he had read Asian philosophers and the Hindu scriptures. He liked living alone on the shore of Walden Pond in Concord, Massachusetts, in close communion with unspoiled nature. Thoreau was strange and childlike, enthralled by the ways of birds, squirrels, ants, and the changing hues of the waters. He was also a mystic, a beautiful writer, and an astute thinker on matters of the spirit. His advice for those searching for peace of mind: "Simplify, simplify, simplify!"[23]

That was clear enough, but Thoreau's writing was sometimes obscure like Emerson's because his goal was obscure—that of self-realization, getting close to God, as it has been for many holy men in the East. Thoreau wanted to search for God directly without intermediaries, and he looked for the divine in his own heart.

13. Dewey: Tools of Religion

John Dewey, 1859-1952, an American educator and philosopher, was an inspired apostle of pragmatism. His theory about ideas was that ideas are tools for solving problems and dealing with our environment. If we get a thought and it's of no use to us, we can ignore it or even declare it untrue. Similarly, we can accept as true a notion that proves practical in solving vital problems. God, Heaven, Judgment Day, and other religious doctrines may not exist in the world outside our brains, yet we accept

---

20. Walt Whitman, *Leaves of Grass* (New York: Penguin Books, 1959).
21. Walt Whitman, *Leaves of Grass*, ed. Sculley Bradley and Harold W. Blodgett (New York: W.W. Norton & Company, 1980), 123.
22. Walt Whitman, *Leaves of Grass: The Death-Bed Edition* (New York: Modern Library, 2000), 35.
23. Henry David Thoreau, *Walden*, ed. Bill McKibben (Boston: Beacon Press, 2004), 63.

them anyway because they can help us improve our minds and behavior to survive the shocks of life.

Thus, Dewey liberated himself from conventional religion but remained faithful to the morality of the Christian Church. Jesus was asked, "How shall we know who is the true prophet among all the false ones?" "By their fruits, you shall know them,"[24] he said. For example, consider the consequences for the German people of their trust in the prophet Adolph Hitler. How about herbs and acupuncture? If they work—never mind how—it's hard to argue against them. Similarly, doctors routinely prescribe medicines and therapies for their benefits, often not knowing how they work.

What works is the approach to knowledge by John Dewey. Who can know the truth? If we are on the right side of the booby hatch, we know how to behave in accordance with truth and justice. If we survive danger, we possess a kernel of reality. Because when something works, it ties in somehow with the universe as it is. What we call reason is nothing but our habitual way of thinking. To break new ground in any field of knowledge or invention, we become irrational, but we cannot ignore the results that follow our thoughts and actions.

---

24. Matthew 7:16 (NIV).

2

SPIRITS ARE IDEAS

My mother, Georgia, a vivacious woman in constant motion unless at rest, charmed nearly everyone with her warmth and love of life. In her thirties, she suffered from kidney stones, and I remember her crying out in the bathroom with pain. She thought she was dying soon from the stones or some other dread ailment and often told us, "Don't cry for me when I'm dead. I'll be with you in spirit."

As a child, I adored my mother, and when she was not at home for a few days, I'd mope around the house depressed and go into her closet to smell her clothes hanging there with her lavender aroma. Often, I had nightmares about her death, her lying on a bed cold and white and still. I'd cry in my sleep with anguish, tears streaming down on my pillow, and say over and over, "I will light candles for you, Mother, and keep them lit until I die too."

One day, when she was thirty-three years old, my mother passed the kidney stones in the bathroom and was never again bothered by them or any other serious illness until she became ninety-two. She was small but tough and strong, a packet of energy all her life, rearranging heavy furniture around the house, working as a dressmaker and fitter, and doing all household chores. At ninety-two, she was complaining of chest pains, and I took her to the doctor, who found no problems with her heart. The next morning, she was hurting again, and I took her for a car ride to a coffee shop because rides usually relieved her anxiety. She didn't touch her coffee or bagel, her favorite food, and I took her home. Outside our door, she suddenly slumped in the car seat, clammy and greenish, wheezing strangely. I called 911.

She had suffered a massive heart attack, which destroyed 80 percent of her heart function. She was in and out of the hospital for the next two months, desperately fighting for her life, but when I took her there for the last time, she looked at the building and said, "I'll never get out of here alive. I'm glad to be the first in my family to go, so I'll not see any of you dead." It was summer, and my sister Alice was vacationing in Greece with her husband. Mother said, "I'll never see my little girl again." A few days later, she was in bed at the hospital, wires and tubes attached to her body, wrists tied to the bed so she would not pull out her life support connections, and she begged me to release her. In tears, I told her I could not.

I kissed her forehead and held her for a moment. Shortly, she was cold and still, that vibrant something gone out of her,

forever.

1. How Was the Idea of Spirit Born?

Seeing life and death up close, it's natural to imagine and believe something animating and vital leaves the body at death. This vital something has been called soul, spirit, or ghost. Consciousness has left the body and gone to some other place or nowhere, depending on your beliefs. People have claimed they have seen something like a spark, radiant emanation, or fog rise up from the body that has just died. Others have said the body weighs a few grams less after death. Scientists haven't measured such things to this day. They have not detected the graviton that mediates gravity either, although theoretical physicists believe it exists. Similarly, I hold the belief supported by its usefulness and some observations: human spirits exist and are imperishable.

I used to think it absurd to believe consciousness survives death. Consciousness, the self being a function of the brain, ceases when the brain decomposes. Consider the instance when you're hit hard on the head: just a concussion makes you unconscious. Or, when you're anesthetized for surgery, some chemicals enter your brain, and time disappears until you're awake. When you sleep deeply, you wake up in the morning, and the night is gone. In sleep the brain only partially shuts down to recharge its batteries and rest—and consciousness, except for some dreaming, disappears. How much more so must be the case in the sleep of death!

Death, then, is the end—or is it? You take up a sledgehammer and give a good whack to your computer. The lights go out, and the humming stops. The hardware is a total loss and the operating system has vanished. Has it really? What about the master copy of it in the Microsoft vaults in Seattle, Washington? Clearly, a spirit is not a computer program, but Heaven has kept a copy somewhere for all eternity if worth preserving.

Now, if a spirit is preserved after the body is dissolved, and thus, it's never lost to the universe, then where was it before it entered the body in the first place? Religious theory says it was at the origin: with God. Was then the spirit the same thing, or was it a different version? It must have been different and less perfect; otherwise, what would have been the point of the pilgrimage to Earth and the trials and tribulations of life?

If it's hard to imagine a loved one lost completely to extinction, it is harder still to believe our own self totally gone. Your mind refuses to accept the finality of death for your personal consciousness, even in battle when many of your buddies are dead, stretched still in their blood or in a hospital with a terminal illness, next to others departing without a whimper in a drugged state.

We see then how the notion of the eternal spirit has come about. When people or animals we love, wonderful beings, die, we cannot imagine that they're gone to nothingness. For me, anyway, watching in old movies Fred Astaire dance, Judy Garland sing, Jimmy Stewart act, and Lana Turner turn on her baby blues, it's hard for me to believe these talented beings are really, truly, totally, and forever dead.

So, primitive man, seeing his beloved mother, father, mate, or child on the ground, pale and cold, covers the body with stones and sees the beloved's image moving and speaking in another world, the world of spirits. He lays a bunch of wildflowers on the grave and kneels, his head bent down. The spirit of the ancestor will live in his memory and that of his children. Ancestor worship, such as in Shinto in Japan, may have been the first religion. It's a very valuable idea because the wisdom of our ancestors continues to guide our steps after they've shed their flesh.

It makes sense then to believe in the existence of spirits, your own included. It's a comforting thought to those the loved one left behind, they also to follow soon to the next world. If (in your mind) you have an imperishable part that continues after your body has decomposed, you can get through some nights with easy sleep and be rested the next morning for the day's struggles. So belief in spirits is a useful notion; but if you start talking to the dead, seeing ghosts, and angels, don't be surprised to find yourself looking out from the wrong side of the monkey bars—you've carried the idea of spirit too far.

Hindus carry the notion of spirit far indeed in their religious philosophy. They believe consciousness permeates the cosmos and resides even in a clod of dirt, the lowest form of life. We know today that the clod is packed with millions of microorganisms. A spirit after death moves to another body with a new birth, and a really evil person ends up as a clod. But overall, there is an evolution and ascent to better bodies until the self eventually, after innumerable lives and much "dharma" discipline along the way, reaches Nirvana: perfection and union with God.

This is all very interesting, but what do we know for sure? Very little! Omar Khayyam wrote, "The rose that once has bloomed, forever dies."[1] Others have likened a life to the flame of a candle. When the candle has burned out, the flame is gone and that is that. But human

---

1. Omar Khayyam, *The Rubaiyat of Omar Khayyam*, 1979 reprint Collins Sherriffs ed.,

consciousness is not a candle flame, a simple form of energy. The spirit is a complex package of information and feelings, a package worth protecting and preserving.

Preserving by whom and to what purpose? Should you wish to leave an observation outpost on a promising planet, would you leave something made of metal and plastic that can corrode and fall apart? Should you wish to leave an important message, would you carve it on stone and have erosion wash it away? No, you would put it in self-replicating, self-preserving units that scatter and cover the surface of the planet. Floods, earthquakes, asteroids, fire, and volcanoes strike and destroy many of these carriers, but enough survive and continue to replicate the message. The message is in the human genes and it's an enduring message to the future.

That's the lesson from the science of evolution, begun by Charles Darwin with the *Origin of the Species*, which is seen by priests to be in direct conflict with religious scriptures. Priests say that man could not have been created by God and also evolved from lower animals. Certainly, our bodies have evolved from ancient apes and before that from primitive mammals and before that from primitive reptiles, amphibians, fish, and one-celled organisms. We see a replay of that evolution in the human fetus. We know today that life's drama began over four billion years ago on the scalding surface of the early Earth—not four thousand years ago, as religious scholars have claimed.

Yet, it's possible that the human spirit was created more recently, about one hundred thousand years ago, with the emergence of Homo sapiens, installed in a body that had evolved from animals. The installation was an act of genetic engineering. You rightly say these notions are nonsense and no evidence supports their validity. I would agree with you, except that our most precious ideas also have no other reason for their existence but their usefulness.

Spirits exist as the integral, the differential, the square, most inventions of mathematics, and so many other ideas like justice, freedom,

---

trans. Edward FitzGerald, ed. George F. Maine (London and Glasgow: Collins Clear-Type Press, 1979), stanza XXVII.

and democracy also exist because we in civilized societies value them in our lives. Their existence is taken for granted because we're also accustomed to them. We conceive them, and because we exist in nature and we're part of the universe, with these ideas, we build material objects that express them: monuments, machines, and other artifacts, and social institutions, libraries, parliaments, and hospitals. Thus, ideas exist, and so do spirits we project into the world, including the Great Spirit. What flows from the idea of God—compassion for the unfortunate among us, love for our fellows, and kindness towards animals—all exist because we bring them out from our hearts into the icy and fiery universe, previously indifferent to all our sufferings.

2. Our Souls are Personality Patterns

Something exists in living things or, perhaps, just in humanity: shining bright, imperishable, apart from the body, connected with God, part of the Divine Source, a mystical quantity, called the soul or spirit. Is this the personality of an individual? Is it a person's special and unique character? The soul is a pattern of energy, held together in a stable state by bonds that cannot be broken, preserved forever somewhere in this universe or elsewhere. As any of the particles of modern physics, equivalent to energy but not the same as energy, the spiritual pattern exists and continues its existence forever.

That is the religious theory. There are many versions of the basic theory, such as the Christian, Muslim, Hindu, or Buddhist. We'll explore some of these versions of the soul in the next chapter. For now, what do you think of the spirit as a tiny spark of light reportedly seen to leave the body at the time of death? Other people have claimed to have seen a kind of mist or small cloud rise up from the freshly dead body. But what about the persons who have suffered brain damage from age, disease, or accident? Did the spirit leave the body before medical death? The personality pattern is gone from what remains; it has already been salvaged and taken away by heavenly authorities.

That's because the thing of value in a person is his or her unique pattern, grown in a life of fruitful action from the nutrients of genes,

Spirits Are Ideas

training, and special experiences. Are identical twins one soul or two? Even identical twins differ from each other, as each has dealt with unique experiences to some degree and the Holy Ghost may have touched them deeply or lightly. Each one is of value to society and to God as a special person.

Individuality is what we value in great art, music, or poetry. That person's unique vision of the world, his or her fresh gift of perceiving the world, is rightly admired together with talent and craft. In a great painting or poem we look for the brilliance of a special style which cannot be forged and duplicated by a lesser talent. We look for genius and inspiration—for something divine.

But what is a personality pattern? A pattern is defined as an organization of elements, so that meaning and information is held in a kernel. A pattern can also be a collection of connected sub-patterns and thus have many levels of organization. Such is the human body, with its tissues and organs, and such is the spirit also. Such also are human populations: clans, tribes, nations, and species.

The individual pattern is a single signature, unlike any other, such as fingerprints, retinal patterns, palm lines, faces, and DNA. Your character is displayed there for the experienced eye to see plainly: your strengths, your failings, your history, and your destiny. Whatever your character may be, as a unique individual, you are valuable and cherished by God.

But does your spiritual pattern include specific memories from past lives? It can't because numerous painful or joyful memories from prior lives would be too disturbing in your current life or make it dull and stale. Using a computer analogy, the soul may be equivalent to the executive program, while specific memories are the data set operated on by the main program. Executable instructions are saved in Heaven's bubble memory, and stored data is deleted with the body's end.

Continuing our computer analogy, how does a computer engineer test a program? The validity of the program is proved by its operation with many different input data sets—a process known as simulation. A soul can be considered a pattern of instructions tested in a world of action for one or many lives. Each test and pain can transform the spirit into a better entity or degrade it. The blow which does not kill makes you stronger if you possess the right attitude. As in a game of chance, the outcome is always uncertain, and uncertainty is the essence of tragedy or comedy. So, the whole world is a staged casino, and all in it are actors and players.

Chance relates to the main feature of a pattern: it carries information. Information was defined by scientists, such as Claude Shannon, as the amount of uncertainty in a message. No uncertainty, no information! If a message is known and predictable, it provides no information. Now, the concept of information implies a sender or transmitter at one end and a receiver at the other. Both sender and transmitter are sentient beings, not devices; the devices simply modulate or transform the message.

Incidentally, information has the same mathematical formulation as the physical quantity of entropy, related to disorder in a system. Physicist Erwin Schrödinger has described the opposite quantity, negative entropy, or negentropy, as the main physical feature of all living things, especially humans. Negentropy permeates us, and we are sources of it as creative beings.

A creative human, like Archimedes, Jesus, Leonardo da Vinci, Albert Einstein, or you, is a special being that breaks down known, established patterns of thought or behavior and creates for a time a state of chaos. Out of the chaos, the creator designs new and surprising patterns that contain information. Every person in action reorders the universe in an area, small or large, and produces a new set of things, an interesting configuration of outcomes. Action waves spread in space and time, affecting everything and everyone, near or distant, even Heaven. Thus, we amuse God, preventing boredom from bringing down his twilight, as in a Richard Wagner opera.

Like Wagner or Mozart, we're all born with some potential for creative action, intimately woven with our basic personality pattern. You, too, are a slave of God, as in the parable of the three servants told by Jesus. Each was given a talent of money by his master: One buried it for safekeeping, doing nothing and thinking of himself as a good servant. The second one spent and wasted his portion. But the third worked it and made it grow.

Since you have a unique personality pattern, you contain deep inside your subconscious mind the possibility of living and acting in a special, creative way, enriching the world with fruitful action and imprinting your signature upon the universe forever.

3. Do Animals and Plants Have Spirits?

Valuable as the personality patterns of humankind are, those of plants and animals are also very precious. We don't know what the destinies are of dogs, whales, chimps, or a million other species on Earth. The same goes for plants. Some plants or animals may have a greater future than that of Homo sapiens—if we allow them to survive our growth and consumption, which leads to the destruction of their habitats. Also, plants and animals carry their own unique spirits, which we ought to respect, though we may eat their bodies to survive.

If, by any chance, I get to be one of the lesser philosophers, I would like to be known as the one who taught love and respect for animals and plants. I have cherished and loved them ever since I was very little. My attitudes towards all living things are those of a Hindu. I abhor the exploitation of animals. The commercial use of our fellow creatures will someday be seen with the same horror as the Holocaust.

But how can it be that animals and plants have spirits when they're so dumb? The ancient Greeks, also Hindus, American Indians, and other peoples have thought that animals are spiritual beings. To kill a living thing is a sin, and we must ask the plant or animal to forgive us if we must do it to survive. Never enslave animals created to be free as we are. Enjoy the fruit, nuts, and shoots of plants; spare the living entity if you can. It's less sinful. (Soon, we'll learn the ways of chlorophyll and synthesize the amino acids we need.) Live with the forest instead of killing it to build dead housing—food for termites. Use stone, brick, concrete, glass, plastic, and metals for construction.

The Greeks called the spirits of trees *dryads*, nymphs that lived in the trees. When a tree was cut down, its dryad cried out and left the land, and the land suffered. The souls of loved animals went to the next world with their masters. Anyone who has known and cherished a beloved pet knows that it had a soul worth saving, almost like that of a human. Plants and animals respond to fine music and a loving touch. They grow and thrive in the care of a person who loves them for themselves.

Because animals and plants on Earth have spirits, let's rethink our idea of mastering this world and all living things on it. We cannot continue to be the destroyers of life for much longer without killing our own species or totally degrading our quality of life. Let's be the caretakers of all beings on Earth. Trees and animals are brothers to us, and we are indeed their keepers. We have evolved together with them from the same origins, and we're all of us together in the web of life. Our destiny is to use intelligence to preserve this living planet, Gaia, before we venture forth to the rest of the universe. God will not allow us to move much further than this world unless we first learn to care for Gaia as Tristan cherished Isolde. Earth is Noah's ark now. The next planet we occupy will be another ark for our menagerie in case a comet demolishes this one.

We have a cat named Whiskers. My family calls him a fur person, someone human in a previous life, now living as a cat. He climbs onto my computer desk as I type this, carefully stepping around the keyboard. He looks at me with clever, knowing blue eyes.

When we adopted him, Whiskers was a mangy stray, full of worms, fleas, and ticks, skin stretched on bones. He came to the door to be fed with other neighborhood cats. He stood quiet, dignified, and apart from the others, waiting his turn at the food.

Whisker is courageous but cautious. A veteran of numerous fights, the king of his domain, he's adored by all the females in his territory. One time he brought food and birds he caught to a pregnant female that we called the welfare mother. When my daughter brought home some baby chicks, he chased them for a while, but after being scolded, he guarded them from other cats as they pecked in the yard until they were grown.

When I drive home, he knows the sound of my car and runs out to the driveway to greet me. "Hi, old boy," I say to him and pat him on the back. As I walk around the block, he follows me, sometimes running ahead a bit, other times following behind, especially when we approach dog territory.

Whiskers hates taking a bath or his medicine like all boys do. In the tub, he sits patiently, his eyes closed, but not fighting the occasion, completely resigned to the inevitable soapy water. To give him medicine, we don't have to force his mouth open. He takes it calmly but with the same mild protest of closing his blue eyes.

I could go on to give you more incidents to show that Whiskers does have a soul, but you know your own animal stories.

The least we can do, as the highly intelligent masters of this world, is strive to preserve our planet's plant and animal species and their evolutionary future. How can we allow the extinction of species around the Earth, which have taken millions of years to evolve? Can we ever, with all our genetic engineering, recreate a Siberian tiger and a panda bear after they're gone? Sure, mass extinctions broke out in previous ages, but these losses are increasing due to our negligence and destruction of habitats. If we have a role in Nature, it is to use our arts and sciences to prevent such extinctions, not cause them. Populations in the developing world are growing rapidly, and the rain forests are disappearing. The industrialized world, on the other hand, is consuming and polluting more each year with its wasteful ways.

I remember the green hills of spring in Greece, my native land: wildflowers on rounded hilltops, red poppies, chamomile, and thousands of other flowers filling the air with their scent. I wander these hills alone or with my brother and friends, picking flowers for my mother, climbing rocks smooth with lichen hair. Sheep and goats are grazing on the slopes. A shepherd walks by, a white newborn lamb bleating for its mother around his neck and shoulders. I sit under a pine tree and touch its rough skin, taking in its aroma of resin. I'm happy. The tree is alive: it touches my skin and knows me as I caress its coarse bark.

My brother and I climb a huge sycamore tree in a village square and lie down on one of its branches to rest, talk, and daydream. A breeze comes up, and the leaves whisper to us a magical story. Often we go to the sea away from town to a quiet beach with some mossy rocks to sit on and talk. We swim in the azure waters, crystal clear twenty or thirty feet down to the bottom, dotted with blue-green rocks, bright tiny fish, crabs, shellfish, and seaweed. We dive in and come up with starfish in our hands.

That's why the spirit out of my dead body will float around the Earth, crying and mourning over the desolation being done until my brothers and sisters change their ways. I will stay on this blue-white jewel of a planet and not go to Heaven or elsewhere until I see it sparkling again with health and beauty.

4. Are Ghosts and Goblins Real?

Ghosts are spirits that linger on Earth instead of going to Heaven, Hell, or Purgatory upon death. Sometimes, they are supposed to do that because they have been murdered or wronged in a serious way and cannot find peace in their graves. Goblins are evil or mischievous spirits; ghosts can be good, but they scare people out of their wits when they appear. Why are we going into this? You may think these are just old superstitions that educated and smart people, properly instructed in modern science, cannot possibly believe. This is the stuff of Halloween, you may say, not real. But let us recall the purpose of this inquiry. It is to explore in a more or less rational manner our notions of God and the spirit world and to evaluate these ideas for practical use. Ghosts and goblins are handy notions; they exist and can be put to use in your life.

For example, consider the Holy Ghost or Spirit. That is a very big concept in the Christian religion, being one of the trinity with Father and Son. It is one with God but a separate entity, as the Son is separate but part of God. Jesus said, "I am in God and God is in me."[2] Also, he said, "I walk in the light."[3] This is not a theological discussion, heaven

---

2. John 14:10-11, 20 (English Standard Version).
3. John 8:12 (ESV).

forbid. People waged wars in the Middle Ages over such questions, or they split their churches into two or more pieces.

The Holy Ghost is a very powerful and mysterious entity. It illuminates and instructs the disciples after the unfortunate demise of Jesus. After the Holy Spirit has visited them, the frightened followers of the Savior are energized and encouraged; they become fearless in the face of persecution, torture, and death, and they become apostles and spread the message all around the Mediterranean. So the Holy Spirit is more than information and more than a message. It's the vehicle of divine power and love.

We may deny the existence of ghosts, but they exist at the Haunted House in Disneyland. The laser phantasms are the concrete manifestation of Walt Disney and his disciples. Yes, I believe spirit entities begin in the inner world, but creative action releases them in the outer world, and there, these figments of the imagination can be studied and analyzed scientifically. Similarly, physical entities in the outer world are internalized in dreams and become possessions of the soul.

Who can deny the awesome power of Hamlet's ghost, the murdered king of Denmark, Hamlet's father? Palace guards see the ghost first in the night mists and bring Hamlet to talk to it. The ghost asks for revenge—not a Christian doctrine. Thus, Hamlet becomes an instrument of the Evil One. Deranged, he causes the death of many people: the guilty uncle and mother but also innocent Ophelia. If any man has ever been in contact with the spirit world, Shakespeare certainly was. The source of any genuine art is one. Shakespeare was clearly inspired by a higher source, and he, in turn, transferred the Holy Ghost to numerous painters, music composers, and literary artists who illustrated his stories and themes.

Do ghosts and goblins really exist? Something is said to exist, which has an effect on something else for good or evil. I remember my mother's bright spirit and her unconditional love for her family. No matter what a nasty thing I might do, her love for me was unwavering. I try, as much as is possible for a man, to be the same for my two daughters. I have a spiritual model that I follow and that is my mother's ghost. It has an effect, like a light that travels in space to infinite reaches.

Once, in a state of altered consciousness, I perceived a message coming to me, telling me I can live a normal life span, but my spirit can never leave the Earth. My spirit will move around the Earth forever like sunlight, following the cool darkness of my loved one's soul. It's a bargain I accept gladly with tears of gratitude. I will dwell like a hawk on a high mountain and glide down with the air currents to emerald treetops. I will dive deep into the cool waters of blue lakes and come up into the air, shedding sparkling drops of water. I will never know Heaven and will be with the Earth forever.

Maybe that is my destiny: to be a ghost on the Earth, protecting her from polluters, destroyers, and the careless. My punishment for the sins and arrogance of my youth: never to see other worlds, other lives, or the City of God.

Ghosts are injured spirits, and they can be frightful or kindly. But goblins are evil and do harm. The notion of evil spirits has been around for a long time in every culture. Are these bad spirits the souls of evil people, lingering on Earth, continuing their unpleasant actions? They are often thought to cause illness and mental distress. Witch doctors fling their colorful powders, shake their rattles, and order them out of the body of the possessed person. Jesus liked to drive the evil spirits into herds of swine. When the demons left the body of the insane, mental health returned. The sick stopped their contortions and screaming. They were at peace with their families again.

You can argue that spirits exist or not, but exorcism helps against goblins and other evil spirits. If spirits are creatures of the inner mind, good ones are beneficial, and bad ones cause damage. It's the old mind-body interaction, about which I will have more to say later on. The witch doctor, priest, or psychotherapist hypnotizes the patient with eloquent mumbo-jumbo and, with a channel to the subconscious open, reprograms the mind to reject the demons and accept the angels. So it is that the lame walk and the blind see, and true miracles occur. It doesn't work every time, of course, only occasionally; otherwise, they would not be miracles. There's a statistical, not a causal, relationship at work here. Quantum physics is in operation, not Newtonian mechanics.

5. Do Spirit Media Tell Us the Truth?

It should be clear to you that we are coming to the acceptance of spirits and such as real things in our internal universe, which can be externalized through the actions of people who experience them. Does Santa Clause, with his reindeer-drawn vehicle loaded with gifts, really exist? Yes, Virginia, he exists as long as there are men and women who overflow with love and generosity for children and needy people. Santa exists when there are joyful people who want to play the game of creating Santa and his helpers and the gentle comedy of shopping and giving freely. Spirit media speak to the heart and tell us beautiful truths, giving us shining wings of love.

There once lived among our people a kind, old gentleman—Santa Claus, St. Nicholas, or St. Basil in Greece—with rosy cheeks and ample belly, who loved children and animals and laughingly passed out presents to the poor during the holidays. This unique person left his immortal imprint in our psyches and on our culture. His character and his spirit live with us and for the generations.

Such spirits are known well by those who focus their awareness inward to the deepest recesses of consciousness. Such persons are the spirit media. Looking at a crystal ball, they can communicate with the spirit world and talk with the souls of the dearly departed. If they must be paid, it is because they need to eat, as you and I do. A group of believers are much help to the medium, all sitting around a table for the séance. The lights flicker and dim, the table begins to shake, the strange shadows move on the wall and the medium speaks in a weird, other-worldly voice. There has to be a bit of a show, after all, to create the proper mood.

Outward appearances mean little. What the medium does with internal events is what counts. The rest are props and aids to the inner search. The medium works with what she knows about the client's departed loved ones and what the client feels and thinks about the afterlife. The linkage is between the medium and her client.

In theory, the medium acts like a modem, linking us to the spirit network. The host computer is God, to be discussed in detail later in this volume. Before you start laughing at my simple-mindedness about my belief in spirits, think of your faith in Jesus, Mohammed, Buddha, Billy Graham, other evangelists and gurus, or whoever your Idol. Spirit media, all of them! Their function is to act as conduits to the world of sacred ideas. They are our guides in a strange and treacherous territory, where a misstep could lead to death, insanity, or hellish torture.

The best of the human media have traveled the road to the mountaintop and have come down whole, strong, and sane. They can be trusted to be our shepherds. Trust does not belong to the official in priestly robes or collar, it is not always the right of the famous person on television, and it does not belong to credentials, erudition, or a high IQ. A simple palm reader, crystal gazer, pyramid dweller, or card-turning gypsy may serve a lost soul better. The spirit medium needs to have a pure heart without guile but with love and knowledge of the great beyond.

The palm reader holds your hand open and studies the lines on the palm. They are unique and characteristic, just like fingerprint and retinal patterns. Then she looks into your eyes and analyzes your face. She listens to the tones of your voice, picking up subconscious signals about your personality, your desires, and your destiny. She's playing back to you. You hear your life story and your future in terms you can accept. You are told what you want to hear.

The ancient seer looks at the birds circling in the sky. The patterns they form have a mystical meaning. Then he takes the sacrificial animal and cuts open its abdomen. He carefully scrutinizes the entrails that come out. Everything in the world is related to everything else. Each tiny pattern is a hologram of the entire universe. The seer plumbs the depths of his inner mind, turns to his king, and gives his forecast of the coming battle.

The strange young man with the divining rod walks over the farm holding the rod in front of him. The rod dips sharply over a hollow near the oak tree. The young man turns to the farmer and points to the spot suitable for digging a well. Is it the rod that found the water? It is the young man's subconscious perception of where water may be. The rod is only a mental aid. It's a prop for the audience.

Sure, there are charlatans, fakers, and confidence men and women in these trades. These types do what they do only for the money. Your state-licensed doctor may also be a quack and your attorney a shyster. Spirit media deal with phenomena that are rare and experiments that are not readily replicated. Their methods work sometimes very well, but not reliably enough to satisfy scientific criteria. However, we cannot deny the benefits that we derive on occasion. If you get a cancer that is declared incurable by the medical establishment and your healer removes it, would you complain? The physician says to you, "This is a spontaneous remission." The healer says, "You have been cured by the grace of Almighty God." What's the difference to you when you are well again?

Here I am full of years, having escaped many disasters that clawed at my life, writing this for you. Who knows what intricate steps Nature or Nature's God has taken to allow me to continue living and finally approach you? Am I doing it for the money? I have enough, thank you. When the stomach is full, why eat more? I have enough money for my remaining years and for my children to give them a start. More would spoil their characters.

I find certain truths beautiful because my character, spoiled or not, was forged in the adversities of my youth: war, hunger, danger, deprivation, and a struggle for survival. Certain spirit media have whispered to me where to find my wings of love and meaning. When in the throes of revelation, I clearly see there's a plan, a design, a purpose, and a meaning to everything that happens. Events are tied together by invisible but unbreakable threads and there are no such things as accidents —only our inability to see the connections in the scheme of things. The spirit media are acutely aware of this and the genuine psychics among them have an uncanny ability to sense these threads and follow them to certain conclusions, spelling destiny.

6. Do Dreams Bring Us Messages?

When we sleep, the conscious part of our mind is switched off, but part of our brain is still active. A mother in sleep wakes up quickly when her baby cries in the next room. A portion of her mind is tuned to receive that message and prods her into waking. Numerous scientists and mathematicians have solved important problems in their dreams, such as the mathematician Poincaré, the chemist Kekoule, and many others. Sometimes inspiration comes when you are in a relaxed and meditative state while bathing, walking, or sitting by the fire, after intense and fruitless effort with a problem. The channel to the subconscious opens when you are relaxed deeply, in a dreamy state, and what was planted for some time may then come up to the surface and be fruitful or thorny.

Relaxing or meditating will not necessarily produce something of value. If the subconscious created nothing, nothing will be the outcome; if it has prepared trash, nonsense is what you get. In the computer field, we say, "Garbage in, garbage out." The subconscious is like the central processing unit or CPU. The conscious mind is like the input-output, I/O, or front-end computer.

Dreams, then, are only as good as the dreamer. It is usually worthwhile to listen to the dreams of a gifted person. Training and discipline are also vital in producing interesting output. Think of Walt Disney and his people dreaming. The dreams of an ordinary person may be extremely boring, as you well know. Your friend starts, "I had an interesting dream last night." You immediately excuse yourself to go to the bathroom and stay there for an hour. That doesn't mean your friend's dreams have no value. They reveal much about your friend. Secret hopes and anxieties vent in dreams, feelings that a person might deny having while awake. Freud and his disciples have made much of the interpretation of dreams in psychoanalysis, and Hollywood has made several memorable films based on Freud's theory of dreams, such as Hitchcock's *Vertigo*. Our interest here in dreams is the ancient one: their relationship to matters of the afterlife.

Do dreams have anything to do with the God connection? Are dreams sometimes messages from the spirit world? My late mother thought so. She often dreamt of her dead father or mother and she received instructions and warnings from them. In her last year, she had frequent dreams of her father, and she felt every time that he was appearing to prepare her for the next world. "He's going to come and take me across," she would say. She always felt very psychic and spiritual. To my father, an agnostic, she was just plain ignorant.

Warnings, messages, and instructions from God were often given to people in the Christian scriptures, both old and new. Quite often, it was an angel from God that appeared, God being too awesome and mysterious for a mere human being to behold, even in a dream. Abraham received a message from God, apparently in a dream, to sacrifice his only son, Isaac, at the altar. He obeyed God, violating parental duty and love. It is generally bad form to kill because of a dream. Fortunately, God retracted his command at the last moment. Isaac lived to grow up with his throat intact and had two sons. When he was very old and nearly blind, his son Jacob stole Isaac's blessing by pretending to be his brother Esau. Then he fled from his angry sibling to his uncle Laban, who had two daughters. Jacob eventually would marry both of them after many years of service to his uncle. Jacob slept on the way to Laban in a place called Bethel (House of God) and dreamed of a staircase to Heaven. At the top of the stairs was God, who told him he was to have descendants, as many as dust, and all the nations of the earth would be blessed through them.

Some people would argue about this, but certainly, the Jews have produced as many prophets in the West as the Indian nation has in the East. A most famous person among Jacob's descendants was Moses, much admired in the Middle East by both Arabs and Jews, and also Jesus of Nazareth, known in the West as the Son of God, the Messiah. Moreover, let us not forget the great prophet of physics, hairy Albert Einstein, and that of music, Felix Mendelssohn, with his revelations in "A Midnight Summer's Dream," beginning and ending with four notes full of the peace of Heaven.

Coming back to Jesus, when he was a baby, according to the Gospels, King Herod of Jerusalem wanted him dead and ordered his execution and that of all babies in Bethlehem. Then Joseph, the Virgin Mary's husband, saw an angel of the Lord in a dream. The angel instructed Joseph to flee to Egypt with Mary and the child. Thus, Jesus was saved, but not the innocent babies of Bethlehem. Divine justice is sometimes very subtle. Life is very precious to Christians, and then again, it is of little value compared to theological ends.

Today, we know dreams are essential to psychological health from experiments in dream deprivation. Dreams are accompanied by rapid eye movements (REM), and by monitoring them, a subject can be awakened when dreaming. Subjects suffer a stress syndrome as a consequence and feel unwell, although they get sufficient dreamless sleep. Dreams help us assimilate the day's experiences and allow us to express our deepest feelings in privacy. Our desires find form in dreams, and later, in the waking state, action may realize them day by day. It is useful to verbalize dreams and analyze them in order to clarify our innermost aspirations, but should we consider these dreams as messages from the spirit world?

If we assume there's a spirit world, our connection to it must be in our subconscious mind. Since when we are asleep, we are unconscious, the subconscious has free rein over our experiences and is properly guided during waking hours, it can lead us to the source of inspiration. In *The Teachings of Don Juan: A Yaqui Way of Knowledge,* Carlos Castaneda goes into the mastery of dreams by the wizard Don Juan. The point made is that dreams can be controlled, shaped, and guided even during sleep with the practice of certain techniques over a period of time. By shaping one's dreams with an effort of the will and patient training, a wise person can master one's nightmares, as well as one's deepest desires, thus guiding one's actions upon waking. And as one's actions go, so does a person's destiny.

While you are awake then, plant good seeds in your subconscious mind, so fruit-bearing vines may surface later. Saying your prayers before going to bed is probably a good start in the mastery of dreams. Another technique for probing the subconscious is to ask an important question with great intensity before bedtime. Then relax and let sleep supply the answer. As a child, I suffered from totally horrifying nightmares. Late in life, through faith and meditation, I've not had any bad dreams. My dreams now are usually sweet and pleasant, although they may sometimes get a little sad. Otherwise, my dreams are so unimpressive that I have no recollection of them upon waking. Nothing disturbs my sleep now, not even aging, loss of bodily functions, or approaching death. I am not exactly sure how I arrived at such peace of mind, but I will try to convey some of my spiritual experiences to you as I go along with this treatise.

7. Are Angels Creatures of Light?

Our inquiry into the God connection inevitably must lead us to angels, often depicted in the scriptures as messengers of God. Sometimes angels appear as ordinary human beings. They are mental constructs acting as our guides, saviors, and messengers of vital subconscious information when we face a crisis.

In the Quran, angels are considered to be below humans in status, and God orders them to kneel before Adam—an order challenged by Satan, for which defiance God banishes Satan to Hell, a nasty place. In Christian mythology, angels are superior beings, sometimes the souls of great martyrs and apostles, such as St. Peter. There is also a chief angel, Archangel Gabriel, who will sound the trumpets of Armageddon. He was the same Angel Gabriel who revealed the Quran or Recital to the Prophet Mohammad, an illiterate camel driver. The Quran is the holy book of Islam and the infallible Word of God for Muslims, a transcript of a tablet preserved in heaven. Through the grace of Allah, Mohammad was able to read it, memorize it, and later recite it to his disciples when he came out of his desert meditations.

Angels in human form were the two that are said to have appeared to Lot before the destruction of Sodom and Gomorrah. Lot received them as honored guests, but handsome angels that they were, the Sodomites wanted to rape them. So, Lot offered his two virgin daughters in exchange for sparing his guests: an intriguing ethical choice. The daughters, fortunately, were saved from a fate worse than death through the intercession of the angels, who, for a time, blinded those eager rapists.

Angels are often pictured with white wings, ready for flight to the heavens. Since their normal habitat is Heaven, which is in the sky, wings seem to make sense. But they are also spiritual beings and creatures of light, having no mass or weight, so wings are hardly needed for levitation. The wings are mostly decorative. Moreover, angels have arms in addition to wings as opposed to birds, so their evolutionary heritage presents a bit of a puzzle.

Gabriel, that famous angel again, appeared to Mary according to the Gospel by St. Luke. He informed her that God had decided to impregnate her with the Holy Spirit, and she would bear Jesus, the Messiah. Gabriel definitely wore wings on this occasion, according to most religious artists. Mary protested that she was a virgin and could not have a baby, but the angel reassured her that with God she could produce the King of Israel who would reign for all eternity. This story reminds me of the Greek legends of Zeus and his dalliances with gorgeous mortal women, such as Leda, on which occasion Zeus turns into a beautiful swan to seduce her. The swan played the role of the Holy Spirit.

This is all in line with the chauvinistic view that men think with their heads, while women with their wombs. Thus a man receives the Holy Spirit with his mind, intellectually, while a woman with her womb, heart, liver, gut—emotionally, as a rule. There are exceptions. Some men take a feminine approach, and some women take the way of the mind. This situation corresponds with the paths of meditation, to be discussed later. There is the path of the intellect, and there is the path of the emotions.

An angel is generally believed to be a creature of light, pure energy, without any material substance. Well, that's what a packet of information is. Light, made up of photons, travels at a speed of 186,000 miles per second. According to Einstein, time freezes up at that speed. So a photon, or a creature made up of photons, does not experience time: it lives in limbo for all eternity until it encounters an object. Then it causes the photoelectric effect—something also studied by Einstein in his early twenties for which he won the Nobel Prize. The effect is on the believer, Hebrew, Christian, Muslim, or Hindu, and the encounter is with a messenger angel, a bundle of coded data and instructions, such as found in fiber optics. Am I going too fast in religious science for you? That's okay. I am going too fast for myself.

In my life, I have never met an angel with wings or other paranormal characteristics. Angels are creatures of the imagination, like Mickey Mouse and Superman, part of the mythology of our culture. However, I have encountered several human beings who stepped in to guide me and help me along the right path at critical times, especially in my formative years in Greece. They were teachers, family friends, or relatives. My mother was more than an ordinary parent for me—she was my early spiritual guide. May her soul rest with God!

My father was always somewhat distant, but he did supply me with intellectual stimulation in my younger years and with the financial support for my education. Then there was a family friend who saw promise in me and supplied me with challenging books and encouragement. Several teachers at Athens College in Greece stood by me and gave me a helping hand with my struggles to study English, to be admitted, to succeed, and to come for university studies in America. Later in life, whenever I was in trouble, someone always came, an angel in human flesh, to stretch a hand to me so that I would come out of the bog.

After all, why should not some humans be like angels? If our spirit has the same origin and the same destination, we're but pilgrims on Earth. We are here for a brief time to act out certain functions and intercede with what goes on in the lives of other people. Certainly, if we possess an immortal spirit, it's far more important than our bodies and the pleasures of the flesh.

When we help other living beings in a proper way, we become angels in human form. Our beneficiaries can be our own family or strangers. We can lend a hand to an animal or a plant. We can join in as guardians of this magical Earth. But let's be cautious in what we do as angels. We shouldn't help when our help isn't needed or can spoil the character of our beneficiary.

We shouldn't do for others what they can do themselves; otherwise, we'll make them weaker and more dependent. Our help to others shouldn't support their bad habits and attitudes, as public welfare systems often do. We shouldn't ask for a return of the favor, or any kind of reward for ourselves, not even gratitude.

Be an angel as other angelic constructs of the world or mind have been for you, surely, in your life so far. But if you're seeking gratitude from those you help, you'll be sorely disappointed. What we do to help others should be done in an unobtrusive, non-invasive way. Our influence should be invisible and unproven, like God's presence. The aid we give should make souls better, not worse. If necessary, burn their bodies at the stake to save their souls, or so the Grand and Holy Inquisition decreed.

8. Do Out-of-Body Travels Actually Happen?

Religious theory says we're more than our bodies, meaning we can exist without our bodies. I find this idea hard to accept, given the evidence of the senses. A dead person doesn't act, doesn't speak, and doesn't stay around. The body decomposes and smells very badly. What was a living thing is gone, and after a while, even the bones disappear, unless preserved in tar or such material. The senses are stilled and gone. The eyes are rotted. The nose and ears are holes in the head. The tongue is food for worms. The skin is dust. And yet, we have the assurances of many wise, highly intelligent, and experienced men and women throughout history and in all lands and all cultures that something imperishable, the consciousness of self and the universe, persists and is eternal. In deep meditation, with senses stilled and shut down, these mystics perceive not a loss of consciousness but its expansion. You possess something that transcends your body.

We have many accounts of out-of-body travels by some special or holy people. And we have accounts of ordinary people who died a medical death and revived to live again and tell us of their experiences. Stories of such travels were presented by Raymond A. Moody Jr. in his books, such as *Life After Life*, *The Light Beyond*, and others.

Near-death experiences are highly personal and subjective, and thus not easily examined by science. But the possibility that they are true cannot be ruled out. Consider an analogy: After a person has lost an arm or a leg, sensations in the detached member often continue, and the patient feels he or she can move it, but of course, that does not happen. The patient has a ghost limb. The explanation is that the brain connections and memories of the limb remain. So if we are connected to a divine host, part of the network of souls, it is perhaps that host, the mind of all life, which maintains the sensations of living after death has seized the body.

Let's look at some of these experiences in detail. According to Dr. Moody Jr., many characteristics of these excursions are common to subjects, although there is great variability in the accounts given, depending on personal history and cultural background. In the first place, many narrators reported much difficulty in putting their experience into words. It was ineffable. It was not an ordinary, three-dimensional world they entered. Time was accelerated or disappeared altogether so that memories of one's past life would appear all at once and in one place, like a complete picture.

Many subjects, while nearly dead, heard a doctor or a bystander pronounce them dead. At the same time, they were filled with peace and tranquility or relief. In many cases, a buzzing noise, not pleasant, was heard and then there was the feeling of being pulled inside a dark tunnel or cylinder, ending with the sounds of beautiful, majestic music. Such an experience is the subjective record of a last transmission burst, the spirit being sent to the Divine Receiver from the local transmitting body about to succumb.

We can assume there are prior transmissions, perhaps during sleep; otherwise, with aging and decay, not much of value would be saved for the next world. At death, the tail end of the personality, the last few bits of information are sent to the host. Incidentally, the spiral tunnel is described by some mystics as a prelude to their vision of Heaven.

Another common account from people with near-death experiences is that of floating out of the body and looking down on it from some distance and on the people attending to the dying body. With this, there is the sensation of a spiritual body that can move anywhere with great speed or even instantaneously, go through walls or ceilings, and float around as in a dream without any time constraints.

This spiritual body can see and hear but cannot touch and interact with material objects or other people. The shape of the spiritual body may be more or less human, a misty fog, or a cloud-like ball. It feels helpless and powerless, observing everything that happens, but unable to act in any way. That is understandable if we imagine that the personality is no longer of this world, that it's no longer inhabiting an active material object, the body, but it is only probing the scene from a different dimension.

Although the spiritual body is cut off from living beings and cannot communicate with them, it encounters in this state other spirits and a great, compassionate being, which religious subjects describe as God. Subjects refer to the other lesser spirits as guardian angels or guides. Angels tell the dying person that it is not yet time to depart and that he or she must return to living for a while longer. The person near death follows this instruction with great regret because the state of approaching death was immensely peaceful and joyful.

Now, assuming that there's a depository of spirits somewhere, it may be possible for one to contact other personalities there and communicate with them, being part of the same system and sharing the same database. It's not surprising then that holy men and women in a deep trance also report such encounters with heavenly creatures when they have detached through meditation from their material bodies.

At this point, most subjects report that they have lost all fear of the occurring death. They feel the release from the body as somebody does being freed from prison after many years of incarceration. When they finally return to life, they do it with much reluctance and sadness in leaving their spiritual state. Thereafter, these revived people are changed drastically for the rest of their lives. They come of their experience totally convinced of the existence of an afterlife and are left with absolutely no fear of physical death. They also become more generous and compassionate towards other people and animals. This is very similar to the results of many mystical experiences people have reported.

Such experiences do occur at death's door or on other occasions, and our consciousness expands—because we're more than our bodies. Although I have not as yet had a near-death experience, my spiritual pursuits have influenced me in the same way. I have, in recent years, gone to surgery without any fear of dying. I used to be terrorized by flying; it's now a pleasure. Heights really bothered me; I can now stand on the edge of a tall building without any anxiety. I consider fear to be an emotion not befitting a thinking human being. Concern about a situation is necessary; fear is not. Fear and anger, I think, are excess vestiges from our animal past, remnants like the coccyx bone in our back.

9. Was Plato's World of Ideas an Illusion?

We'll now examine the theory that spirits are really ideas and ideas are spirits. After all, what is a personality? It's a way of thinking and feeling about things, unique and peculiar to the person possessing it. It's a pattern of thoughts, the essence of an individual which embodied leads to certain characteristic behaviors. For example, for many people a mother is the embodiment of love. For some, it's the father who's the most caring parent, and he represents the principle of wisdom and compassion, blended with discipline, a sort of family God. Such thinking gives rise to a universe of ideas, a reality not of material objects.

God, too, is an idea represented in human form so people can visualize it. As long as He or She shines in the minds of men and women, God exists. Where does the idea of justice come from? That is the idea that we defer to the rights of other people, even if they are weak and cannot defend themselves. As the Hindu scriptures say, "The Self is enshrined in the heart, a thumb-sized being that glows with an eternal light."[4] After all, ideas rule the world: not swords, but pens. Communism, socialism, capitalism, free markets, democracy, Christianity, Buddhism, freedom, feminism, legal rights, social justice, social welfare, human progress, human destiny, science, art, music, architecture, urban planning—all these are simply ideas, spelling human civilization.

---

4. Eknath Easwaran, trans., *The Upanishads* (Tomales, CA: Nilgiri Press, 2007), 351.

That's why Plato, Socrates' chief disciple and scribe, believed in the power and value of ideas and founded an academy in Athens that has radiated the light of wisdom through the ages. So much Plato admired ideas that he believed they represented a reality far superior to the material world we normally inhabit. The classical example of this is the geometric circle. It is a perfect circle where all its points are equidistant from the center. No circle that we can draw or contrive mechanically with the most sophisticated supercomputers can ever approach the perfection of this ideal circle.

Plato also gave us the analogy of the cave. We are in a cave, and on its walls, we see shadows of the real world outside. Our images are nothing but faint and distorted shadows of the eternal truths. We live in a shadow world, a Punch-and-Judy show. This is a notion not unlike that of the Buddha, who awakened to reality.

What is a person if not an idea? René Descartes, a French philosopher and mathematician who helped found modern science in the seventeenth century, wrote, "I think, therefore, I am."[5] He felt that since he, an imperfect being, could think of perfection, it proved that a perfect being, God, existed. What else but God could be the source of these great ideas that occurred to him? Descartes felt strongly his connection to the Divine.

Looking back at the history of all great ideas, each is associated with one man or woman. Revelation does not seem to visit groups or committees. It's a private matter between the Source and the individual receiver, and it's inextricably woven with the unique personality of the innovator. Thus, Einstein *is* Relativity. Mozart is the Magic Flute. Darwin is evolution. Lenin is Soviet Communism. Hitler is Nazism. Jesus is Christianity. Gautama is Buddhism. Mohammad is Islam. Moses is Judaism. Madam Curie is radiation. Walt Disney is Mickey Mouse. Frank Sinatra is the Swinger. Dostoyevsky is *Crime and Punishment*. Gershwin is "Rhapsody in Blue." Leonardo da Vinci is *La Gioconda*. Psychoanalysis is Freud. *La Comedie Humain* is Balzac. *Les*

---

5. René Descartes, *Meditations on First Philosophy*, trans. John Cottingham (Cambridge: Cambridge University Press, 1986), 17.

Miserables is Victor Hugo. Modern Science is Francis Bacon. Think of pasteurization. Consider Lister.

Who said, "Go West, young man"[6]? Remember who said, "We have nothing to fear but fear itself"[7]? Who wrote, "With malice toward none, with charity for all,"[8] "Give me liberty or give me death,"[9] or "We shall fight on the beaches, we shall fight in the streets; we shall never surrender"[10]?

It's no wonder that in the Hindu faith, the self is the individual, and the Self is God. Ayn Rand wrote well about this in her novels, such as *The Fountainhead*, *Atlas Shrugged*, and her philosophical treatise, *The Virtue of Selfishness*. Her character Howard Roark in *The Fountainhead*, patterned after Frank Lloyd Wright, represents the idea of modern, uncluttered, organic, functional architecture as opposed to the stale imitations of the classics. Dominique Francon, intimately connected with Roark, looks at one of his buildings promoted by the second-rater Peter Keating as his own design and says, "Of course!" She knows instantly who the designer is: the building is Roark.

On the other hand, harmonious groups of two or more, but not many, can support, stimulate, and excite individual creativity as in many famous teams, such as Rogers and Hammerstein, Hewlett and Packard, Laurel and Hardy, The Beatles, the New York Yankees. Napoleon Hill called the synergy phenomenon of teams the Mastermind Principle. Jesus said, "Where two or more are gathered in my name, there am I."[11]

Meditation groups can be very powerful, although each person is deep within his or her own psyche. Each member of the team is doing

---

6. Horace Greeley, editorial, *New-York Daily Tribune*, July 18, 1865.
7. Franklin D. Roosevelt, *The Public Papers and Addresses of Franklin D. Roosevelt,* ed. Samuel I. Rosenman (New York: Random House, 1938), 2:11.
8. Abraham Lincoln, *The Collected Works of Abraham Lincoln,* ed. Roy P. Basler (New Brunswick, NJ: Rutgers University Press, 1953), 8:333-334.
9. Patrick Henry, *Patrick Henry: Writings and Biography,* ed. William Wirt (New York: Penguin Classics, 2000), 45-47.
10. Winston S. Churchill, *Winston S. Churchill: His Complete Speeches 1897–1963,* ed. Robert Rhodes James (New York: Chelsea House, 1974), 6:6166-6168.
11. Matthew 18:20 (NIV).

his or her highly personal thing within the framework of the group action.

It's as if there's a sympathetic vibration between the idea and the innovator that inevitably stimulates that person to produce. If you were a super-intelligent being from another time and place interested in accelerating intelligence growth on Earth, what would you do? You would pick a likely local life form with the required potential and install in its genes the design for the cosmic receiver. Messages, constantly broadcast, would be picked up when the time and individual were right for a connection. Messages would be in an ultra-compact code that would be unzipped by the individual in the proper frame of mind: in meditation.

As a vast intelligence that knows the enormous powers available in Nature to those who unlock her secrets, you would want to impart a moral code, an ethical imperative, before you let your protégés loose on Earth and in the cosmos.

So your earliest messages would have to do with proper behavior. People would have to be taught to respect the lives of other living beings, especially their fellow soul mates. Hence the emphasis in early Revelations: "Thou shalt not kill, thou shalt respect, and thou shalt love."[12]

No, the world of ideas is not an illusion; illusion is our little mud ball and the lives we burn on it. But the ideas perceived by us with our very limited minds of the great cosmic truths are very pale by comparison to those of God. They are nothing but reflections of the brilliant Brahma source, as the moon we see is reflecting the light of the sun. Our perceptions of beautiful things are but shadows of the eternal grandeur of God. Michelangelo's Sistine Chapel masterpieces are no more than cartoons compared to the images held by the Cosmic Mind.

---

12. Romans 13:7, 9-10 (NIV).

10. Do Genes and Environment Determine Our Lives?

You've come across the perennial debate on heredity versus environment. Heredity is the genetic information encoded in our DNA. According to evolutionary theory, this information, accumulated in our genes during three or four billion years, represents the sum total of the lessons learned about survival on this planet by our ancestors, human and otherwise. Obesity, sexual orientation, genius, diabetes, sickle cell anemia, mental retardation, musical talent, alcoholism, and manic depression all have a genetic component. Scientists today make much of these genetic influences. But after heredity and environment, there's a third and most powerful tributary of destiny: spiritual enlightenment, also known as the grace of God.

True, a great deal of behavior in humans is instinctive, "wired in," programmed, especially in those less well-endowed with intellect or will. Heredity, DNA in our bodies' cells, is the source of information that determines much of our destiny. We are often inexorably driven to act out the programs encoded in our genes. Sometimes, after years of marriage and children, someone comes out and joins the gay community. After years of good health, in middle age, someone gains weight and, in a routine examination, is found to be diabetic. Or rarely, a stockbroker, the painter Gauguin, quits his job and family, drawn irresistibly to art, and grows into a creative genius.

The information stream from genetics has many surprises, some of which may yet be revealed by the human genome project and its aftermath. Is it possible there is a God gene that is triggered under certain circumstances? There may even be a Messiah gene that produces religious saviors or lunatics. There's a sort of perfection in the carbon crystal of DNA that waits to be expressed. An alcoholic, on occasion, renounces his style of life and becomes a born-again Christian, never to touch the stuff for the rest of his days. He turns to the straight and narrow and becomes a Christian and a model citizen.

Sometimes the spirit of creative action seizes someone who pushes along, a powerful urge within, to achieve a better world. John DeLorean wants to build a new kind of automobile, superior in quality to Detroit's products, "an ethical car," that will last and perform. He's to build it in war-torn Northern Ireland and provide employment for people in a depressed town. A vision such as this is not always fully realized, but the impetus is present and strong.

Nature, as opposed to nurture, is thus seen to be a powerful force that shapes our destinies. Studies have been made of identical twins raised in very different families and environments. Published results show that the twins closely resemble each other not only in appearance but also in intelligence, lifestyles, and ultimate development. Yet, who can deny the value of a good upbringing and an education? A tender and loving parent brings a child to full bloom. A thoughtful teacher opens a student's eyes to the world and its wonders. A tree put in the ground may thrive, but it'll do better if it's cultivated.

A teacher or trainer, however, does best by being a model or letting the student follow his own course and supplying guidance. Think of the master craftsman or artist of old with his apprentice. The apprentice served for years, often living in the home of the master, absorbing skills almost by osmosis. The mere presence of a true mentor can have a profound effect on one's life. Thus we are creatures of our environment as much as we are the products of our genes. Genes supply the potential for growth and nurture the realization of that potential.

So Nature provides and nurture actualizes. Something may be missing from this equation. The green thumb of a good gardener may be more than skill. A third source of information that enters our lives from the spirit world is linked with love, like the care of a devoted mother or father. Remember the effect of holding an infant affectionately. This may be the most potent factor in life. It has been called the grace of God. It has been named the Holy Spirit.

If we possess a modem that can connect us to Divine Providence under the right circumstances, we have the means to contact a totally unlimited source of knowledge and wisdom. Our life's course may change drastically under the influence of a spiritual guide, human or otherwise.

Here is how the Holy Scripture of Hinduism, the Brihadaranyaka Upanishad, puts it.

Spirits Are Ideas

You are what your deep, driving desire is.
As your desire is, so is your will.
As your will is, so is your deed.[13]

So, presumably, we must deeply desire Heaven if we wish to reach it or benefit from it. We tune in to God by loving and desiring God above all else. As Jesus admonished his disciples when asked what to do to find salvation. He told them to follow the commandments. And above all "love thy God with all thy mind and all thy soul and with all thy might."[14] To receive Krishna's blessing, his devotees chant his name over and over again. Christians, too, sing God's praise: "Our Father who art in Heaven, hallowed be thy name."[15] Also, in Greek, *Kyrie Eleison*: God have mercy on us.

Alcoholics at AA meetings don't call on God specifically for help. They hold hands, many of them children of alcoholics with a genetic predisposition to their addiction, and pray to a higher power. From a desperate, hopeless state, a significant number of them rise up and succeed in recovering from their illness. You may think that success comes from group therapy, and God had nothing to do with it, yet grace descended on these poor souls, and the Holy Spirit, a potent healing power, led them back to health.

The most powerful force shaping our destiny, the main tributary of creative information, is not our heredity or environment but the strength of our connection with the Lord of the Universe, who guides our steps. Following chanting, in a state of deep meditation, the devotee receives grace. The flow of information begins in the soul, which guides one to a better life.

---

13. Eknath Easwaran, trans., *The Upanishads* (Tomales, CA: Nilgiri Press, 2007), 1.
14. Matthew 22:37 (KJV).
15. Matthew 6:9 (KJV).

3

PROPHETS: MESSENGERS FROM GOD OR LUNATICS?

Sai Baba is a holy man in India who claims to be an avatar, a reincarnation of Jesus Christ, drawing the adoration and alms of many Westerners to his ashram. A friend of my family, raised as a Greek-Orthodox Christian, travels to India every year to pay homage to Sai Baba, to bask for a few days in the holy man's presence. He has terminal heart disease but is not afraid, knowing death is not the end but the beginning of a better life. A Jewish-American doctor of psychiatry in San Diego, where I live, has made his house a shrine to Sai Baba, with pictures of the holy man on his walls and numerous Indian artifacts. Devotees of Sai Baba gather at the house to chant and meditate together. In India, huge crowds gather when Sai Baba appears in public. He likes to do magic tricks. Once he asked a Western visitor what he wanted most in life, and the visitor joked he wanted a Rolex watch. Next day, Sai Baba materialized such a watch on his palm and offered it to his guest. Guests also offer gifts to the holy man, which have enabled Sai Baba to build his ashram, hospitals, schools, and other facilities for the people in his community. Is Sai Baba a confidence man or a madman? His influence is small from our point of view, and what he does with the money he collects appears to be good for people.

Other prophets had a much greater effect on mankind.

1. What Is God According to the Prophets?

Were the great prophets who established major religions messengers from God or madmen who infected millions of people with their delusions? Moses heard voices and saw bushes aflame without burning. Today doctors would readily certify he was hallucinating and diagnose him as schizophrenic. Jesus declared himself the Son of God with a mission to save mankind from sin and to be the judge of all at the end of the world. Any competent psychiatrist would want to rush him to the nearest mental hospital and treat him for a Messianic complex. Mohammad told his Arabian neighbors God was dictating the Quran's verses to him and urging him to destroy idols and spread Islam throughout the world. Was he a megalomaniac? The answer depends on how we define God. If the prophets defined God properly as an idea guiding us to grow, prosper, and live in peace with our neighbors, then they were messengers bearing good news; otherwise, they were destructive lunatics, increasing the total entropy of the planet.

Most people define God as a Being who exists in a place called Heaven and also everywhere in the universe, has thoughts, feelings, and goals as we do, but is eternal, perfect, unchanging, all-powerful, infinite, all-knowing, and compassionate towards us and other living things. God has been called Lord, Creator, the great Artist of Nature, Great Spirit, and First Cause. God picked up a stone or clod from the earth, breathed life into it, making man and woman.

An interesting entity this God is!

All over the world, most people, foolish or wise, learned or ignorant, rich or poor, highborn or downtrodden, recognize God's existence. However, our eyes cannot see this entity, our ears cannot hear It, our noses cannot smell It, and our fingers cannot touch It. No scientific instrument of the latest design, electron microscope, telescope, Geiger counter, or whatever has ever detected God because God is Spirit and an Idea.

This Great Spirit, according to religious philosophers, is unknowable, unfathomable, and beyond description: a mystery, an enigma, a Sphinx. And yet, God exists for those who have experienced rapture, enlightenment, or *satori*. Nearly every major sage or philosopher acknowledges the existence of such a Being. Among God's prophets, Moses is honored today by three religions that span the globe, and Jesus, with his life and message, did become the Messiah for all Christians everywhere. Mohammed guides the lives of over a billion Muslims from Morocco to Malaysia and beyond. And the ineffable Buddha heals the spirits of countless people in the East and West.

2. How Do We Recognize God?

God is, according to the scriptures of the world, essentially Spirit—not a material body subject to the laws of physical things. So we come to explore what we mean by "spirit" versus "thing." Spirit is something unseen, like the wind, but is felt and can be very powerful in its effects. The closest I come to the notion of spirit is the word idea. An idea is a mental tool for the solution of a problem posed well. For example, the mathematical circle is an ideal geometric figure with all points equidistant from the center. To the naked eye, the moon and sun appear to be perfect circles, but with a telescope, we see mountains on the moon and flares on the sun. You'll find the circle nowhere in the natural world, but the ancients used it to invent the wheel and other mechanical devices.

God is like a perfect circle.

Other notions related to spirit are mathematical algorithms, computer programs, information packets, genes, and data sets—but all of these are charged with emotional content, energy, and forces of control and growth. God is often declared to be the life-giving light, and many peoples have worshiped the sun as the source of life on Earth, as it nearly is with the exception of organisms in the mid-ocean ridges.

Light, like all electromagnetic energy, scatters in all directions at 186,000 miles per second. Light from lasers goes in one direction, and it's of one frequency, while white light travels as a spectrum of many frequencies. We don't know of any electromagnetic energy that possesses the stability of material objects and can hold information. A computer program doesn't work without the hardware. There are some rare instances of momentarily stable energy, such as ball lighting. Crass material objects are the only forms of reasonably stable energy bundles that support life and intelligence on Earth.

But what does all this have to do with God? Most religions assume that God is the Creator of everything in the universe and of the universe itself. This is an incorrect interpretation of God's role. Regarding the universe, we're quite certain—we have much evidence to support this view—that it emerged from a cosmic explosion about fifteen billion years ago and that this primordial energy scattered and cooled in clumps, forming the galaxies. Clusters of galaxies continued to move away from each other in the rapid expansion of space itself. Then atoms and matter were formed from pure energy and galaxies evolved with suns, dust clouds, planets, novas and stable stars, quasars, and black holes.

Everywhere we look in the universe we see simple forms evolving into more complex objects in spite of or because of the law of entropy, also known as the second law of thermodynamics. This law states that all complex systems fall apart sooner or later and reach a state of equilibrium. Even atoms, which are extremely stable, on rare occasions self-destruct without outside interference. However, living systems persist longer and replicate themselves, thus bringing about evolution. This process of evolving things is sometimes called the law of complexity. We can speculate, therefore, that the Supreme Being, the most complex and sophisticated form we can conceive, also evolved after the Big Bang.

A reasonable explanation about God is that He and She evolved from intelligent beings who established close connections with information channels over many millions or billions of years and together emerged as a Super Mind, as we are beginning to behave today with modems and the internet.

After all, what is the mind in the brain unless it's the product of billions of neurons firing impulses and working together for survival? Is there a mind like a computer program separate from the hardware of the brain on which the mind runs? And what is the soul or spirit if it's not part of the mind? Is this spirit something installed by God, or is it simply the product of billions of years of evolution, like the body? When the brain is aged, injured, depressed by alcohol and drugs, tired, or asleep, the mind also suffers deterioration. The mind degrades as the brain suffers, but this could be due to the failure of the hardware while the program is alive and well somewhere, ready to be installed in another piece of equipment by God, Ruler of the Universe.

If God rules the universe, God does so with natural laws, not fiats. Natural laws are absolute and impersonal, having no regard for our sufferings or safety. In all my years, I've never witnessed any breakdown of natural laws. I've never seen a miracle, although I've seen many wondrous things that happened in accordance with these laws. Gravity cannot be defied. The law of Archimedes is never violated, and someone perceived walking on water wasn't actually on it, but by the water. Dead bodies do not revive unless death was actually a coma. Water does not turn to wine but can be a mixture with water appearing as wine to those well enough intoxicated.

Each time we have learned some truth about Nature, we have debunked another religious myth. Thunder and lightning aren't signs of Jupiter's anger; their damage can be prevented with a simple rod invented by Benjamin Franklin. God did not create Nature, but Nature created God. In any case, the forces of Nature are blind and unfeeling. There's no compassion anywhere in the universe except in the hearts of some human beings.

We look at a beautiful sunset, a waterfall, or a forest swaying in the breeze and admire God's creation. In fact, with the sunset, we are really only looking at a nuclear fire that has been burning for billions of years and will continue to burn until its fuel is exhausted. A waterfall is H_2O pouring down a steep drop. A forest is carbon structures pushed around by atoms of oxygen, nitrogen, and other gases. I believe it's not the essence of these things that God created but our own perceptions of beauty in the universe.

God isn't outside but inside our minds and so is Heaven.

You might say all this is quite beyond us common mortals to comprehend and we should believe those wiser than ourselves as to the truth of things. I'm not interested in what I can't understand, only in what I can grasp, even if it takes my whole life to do so. We've not made progress as a species by giving up on the possibility of acquiring knowledge, even if our ability to fathom things seems limited. We cannot stop the search until we're sure we've reached the limits of human knowledge, and we're a long way from doing that. If we continue to grow as individuals and as a species, there are no known limits to our minds or to the knowledge we can command except the limits we set for ourselves.

God sets no limits for us, as Cosmic Intelligence has no limits.

God is an ever-expanding sphere of love and wisdom, existing like the ideal circle with no beginning and no end. Setting no limits broadens life and allows it to grow in all directions, blooming: life doesn't get boxed in. I don't like to live in any box, no matter how luxurious. Neither does the notion of an inscrutable God, beyond my understanding, satisfy me. I would like to look God straight in the face and shake God's hand now that I'm alive or later when I become a spirit.

Now I offer you my personal survey of the world of faith, not as a course in comparative religion, but to relate prophets of the past and their teachings to my idea of a Digital God of the future.

3. Shall We Revive the Ancient Greco-Roman Gods?

Let's begin with a pre-Christian God, a pagan one, to whom the ancient Greeks paid homage: Zeus, the most powerful God, also worshiped by the Romans as Jupiter.

Zeus was primary among the twelve Greek gods and father to many of them. His wife and sister was Hera (Juno), the Earth Mother and goddess of fertility, and his father was Cronus, whom he threw down from the skies in a divine battle. Zeus and the other Greek gods lived on Mount Olympus, and each one represented a different passion or attribute of Nature: Aphrodite (Venus), the goddess of love; Ares (Mars), the god of war; Apollo, the god of light and beauty; Athena (Minerva), the goddess of wisdom; and so forth.

Athena was born from the head of Zeus. He had a splitting headache, then his head split open (or Hera, his wife, whacked it open after one of his infidelities). Out came Athena in full panoply, with spear, shield, and helmet, ready to defend her virginity and wisdom, both always under fierce attack.

The twelve gods, each with his or her special gift, are like Spinoza's conception of the Godhead as a collection of perfect and eternal attributes. If numerous gods seem primitive to you, think of all the Christian saints, each a specialist in granting favors, that we entertain today in our mythology. We can bring back the ancient gods and treat each one of them as representing a unique spiritual virtue: Zeus for restrained power, Hera for abundant fertility, Apollo for artistic performance, Hermes (Mercury) for profitable commerce, Ares for just warfare, Hephaestus (Vulcan) for efficient industry, and so forth. Each god was the personification of some ideal virtue or mental attribute: like the Greeks, we can perfect our lives, modeling ourselves after these ideal entities.

Many of the myths about the Greek gods are found in Homer, the blind poet and singer, whose epics were *The Iliad* and *The Odyssey*. These were histories of princely adventures but also the Holy Scriptures of the day. The poems were recited and sung and later written down—as was done with Hindu scriptures, Hebrew legends, Christian gospels, and the Quran of Islam. Spoken words, like music played, not read in notes, have a life and a power not found in something written.

In ancient times, gods communicated with humans in sleep or through oracles, such as the famous one at Delphi in Greece, where the priestess fell into a trance of narcotic smoke and chanting. Thus, the gods gave their commands, advice, warnings, or instructions to humans, usually people in power, those who could afford to pay for the oracle's gifts. Also, priests divined heavenly messages in the flights of birds, in the guts and bones of animals, and in the smoke of sacrificial fires. The messages were often vague or ambiguous, but the priests did the best they could under the circumstances; it was enough to earn their fees—supercomputers for multivariate analysis not being available then.

The ancient Greco-Roman gods looked much like ten-foot-tall humans but could change form and were immortal. They sometimes fell in love with humans, a favorite pastime of Zeus, and such unions produced demigods, Hercules and Achilles being noted examples of the genre. So, Holy Conception was not unknown before Christ. Hercules fought and won noble battles, and after his mortal body perished, he ascended to Heaven and lived among the gods, much like Jesus and Mohammad. It's a common tale in many religious legends, this climb to Heaven of a great saint or hero to join the Great Spirit. One Greek demigod had a different ending. His story is especially relevant to our inquiry into the God Connection. He was Prometheus, meaning forethinker, son of the Titan Iapetus.

Prometheus took pity on suffering mankind, stole the secret of fire from Heaven, and gave it to humans as a gift.

We know from archeological studies that fire was one of the earliest tools to aid humans in their struggle for survival in a world dense with tigers, lions, and wolves. Fire is raw energy, and its control had many uses right away: fighting enemies, cooking meat and other tough foods, burning clearings in the forest, warming people in cold weather, bringing light to the night, and shaping tools of wood or metal. It was powerful medicine. Zeus was not happy; humans now had this knowledge, and he punished the Titan horribly. Zeus chained Prometheus to a rock on Mount Caucasus, where the Caucasian race had its start, and vultures all day ate his liver, which grew whole again during the night. In another version of the myth, Zeus punished people by releasing Pandora and her box of evils.

It's an old legend that the price of learning is suffering.

In the Hebrew Genesis, Adam and Eve were punished for eating the fruit of knowledge, seeing good and evil and that they were naked. Galileo was punished because he taught what he saw through his telescope: that the moon and planets are material bodies like the Earth. Knowledge is power, and humans shouldn't get too ambitious and try to reach Heaven uninvited. The tower of Babel was a story of human arrogance: God had to destroy the tower to keep mankind under control. The lesson: approach discoveries with humility and respect. Today, the challenges are genetic engineering, nuclear power, and computer intelligence. If we're not careful, we'll open another box of Pandora.

Our debt to Prometheus and his heirs is immense. They have taken us out of the darkness of ignorance and superstition to the light of inspiration and the assurance of knowledge. We no longer have to quake and quiver at night in the dark. When lightning strikes, we need not tremble. When we're injured or sick, there's comfort in medicine and surgery. We can thank Benjamin Franklin, Thomas Edison, Pasteur, and Lister for risking their lives and livers to bring us such benefits. But from whence came their inspiration, fortitude, and persistence? These were human beings like you and me. To say that they were geniuses simply begs the question. They did their work, and they were gone.

The Greco-Roman gods are also gone, but as models of different virtues and attributes for us, they're still immortal.

We admire and praise the beauty and love of Aphrodite, the dignity and wisdom of Athena, the power of Zeus or Poseidon. Similarly, great and wonderful human beings upon death do not vanish completely but are still with us in books, movies, buildings, and elsewhere. Homer, Socrates, Alexander the Great, Julius Caesar, Shakespeare, Beethoven, Mozart, Newton, Einstein, Michelangelo, Leonardo da Vinci, Shelley, Whitman, Emerson, Greta Garbo, Fred Astaire, Sinatra, Roosevelt, Churchill, and so many other inspired and unique human beings are safely preserved somewhere. They cannot have been destroyed forever. Their essence must persist in another world, although their substance has dissolved in Earth's soil. So, Socrates says to his students in Plato's Phaedo, "Don't cry over my death. I'm confident that I go to live with the gods, whose instructions I've always followed in my life; a world where I know I'll enjoy the company of other great spirits and my ancestors that have gone there before me."[1]

4. Visions of Death from Gilgamesh, Zoroaster and the Egyptians

An ancient epic poem from 2,000 BC speaks of Gilgamesh, wise and powerful king of Babylon, who saw the end of his life and could not accept it.

Upon the death of his companion Enkidu, Gilgamesh had a spiritual crisis. "Six days and six nights, have I wept over him. Then was I afraid of death and fled from the land. My friend whom I loved has become like unto mud and I, must I too, lie down like him and never rise again?"[2] Gilgamesh traveled all around the world, like Ponce de Leon, looking for the means to immortality, which he found in some species of seaweed, only to lose it to a snake. Thus Gilgamesh formulated the chief question challenging every human mind: how can I avoid what seems inevitable, the arrival of death? The ideas that arise from this question are the sources of this volume. The answer is now as it was then: keep working, searching, and hoping for the divine light of salvation.

Zoroaster's search was during the great age of Babylon when King Hammurabi laid down a severe code from the gods establishing morality. Zoroaster (or Zarathustra) of eastern Persia (Iran), a great prophet, preached the good god, Ahura Mazda, proclaimed ethics, virtue, and divine judgment, and railed against the evil god, Angra Mainyu, known to the Jews as Satan. Eastern Persia, three thousand years later, gave rise to the Sufi mystics of Islam, such as Rumi, with a clear influence from the neighboring Indian Empire of the Spirit.

Civilizations emerge in areas with extra food supplies, so some talented people have the leisure to sit quietly, meditate, and produce visions.

---

1. Plato, *Phaedo*, trans. Eva Brann, Peter Kalkavage, and Eric Salem (Newburyport, MA: Focus Philosophical Library, 1998), 46-68.
2. Andrew George, trans., *The Epic of Gilgamesh* (New York: Penguin Classics, 2003), Tablet X.

Thousands of years ago this was the case in ancient Mesopotamia, a fertile valley between the rivers Tigris and Euphrates, which produced Babylon. Across the Red Sea in northeastern Africa, the Nile nourished life in Egypt. Osiris, god of the underworld, was said to have introduced agriculture to the land and made civilized life possible for the people. Re, the sun god, was also worshiped as the energy-giving source of all life on Earth: true with the exception of organisms in the volcanic mid-ocean ridges.

Today our answer to the riddles of life and death under the sun is biological research, especially in genetics. The ancient Egyptians' response was the preservation of human remains with mummification. They hoped their loved ones would be resurrected from the mummies —and genetic engineering may do this soon, but the result will be clones or identical twins, and not the original person. We know that the ancient Egyptians also had a moral code and believed in divine judgment. The Hebrews before Moses probably absorbed many religious notions from the Egyptians and Babylonians.

5. Moses: Fountainhead of Three Major Faiths

The Babylonian and Egyptian religious traditions influenced the Hebrew faith, certainly the most ardent in the world, but much of that faith arose independently from mystic sources in Semitic minds. Is there a gene or program in every human everywhere that produces God visions, or is it a psychic broadcast of the same message from deep space?

Some God genes in our species build the receiver in the brain to intercept the divine message.

The Greeks did not know about genes and were often frivolous and playful in depicting Zeus and other manifestations of God. To them, the gods' antics were a source of amusement as well as inspiration. By comparison, the Jews were deadly serious about Jehovah. Try and find one comical story in all of the Old Testament, with the exception of Jonas in the belly of the whale. Later, after the Jewish diaspora, Yiddish descendants developed a terrific sense of wit, probably to escape their dread religion and sufferings in European ghettos.

The Semites, an undistinguished nation in ancient times, except for their fervent faith, had to wait for Jesus and Mohammad to spread their doctrines across the world.

The Jewish attitude was too provincial: centered on the tribe's history and destiny. But Jesus and Mohammad preached for all nations. Jesus was extremely pleased to receive the first Greeks to his Church; they excelled in arts, sciences, philosophy, and music. Similarly, the Romans, and their allied Italian cities, were unsurpassed in military arts, administration, and civil engineering. They conquered many lands and built an empire, which survived longer than any other on Earth. The Roman Emperor Constantine and the Greeks fostered the spread of Christianity throughout Europe. However, the Jews later distinguished themselves in Europe after intermarriage with gentiles and absorption in Western culture. The Jews always had a strong connection with the Divine Source, but it had to be united with Greek reason to bring forth its finest fruit, as it happened with the Arabs at the peak of their culture in the ninth century AD.

The worship of Jehovah by Moses led to our Christian idea of God and Jesus on the cross.

Christians often forget Jesus was a Jew who built his doctrine on Judaism. On account of St. Paul's writings, also a Jew, some people blame the Jews for the Crucifixion and the persecution of early Christians. Now Moses and Jesus in turn inspired the mystical prophet of Islam, Mohammad of Arabia, who spread his faith with word and sword, just like the Emperor Constantine. Not a shred of humor in the whole lot of them! Thousands of years rolled by in Europe and the Middle East, people groveling before the One God, fighting bloody battles to establish one or the other of His versions with very little laughter emanating on any side. I say, give us back the Greco-Roman gods with Bacchus in the lead, and let's have some fun again.

But let's get back to Moses and the Hebrews for a while. He led these people out of Egypt, where they had gone for bread and ended up becoming slaves. Exodus! That was a great spectacle in the movie *The*

Ten Commandments, and a major religious holiday for the Jews. It marks their liberation and beginning as a nation.

With Moses, God becomes approachable and gets more involved with human affairs on an intimate basis. Moses climbed Mount Sinai and got there the Ten Commandments carved in stone. He saw the burning bush in deep meditation and heard the awesome voice of God. Moses had followed a well-established route to the Divine. You climb alone to the top of a mountain, the middle of a desert, or a forest, depending on your habitat; basically, you go away from society. You fast for many days. There in the quiet of nature, away from the tumult of humankind, you get sufficiently light-headed from low blood sugar or lack of oxygen, then you see visions and hear voices.

Today, hearing voices and having other hallucinations would get you a one-way ticket to the booby hatch unless you're an ordained minister or priest from one of the entrenched religions. Back in the time of Jesus, you could have come across as a prophet unless you were crucified, burned, or stoned. It all depended on the mood you stirred in your neighbors; at least you were not locked up with the key thrown away. There were not many asylums for the insane in those days. The theory was that devils or angels possessed you—again, depending on how you struck people with your words and behavior.

Possessed or not, Moses was on a first-name basis with Jehovah. He as often argued as pleaded with God for the sake of his nation. When his people did something wrong, like making idols and having orgies, as was customary back then to break from the monotony of life, Moses would ask God to forgive the sinners and to spare their lives because without the faithful, He would have no worshippers.

Read your Old Testament or Hebrew Holy Scriptures. Moses had a direct channel of communication with God, also known as Yahweh. The holy tabernacle was like a transmitter-receiver, and the presence of God was all around it. Repeatedly, the Lord spoke unto Moses, saying, "Speak unto the children of Israel, and say unto them; this is the thing which the Lord hath commanded."[3] God could not or would not speak

---

3. Leviticus 17:2 (KJV).

directly to the people. He did not care to use a heavenly loudspeaker. He used Moses as his mouthpiece. Moses was either the modem or the interpreter of heavenly speech.

God genes have always been abundant in the Hebrew people.

The message from God found another great voice with David of Goliath fame, warrior, king, dancer, singer, poet, lover of Bathsheba, and father of the foolish Absalom, as well as the wise Solomon; a passionate man and author of the famous Psalm 23. "The Lord is my shepherd; I shall not want."[4] Also, Psalm 24: "Who shall ascend into the hill of the Lord? Or who shall stand in His holy place? He that hath spotless hands and a pure heart, and who hath not lifted up his soul unto vanity, nor sworn deceitfully."[5] The way to Heaven is through good deeds and a reverent attitude.

6. Does Christianity Lead the Way?

Jesus, descended from King David according to the Gospels, a Jewish carpenter, was the son of a carpenter, Joseph. Later, he became the Son of God, delivered from the Virgin Mary by cloning, then modified to take the appearance of a man by hormone therapy because women could not be rabbis. In the entire Bible story, Jesus never showed any romantic interest in a woman, not even Mary Magdalene. He loved men, his disciples, especially Peter, on whom he proposed to build his Church. He was gentle and kind to children. He disliked violence and was very peaceable, except once at the temple, where he chased away the money changers and merchants. Christ's powerful presence in the world has brought more ever-spreading peace and unity to people everywhere. Christianity, the most populous faith on our planet, leads the way to a brighter future for all humanity.

Before beginning his mission, Jesus went to the desert and fasted for forty days and forty nights. He communed with God and saw the power available to him through meditation. Tempted by Satan, he

---

4. Psalm 23:1 (KJV).
5. Psalm 24:3-4 (KJV).

resisted successfully on an empty stomach. At the hands of John the Baptist, he was baptized and received enlightenment. He perceived that he was no ordinary man and saw his great destiny: to show mankind the way to Salvation.

Like the Buddha five hundred years earlier in India, Jesus was happy contemplating God and did not need anything, but he wanted to liberate others from misery. So he sought disciples by the Sea of Galilee, and he began to preach. People seized by the Holy Spirit, like Jesus and the Buddha, as well as lesser beings like myself, have this urge to spread their message and help others.

So Jesus taught people how to pray and reach God through the Lord's Prayer—the protocol of divine communication. He said, "As long as I'm in the world I'm the light of the world."[6] Jesus knew his importance as a conduit of spiritual knowledge: he was a giant fiber-optics channel, a brilliant laser light shining in his eyes. He taught, "Lay not up for yourself treasure upon earth; but lay up treasure in Heaven. For where your treasure is, there will your heart be also."[7] He knew there was little value in material possessions. You cannot take them with you when you die.

The only thing you can take with you to the other world is your soul or spirit; look to the riches your spirit can carry on your way to the next world: understanding, wisdom, love, and compassion.

Jesus declared himself the Son of Man, but his disciples saw him as the Son of God, the Jewish Messiah. Psychiatrists today would certify he had a Messianic complex, but Jesus proved himself to be the Messiah indeed, because his life, his teachings, and his influence for two thousand years all over the world were of immense importance to mankind's spiritual peace, freedom, and salvation.

But then, read your Old Testament: all faithful men are called sons of God and the women daughters of God since God breathed life into their spirits. "I and my Father are one."[8] If one is strongly connected to

---

6. John 9:5 (NIV).
7. Matthew 6:19-21 (NIV).
8. John 10:30 (KJV).

the Divine Network, is he not part of God and therefore, in a way, a god with such knowledge and such powers as God possesses and permits one to employ? When the Hebrews proposed to stone Jesus for blasphemy "because thou, being a man, makest thyself God,"[9] he answered them: "Is it not written in your law, I said, Ye are gods? If he called them gods, unto whom the word of God came, and the scripture cannot be broken; Say ye of him, whom the Father hath sanctified, and sent into the world, thou blasphemes; because I said, I am the Son of God?"[10]

"The Father is in me, and I in Him."[11] A strong channel of communication is a vital link and merges one being into another. The same thing happens when you look into the eyes of your beloved. In this case it was a love between Jesus and the Divine Source of all that's good in this universe and infinite other universes.

In spite of all this divine guidance Jesus received, he lost his temper during his big success in Jerusalem and chased away the money changers at the temple. This action brought about his downfall. The priests were not about to lose their rents from their little arrangement with the merchants, and they plotted his conviction at the hands of the Roman ruler.

While imprisoned and during his trial, Jesus lost practically all his followers. They got scared, even Peter. But after his revival in the tomb and his reappearance, there was a dramatic change in their behavior. Jesus appeared in his own body with the bloody wounds still on his hands and side, which Thomas did touch. He appeared before his disciples three times after his crucifixion and sat down and ate with them, taught them, and gave them his last admonitions.

Then Jesus, aware he could not stay in Palestine anymore and not be caught again as he was now well known, left the country and totally disappeared. The disciples, filled with his spirit, with unbelievable courage and totally fearless of torture or death at the hands of the

---

9. John 10:33 (KJV).
10. John 10:34-36 (KJV).
11. John 10:38 (KJV).

authorities and Orthodox Jews, carried on and spread his message of hope all around the world.

Three centuries later, Emperor Constantine, victorious over his enemies with the help of Christians, converted to Christianity, already his mother Helen's faith. Christianity was officially established, and its practitioners began to persecute others who had different religious views. The Inquisition was on.

Today, Christianity has the largest number of followers in the world —followers who are by far the most powerful. Yet, though it leads all religions in the realm of the spirit, it's waning and in desperate need of revitalization. Muslims are more ardent and are multiplying faster than Christians, except devout Catholics or Mormons. That's fine with me as long as Muslims bury their militants and come out for world peace as broadly and forcefully as Christians have done.

7. Is Islam the Message in Arabic?

Six centuries after Jesus, the Middle East was again the site of another spiritual phenomenon, this time in Arabia: Mohammed and Islam.

Mohammed was an heir to the religious traditions of the Jews and Christians. Mohammed, born in Mecca in 570 AD, was an illiterate camel driver who married a rich older widow and lived a comfortable and ordinary life until his forties. On camel trips to Syria he heard recitations of the Hebrew Scriptures and Christian teachings and was affected deeply at a time when his fellow tribesmen were worshiping idols. If any man ever had a direct line to God, Mohammad certainly did; his message has nothing to do with the current unpleasantness from some crazy Muslims.

By all accounts, Mohammed was a sensible and virtuous man disturbed by the iniquities of his fellows. Being affluent, he was periodically able to withdraw from society and go to the mountain desert, where he found a cave to live. At night, he came out with a cloak wrapped around his body to ward off the chills of night, and under the brilliant desert stars, he fell into reverie and trance.

He meditated, and as he did so, verses of perfect spiritual beauty came to his mind. These verses retold the teachings of Moses and the prophets, including Jesus, and many new things were added in a manner fitting to the culture of the Arabs. Mohammad recited these verses to his disciples, who memorized them. Later, this poetic scripture was written down for all posterity.

So sure was Mohammad of his God connection that the Islamic verses are written in the first-person singular, or plural, or third-person singular, as the voice of God. There are occasional passages spoken by the Prophet or the Angel Gabriel. All of these verses were later compiled in a volume called the Quran. *Quran* in Arabic means "The Recital." Islam means absolute submission to the will of God. Perhaps, this is not dissimilar to the Chinese "The Way," or "Tao."

When Mohammed modestly preached his message, not as God's son but as a prophet or messenger, in the words of the world's Creator, he railed against the iniquities of his fellows. Naturally, he was persecuted by the adherents to the old religion and nearly killed. His own fellow townsmen in Mecca, even his uncle Abbas, became his enemies. "A prophet is not without fame, except in his own country,"[12] said Jesus, Mohammed's colleague.

Besides, people hate getting criticism, especially if it's true.

Mohammad was very strict in his teachings about worshiping only *Allah*, Arabic for God, and no one else. He recognized Moses and Jesus as prophets, like himself. The prophets, angels, and other entities connected with God were to be respected only, not worshiped. He particularly disliked the Christian beliefs in Jesus as the son of God and the adoration of the Virgin Mary, mother of Jesus, who is very big in the Catholic and Orthodox Christian pantheon.

Mohammad preached kindness, tolerance, and compassion.

The prophet of Islam admonished his countrymen to be caring and fair towards women, orphans, slaves, and beasts, and to give some of their wealth to the poor. When it came to the enemies of his religion, however, he was ready to fight and led troops of his followers in a victorious battle against his own tribe, the Quraysh of Mecca, including his

---

12. Matthew 13:57 (KJV).

uncle Abbas, whom he captured and converted to Islam. Following the death of his wife, Khadijah, he married several other women and had a number of descendants. He died in 632 AD, partly from the effects of poisoning at the hands of a Jewish woman, according to legend. Some three years earlier, Mohammed's troops had put the Jews of Khaybar in Arabia to the sword.

Yet, the Quran dwells much on God the Compassionate, Lord of the Universe and Creator of Nature and of man. It strongly exhorts the faithful to mind the prospect of Heaven, Hell, and the Day of Judgment. Legend holds that Mohammad ascended to Heaven after his death and joined God and the angels. Today we would say he was uploaded to the Heavenly Server.

Muslim paradise is pleasant indeed: a garden with running streams and luscious fruit trees, a desert man's dream, and decorated with dark-eyed *houris*, bashful young virgins, eager to please, these being the souls of faithful women—a most enticing vision of Heaven.

God the Creator is said to be responsible for throwing the veil of night over the day, sending forth the winds heavy with clouds over some dead land, and letting waters fall upon it and bringing forth all kinds of fruit. This is again a poetic image of God as Nature, not the physical reality, but our God-given perceptions of the world.

Allah also spread out the earth and placed upon it mountains and rivers. Here we are assuming the Supreme Being engaged in some terraforming of Earth. After all, this is a very unique planet, blessed in many ways among its desolate neighbors: the poisonous and scorching hell of Venus, the frigid, nearly airless Mars, the crushing gravitational well of Jupiter, and the frozen darkness of Pluto.

Life can be wonderful on this blue and white gem we call Earth. But it does get pretty awful sometimes, and it is then that we show our true mettle and prove ourselves worthy of a better world in the next life or a better life in the next world, depending on your cosmological view. We ascend to a better place when we have resisted temptation and are rewarded on Judgment Day by Allah. "Wealth and children are the ornament of this life. But deeds of lasting merit are better rewarded by your Lord and hold for you a greater hope of salvation."[13]

Following this religious guidance, one can prepare his soul for union with God, or one can, through prayer and meditation, achieve the same end directly.

This was the goal of the Sufi mystics who flourished in Persia, next to India, in the twelfth and thirteenth centuries AD. Foremost among these mystics was Jalaluddin Rumi. He was a poet, scholar, and teacher of the first magnitude. His work *Signs of the Unseen*, a collection of his religious discourses, is a good source of Sufism, or Gnostic revelation of Islam. Through knowing Allah directly through meditation, one is said to complement the Prophet's Quran. The Sufis are also famous for the use of the drums and dance in entering a spiritual trance, as in the frenetic dervish dances. Of course, some Sufis came up with novel ideas after communing with God on their own, and inevitably, there was periodic unpleasantness with the orthodox religion of Islam.

From this brief examination of Islam, you can see how close this faith is to Christianity and Judaism. Differences between Jews and Muslims are cultural, not spiritual. Ethnically, Arabs and Jews are cousins and should not be fighting each other. Arabs should embrace Jews in Palestine as long-lost brothers, absorbing some of the Jewish and European intellectual advances. Thus Arab and Muslim culture will ascend again to the heights it had once attained in the ninth century, when it was the most advanced in the world. Oil wealth can allow it to flourish more brilliantly now if put to good use.

Oil and natural gas in huge pools under Arabian sands did not concern Mohammad because he was seeking what was true and beautiful as a messenger of God.

Why does not spiritual knowledge grow from many contributions and become deeper and better as in science? Why must religious practitioners generally be so intolerant and hostile to new notions of life, death, immortality, the Supreme Being, and the soul's relationship to God? Because after a revelation by a prophet, people are asked to

---

13. Quran 18:46 Sahih International.

accept the truth on faith, not evidence. That is a fatal flaw in most major religions and churches. The closest thing to an open and receptive spiritual tradition is found in the Hindu practices, which we'll examine next.

8. The Buddha Guides Us to Nirvana

The Buddha's message was an outgrowth of Hindu religious culture. Hinduism holds many worthy notions. Reverence and love are due for all creation, especially for every living thing in the world. All deities—the Divine Mother included—are really manifestations of one God, Brahma. A part of you survives death and migrates to another living person, carrying along its karma, the consequences of a previous life. Our conduct in each life can lead to perfection and, eventually, to liberation from the cycle of birth and death, entrance into Nirvana—eternal peace, joy, and union with God. Nirvana is our proper goal after we've grown, worked, raised a family, and have aged well like fine wine.

The Buddha's contribution, and that of Jesus, was to provide the means for salvation out of this life through faith, prayer, devotion, right works, and meditation. And the Buddha succeeded more in his mission east from his native land—as Jesus succeeded west of Palestine—in China, Japan, and Southeast Asia.

The Buddha himself, just like Socrates, Jesus, and Mohammad, did not write down his own doctrines. Buddha's disciples memorized his story and teachings, which they later put into writing. Thus it is hard to separate actual facts from legends. His name was Siddhartha Gautama, the son of a king in northern India in the fifth century BC. He was handsome, healthy, and loved by his parents. He was in line to be king after his father's death. He married and had a son. He lived a sheltered life for many years, enjoying the pleasures of a prince: fine foods, clothing, games, and the arts. But he was a sensitive young man who could see the miseries of the world all around him: sickness, accidents, aging, and death. He saw how transient and frail human existence is and his own end someday, in spite of his princely advantages.

Siddhartha became very unhappy. He brooded about the meaning and purpose of life and sought to find a means to escape the common destiny of mankind. Finally, as was the tradition in India for older men, he left his family and household for the forest retreats in search of spiritual knowledge. He cast away his fine clothes and put on the rags of a mendicant, begging bowl in hand. He fasted for long periods and sought enlightenment through deep meditation.

After many years of ascetic living and hard work sitting in the lotus position, reaching into his subconscious, Siddhartha is illumined under a fig tree.

This was a momentous occasion in the annals of mysticism: comparable to Moses' revelation on Mount Sinai with the burning bush, and the experiences of Jesus and Mohammed in the desert. Siddhartha reaches Nirvana, free of time, space, and the evils of the world. He arrives on the other side of the river of life, where illness, aging, pain, and suffering don't intrude; where existence doesn't constantly change and evolve but remains in a state of perfect bliss.

Is this personal happiness enough?

Not for the Buddha! Action is also important. One must abide by one's sacred duty, the dharma. What would be the point of simply returning to the Source, to the original state of perfection without the drama and experience of living? There is something else besides perfection. There is change and growth towards a different and more interesting perfection, and there is compassion for other human beings suffering in loneliness and ignorance. The Buddha is also a teacher and a guide. He wants to lead others out of their lives of quiet desperation to fulfillment, freedom, and joy. So the Buddha abandons his retreat and isolation in blissful meditation and rejoins the world.

The prophet is not an ordinary human being after his enlightenment. He or She has been imbued by the burning spirit of divine love and wants to reach out and touch every living thing and make it well and give it purpose and meaning. The Buddha unfolds to his disciples and all who will listen a clear path to salvation from the soul's misery. That's his message brought back from the other shore. A practical, eight-fold approach to cure frustration and anguish brought about as a result of selfish desires.

First, *right understanding*: to every problem, there is a solution. In every procedure there is a correct technique, such as in every ailment there is a proper cure. The Divine Being, who gives us challenges, also allows us the means to overcome them (if we only think right) because the mind possesses the connection to Heaven or Hell. Right understanding is seeing that the world is transient and what takes material form will eventually disintegrate. One begins the journey to Nirvana by putting away the desire for ephemeral things and attaching oneself to eternal and unchanging ideas.

Second, *right purpose* is required to reach the desired destination. Without a goal, a person is adrift. Our intent steers our lives as a compass guides a ship to the right port. Otherwise, we are tossed by the winds of chance into a random walk like a lifeless molecule. Clear and firm intention unconsciously allows the events of our lives to shape our path to our goal.

Right speech, *right action*, and *right occupation* follow naturally from a correct understanding and purpose. Kindness and compassion for all living things flow from the properly motivated person like pure water from a spring. The dharma of a true human being is to love and cherish, not to harm others.

These actions are worthwhile, but the ultimate goal of a human being is union with the Divine Mind.

The last three steps of the path also have to do with how we should operate our minds to reach Nirvana. *Right effort*, *right attention*, and *right meditation* have to do with training our minds with ceaseless energy like an athlete training for a major competition. Now, attention focuses our effort, just as a laser beam concentrates radiation to one spot, to one thing at a time, here and now, to action that benefits life and does no harm. Meditation and prayer are the means for achieving stillness of mind and purity of thought so that, eventually, contact is made with the Divine Source. Meditation, linking up with the source of all living entities, leads to peace and calmness of mind, essential for a life of devotion to sacred duty. In this life, or some future life, after ceaseless effort, we finally come to complete peace, shalom, and God.

9. Laotse Shows the Way, or Tao

In China there was already a native spiritual tradition akin to Buddhism that was attributed mainly to the great mystic Laotse (born 571 BC) and main disciple and original commentator Zhuangzi (died 275 BC). Laotse was intuitive: he spoke to the heart with poetic aphorisms. Zhuangzi was rational: he addressed himself to the intellect with charming prose. Laotse was playful and witty; Zhuangzi liked belly laughs. They both contributed to a religion that was strange, paradoxical, quaint, intriguing, and intricate. It is to be found in the Book of Tao, the Way or Truth. No religious faith comes closer to a truth in agreement with the findings of modern science than the Tao.

Laotse was a mystic, while Confucius was a philosopher given to moral teachings. Although Confucianism was established as the state faith in China, intellectuals and poets favored Taoism. Laotse taught that God is beyond explanation. The Tao cannot be put into words: it is in a code that cannot be deciphered, only experienced. How can an infinite being be understood by finite minds? It can only be hinted at with signs and words.

A key concept of Taoism is Nature's cycles. Life is inevitably followed by death, and life follows death. The powerful are brought low, and the humble are raised up to might. Plenty ends in privation and privation in abundance. And those who rise will fall. (From the Christian Bible: "How the mighty have fallen!"[14]) Water is Laotse's perfect symbol for the spiritual life. It is clear, fluid, and seeks the lowest places. "Because the sage is able to forget his self, therefore his Self is realized."[15] This is a similar to Hindu teachings and to the Sermon on the Mount by Jesus.

All things are formed from the yin of Heaven, which is silent, and the yang of the Earth, which is active, when they meet and merge. Yin and yang represent the duality we see everywhere in nature: positive

---

14. 2 Samuel 1:19 (NIV).
15. Laotse, *Tao Te Ching*, trans. Lin Yutang (New York: The Modern Library, 1948), Chapter 7.

and negative electromagnetism, matter and antimatter, action and reaction of forces, etc. Spirits, not having substance, cannot act until they enter physical bodies, which they animate. But without the Tao, substance is nothing. Modern physics tells us of the final emptiness of matter. Forms come about in the meaningful bundling of energy packets brought about by cosmic intelligence. These notions of Laotse inspired Fritjof Capra's *The Tao of Physics*.

Thus life comes from a source in the primeval One, divine intelligence, and death is but a return to it in an endless cycle.

The Universe is one; it is whole, and dividing it into pieces is an expedient only for purposes of study. But when we divide, we also destroy its essential form, we dissect a living thing. Laotse warned about the danger of cutting up. Supercolliders, capable of accelerating particles to very high energies, used by experimental physicists, reveal fragments, not the gestalt of matter. The whole picture remains to be assembled by theoreticians.

Zhuangzi, the disciple, wrote: "We go on deeper and deeper [regarding things in separate parts], forgetting to return and finally see a ghost, the externals of things only."[16] It's like looking at molecules, atoms, electron clouds, the nucleus, and finally, quarks. "We imagine we've got it, and what we've got is only a carcass. For a thing that retains its substance but has lost the magic touch of life is but a ghost of reality. Only if we can imagine the formless in the formed can we arrive at the truth."[17] That's echoing Plato: only if we can hear the melody after the harp is destroyed can we know reality.

In the end, Laotse comes to the appreciation of Nature to find and absorb the undecipherable message from God. "There's a great beauty in the silent universe. There are manifest laws governing the four seasons without words. There's an intrinsic principle in created things, which is not expressed. The sage looks back to the beauty of the universe and penetrates into the intrinsic principle of created things."[18]

---

16. Zhuangzi, *The Complete Works of Zhuangzi*, trans. Burton Watson (New York: Columbia University Press, 1968), 125.
17. Zhuangzi, *Complete Works*, 97.
18. Zhuangzi, *Complete Works*, 115.

Prophets: Messengers From God Or Lunatics?

There is much of the philosophy of Laotse in the writings of Rousseau, Emerson, Thoreau, and Whitman. Laotse wrote:

> The spirit of the universe is subtle and informs all life. Things live and die and change their forms, without knowing the root from which they come. The Tao abundantly multiples; eternally it stands by itself. The greatest reaches of space do not leave its confines, and the smallest down of a bird in autumn awaits its power to assume form. The things emerge and submerge, but it remains forever without change. Darkly and without visible form the Tao seems not to exist and yet it exists. The things of the creation are nourished by it, without knowing it. This is the root, from which one may survey the universe.[19]

I am reminded of Jesus saying that the smallest bird does not fall from the sky without the will of God. However, Taoism differs from Christianity because the Tao is impersonal. It's the mother of all things, yet it's strictly impartial. It manifests itself in form and disappears again, just as packets of energy materialize in the bubble chamber of the physicist and produce particles, only later to revert to pure energy.

The Tao is the fathomless and inexhaustible source of all life; it's immanent, present throughout the universe; it operates in cycles by the principle of reversion, which causes the leveling of all opposites, making the same success and failure, strength and weakness, life and death. From this concept comes the paradox that the preservation of the body is important, but it doesn't matter; that success is pleasant, but failure is equally valuable; that fame is sought after, but anonymity is better; that knowledge is to be eagerly pursued, but ignorance is bliss; that life is wondrous and worthwhile, to paraphrase Walt Whitman, but death is sweeter.

Laotse writes, "The universe is everlasting, for it does not live for

---

19. Laotse, *The Wisdom of Laotse,* trans. and ed. Lin Yutang (New York: Modern Library, 1948), 79.

self. Therefore it can long endure. The sage puts himself last and finds himself in the foremost place; he regards his body accidental, and his body is thereby preserved. Is it because he does not live for self, that his Self is realized?"[20]

The lesson of Laotse: your proper goal is the growth of your spirit, the divine program in you, through deep knowledge of Nature's truths. Your body does eventually age, die, and decay, reverting back to earth, but your spirit is preserved with its improved wisdom intact; it goes back to the Source. Your body is useful as a medium for action, service, and achievement. You need to preserve it as long as possible for that purpose.

But you are not your body. Once its mission is accomplished, it's of no value and can be discarded without regret like an old suit of clothing.

10. Zen Teaches Whimsical Enlightenment

When the Mahayana Buddhist monk Bodhidharma came to China in 520 AD from India, the seed was planted for the growth of Ch'an Buddhism, which found its Zen Buddhism culmination in Japan a few centuries later. Zen stresses meditation and the direct experience of illumination, rather than wordy explanations. According to an aphorism from Laotse:

> Those who know do not speak;
> Those who speak do not know.[21]

---

20. Laotse, *Wisdom of Laotse*, 7.
21. Laotse, *Tao Te Ching*, trans. Gia-fu Feng and Jane English (New York: Vintage Books, 1972), 56.

"Direct pointing" with the mind is the method employed to find the truth.

> Outside teaching; apart from tradition,
> Not founded on words and letters.
> Pointing directly to the human mind,
> Seeing into one's nature and attaining Buddhahood.[22]

This is the traditional four-phrase summary of Zen, as quoted by well-known Western exponent Alan Watts in *The Way of Zen*. It is possible, then, that the divine message is in a code not translatable exactly in human words and is best left to direct experience in meditation; in doing so, Zen whimsy and wit maintain a sense of proportion about life and death.

Don't experience and individual wit decide all the important things in life?

We can guide the student in finding out the truth, but the discovery itself must be left to him or her. Consider the acts of love, childbearing and rearing, dying, devotion, worship, pottery making, baking, archery, tea ceremony, flute playing, gymnastics, ju-jitsu, ice-skating, surfing, gardening, swordplay, music making, dancing, painting, basket weaving, and poetry. All these are excellent vehicles for Zen meditation. You can be shown, yes, but you have to do it to achieve any understanding of the process.

Certainly, Taoism and Zen were big influences on Eastern art, and many fine paintings, sculptures, and pieces of music reflect the simple tranquility of meditation—more about that in a later chapter when we examine the powerful influence of religion on art.

Some people in the West have also found connections with modern

---

22. Bodhidharma, *The Zen Teaching of Bodhidharma*, trans. Red Pine (Port Townsend, WA: Empty Bowl, 1987), 2.

physics, such as Fritjof Capra. And more recently, Deepak Chopra and others have shown connections with biology, medicine, and psychology. Certain facts cannot properly be put into words, rational thinking has definite limitations, time and space are relative quantities—expanding or contracting depending on light speed, matter and energy are interchangeable, and matter is periodically destroyed and then recreated (as in the dance of Shiva, the Hindu God). Everything is in a state of flow, changing, as the ancient Greek philosopher Heraclitus also taught.

Zen thinking is known for its close intimacy with Nature. Asian poets and painters have expressed this relationship beautifully. Zen masters spend many hours a day practicing meditation in one form or another and many years to achieve *satori* or illumination. This sometimes comes suddenly, like the conversion of St. Paul to Christianity, and sometimes more gradually. Devices such as *koans*—bizarre word puzzles to be meditated upon—are used to stimulate the student's intuitive powers and elicit the satori response.

The answer the student gives to the *koan* tells the master or *roshi* whether the student has reached a certain level of illumination. When in long meditation, if the student begins to doze off, the master hits him hard on the shoulder with a stick. After about thirty years of this treatment, one may become a master himself and bestow such attentions to a new generation of monks.

Shunryu Suzuki, a Zen master who brought his art to America, collected his teachings in a fine little volume entitled *Zen Mind, Beginner's Mind*. In his last years, he lived and taught in Los Altos, California, near San Francisco, where he founded the Zen Mountain Center.

Suzuki said, "The World is its own magic."[23]

Much attention is given to posture in meditation by Suzuki and other Zen masters, as it is by yogis. Sitting meditation is called zazen, crossed-legged on the floor or mat, head and back straight, spine vertical. It's not a comfortable position unless you're accustomed to it. The idea is to relax and keep the body and mind still and receptive. It makes sense. We know that posture affects the mind. Smile, and you start

---

23. Shunryu Suzuki, *Zen Mind, Beginner's Mind* (New York: Weatherhill, 1970), 39.

feeling better. Keep your head up, and your spirit is lifted; stand at attention, and you tend to become more alert.

There may be a posture best suited for spiritual linking and reception. I prefer to lie down on the floor to meditate in the dead man's posture—legs and arms spread apart, the small of my back against the floor. But not when I am sleepy. Meditation requires that you be relaxed and passive but alert and aware, like a cat in the grass, motionless, observing your prey.

Zen monks are very dedicated to meditation and discipline. That's the Buddhist tradition. The purpose is to achieve, without the aid of drugs, an altered state of consciousness: the Buddha mind. When that happens, you're no longer your little self but part of the Cosmic Mind. This is your true nature, unique and yet merged into the whole of creation. It's the "unitary" experience, feeling you are part of God in your own heart.

Whatever success a Zen student may achieve in meditation, however, he or she should maintain a fresh and modest outlook. That's the beginner's mind of Suzuki. To believe that you have scaled the heights and have arrived at your destination may end your spiritual journey and growth. Even if you've reached Nirvana, you need to revisit it periodically, or you may lose contact.

Nirvana is fine, but I enjoy the whimsy of Zen, also its humor and sense of proportion.

After scaling the heights, Zen Buddhists set other goals. "Although sentient beings are innumerable, we vow to save them."[24] Missionary work is essential to the faith. The saint will go to the world and teach others what he has learned in deep meditation. "Although evil desires are limitless, we vow to be rid of them."[25] It may be impossible to be totally free of sin, but one does not give up the battle against it. "Although the teaching [of Buddhism] is limitless, we vow to learn it

---

24. Zen Mountain Monastery, *Liturgy of Zen Buddhism* (New York: Zen Mountain Monastery, 2024), https://zmm.org/teachings-and-training/four-bodhisattva-vows/.
25. Zen Center of Los Angeles, *Liturgy of Zen Buddhism* (Los Angeles: Zen Center of Los Angeles, 2023), 2.

all."[26] The pursuit of knowledge is never ending because new findings appear constantly like branches on a tree. "Although Buddhism [becoming a Buddha] is unattainable, we vow to attain it."[27] To attain the full perfection of Buddha nature may be impossible, but a disciple will try to achieve it as long as he or she lives.

After all, a human being has innumerable lives to keep trying for this perfection, according to the scriptures handed down from Hinduism.

11. The Mormon Tablets Are Sources of Discipline

Many centuries later, in America, a young man named Joseph Smith had a vision of an angel with the name Moroni. The angel gave Joseph Smith instructions on where to find some golden tablets buried in a hill. The tablets had hieroglyphics, which Smith was able to translate into English with the help of Moroni. Then the angel buried the golden tablets again in an unknown place for future generations, but not before they were witnessed by several men who swore to their testimony in writing.

The translation of the golden tablets resulted in the Book of Mormon, a new Christian revelation for America and the world. Some people, more women than men, believed Joseph Smith, and the Mormon faith was born. Of course, other good Christians hated the Mormons, who practiced the custom of polygamy. Joseph Smith was killed in a riot. The Mormons were forced west to the Great American Desert near the Great Salt Lake of Utah, where they found the Promised Land and underground water. A new religious culture bloomed there and has spread around the world, which numbers millions of adherents. Mormonism is a powerful Christian sect leading people to better lives for themselves and society.

When Jesus was asked about prophets that were to follow him, how

---

26. San Francisco Zen Center, *Liturgy of Zen Buddhism* (San Francisco: San Francisco Zen Center, 1970), 2.
27. Zen Mountain Monastery, *Liturgy of Zen Buddhism* (Mount Tremper: Zen Mountain Monastery, 1970), 3.

the people would know the true ones from the false ones, he answered, "By their fruits, ye shall know them."[28] The Mormons are disciplined, hard-working, thrifty, good family men now that they have fewer wives, and charitable to their own unfortunate co-religionists and to others. They are honest, loyal, and faithful. Not surprisingly, Mormons are successful in business and the professions. Believe the golden tablets story and the Book of Mormon or not, but you have to believe the Mormons have a culture and a tradition worthy of note.

Mormon Church culture fosters family values and personal accountability for one's behavior—clean living with no drugs, cigarettes, liquor, gambling, or illicit sex. Mormon teachings emphasize direct communion with God and the Holy Spirit by each believer and the full support and cooperation of the Church in every phase of life. If this is a cult, then the word has a new and better meaning.

You may consider the teachings of the Church of Latter-Day Saints as moronic myths. Think then about what you believe, if anything. A myth or legend holds symbolic meanings: it's the quality of the content in the message, not the symbols, that is important. As a reference, look up Joseph Campbell's books, especially *The Hero with a Thousand Faces*. If there is a cosmic message, it's probably indecipherable in our human languages. The closest we come to its content is through great poetry, like that of Walt Whitman, Shakespeare, Dante, Goethe, Shelley, and Milton, or through the paintings of El Greco, Michelangelo, da Vinci, Rembrandt, Van Gogh, and other artistic geniuses.

What myths do I believe in?

If my mind must be boxed in any creed or spiritual practice, my choice would be Zen Buddhism because it demands the least amount of credulity. If there's a Supreme Being, speaking through the great prophets, He and She did not create the universe—a messy place, though splendid in many ways, with brilliant suns, galaxies, and clouds of luminescent gas. There's no fairness, justice, or compassion in the universe outside; these paragons exist only in the world within our minds.

---

28. Matthew 7:16 (NIV).

What we find studying the universe is a huge indifference to our sufferings, concerns, and hopes.

Galaxies are formed, evolve into suns and planets, perhaps with living and intelligent beings, and then randomly collide, destroying worlds without a trace of magnificent civilizations. Blind and irrevocable laws govern most of what happens in the universe: gravity, entropy, complexity, electromagnetism, atomic forces, weak and strong, birth, death, and dissolution. Miracles occur only in the minds of believers.

Religious faith offers security or safety to no one, although it does give some emotional comfort to believers. Invariably, people running to a church or temple during an air attack are bombed to smithereens. In 1453, when Constantinople fell to the Turks, thousands of people seeking refuge in Saint Sophia were butchered or raped, and the inner sanctum was desecrated. Presumably, the Christian God stood by and did nothing to defend the second-largest center of the Christian faith while Allah cheered the Muslims and enjoyed the show. God, being one and the same being with different names, simply set the heavenly clock back a few centuries for the evolution of human culture.

4

GURUS, SAINTS, AND PATRIARCHS: ARE THEY CONDUITS TO GOD?

I was moved deeply years ago when I read the inspiring story of Helen Keller, born blind and deaf. She was almost wild, dumb, as well as deaf until a teacher dedicated to the handicapped took Helen under her wings. The teacher saw in the withdrawn little girl some sparks of intelligence and spirit; the teacher, after many setbacks and disappointments, finally broke the wall of Helen's isolation, teaching her pupil to communicate with hand signs. The breakthrough came suddenly when Helen asked with hand signals, "Who are you?" and the teacher answered the same way, "I am teacher."

1. Teacher and Guru: Ladders to Heaven?

Are we not all born blind and deaf in a spiritual sense until we come across a teacher who can reach us? Remember, the crowds that followed Jesus called him rabbi before his disciples named him the Messiah or King of the Jews. Rabbi means teacher in Hebrew. There is a very special relationship between an inspired teacher and rapt students. The field of study is unimportant. Good teachers, a small percentage of those in the profession, make history, math, science, or medicine come alive with excitement and wonder. Learning from them is an adventure. The knowledge they impart is not dry chaff, but the stuff of life. It's spiritual food. As a great chef prepares a dish that's a delight to the senses and a work of culinary art to be remembered, so a great teacher guides his devoted students in the realms of discovery and wisdom. Choose your teacher with at least as great care as your surgeon.

Students who chose me as their professor at California State University, I confess, got short-changed. For me, teaching was easy work that promised me free time to do other work to make myself rich. I missed the wealth and beauty of bringing new souls to my field of computer science. What I taught was interesting to me and to a few students, who were patient enough to put up with my high-handed methods, but most were lost because I was too arrogant to reach out to them. Thus I remained a marginal teacher. I sorely regret those ten years of grinding out lectures for a minimal salary. I would have done better on the street with a robe, sandals, and a begging bowl. And my students would have fared better with a teacher that looked to their interests and capabilities.

When assigned to a class, the teacher faces an emotional gap with the students squeezed into the lecture room seeking a degree or diploma. As a first step, the teacher bridges this gap for anything to happen. Thus, the teacher establishes rapport, and the student is open to communication and can be helped. Like Michelangelo's Adam reaching out to God with his finger on the Sistine Chapel ceiling and God floating down to Adam with his finger extended, there is some space between. That space is the essence of personal freedom, just like the gaps between the neurons in the brain. The gaps allow for different connections to be made—connections to God or to other entities. Thus the student comes to the lecture prepared to believe or disbelieve the teacher, not as to the facts so much, but as to the meaning behind the information offered.

The teacher should not violate his student's personal freedom. The student in turn must come to agreement or disagreement with the teacher on his or her own terms, and in his or her own time. If you are the teacher, never pose as an authority; authority resides in the message alone. The teacher parts the curtains and lets the light shine. If you're the student, abandon any teacher who lacks humility. The universe is vastly more complex than any human mind. It's forever capable of surprising us with subtle truths, upsetting our firmest beliefs and convictions.

The teacher is, therefore, a simple conduit for truth and love. A true teacher can be a parent or grandparent—if he or she is not the usual controlling type. A godfather or godmother, in the tradition of the Orthodox or Catholic Christian Churches, may serve quite well in guiding a young mind to the light. Sometimes the first spiritual teacher is an uncle or an aunt or a family friend who notices a spark in your eyes and nurtures it. A teacher opens your inner eye and ear to messages from a different world than the one we perceive with our mere senses. Thus our perceptions of sense data change and become more meaningful. As Jesus said, "Let those who have eyes see, and those who have ears hear."[1] That's a cryptic transmission from another dimension. The teacher supplies a piece of the Rosetta stone for the God connection.

Now, is a teacher necessary for one's spiritual awakening and enlightenment? The holy words and scriptures in all cultures are passed down from generation to generation, with new prophets adding refinements before these messengers are duly burned, crucified, butchered, shot, or otherwise freed from their material bodies. But who taught the first teacher the secrets of the spirit? God contacted the first teacher directly, as God did with Moses on Mount Sinai.

And what happens if you don't bother to be taught the moral code or after being taught, you reject it? Then you remain a beast, even if you're highly intelligent. You may possess intellect, knowledge, and power, but you have reverted to a sophisticated beast of prey, like Adolph Hitler or Genghis Khan.

To avoid becoming a human beast, see a guru; in India that's a spiritual teacher. A guru teaches you Asian philosophy and meditation, leading you to inner peace, quietness, and the avoidance of violent

---

1. Matthew 13:9 (NIV).

actions. How does one select a guru and why bother to have one? Would you attempt to climb Mount Everest without an experienced guide? Surely, you can read about the experience, and you can climb smaller peaks for practice, but your chances of survival on Annapurna are far better with a good and experienced guide who's made the climb successfully many times before you. Or, you can be like the first men who scaled the peak and take your chances. The trip to self-discovery and realization is like a razor's edge, fraught with bloody cuts.

You can do one thing, however, that's more dangerous than attempting the journey without a guide: trust one who's incompetent or evil. I'll devote a whole chapter to this matter later on. For the present, let me say that I've learned to bypass someone who demands my trust as a condition of being my guru. "Have faith in me and don't question what I say" inevitably turns me off, and I go elsewhere for guidance. I prefer to put my trust in truth, love, beauty, justice, compassion, and the power of my own mind to think clearly and surely. You have a genius in your heart as your true guiding spirit. Put your trust in your own insights, if an honest guru is not in view.

2. How to Be a Good Master or Disciple

A master has a thorough working knowledge of a particular discipline, an intimate grasp of his particular field of skills and facts, more extensive than anyone else around. Someone who's reached a high pinnacle in the art of living a particular religious philosophy is a spiritual master, *roshi* in Japanese. Fervent and devoted students follow the master and listen and observe and emulate to learn an art or discipline—they become disciples. The roshi's students have enormous respect for their master, and they're devoted to his or her person because students know he or she is the gateway to spiritual knowledge but must guard against thinking their master knows everything and is infallible.

Whatever the master says seems like a revelation from God. Rembrandt was such a man in the art of painting. He had apprentices who learned the craft from him. He was a conduit for inspiration and was closely imitated. A master is connected with the Source, as were the geniuses Archimedes, Leonardo da Vinci, Newton, and Einstein. The master is highly idiosyncratic, a unique blend of traits, very rare in any age. Such a teacher can't be imitated, and those who copy the master are doomed to mediocrity. The master is an overpowering influence whom the spirited disciple will confront and oppose at some point in his or her career.

To the disciple with the potential to become great, the master is someone to be challenged, eventually surpassed, and left behind. This student learns as much as possible and begins early in the relationship to question the master's ways and thoughts. When conflicts become bitter, out of respect and gratitude for the master, the disciple moves on and gets away from the master's influence to another place. Any other course would spell the student's doom as a flower in creativity. It's a difficult choice because the disciple loves and respects the master deeply.

The reason for such a choice is that learning interferes with discovery. What we know seems rational and right, but it's often simply what is familiar to us. Knowledge of the laws of motion, as expressed by Newton for a long time, inhibited the discovery of relativistic mechanics until the coming of Einstein. Great respect and admiration for a particular style of art tie down the young artist to imitative ways. Genius, at the time of flowering, is likely to be disrespectful of what has passed before and of the incumbent master.

Inevitably a new master will fight his old teacher for creative supremacy as a young lion does the old ruler of the pride. It can't be otherwise; two virile roosters will not share a hen house. Paul Gauguin could not live in the same house as Van Gogh. In the world of creation, one cannot serve and obey as well as command. Is it possible, then, for a potential master to learn from his predecessors? Yes, but certain difficult conditions must be met in the process.

The disciple who wants to grow, respects and admires the skills of the master without imitating the master's work. The student seeks a special path and pattern of growth; the master allows that growth to occur and doesn't stifle it. It's hard for most people to accept strange new ideas. The master may feel new ways are a threat to his integrity and oppose them. In this situation, the budding master will walk away. The old master may be grand enough to forgive uppity ways. In the end, the old master should send the talented disciple away to another place, as the beavers chase away their young to another stream to build their own dam and lodge.

When a master, who's also a good teacher, takes a student, the master shows the student how to fish but doesn't provide fish. The master shares the spirit of discovery and allows the student to seek its rewards. Often the master influences with presence and dedication, not talk. The master stands aloof and distant while opening doors to the universe of ideas. He or she is silent and waits. A gleam appears in the disciple's eyes, and the master turns away.

Inevitably, a master represents authority. J. Krishnamurti wrote, "Authority in its very nature prevents the full awareness of self and therefore ultimately destroys freedom. In freedom alone can there be creativeness. There can be creativeness only through self-knowledge."[2] There's a paradox here. The master imparts inspiration and, at the same time, thwarts it. He or she provides ideas and inhibits new ones. Such was the case with Aristotle, the teacher of Alexander the Great, who collected in his books all that people of his time knew or thought they knew. Aristotle's authority dominated the Middle Ages of Europe, otherwise called the Dark Ages.

The student learns mostly from his or her own observations. Krishnamurti again: "I have to observe and see the fact, the actual, what is. If I approach it with an idea, with an opinion—such as I must not or I must, which are the responses of memory—then the movement of what is hindered, is blocked; and therefore, there is no learning."[3]

If the master is bathed in the admiration of his fellows, you get the makings of a prima donna and there's room for only one such in a theater. Such a master, like the great actor and director Orson Welles, indulges in self-adoration and gets fat in body and mind. A regular

---

2. Jiddu Krishnamurti, *The First and Last Freedom* (New York: Harper & Brothers, 1954), 42.
3. Krishnamurti, *Freedom*, 24.

dinner for him was two steaks, a whole pineapple, triple pistachio ice cream, and a full bottle of scotch. Welles had the means to satisfy his appetites, and he knew his uniqueness. He could not be easily replaced, and he took advantage of it. It's far better for such a master to remain unrecognized and despised until after his death, like Vincent van Gogh. Let this master live in an attic and starve until he or she learns the value of humility.

On the other hand, a true master has a beginner's mind. S. Suzuki spoke well about this in his *Zen Mind, Beginner's Mind*. "The goal of practice is always to keep our beginner's mind . . . if your mind is empty, it is always ready for anything; it is open to everything. In the beginner's mind there are many possibilities; in the expert's mind there are few."[4]

You have not chosen your own master well if he or she is full of ego and an established expert who's stopped growing. Such a master is ready for the attic heap. The disciple needs to run away from such a person. Socrates said, "One thing I know, that I know nothing!"[5] That's an exaggeration, but it's a good attitude to have if the world applauds you and your disciples adore you. It's beneficial for a master to be laughed at once in a while. Laotse wrote: "The Tao would not be Tao if it were not laughed at."[6]

3. Saints and Swamis Salvage Our Souls

In every religious tradition appear personalities who are especially revered by the faithful and are seen as holy men or women, martyrs for the faith and sainted souls. In India, they are called swamis, and you can find large numbers of them in the streets and the forests. A genuine swami or saint is a lifesaver for your spirit in turbulent waters, but you still have to swim to the other shore on your own.

A saint is usually a martyr (witness in Greek), someone who's been tortured and killed by those holding opposing religious views. Thus a

---

4. Shunryu Suzuki, *Zen Mind, Beginner's Mind* (New York: Weatherhill, 1970), 21.
5. Plato, *Apology*, trans. G. M. A. Grube (Indianapolis: Hackett Publishing Company, 2000), 21d.
6. Laotse, *Tao Te Ching*, trans. James Legge (New York: Dover Publications, 1997), 41.

saint is a witness to God's truth. In other words, he or she's a fanatic, a true believer, and cannot be tolerated among decent people. For the good of society, it's imperative to kill such a person as soon as he or she appears and starts preaching so that he or she will not infect impressionable young people with nonsense. Moreover, as the Inquisition aptly demonstrated in a past age, by burning a heretic believer you save his or her soul for all eternity, the loss of a transient body being a mere trifle.

In the Greek Orthodox Church in which I was raised, a saint's picture has his or her head in a halo or radiant light. Saints, enlightened souls, emanate spiritual energy that surrounds their bodies, and around the head, it's called a halo. There are reports that the aura can even be photographed using special techniques and Kyrilian film. The Buddha was said to be glowing after his awakening. He was emanating so much of this charismatic light that bystanders thought he was a god. He declared that he was not, but many followed him anyway, drawn by his magnetism, and became his disciples. So, the Buddha qualifies more as a saint rather than as a Messiah or a Son of God, and his practice was primarily that of a healing saint for spiritual ills.

In the Greek Orthodox Christian faith, saints are specialized entities. Not unlike the deities of the dodecatheon of ancient Greece, each saint has a special function and bestows particular blessings to the faithful. Each trade has its patron saint, and there's a blessed protector for each locality with a church dedicated to his worship. For example, Saint George, who used to be a soldier before he was martyred, protects the military. He's a dragon slayer, a killer of evil enemies. The patron saint of Corfu, Greece, where I was born, is St. Spyridon, who brought the Christian faith to the islanders and was martyred. His remains are said to defy decomposition, and they emanate an aroma due to his great holiness. The islanders call for his protection in any disaster situation, not unlike the practice of the Irish with St. Patrick.

Saints are not gods but are worshiped as such by many people. They are mortals who were close associates of the religious innovator and will sit close to him in Heaven. They are true followers and devotees, kind and compassionate. They reflect the light of faith rather than

Gurus, Saints, And Patriarchs: Are They Conduits To God?

radiate it. They perform miracles and healing acts because spiritual power is passed on to them by their leader. They are apostles of the faith and spread it among the infidels even at the cost of their bodily form. It is so in India, a land replete with saints. I was amazed to read about many such in the famous *Autobiography of a Yogi* by Paramahansa Yogananda, founder of Self-Realization Fellowship. Saints or swamis possess fantastic powers in his book. One swami is able to project his physical body, or copies of it, to distant places. Another saint, a woman, lives for years without eating, absorbing energy directly from her environment. There's also a levitating saint. Most importantly, there's a saint who travels to the next world and brings back reports of what it's like. This other world is peopled by beings of radiant light; they live as pure spirits in an ideal environment and in the company of other magnificent souls. This isn't unlike Socrates' account of the afterlife in Plato's *Phaedo*.

As a rule, the connection of the saint is with his prophet, not with God. The Spirit and mystical powers are transferred from the Godhead to the prophet or Messiah and from the Messiah to the saint. The case of St. Paul of Tarsus is typical. On the road to Damascus, Jesus spoke to him and berated him for his persecution of Christians. A light blinded him from the Messiah and God. Yet Paul was greatly inspired and began his mission with such zeal that he traveled all over the ancient world in search of converts. Paul's teachings, letters, sermons, and deeds are credited with establishing the Christian religion. So reflected light can be as brilliant as the light from the source, if the mirror of the soul is bright and clear.

It's clear that an essential feature of sainthood is the experience of great suffering in life and a painful death, both cheerfully accepted by the saint, confident in his faith in the afterlife. St. Paul suffered much in his travels for Jesus. He was imprisoned, tortured, stoned, and persecuted, besides being shipwrecked and almost drowned. Eventually, Paul was martyred and moved to Heaven. Why is suffering of such value to potential saints, while most people are demeaned and degraded by it? Under what conditions does suffering make one nobler, wiser, and kinder rather than mean, cruel, and bitter?

Recall the story of Job and his trials. God tested his faith by allowing fate to rob him of his wealth, family, and, finally, his own health. Yet Job did not lose his faith in God and His righteousness. In the end, he was rewarded for his patience by getting back his health, wealth, and another family (the previous family was only a prop anyway and completely interchangeable.)

The moral you gather from Job's story and the lives of the saints: pray for salvation, but also accept all your sufferings and misfortunes with equanimity, using them as lessons and tests to improve your character and soul. After all, it's only the body that may suffer from earthly blows, not your faithful spirit. The godlike spirit shines brighter after bitter trials and emerges into the next life purer than gold. The spirit is something like a computer program, carefully guarded by God in heavenly archives: only a copy of your spirit runs in your body—to be improved in the random hazards of life.

4. How to Apprentice to a Sorcerer

A sorcerer is a master of illusion, a manipulator of reality, a miracle worker, a mechanic on the minds of his subjects and his audience. A sorcerer is feared and admired. There are good and evil sorcerers, but in any case, this person has power and is willing to exercise it over other people. He may be a leader, like Hitler, or an adviser to the seat of power, like Merlin the Magician was to King Arthur in the English legend. Go slow, be cautious, and ever careful when you apprentice with a sorcerer.

Any expert is a sorcerer to the rest of us, like the mechanic who fixes your car or the surgeon who cuts and stitches your body when you're sick with a tumor or injured. The expert possesses knowledge and tools that are mysterious and miraculous to the uninitiated. In times past, this knowledge was kept as trade secrets in the guilds. Now corporations protect their competitive edge with patents or secrecy, as in the case of Xerox Corporation, Coca-Cola Company, or Microsoft. The company has franchises and exclusive rights, allowing it to grow with some basic advantages and earn more profit. It's often not clear where commercial creativity ends and the magical or miraculous begins.

Magic is more than illusion. It is also competence. An incompetent magician has no power. There's a thin line separating illusion from reality. They are not as different as they appear and, in the twilight, they merge, as Rod Sterling demonstrated in his series, the *Twilight Zone*. Technical know-how appears like magic to the naïve or the uninformed native.

Magic and the source of all new ideas in the world is the human mind connected to the Cosmic Mind or "Self" deeply in the subconscious. Also, our perceptions of reality constantly change and what's known is essentially what's habitual. For many centuries, the Earth was thought to be flat; a flat Earth was perfectly normal, and that concept worked very well for people. Nobody for many centuries got into any difficulties on account of the flat Earth concept. The notion of a round Earth simply worked better for those who wanted to reach the Indies by sailing westwards.

Similarly, nobody in science and engineering can deny the usefulness of Newton's laws. They do very nicely for speeds not close to that of light, and most engineers use them in their work. Young Einstein, however, traveling in Italy, perceived the universe somewhat differently and saw the usefulness of constant light speed and variable time frame. His concept made atomic energy possible and solved numerous riddles of the cosmos.

Einstein was a wizard and published his major papers when he was twenty-five years old. Any one of those early studies was worth a Nobel science prize. What was the source of his inspiration? We can't be sure, but he certainly wrought miracles. Einstein said, "Imagination is more important than knowledge"[7] because a fruitful imagination may give rise to new realities, while known facts are sterile.

Science does seem like magic, indeed. To a simple tribesman untouched by the modern world, a mirror is a magical tool. So is a

---

7. George Sylvester Viereck, "What Life Means to Einstein," *Saturday Evening Post*, October 26, 1929.

camera. It's not an accident that science fiction often predicts new inventions. Watching old *Star Trek* episodes with flip phones, one is impressed with their similarity to Motorola cellular phones. Has art imitated the future, or has the future—our present—imitated the art of Gene Roddenberry and his associates?

One is led to the theory that past, present, and future are one, and an intricate web runs through it all rather than an irreversible stream of events. In this type of universe, a creative mind is like the sorcerer's apprentice of Paul Dukas. One must be careful not to end up becoming Mickey Mouse in the water works as in Disney's Fantasia.

One cannot help but feel sometimes the scene we live in is like a grand illusion, a "holodeck" on the Starship Enterprise of the New Generation *Star Trek* films. "Scene" means stage in Greek. We are all more or less like the Duke Prospero in Shakespeare's *Tempest*. "Such dreams are the stuff our lives are made of."[8] Or we're like the unlucky hero of John Fowles' novel *The Magus*, enticed by a beautiful accomplice to an island in Greece, where a contrived drama takes place at his expense for the amusement of the host's guests.

In the most momentous events of our lives, at the time of marriage, critical danger, death of a loved one, or the birth of one, we feel like we're in a dream or play, a situation contrived in another dimension.

Carlos Castaneda has written beautifully about this matter of unreality in his books, such as *A Separate Reality*. Don Juan, a Yaqui Indian sorcerer, leads Castaneda, the narrator, through a sequence of religious experiences of alternate realities. Sometimes the trips taken with Don Juan are with the aid of mescaline, sometimes with the imagination unaided by drugs. A stark desert scene is the backdrop for actions involving various potent psychic symbols, such as a hawk, a cactus, or a rabbit. It's a journey of self-discovery for Castaneda, helpless in the hands of Indian magic.

Jesus also performed numerous magic acts, and so did his apostles. Many in Jesus' audience were there to watch his act rather than listen to his sermons. This irritated Jesus, and he often declared he would

---

8. William Shakespeare, *The Tempest*, 4:1.156-157.

show no more miracles. But his compassion and pity for people made him forget his resolution, and he continued to heal the sick and make the lame whole.

Christ turned water to wine for the wedding feast and multiplied loaves and fishes to feed the multitudes that followed. He cured many supplicants but did not take credit for it. "Your faith has healed you,"[9] he said. He understood that the healing took place in the mind of the sick person before it transferred to his or her body. He was only the medium for the healing energy.

But be careful in using this sorcerer's magic, and don't use too much of it before you've mastered enough magic art. Do you want to believe Jesus healed lepers, an incurable disease at the time? Be my guest. I'm sure the lepers felt better after Jesus shone his compassion on them; those poor souls went through years of being avoided, isolated, and despised by other people. Compassion and sympathy were His magic. Let it be yours too.

5. Do Oracles and Prophesies Tell the Future?

From time immemorial, people have tried to solve the riddle of the future. A king wanted to know if he would be victorious if he went to war. The Oracle of Delphi replied that he should go to war because he would not die in battle. The priests of Delphi neatly packaged the prophecy to cover both eventualities. You notice the comma before or after the word "not" is missing. As it turned out, the unfortunate king lost his life in battle and his sizable gift to the priesthood. In ancient times, it was also the custom to offer a sacrificial animal to the gods and cut up the abdomen to look at the insides. The priest studied what was in the guts and pronounced the likely outcome of an important occasion. Better than supercomputers, the mind of an astute and sensitive individual was at work here. Other omens were in the flights of birds. The patterns the flocks formed in the air could reveal the outcome of a coming battle or the illness of a king. The key to predictions and our

---

9. Mark 5:34 (NIV).

future, though, is not in omens, but in our innermost mind. Use that source of foresight, remembering it's no more certain than most scientific predictions.

In every culture, in every age, in any locality, there were devices to aid in perceiving the future. For example, the movement of birds in the sky was used to forecast the future of human events. The behavior of birds naturally reflects weather conditions and hidden predators in the bush. At work, the trained mind of a priest or seer revealed the future. There was no multivariate statistical analysis then, with supercomputers and earth satellites, to predict the weather and other vital events. Tea leaves, demitasse coffee cups, bones, dice, crystals, playing cards, palmistry, star gazing, astrology, and iris patterns were all used. Any device or phenomenon with a mixture of randomness and order would do. In a microcosm or macrocosm, our own random lives were reflected in the mind of the sensitive seer.

If the universe is one, its holographic nature allows for a piece of it to contain a glimpse of the whole. No wonder games of chance hold such fascination for the gambler. Is there fraud, deception, duplicity, or cheating in such games and forecasts? Yes, but there's an element of truth in such things that needs to be considered seriously. Think of the three wise men: they saw in the skies the star of Jesus and found the road to Bethlehem. They forecast the future of Christianity and the world. A new beginning of time began that day.

Naturally, we have a keen interest in our future, and yet we're afraid to know what will happen to us. So the wise oracle will give some ambiguous answers and much reassurance. Don't worry, everything will be all right. One thing is certain. Someday each one of us will be a heap of bones or dust. The oracle always boils down to this basic question: "Will I, my consciousness, disappear or my material body only?" Some people say it's only fear of death that prompts us to think there's an afterlife. "The rose that once has bloomed forever dies."[10] You were wrong, Omar Khayyam. The wisest of men that have ever lived, like

---

10. Omar Khayyam, *The Rubaiyat of Omar Khayyam*, trans. Edward FitzGerald, (New York: Random House, 2004), 45.

Socrates and Jesus, reached a time in their lives when they had no fear of death and they showed it by their actions. These enlightened men gave us their absolute assurance there's an existence after death. They knew.

Often, our questions to the oracle have nothing to do with our spirit or consciousness but with the random events in our temporal lives. We want to know how our earthly fortunes will proceed, but we would be totally bored if we knew every outcome. Could you enjoy a game of chance if there were no uncertainty in it? Who would play with you? The essence of excitement springs from the possibility that we may lose —sometimes even our lives. What is adventure if it's not risk taking? Without randomness, there's no freedom of action. When everything is pre-arranged and certain, that's the end of possibilities and growth. That's the perfect crystal of Heaven. On Earth, we respond to challenge and risk. Thus we grow.

Societies and cultures grow in a similar way. We desire to know the future of our families, posterity, and society as fervently as that of our own lives. After all, we can see the end of our personal life, but our posterity stretches out into the unlimited future. This desire gives rise to prophets. Moses was one for Christians and Jews. He led his people out of captivity in Egypt and in their wanderings through the deserts, but he also had a clear vision for them of the Promised Land. So did Brigham Young for his Mormons after the founder of the sect, Joseph Smith, was killed in a riot. He settled them in the Great Salt Lake valley where they still thrive.

Jesus also thought of himself, among other things, as a prophet. He lamented, when he returned to his town of Nazareth, that prophets are despised in their own home while they're honored everywhere else. His prophecies were very big, involving the end of the world, his Second Coming, and Judgment.

Mohammad produced similar prophecies in Arabia and was almost killed by his own townsmen. He didn't care to be a sacrificial lamb, though, and took up arms against his enemies over whom he prevailed in the end. Some of his descendants still rule today in Jordan and other places. This was a man who prophesied and then went to work to realize his visions.

Hitler was also a prophet in his own unique way, and his prophesies are well documented in his book *Mein Kampf*, which I have read with great interest if not pleasure. Germans who lived in the thirties with him held a different view of him then than we do today. He came to be known as The Leader, but he was also a man of vision for the German people.

In his inner mind, Hitler saw a future for the German people far different than their miserable condition after the armistice of World War I, reparations, inflation, and depression. The future was to be a Third Reich, lasting for a thousand years. He largely realized his dream in the thirties and early forties. It was his astounding early successes that deranged his mind and led to the attack on the Soviet Union at a time when German forces were still fighting the British Empire. Hitler's goal was to drive through Russia and send his troops south to the Middle Eastern oil fields in a pincer movement with Rommel's troops in Africa. The ancient Greeks had a saying: "Those whom the gods wish to destroy, they first drive mad."[11]

6. Holy Men and Apostles Light Our Path

Holy is something coming from God; something that has part God's essence, belonging to Him and Her. Places may be holy or sacred. Moses saw the burning bush that was not consumed by fire and was told, "Remove your shoes. You are on holy ground."[12] A special light imbues such a place. Such as Delphi in Greece, the Isle of Man in Great Britain, and Taos in New Mexico. Then we have holy cities: Jerusalem, Mecca, and Rome. Catholics judge the Pope to be holy. He's the Holy Father. The Holy Mother, on the other hand, is Mary, mother of Jesus. Permeating all such sacred entities is the Holy Spirit or Holy Ghost.

---

11. William Anderson Scott, *Daniel, a Model for Young Men* (New York: Carlton & Phillips, 1854), 115.
12. Exodus 3:5 (NIV).

Gurus, Saints, And Patriarchs: Are They Conduits To God?

The holy spirits of men and women of God guide us to a nobler spiritual and bodily existence.

But what is holy? It's something or someone pure and perfect in a spiritual sense; someone free of sin, beyond the common failings of mankind—someone who can't do wrong because his sense of morality comes directly from God. That's a holy man or woman. He or she is without blemish, simple, direct, at peace, quiet, and gentle like a young child, innocent and without guile. "Suffer the children to come onto me,"[13] said Jesus to his disciples. Children's souls are fresh from Heaven and haven't suffered any corruption on Earth as yet. A perfect example of a pure soul is the young Christ child, born in Bethlehem, so much admired by Christians. The sky's clear, and the stars are bright. A deep quiet, stillness, pervades the countryside. The air is cool and fresh. Most people and animals are asleep. Mary labors and Joseph is standing by. Three wise pilgrims and shepherds approach, guided to the stable by a bright star.

An older person sometimes also approaches this holy state, if he or she has led a good life and has nothing to fear from the next one. As such a person approaches the Source again, a blessed innocence and purity descend on him or her, and they become a child again with a fresh glow. I have seen this look in the faces of old men and women of simple faith and open heart; people who have served their families and communities without selfish passions. I have seen it in the faces of dedicated artists or artisans who have achieved complete mastery and intimacy with what they create. They're happy and trusting. They have no fear of aging or death.

Such people are focused and sure. Their thought is like a coherent light beam, like a clear crystal directing their destinies. Any flaw in the soul would distort the transmission from Beyond and be amplified many times in the outpouring of Cosmic Energy. Yet the power would be there and lead to horrible acts, thus the need for purity and holiness. A holy person puts away all selfish desires for himself or his community and moves in perfect grace. The slings and arrows of outra-

---

13. Matthew 19:14 (KJV).

geous fortune do not really touch the holy. In a den of hungry lions, the holy one is undisturbed, like Daniel. Even if he's torn to pieces, he goes to the next world in perfect equanimity. "Though I walk in the valley of the shadow of death, I shall fear no evil,"[14] the psalmist sang.

Now, some holy men become apostles. The blessed person is fired up about helping others and spreading his or her message of good news far and wide. A prime example of the apostle was St. Paul; he effectively founded the Christian Church in the ancient Mediterranean region. Another great apostle was Mohammad, who called himself God's apostle in the Arabic language; still another influential apostle was Bodhidharma, a Buddhist disciple, who left his native India to travel and teach in China. His message blended there with Taoism and spread to Japan, where it flowered as Zen Buddhism.

Apostle means messenger in Greek, a messenger from God. The apostle is the receiver of a transmission from the Ideal World or from an Ideal Person, such as the Christ. The apostle has to be capable of speech or other means of communication to do his job. Bodhidharma used other means. In China, he lived in a cave and stared at a wall for most of the day, deep in meditation. According to legend, he was a rather sullen fellow with big, glaring eyes. Yet he impressed many disciples who became devoted to him.

Any brand of faith would not be around for long without apostles. Religions spread because some people will sacrifice their comfort, possessions, and even their lives to communicate to others what they passionately believe is vital and true—that is, their particular brand of faith or illusion.

Apostles and missionaries seek converts, new believers, as lions want fresh meat every day or so. Established believers often become complacent, especially if they inherit their faith from parents. New converts are more enthusiastic and eager. So apostles and missionaries set out continuously from the holy cities and other faith centers to the boondocks and beyond to gather up the grain for God's mill.

Another version of the apostle is the evangelist, such as Billy

---

14. Psalm 23:4 (KJV).

Graham, and lesser players, such as Taggart, Backer, and Koresh. The spirit of God seizes them, and out they go to save the souls of men and women. These evangelists are mostly concerned about reviving the old faith, rather than spreading a new one. They remind people of the delights of Heaven for the righteous and the fierce punishments of Hell for evildoers and unbelievers. Are the evangelists really inspired? Are these people connected to the Source of Goodness? Or are they rabble-rousers and demagogues of religion? Their personal conduct and the fruits of their actions supply the answer.

Follow in the path of your holy fathers to a brighter future, being careful whom you follow. False prophets abound, spreading deceit, theft, fraud, death, and destruction in their wake. Such leaders are not followers of the Lord of Love, Creator of Life. Some other entity is the master of false prophets, who sow the seeds of bad religions, as I shall show at length in Chapter V of this volume.

7. Popes and Patriarchs Guide the Faithful

The Pope is a patriarch or chief father. His seat is in Rome as the head of the Catholic Church spread around the world. But we'll use the term loosely here to describe the head of a major church or religious faith. In this sense, the bishop of Constantinople (Istanbul now) is the Pope of the Greek Orthodox faith and head of the Eastern Christian Church. Popes and Patriarchs guide us according to Church tradition and have a direct line of communication to God to ask for explanations when moral problems arise among the faithful, such as birth control or abortion.

There was a time when the bishop of Constantinople was as important as the bishop of Rome, or even more important. After all, Emperor Constantine brought the seat of the Roman Empire to Byzantium on the Bosporus, and there established a Christian state. Being near Greece and Armenia, the new empire was soon dominated by these two cultures. Many of the Byzantine emperors were of Greek or Armenian origin and the official language of the empire became Greek. Little by little, the Byzantine Empire gave way to the Barbarian hordes, and eventually, the capital itself fell to the Turks. The Ottomans became rulers of that region of the world.

In the West, the Roman Empire also fell to barbarians from the North, but the Catholic Church conquered their savage minds and converted them to Christianity. The Pope became more important now than the Patriarch in Istanbul and the two Churches split in the Schism. The Catholic Church became ascendant and, through Spanish and Portuguese conquests, spread to the New World. The Eastern Church shrank dramatically, but not before converting the Russians. The Czar had considered Islam for his people, but the Eastern Bishop promised the Russian Church full autonomy and equal status.

Meanwhile, the Pope ruled over the kingdoms of the West, and his power was supreme in religious matters. It was during this period that the doctrine of the Pope's infallibility emerged, which is of interest to us. The Catholic Church does not advertise this doctrine much today, but the idea is that the Pope can talk to God and get advice. When he issues an encyclical, a letter to the bishops of the church, he's providing instructions given to him by the Almighty. The Pope has a connection with God not disturbed by any static or error. His cellular phone to Heaven is digital, not analog, and does not suffer from interference.

The Holy Synod, a council of cardinals, convenes periodically and also rules on issues of faith. Whatever the decisions handed down from the Pope and from the Holy Synod, all good Catholics must follow or face the peril of excommunication, a cutting off from the body of the Holy Church. In the old days, the apostates could face trial at the hands of the Inquisition and fire at the stake. That was the punishment for questioning anything at all with regard to religious teachings. Now the way of modern science differs greatly from old religion. Science invites questioning and scientists consider new ideas freely, although often with resentment. Old religion puts fingers in ears and declares any questioner to be a traitor to the faith.

Why is this so? It's a method of control over the faithful. A leader appears stronger if he's not questioned. Hitler didn't allow opposition to his ideas from the German generals in World War II, even when his decisions were disastrous. When the leader has absolute self-confidence, this leader wields almost magical powers and, when gifted, is capable of extraordinary achievements. Consider, for example, Alexander or Napoleon. There is, of course, a flip side to this situation.

Remember Nero and Caligula of the Roman Empire? If you want total obedience from your followers, it helps to declare that you are infallible and have them accept this claim. It's what a doctor, attorney, or accountant does when you walk into his or her office on business. As a result, the fee is larger, your cooperation is assured, and the chance of a malpractice lawsuit is lessened. The monarch cannot appear naked in ignorance.

This prestige and assurance of the great leader may be transferred to successive heads of the institution. Then the leader is called a patriarch, meaning fatherly ruler in Greek. Eastern religions also follow the tradition of patriarchs. In Tibetan Buddhism, the patriarch is also an incarnation of past spiritual leaders. In Zen Buddhism, Bodhidharma was the first patriarch that brought the faith to China. A patriarch passes the mystical torch of faith to his disciple and successor by some invisible, esoteric means. The transfer of the Holy Spirit is not by means of words or acts but by osmosis between the patriarch and his successor. One day, the successor simply becomes aware of the message from God and carries that transmission forward in time to the next patriarch.

What exactly happens in this mysterious process of religious transmission? One would need to be a patriarch to know, and then he would not be able to explain it to others because it's a matter beyond words, encrypted in a code that must remain indecipherable even by the best cryptographers in the world. Consider an analogy. If you have known sexual union with your beloved, you know what it's like. No lecture, no analysis, no description will communicate to anyone who has not known sexual love the experience of blending physically with the beloved. Poetry can hint at the feeling as it does for religious ecstasy.

Legend says that when Bodhidharma meditated in his cave, a man named Huyku approached him and wanted to be his disciple. The first patriarch ignored him. Huyku pleaded repeatedly outside the cave in the snow for many days. The patriarch kept staring at the wall of the cave. Finally, Huyku cut off his arm to show his earnestness, and the patriarch admitted him. Thus Huyku became a link in the chain of Zen patriarchs in China and Japan. Huyku offered his arm as a sacrifice to his search. Others have offered their testicles, physically or mentally.

Although possessing testicles, a priest in the Catholic Church is not allowed to marry and have a family; the same restriction applies to a Greek Orthodox churchman of higher rank, bishop or patriarch. When such a man dedicates his whole life to dreams of the Other World, he puts away sexual passion and children, even parents and siblings, his entire biological linkage, and changes his name to something like Pious. He devotes his life to spiritual ancestors and descendants: the flock of humanity he's guiding on the path of righteousness.

Such a truly pious patriarch, in some religions a matriarch, the faithful can follow with confidence in their moral conduct. He or she takes the long view of life, looking to generations in the past and future, unwavering in the winds of fashions and enthusiasms of ordinary humans. If a change needs to be made in morals, the patriarch or matriarch looks to God for guidance through devout prayer and, after lengthy counsels with other high-ranking church people, deliberately and wisely recommends a new way of behaving, such as to allow abortion or to ban it. Or at least that's the theory to which religion should adhere.

8. Music, Mathematics, and Mysticism May Make Meaning out of God.

We'll now explore the connections between great musical scores, deep mathematical concepts, and mystical experiences. Other arts besides music give us insights into the God connection, such as dancing, painting, sculpture, and architecture. Music, however, has an abstraction, a purity of form, and a detachment from material objects, lending best to spiritual endeavors. Mathematics and good music resemble each other in structure and feeling. It's common for mathematicians to be amateur musicians and vice versa. Mathematical abstractions, moreover, best describe natural laws and engineering principles; some people have said God is a mathematician. For more speculations along these lines, you may want to refer to Paul Davies' *The Mind of God*. Abstract mathematics, good music, and sound mysticism with meditation may bring us to an understanding of God and God's ways.

One of the earliest thinkers about math and God was Pythagoras, known to every school child for his famous theorem relating the sides of a right triangle. He was an ancient Greek philosopher who believed everything of interest in the universe expressed in numbers leads to wisdom and God. Every year that passes with advances in the quantitative methods of science, the Pythagorean idea of a mathematical explanation for all phenomena of Nature and Divinity comes closer to realization. Even the descriptive or soft sciences, such as economics, sociology, and psychology, are becoming increasingly mathematical in their theories.

Mathematical notions begin in the heads of original thinkers who set them down with precise and unambiguous definitions and then proceed to show inevitable logical connections among the objects defined, such as lemmas, theorems, and corollaries. So, mental constructs that originate in the subconscious and are verified by conscious thought turn out to correspond closely to laws of the universe outside the mind. The inevitable conclusion: the universe and our minds have a common locus, an area of intersection. In some fashion, the universe and our mind are one. The number one, unity, is central to the Pythagorean mystical system. Today, with computer science, we are reducing information to ones and zeros, creating a digital world, and approaching God, the One, and Satan, the Zero: Light, and the absence of it, Darkness.

Another mathematician-philosopher of major magnitude was René Descartes in seventeenth century Belgium, whom we discussed earlier for his thoughts about God and the foundations of modern science. He devised a mathematical tool, called today the Cartesian coordinate system, which united the refined geometry of Euclid from ancient times to the algebra of Arab thinkers. Now, mathematical equations and algebraic expressions can be converted into graphics: two-dimensional, three-dimensional, or multidimensional images, and such graphics are implemented as machines and structures in the physical world.

Modern mathematics emerged with the calculus of Newton and Leibniz and employs the notions of the infinite and the infinitesimal, the infinitely small. Infinity is commonly offered to be an attribute of God by religious philosophers. God has no limits. He is the limit. The universe was until recently thought to be infinite and then our radio telescopes detected its limits in the background radiation of the Big Bang. At the same time, theories are now proposed of multiple universes, an infinite number of them.

Infinity is hard to comprehend and handle. Yet in calculus it's used to solve problems that were intractable for ancient Greek mathematicians. For example, the slope of a curve may be calculated by taking the ratio of infinitesimal distances to the limit of zero. Some terms in the expression of the slope disappear in the limit, and what remains is a formula for the slope. Similar calculations allow us to derive the value of the mathematical constant Pi to any degree of accuracy and achieve the squaring of the circle, a famous problem from antiquity.

Two other mathematical developments occurred about one hundred years ago that are of interest: first, the development of probability theory and statistics, which deal with random phenomena. These were thought to be impossible to formulate in mathematical terms. Gambling was the activity that stimulated interest in this area. Russian mathematicians pioneered many of the theorems of probability, which bear their names. Probability theory was an essential tool in the development of atomic physics and especially quantum mechanics. Max Planck showed that we live in a quantum-mechanical universe, where particles are probabilistic waves.

A second development of interest was the mathematical theory of Fourier functions, made up of series of sine and cosine forms. Fourier showed that most mathematical functions (relations between variables) can be expressed as such series, summations of sine waves, by integrating the functions to infinite limits. Nobody made much use of Fourier theory until electrical engineering science gave rise to electronics and communications. Acoustics, sound wave science, also makes use of Fourier theory in understanding and manipulating sound waves. Any system that absorbs energy vibrates with waves and emanates some radiation to the environment, from an atom to the engine of your automobile. Your mechanic listens to the sound waves carefully because they give clues to the structural condition of the engine. Molecules vibrate in the so-called random walk, and it is said that the entire universe also vibrates. The Hindus call this vibration the holy sound of OM or AUM, which they chant in their prayers and meditations.

Music is made up of sound waves of a particular kind. Physicists call them standing waves. Standing waves possess structure and integrity, as opposed to noise. A sound and well-tuned engine will hum with beautiful sounds, while a failing engine emanates noises. Good music is the same. It's not the air medium of sound that's important but the structure of these waves and their architecture. Beethoven was deaf when he created some of his greatest symphonies. He conceived the majesty of his musical artifacts without hearing. Listening to Puccini's great arias in *Madama Butterfly* and other works, you're transported to a spirit world of passion and light.

To reach the spirit world, people chant and sing in practically every religious practice around the world. Music puts the participants in a meditative state to contact the Cosmic Mind. Consider American Indian chanting and dancing, African American spiritual songs, Protestant chants, and Gregorian singing. In the Islamic world, the Imam sings praises to Allah in the minaret with high notes that vibrate through the town. *Allahu Akbar*: God is One.

9. Four Great Christian Mystics Lead Us to the Light

There are many famous Christian mystics. St. Paul, St. Augustine, St. Francis, and Meister Eckhart are four I admire especially. These men were major channels for God's cryptic messages. A steady source of wisdom illuminates their writings or sayings, derived from a source outside their minds. The lives of these saints, separated by many centuries and long distances, are like beacons of bright light. You can go far in your travels across the oceans of spirit, following these old souls as your models for living, thinking, and feeling.

St. Paul is generally credited for taking a tiny Jewish cult of Christ's followers and turning it into the world's major religion. After his divine enlightenment on the road to Damascus and indoctrination by Ananias, Paul began his mission. He traveled extensively in the eastern Mediterranean region delivering his message. He spoke and wrote Greek and Latin and was a Roman citizen. Christianity was a culture that grew in the soil of Greek letters and Roman laws. Greek was the *lingua franca* of that age. Roman roads and Roman officials crisscrossed the empire.

The diminutive dynamo that was St. Paul made good use of his Hellenistic education and Roman citizenship. He established many Christian congregations in Greece, Asia Minor (today's Turkey), Syria, and Lebanon in the manner of Hebrew synagogues abroad. He was an untiring letter writer to these clusters of Judeo-Christian faith, and his epistles are incorporated in the New Testament.

St. Paul's story of conversion is one about spiritual possession. Jesus, the Son of God, entered his body and guided his actions and words. If Jesus was one with God, St. Paul was one with Jesus. If the Divine Spirit is something like a living computer program, it was running in St. Paul's brain hardware after his sudden conversion at the speed of light.

He first preached in the Jewish synagogues, but his language offended orthodox Hebrews, who invariably chased him away with whipping and stoning. So St. Paul turned to the Gentiles (Greeks, Romans, Levantines, etc.), enlarging upon a Christian theology that was somewhat different from Judaism, making light of some sacred customs of the orthodox Jewish faith, such as circumcision.

St. Paul's letters are often bitter about his treatment at the hands of his fellow Jews; thus his mission resulted in a Christian Church distinct from the Jewish cult of Jesus. The Early Christians were severely persecuted by the Romans and other pagans, fed to the lions in the arena, dramatized colorfully in Hollywood movies, and imprisoned and enslaved until the arrival of the Roman Emperor Constantine. Emperor Constantine recognized Christianity as the official state religion. After

Christians became the establishment, they, in turn, began persecuting Hebrews and others of different faiths, and St. Paul's epistles in the Gospels gave them plenty of material for religious hatred, even to this day, against the tribe of Jesus.

Another early believer possessed by God, St. Augustine, flourished in the fourth century AD. He was the son of a pagan father and a devout Christian mother. A literary man well versed in the Latin of Cicero and Virgil, a teacher, and scholar, a youthful St. Augustine lived in sin, enjoying the pleasures of eating, drinking, and sex until a day of personal crisis, conversion, and baptism. Later, St. Augustine became a bishop and wrote two theological treatises, *The Confessions* and *The City of God*, both literary masterpieces.

St. Augustine's *Confessions* is autobiographical. In the book he passionately confesses his early sins and regrets for a misspent youth and declares his undying love for God. It's nearly poetic work, in the style of the Psalms. He writes, "How shall I call upon my God, my God and Lord? Surely when I call on him, I am calling on him to come into me. But what place is there in me where my God can enter into me?"[15] The confessions are addressed to God as a lover towards his beloved. Union with God fills his heart with sweet joy and splendid peace. What went on in the mind of St. Augustine? What's this ecstasy that thrills a saint like him? Does prayer of this sort stimulate the pleasure centers of the brain like spiritual masturbation or does it lead to the beatific vision, a glimpse of Heaven?

Similar events occur in the life of St. Francis of Assisi. He lived in turbulent thirteenth-century Italy, ruled by the German princes of the Holy Roman Empire. In the midst of a drunken party with his young friends at Assisi, Francis starts praying. He's in a trance, filled with sweet happiness as his soul unites with God.

The son of a wealthy but crude merchant, St. Francis leaves home and begins his life of poverty and dedication to the poor and sick. He loves to rebuild old churches abandoned in disrepair and becomes inti-

---

15. Augustine, *Confessions*, trans. Henry Chadwick (Oxford: Oxford University Press, 1991), 3.

mate with Nature, especially birds. St. Francis experiences a very personal God that he knows through meditation, as a lover knows his beloved. He's possessed by a sort of madness at first ridiculed by his townsmen. But over time he attracts to his way of living his old drinking friends and wins the admiration of the world. His close disciples form a monastic order known as the Franciscans, dedicated to serving the poor and unfortunate.

A few years after St. Francis, Meister (Master) Eckhart (1260-1326 AD) appeared in northern Europe. He was a profound theologian and mystic, a member of the Dominican Order, academician, administrator, and lecturer. He was intensely interested in the reach of the intellect to the divine realm through meditation and prayer.

Eckhart was skilled in meditation and used the insights he gained from this practice to explain in a novel and unique way the mysteries of the Christian faith. Many of his sayings ring in my ears like the basic teachings of Eastern Philosophy: Hindu, Buddhist, or Zen. He writes, "When is the will a right will? The will is perfect and right when it has no selfhood and when it has gone out of itself, having been taken up and transformed into the will of God."[16] Again, he writes, "If someone were to go entirely out of themselves with all that is theirs, then truly they would be so rooted in God that if anyone were to touch them, they would first have to touch God."[17] This is the idea of the atman, which is divine or of the same substance as God.

In his essay, "The Noble Man," Eckhart writes of the noble, inner man in each of us. "He is also the field in which God sows his image and likeness and in which he plants the good seed, which is the root of all wisdom, all skills, all virtues and all goodness: the seed of divine nature . . . God's Son, God's Word."[18] Remember now, a seed is a package for information in the DNA; it transmits a message of life and growth, as Christ did, and any man who takes up the imitation of

---

16. Thomas à Kempis, *The Imitation of Christ*, trans. Robert Jeffery (London: Penguin Classics, 2013), 3.9.
17. Meister Eckhart, *Selected Writings*, trans. Oliver Davies (London: Penguin Books, 1994), 41.
18. Eckhart, *Selected Writings*, 41.

Christ. Eckhart tells us "the eye with which I see God is the same as that with which he sees me."[19] A mystic like Eckhart tries to see Heaven through a kind of keyhole. It's a two-way channel of communication. What you see through the keyhole is God's eye looking at you, and that eye is the mirror of your soul.

10. God and His Sons Bring Salvation

When Jesus spoke of himself as the Son of God, the Messiah, he outraged Orthodox Jews. They cried, "Blasphemy!" His disciples, apostles, and followers were stoned, martyred, whipped, and otherwise kicked around for making the same claim for their leader. I fail to see why the Orthodox Jews got so upset with this claim. In the Old Testament, the children of Israel are often referred to as the sons of God or the daughters of God. After all, it was taught that God created them in his spiritual image. If you are closely connected to God and can receive God's message, you are a god too, and you can achieve God's powers as far as your mental capacity and fortitude permit.

Before Christ, many men and women claimed to be gods or goddesses or God's offspring. If these people had power and prestige, their claim was respected. If not, they were summarily knocked down and killed. Today such individuals, regardless of rank, are transported quickly to the nearest mental hospital and placed in the hands of a registered shrink, authorized to perform lobotomies and other such ingenious attentions.

Alexander the Great declared himself to be a god after conquering a huge area of the ancient world. He founded several cities, which he named Alexandria, to honor his own person, and died quickly at thirty-five following an infection. Being, at the very least, a great hero, he ascended to Olympus to live for all eternity with his fellows. Spare me such a fate and let me celebrate my hundredth birthday like my father.

Other celebrated men-gods were, of course, the Roman Emperors

---

19. Meister Eckhart, *The Essential Sermons*, trans. and ed. Bernard McGinn (Mahwah, NJ: Paulist Press, 1981), 208.

Nero and Caligula. They were not much admired, but their removal from office and the world stage was somewhat delayed due to technical considerations.

Napoleon the Great and Hitler, The Leader, were men who did not claim divinity but felt they possessed destinies given to them by God that entitled them to worship and adoration. These two believed that they were also the Word made flesh with the attendant rights and privileges. Their problem was their lack of humility and the realization that they were tiny appendages of the Cosmic Being.

Now let us return to the notion that the human spirit is a sort of computer program that has been installed in the brain and executes there various advanced operations, different from those of animals, such as creative and compassionate acts. All of the information may be inside this program package, or there may be a link to an outside source that may supply new and more advanced messages as humanity progresses.

Each Messiah, Son of Man and God, is put through a series of bitter trials and extreme anguish as a way to perfect his or her soul. That was the fate of Hercules, Prometheus, Theseus, Siegfried, and countless other heroes from all cultures. Iron takes its shape and function at the forge, with heat and pounding.

> Tiger! Tiger! burning bright
> In the forests of the night,
> What immortal hand or eye
> Could frame thy fearful symmetry?
>
> What the hammer? what the chain?
> In what furnace was thy brain?
> What the anvil? What dread grasp

Dare its deadly terrors clasp?[20]

Thus the mystic poet William Blake scripted. Character emerges in adversity. An easy life does not support much self-improvement. The road to Heaven may be through Hell on Earth, and few are the men or women who get through only by the grace of Almighty God. Acceptance of pain and willingness to learn from it as we grow are basic requirements. The phoenix emerges winged from the fire, but a turkey just gets roasted there. The soul is purified in pain and suffering and ascends to other spheres. So it was with Jesus, our prime Western World hero.

Jesus said, "I have come not to change the Law of Moses, but to add to it."[21] That was a perfectly legitimate claim, which prophets had made in the past. He began his mission by preaching in synagogues and when he was not welcome there, he taught in the streets and open country, even from a boat on the water. The Sermon on the Mount was in a modest mode. He praised humility and compassion and promised the rewards of Heaven for the truly righteous. It was an extension of Moses' law.

Later, Jesus gathered large crowds and declared he was that very special individual, the Messiah and the Son of God, to sit in judgment of everyone at the end of the world, arriving soon then and still arriving. He said, "I am the Way, the Truth, and the Life. No one shall go to God except by me."[22]

Jesus also performed acts of wizardry, healing, and exorcism. He felt the powers of Heaven within his heart; his faith could move mountains. He was charged up from the adoration of the crowds and the energies of the inner gate. He was bursting with the light, and at the same time, he was filled with anxiety regarding the sufferings he foresaw for his body. After all, he was not unaware of the customary treatment of revo-

---

20. William Blake, "Songs of Experience," *The Complete Poetry and Prose of William Blake*, ed. David V. Erdman (New York: Anchor Books, 1988).
21. Matthew 5:17 (KJV).
22. John 14:6 (NIV).

lutionaries at the hands of the authorities. Rome's standard punishment for such men was crucifixion. The Hebrew Priesthood led Jesus to this terrible death. They were disturbed by his teachings, following the eviction of the temple merchants.

Crucifixion was not unique to Jesus. Later on, Spartacus, the Greek slave leader in the revolt against Rome, had the same honor. What was unusual with Jesus was that he had a large following in Jerusalem, and he refused to use his men in a fight. He employed passive resistance. Also, his body revived after the crucifixion and coma. Thereafter, he left for parts unknown after charging his followers with detailed instructions on how to spread his message. He was not a spirit or ghost after his burial because the body was gone from the grave, and Thomas touched his wounds according to the evangelists.

Where did Jesus go after he left his disciples? That depends on your faith or lack of it. His body went away from Jerusalem, and any other place where he could be recognized and seized again by his enemies. Eventually, his body followed the way of all flesh. As to his spirit, would God allow such a magnificent specimen to be lost to the universe? The spirit of Jesus was carefully preserved in Heaven and will return again to carry on with his mission.

How far can you take your mission connected with God? The answer is clear. How heavy a cross can you pick up and carry to follow Jesus?

5

THE FRUITS OF BLIND FAITH ARE ROTTEN

In the city of Huntington Beach, California, where I lived for many years, a Hispanic man used to walk up and down Beach Boulevard half naked, gesticulating towards the heavens, yelling in Spanish about God and His angels. He was harmless, and the police didn't bother him, as his family looked after him well. Was he driven insane by religion, or was uncontrolled religion a symptom of his illness?

People often talk about someone getting religion as if it's invariably a good thing. Is there a practice such as bad religion? Yes, Virginia, there is a Satan who's the source of bad religion. Satan, like God, is an idea we have projected from our minds to the outside world and have realized. Satan rules in Hell, a parallel universe, and from Hell, influences life on Earth and other spheres. On Earth, we suffer from bad medicine, law, business, and government. But none of these gets as nasty as misguided religion. Because religion has to do with the core of our being, when religion is rotten, it stinks indeed. I read in history books that the boys in the Vatican choir were emasculated, so with puberty, their sweet voices would remain angelic.

How far do you want to go back to see examples of horrible religious practices? Consider the glorious Crusades against the Saracens of the Holy Lands. The European Christians waged wars against them for many decades in the name of Jesus Christ in order to evict the infidel Muslims from Christ's birthplace. Islam being roughly the same as the Judeo-Christian message, translated into the Arabic language and culture, meant nothing to them or their adversaries.

1. Bad Religion May Serve God Too

Jesus Christ warned us about false prophets. He said many would come after him and claim to be messiahs. He was asked how then we were to distinguish the true from the false prophets and he said, "By their fruits you shall know them."[1] Adolph Hitler, who brought many benefits to the German people in the beginning of his rule, finally wreaked havoc and desolation on them. As the Russian armies approached Berlin in 1945, he would order existing and destroyed military units against the Soviet juggernaut. He would say to his aids, "If the German people are defeated under my leadership, they deserve to be destroyed."[2] At first, false prophets appear benevolent to deceive us, but eventually, their fruits are death, despair, and destruction. After havoc has run its course, however, repair, rebuilding, and redemption lead people again to the path of God.

Another example of rotten religion is the warfare between Irish Christian Catholics and Irish Christian Protestants in Northern Ireland. And what of Milosevic's ethnic cleansing of Muslim Slavs by Christian Slavs in Bosnia and Kosovo? The Muslims were called Turks (not their ethnicity) and butchered in the name of the Father, the Son, and the Holy Ghost, because they worshiped Allah, the Arabic name for God. Of course, the real Turks did attack and conquer Christian countries centuries ago, putting the infidels to the sword or servitude in the name of Allah the Compassionate.

Consider also the atrocities and wars between Muslim and Hindu Indians that led to the division of that country into Pakistan, India, and

---

1. Matthew 7:16. (NIV).
2. Ian Kershaw, *The End: The Defiance and Destruction of Hitler's Germany, 1944-1945* (New York: Penguin Press, 2011), 359.

Bangladesh. The Holocaust also was a religious persecution of Jews by Aryan Nazis, believing themselves descendants of gods that had mated with common humans. With such examples in mind, you may wonder whether, on balance, religious faith has been a good idea for mankind or a disastrous one.

Yet, true religion establishes the unity of all life and the brotherhood and sisterhood of all men and women. It has brought greater, if not perfect, peace in regions of the Earth where it has spread. The Vikings, for example, were murderous raiders all over Europe before they accepted Christ. Now they prefer to stay out of all wars. The Swiss, famous in recent centuries for their neutrality and peaceful pursuits before becoming Christians, were warlike and served as mercenaries to the Romans.

So, generally, religion is beneficial to humanity, but when faith leads to war and the murder of people or other living things, it's not useful anymore but evil and blind. When religious fervor becomes extreme, it's madness—one of the worst evils that blights humankind. Evil religion is Satanism, faith in the power of dark cruelty: the stuff from which priests make human sacrifices to the gods, hearts taken out of chests and held up for all to see while still beating.

What is evil? We call evil that which is obnoxious and destructive to us or our possessions. For example, we hate and treat evil animals such as mice, rats, wolves, and bears when they come close to our dwellings, although we accept them in the wild. Some unpleasant or destructive processes are necessary for new growth and improvement. Excrement is smelly and disgusting, but serves beetles well as food and, once cured, provides excellent nutrition to plants. Death is the ultimate evil for most people, the grim reaper to be avoided at all costs. But death is the sculptor of evolution and advanced life would not have been possible without it. Death is the chisel of natural selection, sculpting new species as it makes old ones extinct.

Predators such as lions, tigers, and ferocious crocodiles are evil, right? Today, we know that they're very useful for culling the herds of grazing animals and fostering health and well-being in the prey species. In our age, humans have no natural predators other than bacteria, viruses, and other aggressive humans. So, Darwinians might say that disease, pestilence, murder, and exploitation are good for the ultimate welfare of society by removing defectives and improving the gene pool.

Darwin showed that old life forms are destroyed giving up territory for new and improved, or better-adapted, species to emerge. To Hindus, Krishna is the creator and also destroyer of worlds. Could it be then that we advance through wars, killings, and suffering? It was before wars became so technologically advanced that they killed blindly and caused nuclear contamination of the whole planet. Atomic war is then the ultimate evil as it brings no benefits—unless it eliminates cultures not fit to survive in the galaxy, provided planetary populations can travel beyond their solar systems and propagate elsewhere.

In good religion, God is kind and compassionate. Widows and orphans are looked after by the faithful and alms are given to the poor, deserving or not, by those more fortunate. The holy Buddha, beyond suffering himself, sheds tears for the afflictions of humanity and seeks to free them from pain. But pain has its uses. And every activity that exercises our organs to function for survival can be associated with pleasure by means of rich nerve endings. Sexual expression, eating, running, defecation, hunting, socializing, sleeping, waking up, stretching, and washing—all these are pleasant and good. Pain, irritation, fighting, aging, and defilement are evil—so most people think. Yet, with a little imagination, humor, and a dash of masochism, these pains may also be enjoyed, turned to some advantage, and thus serve survival functions.

Even false prophets, such as Hitler, in the end, serve God's purposes after death and destruction have run their course; an exhausted and chastised people finally see their leader in the cruel light of sanity—and reform. So did the German people in 1945 amid the ruins of their cities, rising up to rebuild a more just and fruitful nation and, in the end, leading Europe and the world towards justice and peace. The nature of evil is not so clear-cut. The Supreme Being, or Nature, has two faces, and the evil we see only serves to make good stand out and shine even brighter, as darkness makes glowing objects more beautiful.

Liberty is never so dear as when we have been oppressed, health never so vibrant as when we have recovered from illness, and life never so sweet as when we're dying and hoping to be born again.

2. Insanity and Religiosity Often Go Together

Insanity is mental dysfunction of an extreme form. The mentally ill are unable to reason effectively, and their emotions are exaggerated, distorted, and inappropriate. We feel revulsion and horror watching their behavior. We fear insanity more than other serious illnesses because it damages those afflicted, their family, friends, and society at large, and it's eerie. Any pain can be controlled with the mind, but when the controlling mind is not working, suffering is without limit— the mentally ill descend to Hell. Now, religiosity is fanaticism in a particular faith and often turns to insanity with disastrous results, such as the acts of al-Qaeda. Religion is the basis of our value system and our relationship with the universe of ideas. When your religion is distorted, your personality becomes warped, and madness follows. To possess a sane life, take to heart a sane religion—because if you don't, you are at risk of serious error and insanity. Denying religion altogether will not protect you, leaving you open to evil influences: an empty vessel will fill with something, fine or foul.

Consider the stories of William James in his fine book *Varieties of Religious Experience*, filled with fascinating examples of bizarre religious behavior. James tells us of the queer behavior of Quaker founder George Fox in the throes of revelation. Under an irresistible compulsion, not unlike that of a psychopath, Fox removed his boots and went barefoot into town to preach. St. Francis of Assisi, when the Spirit seized him, bartered his fine clothes with a beggar, draping himself in filthy rags, just as Gautama, the Buddha, is said to have done when he gave up his princely state to seek enlightenment.

The region between insanity and religiosity is well-populated. Schizophrenics are tortured by hallucinations. They hear voices and see devils that sometimes direct them to kill or commit suicide. Saints are exalted by visions of the Holy Mother, angels, or God who urge the holy human to plunge into a mission of service and sacrifice. Messiahs, gods, and other deities also heavily populate mental hospitals. In the streets of our cities, unwashed evangelists gesture wildly and talk to the sky, while people walk by unheeding. They exhort the public to prepare for the end of the world and the Second Coming of Jesus. Belief in flying saucers and little green men with huge eyes haunts the imaginations of millions of people in and out of mental institutions.

What about St. Joan of Arc? Was she mad? She had a vision of the Holy Mother, which led her to take up the sword and lead the French against British invaders. She was convicted of heresy and burned. What of the sighting of the Mother of God by the peasant girl that led to the discovery of the healing waters of Lourdes in France? And what do you think of the appearance of the Lady of Guadeloupe in Mexico? We can lock these visionaries up in the booby hatch for treatment, preferably shock treatment, or better still, lobotomy, or declare them saints, especially if this way they're useful to us.

The question is this: does great religious fervor breed insanity or does madness make one into a religious extremist? Legend has it that when Mohammad went home to Khadija, his wife, after his encounter with Angel Gabriel and Allah, he told her he had become a prophet—or a man possessed by madness. She loved him, fifteen years her junior, and proclaimed him a prophet to his people. Mohammad launched his mission. Hardship, persecution, insult, and outrage would not stop him for twenty-three years.

Genius is close to insanity. The same applies to religious fervor, perhaps for the same reasons. A maniac quivers with energy and excitement when seized by passion: so did St. Paul upon launching his apostolic mission. Van Gogh, a manic-depressive painter, produced a series of masterpieces during a productive period of five years. Some paintings he sold for a few francs to buy materials, others went to his brother Theo who supported him, and the precious little canvasses waited there in Theo's attic to be discovered later and sold today each for fifty million dollars or more. In the end, van Gogh, in a fit of depression cut off his ear and eventually put a shot to his head.

The Russian composer Pyotr Tchaikovsky also suffered from manic depression and came close to suicide many times. He also composed *The Nutcracker* ballet, a perfect musical delight. Are the causes of such suffering some faulty biochemistry and hidden defects in brain structure, appearing under the pressure of a secret dilemma that can't be faced? Or is the cause an encounter with forces of such power that the human mind can't handle sometimes, leading to emotional breakdown?

Mystics have described a deep expedition into the hidden mind as a perilous voyage. In a trance of creative work or religious experience, you enter a realm of such wild excitement you can't safely contain your joy or disappointment. If your mind is not well prepared and guided, you're at risk. You should have a stable personality core for such explorations into mystical imagination, just as a ship crossing violent seas needs ballast.

The further you reach into the unknown, the tighter must be your hold on reality. As a rock climber secures his or her place before reaching upwards, so should your mind venture into the mystic realms of the gods. Depend on firm knowledge possessed with absolute sureness. If you do otherwise, you invite madness and religiosity.

That's because there's no clear dividing line between insanity and normal behavior, or acceptable religious practice and religiosity. There are armies of eccentrics in every land, and some of them are wealthy and famous. An eccentric is a nut we're willing to tolerate. There's, for example, the case of the little old lady who lives with fifteen cats in her house and leaves her fortune to them in her will. Many faithful are convinced they talk with God daily and declare it openly to all those who'll listen. These people are not usually locked up unless they cause unacceptable trouble: if they pose a clear threat to their own life or other people's lives and property.

You cross over the boundary of sanity suddenly or gradually without being aware of it. Your frame of reference with reality, your vision, changes and you know you're right and everyone else is wrong. This also happens to great innovators; except they know intimately how things are in Nature and how to project outwards their inner reality. If, however, you're not so sturdily sane, a basic flaw in your character, magnified many times by the intensity of a mystical experience, can lead you to mental confusion and dysfunction.

Denying religious feeling is not the answer. Much of life's meaning will go out of you, or evil vibrations will begin to hum in a heart empty of good spirits. Like a diamond with a fatal imperfection crumbles under the cutter's chisel, so does a soul, like that of Osama bin Laden, disintegrate in the cauldron of a spiritual blaze. Such a soul is often powerful and charismatic. Such a soul eventually emerges as a leader who learns to drive her or his mind hard, achieving through force of personality feats others shrink from. Such a soul applies magic on others and acquires followers, ready to do his or her bidding. Thus, a new cult, such as al-Qaeda, emerges in the world, bringing forth blood, tears, and deadly anguish to us all.

3. The Cults Will Be with Us Always

It's been said that every major religion started out as a hated cultist movement. But there's a clear distinction between a genuine religious movement and a cult that has nothing to do with its size or tradition. A cult has fundamental flaws in its message, which I'll take up shortly, but mainly cult leaders use compulsion to hold on to members; a great religion, while growing, doesn't restrain followers, attracting fresh minds with an ever-spreading message of value and hope. But what is the source of cults? Do cult leaders receive a sinister message from Beyond? Or is the same cryptic message, beamed to us all from outside time and space, being distorted by the cultist leader's faulty receiver in a sick mind?

We explore these questions by recalling some news headlines about disastrous cults of not long ago. The Reverend Jim Jones got his start in San Francisco in 1955 by preaching racial harmony and help for the poor. He established the People's Temple, which attracted many blacks and whites who sought to heal the wounds of civil unrest in the sixties. Allegations of wrongdoing in the Bay Area prompted Rev. Jones to move 900 of his followers to Guyana in South America to escape what he perceived as religious persecution. On Nov. 18, 1978, a paranoid Jim

Jones ordered the killing of US Representative Leo Ryan and three newsmen and then the mass suicide of his followers. Grape juice spiked with potassium cyanide was used for most, while the rest were shot to death, including Jim Jones.

This prophet's delusion was that his life and the lives of innocent followers were unimportant as long as he could make a statement against the government. What garbled message did Rev. Jim Jones receive from Satan leading to his death and the horrible slaughter of his faithful flock? Other cult leaders have, in recent years, followed the same path to destruction. God talked to David Koresh in the nineties, and he organized the Branch Davidians into a close-knit clan with himself as messiah. Koresh took many wives from among his followers and the children of his faithful, girls as young as eleven years, and had many children from them.

His group was well armed and fortified in Waco, Texas, when they were confronted by agents of the federal Bureau of Alcohol, Tobacco, and Firearms. After gun battles and killings, the compound was set afire on orders from Koresh on April 19, 1993. In the end, eighty Branch Davidians committed suicide or were killed, including many children. Koresh had prayed frequently during this tragedy and claimed to have received messages from God. He said he had waited for detailed instructions from God before making any of his moves, including the rebellion and suicide.

The act of mass suicide reminds me of the villagers of Souli during the Greek rebellion against the Ottoman Turks in 1821. Their village encircled by the troops of Ali Pasha, the rebels climbed to a mountain over a canyon. Singing their songs of freedom and dancing, they threw themselves and their children into the abyss to die rather than be enslaved. Is there a noble way, for a good purpose, to shed the mortal coil? We'll examine that later. We have, for now, bad cult behavior to consider further.

The purpose of Heaven's Gate disciples was to escape Earth's misery and go to a world one level above humans on a UFO trailing the Hale-Bopp comet. On March 26, 1997, Marshall Applewhite and co-founder Bonnie Lu Nettles convinced thirty-nine of their followers to ingest alcohol with phenobarbital—a decisive mixture. Covered with purple shrouds and wearing Nike sneakers, they took off for the skies from a rented mansion in posh Rancho Santa Fe, near San Diego, California.

This was a technical cult with profitable work and a website on the internet. They knew computers, high technology, and astronomy. They believed that their immortal spirits were simply held in bodily containers of little value, and once these were shed, they would be free to travel to a better world. Their leader assured them he had made all the travel arrangements with friendly aliens in a spaceship with whom he was in close communication.

Less publicized were the collective suicides by members of the Order of the Solar Temple in Quebec, Canada, and Switzerland in 1994. Inspired by their guru, Luc Jouret, and led by French-Canadian Joseph Di Mambro, members believed their deaths were an illusion and they were leaving Earth for a better planet. It was murder-suicide again of fifty-three people who were shot, asphyxiated, or given poison laced with sedatives, then burned in buildings set afire by a remote-control device. Anyone not wanting to join in the fun was declared a traitor. Those wanting to die with their leaders were praised as immortals. Their faith was based on a centuries-old Roman Catholic society. They believe that death is an illusion and that life continues on other planets.

Another apocalyptic cult, Aum Shinri Kyo, directed their attention to killing others rather than themselves. They produced sarin, a deadly gas, and released it in Tokyo's crowded subway system in 1995. Shoko Asahara, a blind guru, founded his dogma on elements of Buddhism and Hinduism and centered it on the worship of Shiva, god of creation and destruction. It was reported in court that he once quietly listened to the screams of a member being strangled on his orders.

The cult had a compound on the slopes of Mount Fuji where tons of lethal chemicals were found. The cult even sent a team to Zaire to obtain strains of the deadly Ebola virus. After the Tokyo subway attack, Asahara celebrated with his disciples, praising them for the nerve-gas killings. The leader practiced frequent meditation in the Buddhist manner.

What were the messages Asahara received from the World Beyond?

Meditation gave him powers and influence over people who, having eyes, became his blind followers. The cult was well organized, with a chief for every department and plenty of resources, which were eventually directed towards destructive purposes.

September 11, 2001, brought home to everyone the power and malice of the cult called al Qaeda, spawned in the Islamic hatred of the West, especially America and Israel. The destruction of the World Trade Center was costly, but the damage to the US and the world economy was far worse. A wealthy Arab guru and his close associates planned, financed, and directed this massive assault on civilization using the West's own high technology of jet aircraft against the world's center and symbol of free trade and progress.

Such a tremendous coup could only be conceived in a very sick mind, a faulty diamond of a mind, distorting messages from the Spirit World and projecting them on followers and sympathizers of extreme Muslim thought in the world's crescent of Arab culture. September 11, 2001, was a watershed event in the struggle between enlightenment and peace versus evil, destruction, and darkness. It presented us in the civilized world with an enormous test, shaking us out of our complacency and moral idleness.

4. Crusades, Holocausts, and Gulags Continue Today

On September 11, 2001, America absorbed the shock of jumbo jets smashing against the World Trade Center and the Pentagon, flown by Arab suicidal-homicidal Muslim extremists. Now we are in a war of terror, and it's a religious war, a *jihad*. Humans have, in the past, indulged in many religious wars and such conflicts continue today in an age of global trade, science, and space. Case in point: the conflict between Pakistanis and East Indians in Kashmir, a disputed territory. Consider the attacks against the pagan Indians in the Americas and their forced conversion to Catholicism. Study the bitter feud between Catholics and Protestants in Northern Ireland and derive, if you can, the causes of the conflict and the cure. But the roots of 9-11 are in the Crusades against the Muslims in the Holy Lands. And in those lands, world leaders need to find the resolution of the conflict between Muslim fanatics and Judeo-Christian extremists.

With the rise of Islam, Arab military and political influence expanded in the Middle East, Africa, and Asia. Arabs captured Jerusalem in 638 AD and built a beautiful Muslim shrine, the Dome of the Rock, at the site of the Hebrew temple, which had been demolished by the Romans six centuries earlier. Arab armies took Syria and other provinces from the Byzantine Christians and then the Jihad moved along North Africa all the way to Spain, where Arab culture flourished for many centuries in Alhambra and other cities.

Following the dictates of the Quran, basically a translation of the Bible's messages into Arabic, Muslims generally respected Jewish and Christian populations if they caused no trouble and allowed them to practice their religions freely. The Arabs absorbed and expanded much of the ancient Greco-Roman culture and translated the classics into Arabic, while the West descended into the Dark Ages.

Then the first Crusade was launched in the eleventh century AD. Jerusalem fell to the Western Christian Knights in 1099. The Christian Knights butchered Muslims without mercy—men, women, and children—and burned synagogues together with the Jews who took shelter there to escape the attacks. The Christian Knights built castles and tried to hold on to the Holy Land, but Saladin recaptured Jerusalem in 1187. The Muslim prince treated the Christian inhabitants of Jerusalem mercifully.

There were further crusades. In 1202, the fleet of Venice took the crusaders to Constantinople on the way east. The Byzantine Christians received them as guests. The Western Knights stayed in the city for ten months, eventually turning to violence, looting, rape, and desecration. The Byzantine Empire was seriously weakened and became easy prey for the Muslim Turks later on. The Pope publicly rebuked these crusaders for drawing their swords against Christians, not infidels, and capturing Constantinople rather than Jerusalem.

During the Crusades, and at every good opportunity thereafter in most Western lands, Semitic Jews became targets of persecution and slaughter. We are conditioned to hate certain people and kill them periodically: "they" with a different color or features, the hated enemy across the border or among us as immigrants, these "sub-humans" who also practice an abhorrent faith with obscene rituals.

Everyone knows "they" cannot be trusted. They're evil and want to defile our pure women and mix their foul fluids with our noble blood. So the Nazis passed anti-Semitic laws at Nuremberg in 1935, and the persecution of the Jews began in earnest. Paragraph 1 of the laws stated that marriage between Jews and citizens of German blood was forbidden, and if performed abroad, it was void. The punishment for violation of this law or extra-marital intercourse with a Jew was prison or forced labor. It didn't matter if two young people loved each other and were a perfect match. The high ideals of the Third Reich had to be upheld.

Most Germans were deeply moved by the message of hope and pride in the Nazi propaganda. They overlooked that the Nazi leaders were hoodlums. The new order promised good jobs to displaced workers and fat contracts to greedy industrialists. The Nazis delivered. The Nazi extermination camps, with the inhuman treatment of Jews and other enemies of the Third Reich, will remain forever seared in the consciousness of mankind. The Nazis had a religion: swastika, torchlight parades, and salutes as rituals; Adolph Hitler, as prophet, leader of civilians and military troops, and the priesthood was the party hierarchy.

It was a faith that submerged their Christianity and made it irrelevant to the crimes the Nazis committed. Hitler and his disciples followed clear guidelines from their Source, Satan's universe, and proceeded to build Earth's contribution to that sphere. They were stopped here. They succeeded in another dimension by delaying the attack on Russia and waiting for the procurement of nuclear weapons and rockets before conquering the world.

In our universe, the invasion of England was canceled, and Operation Barbarossa was implemented prematurely. Joseph Stalin, another messiah, successfully rallied the Soviet people in a heroic struggle against the cruel invaders of their land. President Franklin Roosevelt gave the Soviets the lend-lease program. With Stalin's "divine" guidance, the Soviets defeated the Nazis in gigantic battles for Stalingrad, St. Petersburg, Moscow, and other places. Stalin's armies repulsed Hitler's divisions and swept through Eastern Europe to lodge there for forty-five years. Once, when the Pope in Rome chastised Stalin, the great dictator said, "And how many divisions does the Pope command?"[3]

Another religion had been brewing in Russia and its satellite countries since 1917: Communism. The Central Party Committee was its highest priesthood, and Party Secretary Joseph Stalin was Communism's embodiment. His image, in huge proportions, was everywhere, and faithful Communists worshiped and loved him like Christ. Those who opposed Stalin and his party were imprisoned in the Gulag or liquidated by the millions. It wasn't necessary to commit treason against Communism. Suspicion and accusation in the right quarters were sufficient to get you put away for years and often killed. Eventually, Communism, like Nazism, collapsed not from an assault by the Western Allies but under its own rotten weight. Yet some of the evil from both of these inhuman doctrines persists in the hearts of many men in Europe and the Middle East and drives hatred against the United States and Israel, a beacon of light in the midst of darkness. This evil continues because the United States is the hope of the world. This evil foils US and UN peacemaking efforts around the planet.

The heart of Darkness throbs in the Middle East, birthplace of Judaism, Christianity, and Islam, and there it must be confronted by all sane men and women and excised. The essence of bad religion is blind faith and dogmatism, coupled with intolerance towards other people's beliefs. The Nazi and Communistic doctrines fully qualified, and so does Muslim fanaticism and Judeo-Christian extremism. Hitler was a nationalist, Stalin an internationalist, Iran's Khomeini was a theologian, and Rome's Constantine was imperial. But their objective was the same: to regiment people's bodies and minds in the bonds of a rigid and authoritarian social system forever or at least for a thousand years.

---

3. Winston S. Churchill, *The Second World War, Vol. 1: The Gathering Storm* (Boston: Houghton Mifflin, 1948), 105.

5. Heretics: To Save Their Souls, Burn Their Bodies

There comes a time in every religious tradition when someone will be inspired to challenge the official dogma and declare a faith somewhat different from what's authorized by those in power. That person is usually branded a heretic or traitor to the orthodox religion and vigorously persecuted by the established priesthood. It's vital for the future of mankind to study this phenomenon and compare it to procedures in science when new theories or inventions are proposed. As science has grown and prospered so brilliantly in the past three hundred years, so can religion by avoiding the reflexive shunning of new ideas and the killing of those who devise them.

It is written in the Old Testament that Moses received regular messages from God, emerged as the leader of his oppressed Hebrews in Egypt, and taught them the faith of their ancestors, Abraham, Jacob, and Isaac. But when he went up to Mount Sinai to meet God in person and obtain the Ten Commandments, he was shocked to find that many of his people during his absence had gotten into some religious practices, such as worshipping golden calves, that Moses found abhorrent. His loyal followers waged a battle with the heretics, and God opened a chasm in the earth, which swallowed up the bad guys.

The commandments from God did not include anything regarding religious tolerance. An eleventh commandment was missing: Thou shalt not prosecute others for their faith as long as they do no harm to others. This rule of forbearance had to wait for the Constitution of the United States to be declared, and it's still waiting for its full acceptance in America and elsewhere.

Remember that Orthodox Jews also branded the early Christians as heretics, and Jesus himself was almost stoned as a blasphemer for announcing himself as the Messiah. Later on, Roman authors commented. Suetonius: "The Christians are a class of men given to a new and wicked superstition."[4] Tacitus: "There is a group, hated for

---

4. Suetonius, *The Lives of the Twelve Caesars*, trans. by Robert Graves, rev. J. B. Rives (London: Penguin Books, 2007), 251.

their abominations, called Christians by the people. Christus, from whom the name comes, suffered the extreme penalty during the reign of Tiberius at the hands of one of our officials, Pontius Pilate."[5] Pliny the Younger: "It's their habit, on a fixed day, to assemble before daylight and recite by turns a form of words to Christ as a God. The contagion of this perverse and extravagant superstition has penetrated not the cities only, but the village and country. Yet it seems possible to stop and set it right."[6]

Eventually, Christ's disciples, well-trained in his methods and message, prevailed in the decay of the Roman Empire and built the western Holy Roman and eastern Byzantine Empires in Christ's vision. In 380, Emperor Theodosius I made belief in Christianity a matter of imperial command: "It is Our Will that all the peoples We rule shall practice that religion which the divine Peter the Apostle transmitted to the Romans.... the rest, whom We adjudge demented and insane, shall sustain the infamy of heretical dogmas."[7]

The Age of Faith and Darkness followed and lasted a thousand years until ancient Greco-Roman thought revived in Italy and much of Europe. The reformation of the Catholic Church came with the Renaissance of culture, but not before the Grand Inquisition had its way with heretics for several centuries.

In the thirteenth century, the Church of Rome was in full power and splendor when St. Francis of Assisi carried out his mission in Italy. He was the apostle of poverty, humility, and utter simplicity in the midst of a wealthy and proud Church. He established the Franciscan order of monks and his friend St. Clare the order of the Poor Clares. He loved nature, birds, flowers, animals, the wind, and the sun and praised them in his poems as God's creatures and blessings. In the end, when he was dying, he even praised Death, the deliverer, as God's final gift.

---

5. Tacitus, *The Annals*, trans. A. J. Woodman (Indianapolis: Hackett Publishing Company, 2004), 15.44.
6. Pliny the Younger, *The Letters of the Younger Pliny*, trans. Betty Radice (London: Penguin Classics, 1969), Letter 10.96.
7. Clyde Pharr, trans., *The Theodosian Code and Novels and the Sirmondian Constitutions* (Princeton University Press, 1952), 440.

His teachings were very much in conflict with the ways of the clergy in his day; he escaped being branded a heretic because of the orthodoxy of his beliefs and his sweet nature. The Church hierarchy made good use of him. However, four of his Franciscans were burnt as heretics in 1322. They had been too vociferous in their denunciations of riches for the Church. Afterwards, the Pope abolished the Franciscan doctrine of "poverty in Christ."

About the same time, St. Dominic, a Spaniard, preached strongly against heresy. His Dominican friars served as judges in the Catholic Inquisition, and Spain was the best hunting ground for heretics. Muslims and Jews were given the choices of converting to Christianity, being exiled, or burned at the stake.

In 1492, Columbus set sail for Ferdinand and Isabela to the Indies to find trade, gold, and souls for Christianity. About the same time, in Florence, Italy, a fiery Dominican friar, Girolamo Savonarola, put crowds into a frenzy with his sermons against the mansions, jewels, silks, perfumes, servants, and fine horses of the priesthood. He railed against the revival of Plato, Aristotle, and Greco-Roman art. He urged people to throw the artworks and the books of antiquity into the fire. In the end, into the fire went himself as a heretic.

In 1517, however, a protest against the abuses of the Roman Church was successful. Martin Luther, a German theologian in Wittenberg, posted his ninety-five theses on the door of the castle church and got away with his life thanks to the protection of the local prince Frederick the Wise. He continued to publish pamphlets attacking the Roman Church for selling indulgences to secure the release of souls from Purgatory and other corrupt practices. The Pope called Luther a child of Satan.

Luther's escape from the Inquisition was the beginning of the Reformation and Protestantism. A Protestant, by definition, is a heretic who escapes burning at the stake. In England, they were called Anglicans. In Switzerland, the Netherlands, and Scotland, they were Calvinists, after John Calvin, a church reformer exiled from France. In Geneva, Calvin established a "City of God," where government and religion supervised and controlled the lives of citizens. No moral laxity was allowed, and adultery was punishable by death.

With greater religious freedom in America and later in Europe came a proliferation of sects in the Protestant movement: the Methodists, Presbyterians, Quakers, Baptists, Christian Scientists, and Mormons, which continue today, and many others which disappeared, such as the Shakers and the Oneida community.

When it comes to religious beliefs, no method exists at present for reaching an agreement as to what is true or false as does in science. Those who have different opinions from the established dogma are usually persecuted. But it doesn't have to be that way: science is also dogmatic in principle, but in practice, it is very liberal, and religion can be such also, allowing for differing opinions to be tested for truth and value. Religion, like art, is largely a matter of taste. I find some art fine and great, but most is sleazy and crass, even demeaning and damaging. Great art elevates, inspires, enthuses, refreshes, exhilarates, and nourishes our spirit; poor art degrades us. Artistic masterpieces cultivate our senses and make us healthier and more effective. Base art, like bad rock music, assaults the senses or titillates us to exhaustion, while good art refreshes and renews our energies. Similarly, we should judge new religious ideas by examining their consequences. In science we accept as true what works in Nature. In religion we should accept as good ideas those that serve well the individual, family, society, humanity, and all life on Earth, in increasing order of importance.

6. Drug Heavens are for the Unwary

Our bodies are biochemical machines. Drugs and other chemical agents, both natural and designed, can affect our every function strongly. It's not surprising then that some drugs are psychoactive and stimulate or depress that organ of consciousness responsible for religious feelings, the gate to the heavens. From ancient times and in every culture, people have sought a quick and easy release from the constraints of mind and body to the spaces beyond. But drugs lead not to Heaven, but to a far different place.

Alcohol from fermented fruit juices or grains must have been a very early discovery because it's easy to find it as an accidental process and duplicate it. The fruit of the vine brewed was a favorite alcoholic drug for ancient Greeks, Hebrews, Romans, and other southern Europeans. Northerly tribes indulged in beer and other brews made from grains. Ancient peoples attached a spiritual content to wine and other alcoholic beverages, and many do so today.

The Greeks and Romans celebrated their Bacchanalia, religious revelries and orgies that took them away from daily conventions to a sphere of free expression. They also had their symposia, men alone drinking watered wine all night long and in its pleasant haze discussing the deepest questions of life and death. Jesus offered wine as his symbolic blood to be drunk reverently at communions and bread, his symbolic body. Thus Jesus enters the bodies and consciousness of the faithful with his Holy Spirit.

American Indians used smoking tobacco to cement treaties and for religious purposes. They also made use of marijuana and peyote for rituals and to help establish contact with the Great Spirit. They passed on these practices to the European conquerors, and the Europeans returned the favor with strong liquors. Thus many are dying on both sides from indulging in these blessings. There's something mystical in the swirling smoke and the glowing end of a cigarette. Nicotine works well also as a stimulant and has the power to change your consciousness. And a big cigar, a phallic symbol, tends to make you more aggressive and domineering.

Next comes chocolate, tea, and coffee, used extensively in coffee shops or tea shops where important intellectual discussions are carried out and people make contact with others. Coffee is psychoactive for many people who get overly excited after a cup or two of strong coffee. These beverages, containing the active ingredient xanthine, are often combined with refined sugar, also a very potent drug with the added benefit of contributing to obesity and diabetes.

Anyone watching the devout sitting down and munching chocolate chip cookies with strong coffee cannot miss the look of perfect bliss as their souls make contact with the Spirit. Which Spirit is that? It depends on the consequences.

For children, there are, of course, carbonated beverages, which quite often have more caffeine than coffee with plenty of sugar and artificial acids and colors. In our society, children slip into the use of such drugs quite naturally and quickly become hyperactive and unable to concentrate well on anything except smash-blast video games—another addiction.

Back in the sixties, the use of drugs for spiritual liberation was fashionable. Harvard psychologist Timothy Leary then delivered this mantra: "Turn on, tune in, drop out."[8] He and his followers turned on with the synthetic drug LSD, d-lysergic acid diethylamide. To what broadcast station was Leary and followers tuning in? Millions of young people were embroiled in drug use for pleasure and profit. Sex and rock & roll were freely dispensed to all and sundry.

Great religious happenings, such as Woodstock, thrilled the faithful. Psychologists and psychiatrists experimented with drugs on their patients. Reports were written such as *The Varieties of Psychedelic Experience* by R.E.L. Masters and Jean Houston. These researchers generally concluded that psychoactive drugs "afforded the best access yet to the contents and processes of the human mind."[9] It was not a fruitful approach, but the interest in biochemistry in treating mental illness led directly to the more extensive use of medicines rather than talk by psychiatrists. Thus it was possible for the welfare mechanics of the Reagan administration to release millions of "cured" mental patients to the streets and parks of the nation.

In fact, there are unlimited numbers of psychedelic drugs in plants and laboratories. Derivatives, such as hashish or marijuana, of the hemp plant were used by ancient Chinese, Scythians, Assyrians, East Indian holy men, and Muslims since Islam forbids alcohol. The ancient

---

8. Timothy Leary, *Flashbacks: A Personal and Cultural History of an Era* (New York: G.P. Putnam's Sons, 1983), 253.
9. Robert E. L. Masters and Jean Houston, *The Varieties of Psychedelic Experience: The Classic Guide to the Effects of LSD on the Human Psyche* (New York: Holt, Rinehart and Winston, 1966), 3.

Greeks knew of daturine or atropine from thorn apple and probably used it at Delphi to induce possession by the god of the priestess and divining oracles for the supplicants. Aztec priests used peyote to produce visions and commune with their gods. Also used was the sacred mushroom teonanacatl.

Witches in the Middle Ages used mixtures of henbane or belladonna to fly to orgies and visits with demon lovers. Viking berserkers made good use of the mushroom fly agaric, which is highly toxic but was specially prepared to induce a simple frenzy.

Most psychoactive drugs are toxic or poisonous, and in plants, they're defenses against animals that would eat them. Many cause nausea, confusion, and hallucinations. An animal is unlikely to sample such plants a second time, and if it does, it will not continue feeding or survive for long. Survival in the face of enemies depends on a clear mind, unclouded senses, and quick responses, which are not available when you're spaced out. The sacrificial victim may enjoy his or her moment of union with the gods but is unlikely to leave descendants with the same proclivity.

It's not well understood what happens when a psychoactive drug enters the brain. Many of these chemical agents affect the amygdala and hypothalamus, organs that mediate emotions. Other organs may also be affected, including the one that is responsible for the perception of God. In that case, contact with the Cosmic Mind is quick and forced by the action of the drug.

Contact with a deity through the use of drugs does not involve years of preparation and discipline, such as in Zen practice or other religious traditions, and without self-control, the drug user may come to spiritual blind alleys and, eventually, to dark places of the mind. Did Moses, Buddha, Laotse, Jesus, or Mohammed make use of drugs? We're told they removed themselves from the crowds, fasted, and meditated for long periods before their revelations. Then they returned to the world to bring their message to the rest of us.

7. What Good Comes from Evil?

"The end justifies the means": it's okay to do evil, if the end result is good. In his book *Beyond Good and Evil*, Nietzsche preached that evil in the hands of noblemen is justified so they may achieve their great goals. Niccolò Machiavelli, in *The Prince*, essentially proposes the same doctrine. In the thirties and forties, total brutality against enemies was the doctrine of Nazi theorists to bring about their wonderful New Order in Europe. A surgeon cuts off an arm or a leg if gangrene has set in to save a person's life: the greater good justifies damage to a lesser part. Killing is a sin and unlawful, but not against enemies of the state. A war to defend your country is morally right. A body organ may be excised if cancerous. A criminal is executed because he did evil; society orphans his children and leaves his wife a widow if the crime was heinous enough. There's an evil result from every righteous deed and some good coming out of every foul one.

In Nature, a predator needs to kill in order to survive, and the herd benefits from the culling of its weaker members. In any case, adversity builds character if it doesn't kill you and strengthens your faith in God's wisdom as it did for Job. The death of Job's children was not important because he got a new family after his trials, and his original family was a prop in the picture anyway.

We need to take bitter medicine sometimes to cure an illness. Chemotherapy decimates your hair and makes you feel like excrement, but it may cure your cancer. On the other hand, when you take good antibiotics, you're likely to breed in your body evil super-bacteria, the tough ones that survive the medicine and multiply their kind. If you spare the rod, you spoil the child, so vent your anger on your children when they do something that displeases you. After all, you're beating them up for their own good. Burn the witch to save her immortal soul. "My country, right or wrong."[10] It was necessary for the US to devastate Viet Nam in order to save it from Communism. It was right for the

---

10. Peter T. Lubrecht, *Carl Schurz, German-American Statesman: My Country Right or Wrong* (Mount Pleasant, SC: Arcadia Publishing, 2019), p. 224.

Soviet Union to rain bombs on Afghanistan and Chechnya to keep fanatic Muslims under control and save Communism. After September 11, 2001, America picked up the killing work in Afghanistan and Iraq in order to bring to their peoples the blessings of democracy and freedom.

"Thou shall not kill." The instructions from the Scriptures are clear: "Love thine enemy." But let's suppose aggressive neighbors attack your country. Enemy soldiers break into your house, rape your daughter, and butcher your mother. Be quiet and love them. Do not take up your gun and shoot them dead. Moses brought down the word from Mount Sinai. Honor your father and your mother. Socrates added, higher and holier than father and mother and all your ancestors is your country. If your parents turn out to be traitors to your country because they protest Nazi propaganda, you report them to the authorities, and you will be a good Hitler youth and get a medal from the Fuhrer himself.

Ah, you say, I may kill in self-defense. A tooth for a tooth and an eye for an eye, say the Hebrew Scriptures. In defense of your home and country, you kill, burn, and pillage. Moreover, everyone knowledgeable in human conflict agrees that the best line of defense is attack. So attack and kill a potential enemy before he does it to you. A preemptive war is justified in the face of enemy terrorism. Shoot first; ask questions later. If a wild dog growls at you and bears its teeth, get a big stick and hit it over the head. Don't wait for the teeth to reach your throat.

Consider the plight of the American Indians at the time of colonization. If they received the European settlers in peace and trade, the Indians were defrauded with beads, trinkets, and whiskey. If they dared fight the Europeans, they were exterminated like vermin. In any case, the natives contracted smallpox and died in droves, and their lands were taken. The Europeans spread further and further West, cutting down the forest and the buffalo, fighting Indians, perishing in large numbers from poor nutrition, filth, frigid weather, lack of medical care, and feminine attentions, as well as gunfights among themselves. From this cauldron emerged the American race, a tough breed of people, mongrel but not degenerate.

It appears then there's much good in most evil events. Even Death is the great sculptor of life. Without death, there would not have been evolution and advanced life forms. Without dying, there would be little breathing room on the surface of the Earth: living things would pack in everywhere and could not be removed. The thing to avoid is universal destruction and death of all individuals and all species, a nuclear holocaust, the ultimate evil from which no good arises.

What about the dilemma of a loved one of yours dying from a painful illness, accident, or advanced age? Do you follow the example of Dr. Kevorkian or use every available scientific torture to prolong your loved one's life? Remember that you can't really save any life, but only stretch it a bit. You may use the criterion of comfort or pain. Is the pain too much? Let them go. Is there a chance of happiness or comfort for your loved ones with terminal illness? Try to keep them alive. You may also employ the rule of usefulness: Are they likely to contribute anything further to society and mankind? Let them suffer more as a necessary evil and survive a while longer in order to continue creating things of value.

Then there's the consideration of cost. How much should you or society spend on high-tech hospital treatments to keep those alive who are of no use? We're approaching a point in medical science when billions might be spent to extend one broken or aged life just for a few days or months. Eventually, society will have to say, That's how much we'll spend and no more. Thrift is also a virtue, and at times, charity becomes a vice.

I don't know the answers to such cruel dilemmas as these. But I do know I can turn every unfortunate event befalling me into something good; I know I should be wary, as a physician should be, when helping others for my aid may do harm to them as a side effect. I don't think anyone else really knows all the answers, even when they claim to be prophets, apostles, and awakened ones. I search, I pray for answers, for guidance. Now, I am guided to believe that a truly noble person avoids killing and evil, no matter how great the ultimate purpose is; a great prince is especially kind and loving. I want to lean on the side of compassion and understanding; in the face of cruel enemies, I want to use restraint and patience, even as Neville Chamberlain did with Hitler. I want to understand my bad neighbors and reach their hearts before I charge at them with ferocity. I may even learn their horrid idiom and talk to them with their own manners, before I start shooting. Let me use love for my fellow man as the first and last tool of diplomacy—and put away war forever, for "with God all things are possible."[11]

8. Evil: Is It Dysfunction or Possession?

The question now is what causes evil? For example, is a criminal simply a sick person, a sociopath, or is he evil as in a tool of Satan? If a person sees evil, speaks evil, and does evil acts, is he simply deranged, with damaged and malfunctioning brain circuitry, or is that person possessed, inspired, or guided by the Great Deceiver? In the time of Jesus and until modern science arrived on the scene, it was believed that mentally ill people had been invaded by demons. Driving out demons was exorcism, practiced by holy men, priests, and witch doctors. I think evil, such as killing, is a dysfunction: a faulty mechanism in the brain of the wrongdoer, made up from unbalanced biochemical reactions, and an influx of bad ideas. It may be our entire species is so controlled by this original sin, our thirst for killing, which we must drive out from our brains to safely reach the stars.

The prophet Jesus did drive out from people many rotten ideas with exorcisms, such as in the case of the man called Legion. The demons ended up in a herd of pigs, filthy animals abhorrent to faithful Hebrews —and the pigs died by falling over a cliff. What happened to the demons then after they left the bodies of the pigs? Demons, being spirits, are not eliminated by the death of their hosts. They set up residence elsewhere, but at least Legion was freed of them and went home to his family in good health.

In the old days, sickness meant invasion by bad spirits. The holy man or witch doctor would bless the patient and drive out the evil spirits with incantations and other magic. He was a healer, not a doctor. Jesus is said to have cured many desperately ill people this way, giving sight to the blind and locomotion to the lame.

---

11. Matthew 19:26 (NIV).

Sigmund Freud would mutter at such stories and declare the patients in a state of hysteria, which could be cured after only a few years of psychotherapy at $200 per hour. Spirits are stuff felt but not seen. Pathogenic agents, such as bacteria or viruses, often cause illness by invading and possessing the patient's body. These could not be seen before the invention of the microscope. Probably other infectious agents exist, which we still can't see today. We could call these spirits until they can be seen with some new instrument of observation. So, is there no efficacy in blessings and incantations? That depends on the power of the body-mind relationship in the subject and how well it's evoked by the healer.

As to the cause of evil, we consider the causes of human growth, heredity, environment, and possible spiritual guidance. In other words, is a human being only body and mind nurtured by the environment, or also spirit from a third source? Watching the movie *The Silence of the Lambs*, you see an evil spiritual influence in Anthony Hopkins' chilling portrayal of Hannibal Lecter, the brilliantly cruel psychiatrist. He ate one victim's liver with a nice bottle of Chianti.

How is it possible for a world-renowned medical doctor to sink to this level of bestiality without Satan's influence? You say, well, that's fiction. Here's what David Berkowitz, Son of Sam, serial killer, declared dead in 1999 at a maximum-security prison in New York, said: "I'm absolutely convinced without a shadow of a doubt that I was demonically possessed and controlled. I allowed these spirits, through my own ignorance, to control me. The murder and mayhem was a result."[12]

You have also read about Charles Manson and his disciples in California, famous for the Tate-La Bianca murders in Hollywood. His group was a drug and Satan-worshiping cult that sought the destruction of social order by blaming the murders on African Americans and instigating a civil war. His hypnotic influence and control over female and male cult members were well documented. Was he deranged, or was he under an evil spell?

Events in the real world often parallel literary documents. Jack the

---

12. Jimmy Breslin and Dick Schaap, *Son of Sam* (New York: Berkley Books, 1978), 252.

Ripper, the killer of prostitutes, did exist in London but was never caught. The infamous Mr. Hyde was only in Robert L. Stevenson's imagination, the satanic alter ego of the kind and gentle Dr. Jekyll. Hyde emerged after the good doctor concocted and imbibed a chemical potion. The implication is that the biochemical balance of the body decides which of the many personalities present in a person will be dominant. Spirit is in the flesh, and that is the way all things go. But the truth lies elsewhere. There's a Satan connection, after all, and the drugs simply establish the junction to it.

If, by any chance, crime is not solely due to failure in the machinery of the brain but also due to an invasion from the evil spirit world, that has implications for social policy. Don't exact capital punishment on criminals. If you do, you simply release the demons to enter another host. Keep the criminal alive as long as possible to keep the evil one entrapped and harmless. In other words, don't let the porkers go over a cliff to their death, but keep them and their resident demons penned up.

If the Hindus are right, bad guys come back into other bodies, human, animal, or alien; good guys do the same. So, evil can never be eradicated, neither can good. It will recur in another embodiment, another form, another time and place. This theory could explain why, in spite of all our social progress, there doesn't seem to be any improvement in the frequency of evil actions and evil people. Ethnic cleansing continues. Serial killings and mass murders are in the news almost every day. Poverty, ignorance, injustice, and prejudice are found around the globe.

If you are human, you are a killer deep in your mind, a burden of your heredity as a member of the Homo sapiens species, but killing itself is something you can control, restraining yourself when tempted. Crime is a failure of the control machinery of the brain, so an evildoer, while incarcerated, should be treated and given training to prevent a relapse and released when fully cured to become a contributing member of society. In the case of criminal insanity, this is the law. However, when a criminal is found sane by qualified psychiatrists, that criminal is imprisoned and sometimes executed. Is this right? Sanity is obedience to reason. Does reason ever dictate thievery, assault, and murder? The commission of antisocial acts is evidence of unreason and, therefore, insanity. Did you say these criminals are animals, having no reason? Then let's put them in an isolated wilderness area, where they can live freely and happily among other animals, saving taxpayers large sums of money.

Two centuries back in England, authorities emptied prisons by shipping them (and debtors) to Australia. Castro unloaded his Marielitos on the United States. The moon would make an excellent place of exile for the most dangerous people on Earth, such as the al-Qaeda fanatics; they would have to behave well there or perish.

9. Witchcraft and Human Sacrifices Appease Satan

A witch, usually female, is the opposite of a fairy godmother. She's ugly, mean, old, and does harm to you or yours, just as the evil witch queen did to Snow White. She gives you a poisoned apple to eat or some brew that turns you into a frog. A witch has supernormal powers derived from the Lower Source, but, according to Hansel and Gretel, her eyesight is very poor. If caught by the religious authorities in the old days, she was burned to a crisp at the stake for her evil deeds and ways, and every good citizen danced around the bonfire. Witches were persecuted in the Middle Ages and in early New England colonies.

Witches perform rites to honor Satan and chant strange incantations to establish contact with their deity, such as a fax machine does to make a connection with another fax machine. One has to follow a certain communication protocol for this thing to work. In Godly circles, such communication sounds are AUM, hallelujah, Kyrie Eleison, Allah is Great, Hare Krishna, etc. It's not important what you chant as long as it goes with the right emotion of reverence; if you do it wrongly, you could end up contacting Satan and receiving wicked advice. In Satanic circles, the High Priest chants, "In nominee de nostra Satanas: Lucifer Excelsis."[13] The congregation responds with "Bagabi laca bachabe," or

---

13. Anton Szandor LaVey, *The Satanic Bible* (New York: Avon Books, 1969), 144.

"Lamac lamec bachalyas."[14] The first phrase is Latin; the others sound African in origin.

In Africa, witch doctors, usually men, guide the spirits of the people. They dress up in horrific costumes and paraphernalia and dance around the sick with painted bodies. They sing strange incantations and perform weird acts. To us, they appear evil and abhorrent. However, our own priests in their robes and hats must surely appear the same to the Africans. When Europeans came to America, they found medicine men and Aztec priests and despised them as pagans and followers of Satan. It was a shock to them to find human sacrifices routinely performed at the temples.

It is shocking today this trend to describe witches as innocuous and even beneficent. A person that uses spiritual powers for good is a saint, true holy person, or genuine priest. That person does ceremonies and rituals for a certain effect over the mind of the subject and that effect should be beneficial, not harmful. The term "good witch" confuses the issue.

In a way, a Mafia Don, such as the Godfather or the Don in the movie *Prizzi's Honor*, is a charismatic person who uses occult powers, blood rituals, and secret oaths to control his subjects. His empire is based on compulsion, fear, intimidation, and bloody punishment. As a mild chastisement, he breaks arms or legs. For more serious offenses, the Don puts people into concrete and drops them in deep waters. He shoots enemies dead without mercy. Such actions by dons, tyrants, and other powerful witches lead to a universe of an Evil Empire.

A major witch is clothed in great power derived from the subconscious mind and the evil spirit world. Such a person was once tempted, as Jesus was tempted in the desert by Satan. Unlike Jesus, who was told that he or she would be given the whole world if he or she obeyed Satan's commands, this person accepted the offer: a contract was made, and a witch was born.

The way of Satan: do what is needed for success regardless of injuries caused to others or your own person. Christians believe that if

---

14. Gerald Gardner, *High Magic's Aid* (Cornwall: Godolphin House, 1949), 123.

you go this way, your soul is lost to Heaven; it will exist in Satan's universe for all eternity. Is there happiness and joy in such a course? There may be triumph for a while, gloating, pride, pleasure, and satisfaction, but ultimately the reward is pure torture. God created our souls in His or Her image, and they properly belong to God.

Our bodies evolved on this earth and are the product of chance and selection of the fittest, but our spirits were hatched in Heaven. Satan can't create anything. Satan is the destroyer of worlds. Souls that go to Satan are stolen through deceit, cunning, and oppression. Satan is the Great Fraud, and those who defraud others imitate the Horned One.

We're told God demands sacrifices from us in order to perfect our souls. Satan also makes demands on us to destroy our souls. In the Hebrew Bible, Abraham, who had an only child from his wife Sarah when he was one hundred years old, was asked to sacrifice Isaac at the mountain of Moriah as a burnt offering. God used to speak to Abraham quite a lot, and Abraham always obeyed. This command was only a test. An Angel of the Lord stopped the sacrifice of Abraham's beloved son and a ram, caught in a bush, took his place.

The point is that God, or Satan, demands the sacrifice of our most valuable possession before we may be promoted to the next stage of spiritual existence. If money is what you value most highly, then Jesus would say to give it up and follow in the path of salvation. And similarly, in order to become a captain of Satan, sacrifice your most valuable possession, which is your own soul. The Aztecs and Mayans had substitutes. Their priests tied captives without a blemish at the altar, took out their still-beating hearts with a stone knife, and held them up for the crowd to see.

Also, virgin girls were sacrificed in the bloom of youth, and young men as well, those perfectly formed. Their beautiful bodies were discarded thus, and their spirits went to the gods. Men in the Heaven's Gate cult sacrificed their testicles first and eventually their earthly "containers" in order to leave for a perfect world in an alien spaceship.

These cultists were thinking and praying in the wrong way and ended up on the lap of the evil deity. There's much craziness in occult beliefs. What's genuine must be carefully sorted out from all the garbage. Look at the fruits of a witch's actions to see if they are a good witch or a bad one. And wait a while before deciding about the outcome. Good stuff may come out for a while, but it could be only the bait. It's only in the long run that the fruits of true righteousness can be appraised.

10. Satan in Hell Watches Under Us

If evil witches and wizards abound and administer to demons, it follows there is a principal source for such entities, and that would be Satan, prominent in the Christian religion. Christian nuns are said to be the brides of Jesus, spiritually. Their devotion and loyalty are given to Christ, and Christ possesses them. It follows that witches have intercourse with the Devil and, if intercourse is spiritual as well as physical, witches belong to Satan to do what they're told. Through the eyes of witches, Satan watches under us.

In exchange, witches receive many magical powers, including the power to fly on broomsticks. Witches are said to celebrate the Sabbath, an orgy of sex, drugs, drinking of blood, and eating of stolen babies when they worship the big ugly one with the horns. It's a sort of leftover Bacchanalia from pagan times, according to Christian sources.

Most religions give some space in their scriptures to the Evil One, although with less emphasis than Christians. In Judaism, Satan takes a back seat to God. Islam trivializes Satan and teaches about a paramount God ordering the disobedient angel to kneel before Adam of Genesis. In Hinduism, Krishna provides the cycles of creation and destruction, and Mara, the Deceiver, is of minor interest. It was natural that the Christian message, which makes much of goodness, would also entertain us with the apotheosis of evil.

A Christian novelist, C.S. Lewis, fantasizes in *The Screwtape Letters* about a world in which guardian demons battle angels for the possession of people's souls. The devils' efforts are geared towards stimulating our egoism, pride, self-complacency, and pleasure-seeking at the expense of true Christian virtues until our spirit is completely possessed, thus easily captured by the demons. Then the soul is taken to Hell and consumed there with relish. By comparison, God allows freedom with dignity for each person and each unique spirit is preserved in Heaven with its full individuality.

Whether you believe in the actual physical existence of Satan, or God, the notion is a powerful one, capable of driving people to outrageous behaviors. When Ruhollah Khomeini of Iran declared America the Great Satan, he stimulated hatred in millions of Muslims against our country and many acts of terrorism. As we saw, ferocious witch persecutions were carried out in Europe and America in the sixteenth and seventeenth centuries and thousands of people were hanged, burned, or imprisoned because of the specter of Satan. Today we continue to look upon murderers and other criminals as inspired by the Other Deity and thus deserving punishment with death or imprisonment. Otherwise, we would diagnose such people as ordinary human beings afflicted by social personality malfunctions, treatable with medication and therapy. The killing of criminals would not be allowed. The courts would order only humane restraints.

Alternately, there exists a Satanic Universe, one of the infinite possibilities in space-time expansion. All material in such a cosmos is converted to living brains that are connected into a whole. However, the integration of living entities is by force and compulsion, not eager joining with affection or self-interest. So, you have structures like the Third Reich or the Soviet Union rather than the European Union or the United States. This Satanic Universe is ruled by collectives such as the Borg of *Star Trek: The Next Generation*. "You will be assimilated! Resistance is futile!" This universe is controlled by such as the Evil Empire of *Star Wars*. It's ruled with fear and compulsion. Hatred, anger, and intolerance are fostered, and those who do not obey are put in prison, brainwashed, tortured, or killed. This is the vision of Aldous Huxley's *Brave New World*, or Orwell's *1984* actually having happened.

Such a universe coexists with ours, and messages go back and forth with it through the spirit media or wormholes. Dead souls travel there when freed from material bodies, inexorably driven in the direction of Hell because of their emotional and intellectual orientation towards evil. Hell is not a punishment for sinful and non-repenting beings, but their just reward for their actions and thoughts. It's what they desire, and as the Upanishads say, "As your deepest desire is, so is your destiny."[15] So, a gangster ends up in the Evil Empire and is very much at home, cursing and kicking, torturing those weaker, and being abused by those of superior power. Gluttons are served daily feasts, which blow them up to five hundred pounds or more. Sex offenders continue their trade and become children again, in turn receiving the same treatment. Killers are killing and being killed, thus perfecting their skills, until they are sent again to another world to practice their profession.

On Earth, meanwhile, witches are the eyes and ears of Satan, watching under us, tempting us to sample evil and satisfy our appetites. In Dante's *Divine Comedy*, each spirit sends a message to the appropriate destination while in a body. "Beam me up, Scotty," called up to the Enterprise the teammates of *Star Trek* ready to leave a planet. You do the same in your prayers while dying and much earlier. Each of your decisions for good or evil, each of your actions, each of your feelings, and each of your thoughts channels your spirit into God's or Satan's time-warp tunnel, death simply ending the transmission.

---

15. Eknath Easwaran, trans., *The Upanishads* (Tomales, CA: Nilgiri Press, 2007), 4.4.5.

6

MEDITATION: GATEWAY TO HEAVEN?

My mother, Georgia, would often pray, meditate deeply, and go into a state of hypnosis. She was awake but not alert to what was going on around her, talking to herself and expressing deep feelings, inner thoughts, and images. She would ramble on and on, spouting deeply perceptive thoughts together with nonsense in a stream of words. When I touched her arm to get her attention, she would be startled. "What, what?" she would say.

If she fell ill or had an accident, her first move was to pray for recovery. "I'll be fine. I'm going to be fine," she would tell herself. Then, go to bed, sleep, or close her eyes in meditation. Usually she was well again in a day or two. Late in life, she would not hear of going to a physician for her problems. I took her to her doctor's office for treatments, but once she realized where she was, she stood up and said, "Take me away from here, or I'll start screaming." Finally death took her away with a massive heart failure at ninety-two years of age.

1. States of Consciousness: A Stairway to God

I used to think that death destroys consciousness, and my reasoning was simple. The brain produces consciousness. If it's asleep, much of awareness disappears, and sometimes we wake up in the morning as if an instant has passed during the night. A concussion blanks you out, and you appear to be dead. Brain injury damages consciousness. And so do some drugs which enter the brain, such as anesthetics, and put you into deep sleep, so pain isn't felt. What happens then, if the brain is destroyed by death and decomposes completely into dust, how can any consciousness remain? Now, I hold a different opinion, and you'll hear why. Imagine your consciousness as a sort of super-sophisticated computer program that executes in the circuitry of your brain. You are not your body. The hardware of your brain is needed to run the program of your soul but not needed for your soul's existence; the program of your soul can run in some other hardware, somewhere else, at another time.

There has to be a process that transfers the program of the personality, but not the data set of life's memories, to another living entity, sometimes on another planet and to a different organism. This could explain why certain people are just able to do some things without knowing exactly how they do them. Idiot savants and geniuses can compose masterpieces, produce great paintings, or write fine poems simply through "inspiration."

Such people, when asked how they get their information, reply, "I just know. It comes to me; it's a natural action." Have you seen the film *Good Will Hunting*? The story is about a poor and uneducated young man who works at MIT as a janitor. During his spare time he fills the blackboards with the proofs of tremendously difficult mathematical problems. He's discovered by one of the professors. The professor had advanced his career in mathematics through hard scholarly work over many years. The professor asks the janitor, after an especially brilliant solution to a difficult problem, "How do you do it?" The answer: "It just comes to me." The explanation for this phenomenon is that specific memories from previous lives are not retained, but you do the work in an automatic fashion as the main program executes in your brain. Or else, you're acting out the directions from the spiritual world, often in a trance-like state of mind.

A specific state of consciousness, the meditative state, is critical to highly inspired work. In all activities, we perform according to our mental state. When we need to rest, we feel drowsy and fall asleep, ceasing activity. When feeling hungry, we eat or go in search of food. When we're in love, we seek union with our beloved. When angry, our blood pressure, heart rate, and energy move up, and we fight. When we're alert, we're open to sensations and occurrences.

So with trained meditation, we enter a state of mind, called the "relaxation response," finding inner peace and calm while the body recovers from stress and strain. Physiologically, neurons fire less vigorously in the action-producing sympathetic nervous system, while the parasympathetic brain cells produce inhibitory signals to reduce adrenaline production and slow down breathing and blood flow for rest and recovery from stress. It's the beginning of meditation, the looking-inward consciousness, and the avoidance of external stimuli. Material objects cease to be important, and we swim in a stream of feelings and ideas from our inner world.

Some people reach a state of high jubilation through dancing, as the Sufis and American Indians do, or some other rhythmic and steady activity, such as wheat harvesting, hauling in nets full of fish with song and a string of your fellows in line. The women at the river, washing the family's clothing, singing, and scrubbing with steady motions on their washboards, find some of this feeling. It's a state of union with God, bringing the joy of Heaven here on Earth.

You can reach many degrees or levels to such exaltations of consciousness. Buddhist doctrine recognizes seven levels in meditation, which have been named and described. The highest level is complete awareness of some higher reality. The Gautama Buddha reached this level after many years of mental discipline and thus became the Awakened One, or the Buddha. He returned to normal life from this state of consciousness but was no longer the same man. After his experience, the Buddha's face glowed with such brilliance that his companions thought he was a god. Most of us have a bit of this glow after sexual union with our beloved. After union with God, you see the world differently and react to people as an enlightened person who has known perfect inner peace, if only for a short while.

A basic tenet of Asian religious philosophy states that consciousness is at the source of the universe, not material things. The master, trained and disciplined in the use of the mind, controls consciousness; therefore, the physical world is also under his or her control. No task, no feat, is beyond the master's ability, even the moving of mountains. The master, however, may not succumb to arrogance, greed, possessiveness, or any of the common sins of mankind, or the empire built with his divine powers will come crashing down on his head. The mastery of a higher consciousness provides an explanation for the healing miracles and other feats of the great saints and prophets, such as Jesus Christ and Mohammad. Mary Baker Eddy built a modern movement based on this view of the world, promulgated in her book on Christian Science, *Religion and Health with a Key to the Scriptures*. In her view, Mind is everything and Faith can provide the cure to any illness, curable medical science or not: the ultimate placebo effect.

If true, Mind and Faith can also provide for the salvation of your soul by directing it to a secure haven after death. That would be God's supercomputer, where your spirit is installed in an indestructible and eternal hard drive and is saved for execution at God's will or for beaming back to Earth to be placed in a new living body. According to Buddhist doctrine again, if your soul has been perfected during your sojourn on Earth and can't be improved further, it doesn't make sense to send it back to the forging material world, so your spirit stays in the company of God and other perfect spirits.

2. Spirit Channels are Information Valves

If there is a spirit world, how can you know about it? You possess a channel of communication with spirits, an information linkage. Information is the stuff that makes up ideas, and we can think of the Beyond as an ideal world where harmonies and rhythms dwell in God's crystal lattice. You have an information valve in your brain, opening, and closing as needed, and with patience, practice, and prayer, you can use it to connect with God and His universe.

You've heard of channeling to previous lives, a Hindu notion popularized by Shirley MacLaine and other luminaries. If our personalities are unique packets of information, like computer program packages of an advanced sort, they're uploaded or downloaded through these channels to the Ideal World. So are messages, back and forth, and mystical contacts with ancestors and other spirits.

Consider the first telephones: the wiring was ponderous and the apparatus crude, but it was a beginning for earthly communications beyond the reach of the human voice. Then we went to fine copper lines and wireless transmissions, which are now reaching their full fruition. Today, we also have fiber optics, microwave, and radar networks for our communications labs. Imagine a civilization that matured billions of years ago in our universe or, beyond time, in another universe. What means of mental contact such a civilization might have developed in its immense time frame, which exists even now and is available, but is incomprehensible to us? After all, how many people understand the intricacies of the cellular phone although they use it daily?

This hypothetical channel to the World Beyond is of critical importance in our discussion. We have some indications about its nature. People who have had near-death experiences describe it as a tunnel into which their minds spiraled. Hieronymus Bosch, a medieval artist, made a famous painting of it, showing the souls of the departed moving along this tunnel.

Claude Shannon, one of the founders of information theory, working at Bell Labs during WWII, defined information as a measure of uncertainty—more specifically, the logarithmic sum of probabilities in the message. Using this definition, he calculated the information capacity of communication channels. We can imagine the Ideal World as a source of information with immense content, holding many surprises for us, the receivers. For God, the Crystal Universe holds no uncertainty. It's perfectly known to God and has zero entropy. But when the information flows to us, the receivers, it's often turbulent due to compression to accommodate our limited-capacity channels. Hence, the danger of meditation: the way to the "other side" is like a razor's edge.

Meditation: Gateway To Heaven?

It seems inescapable that there's an information valve at the beginning of the mystical channel, deep in the subconscious mind. The reason for the valve is to provide a suitable barrier between our world and that of the spirits. The Crystal Universe has to keep out psychic viruses from the material spheres from infecting its absolute perfection. And the spiritual traveler needs protection from the flood of heavenly information into his mental framework.

The valve opens only after much effort and self-discipline in meditative practice, and the results are often unpredictable. Contact may occur during prayer with the Universe of Evil, where compulsion and discord have crystallized in the temple of the ultimate acid rock. We believe we're in the presence of God when, in fact, Satan has taken possession of us. We're tempted with power, fame, and success and led to destruction and absorption by the Evil One. Be pure in your heart and humble in meditation. Put away your ego and selfish desires. Thus, the valve opens with relative safety, and divine inspiration flows in like the light of a brilliant day.

What's the nature of the spirit valve? It's a mental gate that is enabled by faith. We cannot directly control it without conscious mind, as we control the valves to the material world by focusing our senses. Relaxation is the first essential step in opening the valve, as it is with the vagina in the female body, the rectum, the urethra, the mouth, the throat, and the stomach's duodenum in all of us. The body holds its wastes to release at the proper time and place. Materials coming into the body are screened at the mouth, nose, and ears.

In other respects, the spirit valve resembles a radio or television tuner. This device allows one particular frequency in the electromagnetic spectrum admission to the receiver and all others are blocked out. If not blocked out completely, there's said to be interference or static. So messages come to the psychic person from regions of the spiritual spectrum, and there's usually a great deal of mental static to be avoided. Again, you can easily lock onto the wrong source and get disastrous guidance.

There are proven techniques for tuning to the Divine Source as well as for contact with other sources, which I'll discuss later. For example, a meditation mantra is like a guidance beacon. Seekers often employ purification rites and train their minds to accept peace and love and reject selfishness, anger, and hatred. Drinking water or bathing may be useful symbolic acts in these preparations in many religious practices. Catholics sprinkle holy water. Buddhists and Hindus drink it and wash their bodies with it and so do Muslims before their prayers. In Christian churches, a person is ceremoniously baptized to indicate purification before admission to the faith. Nakedness is often an important element in communion with the Divine. Supplicants remove their clothes during baptism and other rites as a symbolic act of baring their souls to God, as did St. Francis of Assisi when he dedicated his life to Christ.

Well prepared with solemn rituals, you open your heart and mind, allowing information to flow through your spiritual valve to and from God. You go to the Source like a baby just born, with simplicity, humility, and candor, exposing all your sins and imperfections before the supreme judge before being admitted to the sacred light of Heaven. Thus opens the gate to the next world.

3. The Faith Switch Turns the Light On

Jesus taught that "If you have as much faith as a grain of sand, you will say to the mountain, 'move aside' and the mountain will move."[1] What did he mean by that? Can faith move mountains? What is faith, anyway? Moses also exhorted his followers when they were discouraged in Egypt and in the desert that God would come to their aid. Faith is a psychic switch you turn on, bringing to mind and soul the pure light of God.

Mohammed's movement was nearly wiped out in the beginning, but the apostle never lost faith in ultimate victory and thus inspired confidence in his followers. Who can doubt Winston Churchill's faith in the darkest hours of WWII, when England alone stood against the Nazis? Churchill knew the outcome would be victory for the Allies and

---

1. Matthew 17:20 (NIV).

transmitted that feeling to the British. What do you think about Franklin D. Roosevelt's speech after Pearl Harbor? Saying that the day, December 7, 1941, would "live in infamy" implied absolute confidence that America would win the war and write the history books accordingly. He also said, "We have nothing to fear but fear itself,"[2] in the depths of the Great Depression, as he knew full well that confidence had to be restored in the people before economic recovery could come. Rich people had to put away their fears and spend money, while the poor had to have faith and go looking for work, scarce as it was then, or create their own productive activities.

Faith implies that you believe something to be true although you have little or no proof. It means you know the existence of something without seeing, hearing, or sensing it by any other physical channel. Faith is an unconscious memory, surely guiding your steps. You're not aware of this memory, but you rely on it as you rely on your steady breathing and heartbeat. As you walk into a dark room in your house, you open the door to the right, and you reach for the switch on the wall to the left and flip it on. Light comes to flood the room, and you see. Faith often derives from absolute trust in another person and dispels fear. When I bounced my little daughters in the air, they giggled and laughed with delight. They would have acted differently handled that way by a stranger.

In the same way, people will follow a great leader, religious or political. The leader knows the truth from personal experience, and followers know through trust in the leader. Jesus said, "I am the way, the light and the life, and whomsoever believeth in me shall never die."[3] He experienced the existence of Heaven in his meditations and knew the way there. He was referring to life in the next world for his followers, not life on Earth. Many of his martyrs followed him to bodily death in the Hebrew, and later Roman, persecutions with absolute

---

2. Franklin D. Roosevelt, *The Public Papers of Franklin D. Roosevelt, Volume Two: The Year of Crisis, 1933*, ed. Samuel I. Rosenman (New York: Random House, 1938), 11.
3. John 14:6 (KJV).

confidence in the resurrection of the spirit. They would go into a trance and accept horrible pain with a blissful smile.

Who has not played a game, from solitaire to tennis, when everything is clicking just perfectly? There's a flow of inevitability to events such that we simply know the outcome is going to be a win. Is it prescience? Is it a replay of previous circumstances? The signs are there, and though we see them not, we feel they'll lead to success.

A salesman experiences this situation many times in his practice. In marketing courses, one is taught to believe that the prospect's objections are really indications of interest or requests for explanation and that the salesperson will close in the end. When a salesperson proceeds with great confidence, the result is a much higher percentage of sales. The fellow without such an attitude is reduced to a mere order-taker.

How many entrepreneurs would succeed without the absolute confidence derived from faith in the eventual success of the company they have created? A start-up business almost always faces almost impossible barriers to surviving and growing. The business may not have enough capital, credit, trained people, or management expertise. Customers resist a new product or service; at all levels, government officials interfere with fees, charges, fines, and taxes. The founder of the enterprise needs to be like an evangelist, with the utmost charisma, confidence, and faith. Any negative thinking will quickly sink the team spirit of his people and the enterprise.

Faith then generates positive feedback in the minds of believers. Positive feedback is a term from engineering practice that means some of the positive output signal is channeled back to the input of the system to amplify the signal. With positive feedback, energy is increased in the system, like movement on a swing, and more action and effort are the outcomes. The system vibrates vigorously, like the old unfortunate Tacoma Narrows Bridge in the wind, energy piling up and resonating until sometimes it all falls apart.

Resonance is a function of the sympathetic nervous system in the body when aroused. In a liberal mode of operation, the leader takes risks and gets things done. Any thoughts of doubt or indecision are put away. A follower or bystander who questions the inevitability of success is like a monkey wrench in the works. In this mode, the leader can't tolerate a Doubting Thomas; he's worse than a Judas Iscariot.

Inevitably, the leader and his supporters pay a heavy price if the venture falters and crashes. People may lose all their money, time, and even their health and life. Napoleon the Great was filled with absolute confidence when he invaded Russia with his Grand Army. He believed in his Destiny. So did Hitler when he smashed against the Soviet Union in 1941. So there's a big downside to much faith and positive feedback.

Negative feedback too has its uses: doubt and the parasympathetic system maintain a stable operation. At the right time, the body and mind need to stop action, return to rest, recreate, and consolidate gains. To succeed in the long term, know how to enter the relaxation response; asking for your massage, hot bath, your time of quiet and withdrawal from the world—return home in meditation to renew for the next battle.

Your renewal begins when you turn on the psychic switch of God's light in your heart with faith. You know you're in good hands when you relax in deep meditation; nothing can hurt you. Like an astronaut lost and floating in a space suit alone, away from your mother ship, you're still with God in this bright state of being, unafraid, confident, and secure.

4. Is Your Soul Immortal?

A mechanism exists for preserving consciousness and personality in the data banks of the Divine Engineer. Earlier, I compared such a mechanism to an operating system program's saving of its original, bug-free, and virus-free (sinless) code in the safe of the software engineer who created it. The soul doesn't blow out like a candle; it doesn't wither like a rose that once had bloomed. Why is this so? Look to the sense of immortality experienced by so many great mystics around the world, brilliant men and women in deep meditation and a state of cosmic consciousness.

Mystics have a common experience as they enter the innermost recesses of their spirit. They sense the existence of another universe, the ideal one, where everything is in a state of perfection and peace; they feel the presence of an all-powerful but loving being, and they experience an alternate reality in which death does not exist, where one is immortal in spirit. They perceive that the body and its life here on Earth are an illusion, a tragicomic act on an intricately contrived stage. Shakespeare, a most inspired individual, said it well. "All the world's a stage and the men and women on it merely actors. They have their entrances and their exits."[4] Many other inspired people have also said, "There is no death!"[5]

Listen to the words of Walt Whitman, the mystical poet of America, in "Song of Myself."

> The smallest sprout shows there is really no death,
> and if ever there was it led forward life,
> and does not wait at the end to arrest it,
> and ceas'd the moment life appear'd.
> All goes onward and outward,
> nothing collapses,
> and to die is different from what any one supposed,
> and luckier.[6]

What did Whitman mean by such a statement? All of us hate death and want to live forever, except for a few desperate souls who have suffered the slings and arrows of outrageous fortune. Even those who are bored and disgusted with their lives hate the idea of shedding the mortal coil. Yet it's easy to see the benefits of death if one believes that it's the gateway to a new and more rewarding existence.

In the great Hindu epic of the Upanishads, the spirit is compared to

---

4. William Shakespeare, *As You Like It*, ed. Barbara A. Mowat and Paul Werstine (New York: Simon & Schuster, 2004), 2.7.139-166.
5. John Luckey McCreery, "There Is No Death," *Famous Single Poems and the Controversies Which Have Raged Around Them*, ed. Burton E. Stevenson (London: George G. Harrap, 1924), 11-12.
6. Walt Whitman, *Leaves of Grass: The Death-Bed Edition* (New York: Modern Library, 2005), Section 6.

a caterpillar that stretches out on one leaf and reaches to another; so does the human spirit leave one body and just as easily enters another. This is a system of faith in which souls are recycled.

In the Christian vision, the souls of the faithful are preserved in a special place, Heaven, where they dwell in perfect bliss near the presence of their Creator. But in the Buddhist tradition, death for the awakened ones is liberation from the bonds of separate existence and entrance into cosmic consciousness. Nirvana is the end of the tortuous cycle of birth and death. The poet John Donne created a beautiful image of the raindrop that rolls into a stream, then a river, and finally flows to the sea (the main), whence it came. The ego is lost, and a new awareness is found in the ocean of universal love.

Expressing in words such feelings and visions, is more than difficult. It's true that the people we know and love—relatives, friends, admired heroes—all die someday and are never seen again, except in dreams. These characters stop acting on our world stage. They're gone even from behind the scenery. Not even their voices are heard in the theater of life. Never again shall we hold our mother's hand or kiss our father's forehead. Never again shall we hear their voices, their loving counsel, or feel their caress.

How do we know then that they still exist somewhere? We go to their gravesides and pray for their departed souls because we rely on the assurances of wise and enlightened men and women who have seen beyond the veil of death into a different world.

True, no matter how improbable the idea seems to you. When you, in disgrace or in protest, kill the body for the sake of the spirit, as did the early Christians of the Roman Empire in defense of their faith, then death is a doorway, a portal to another dimension, to a better world. That's what we learn from near-death experiences documented by scientists. A person, quite often not of a religious bent, is declared clinically dead by physicians while at the same time experiencing a different sort of consciousness. The patient remembers leaving his or her physical body and floating above it, looking down upon his corpse and the concerned doctors trying to revive it.

The soul of the dead person sees relatives crying at their deathbed or in the waiting room. Then the bodiless spirit passes through walls and ceilings freely, hears and sees clearly, but cannot communicate with the living or act on material objects. Time is compressed or stretched out in this universe, and events may happen instantaneously. The disembodied spirit sees past life whole, not as a sequence of events. The soul moves into a spiral tunnel, a light shining brightly at the end. He or she feels strongly the presence of a compassionate, forgiving, loving entity and is completely at peace and happy.

Looking to such experiences and the sayings of great seers, such as Pythagoras, Socrates, Jesus, Mohammed, Gautama, Laotse, and other brilliant men and women, you can rely on a chance for immortality in Heaven. Rest your hope, not for the immortality of your body, mere fertilizer when dead, but for the eternal life of your soul, looked after by God and His saints in a perfect universe of peace and harmony.

5. A Cosmic Computer Saves All Events of Your Life

A mechanism exists for preserving our souls and a record of our experiences. A Cosmic Being, God in Biblical terms, has established a communication link from the individual mind, the self, to this universal mind, the Self. Then, Heaven watches what we do and records all our activities in God's infinite memory. These recordings of God are three-dimensional and include all impressions from sight, sound, touch, taste, smell, and the full spectrum of feelings and emotions evoked in a given living adventure. Like a benign Big Brother, God then can observe your behavior as you are acting on Earth in real time or later at leisure from the recordings made by the Cosmic Computer.

Life's scenes are edited and enhanced in Heaven and made into a show for the entertainment and edification of angels and saints. Guardian angels study our experiences and behaviors and come to our aid and support as needed. Of course, the other side of the spiritual universe is also keeping track of us with a different purpose in mind. Satan's disciples study us and look for weaknesses in our characters to point their attacks.

Remember Omar Khayyam's poem? "The moving finger writes, and having writ moves on. Nor all your piety and wit shall lure it back to cancel half a line, nor all your tears wash out a word of it."[7] Mystics have sensed Heaven observes whatever we do in this life and makes a complete record and accurate record of events. Else, how could Judgment Day be conducted? As in court, the judge takes testimony about the course of our lives and accepts a compact disc as evidence.

You are charged with the operation of your body, a probe, a surveyor craft, on planet Earth. The link to the Source is the key thing and the probe is expendable, although very valuable. As an engineering probe telemeters data to central control, so does our body. Heaven's universe coexists with ours. Contact is intimate. Hindus believe there's an ethereal body that corresponds to our body on Earth. Our earthly body is but a shadow of the ethereal one. Information from our experiences, with sight, sound, and all the other sense impressions, transfers to Heaven directly, body to body. All spirits in Heaven are closely merged. What one soul knows is shared by all, and it becomes common play and entertainment; thus eternal and unchanging Heaven avoids boredom.

Consider this: Every organization has to have records. A business operates with a general ledger, which records income and expenses. It's recorded in the general ledger who paid money to the company, to whom money was paid, and how much. If there's a divine order that allocates psychic resources, that order has to keep accounts, not in money, but in blessings. You give a blessing without thought of recompense, and you receive a blessing from God, without asking for it. It's a magnificent obsession with doing the right things in your life. You succor the poor and unfortunate in real need of help, and you laser a record in the heavenly accounts. You act with cruelty or callousness—again, you cause an entry in the divine ledger.

This is also how the mind operates with regard to useful or destructive actions. A memory trace is generated in the conscious, temporary storage registers of your brain and later transferred to permanent,

---

7. Omar Khayyám, *The Rubáiyát of Omar Khayyám*, trans. Edward FitzGerald (London: Penguin Classics, 1989), verse 51.

chemical memory of every act in which you engage. A constructive action leads to more good things, and a negative one leads to the downhill side of life. For example, suppose that you get into the habit of sipping hard liquor in the evening to relax; after a while, the time of drinking shifts earlier and earlier until, eventually, you wake up and have to have a shot of whiskey for breakfast. After a few years of this, your liver decides to call it quits.

It's what that unforgettable character Napoleon Hill called the law of Cosmic Habit Force. It's how we get accustomed to degradation or improvement: one step at a time, one day at a time. Such a way continues to the next life. The actions we take today and tomorrow and the next day are inevitably recorded and determine our fate in the next one. It's Karma. In the Hindu view, there's no reward or punishment really, but a natural process leading to the consequences of our actions, good, bad, or indifferent. For example, if we're gluttons in our food choices, we become pigs in the next life, since that's the character we practice in the present one.

The reason behind this process is in the Cosmic Recorder. Everything we do is registered there and when our next body is issued to us, we receive a fitting vehicle for our actions. There's no punishment in this. It's what we have desired and sought to have and what we have earned. In the long run, we end up with what we deserve and have earned with our thoughts and actions. We get the income we have truly earned, the health we have cultivated, the friends we have sought, and the afterlife we have foreseen and worked for while walking on this earth.

6. Judgment Day is Coming

A common feature in most religions is the notion of Judgment Day. At the end of our life on Earth, the Supreme Being sits in judgment of our total behavior after our maturity, when we could tell right from wrong. Persons who died when they were children are exempt from this process and go directly to Heaven. Animals are also exempt from punishment or reward since they're driven purely by instinct and can't make moral decisions. The feeble-minded and insane are excused too, as they're treated in the courts of civilized nations. You and I are responsible for all our actions here on Earth from adulthood to the end of our lives. You are a free agent; you'll be held accountable for deadly sins you have done, as well as acts of kindness you missed doing.

You can see how the notion of Heavenly Judgment came about. Here on Earth, people who do evil deeds are eventually caught and, as a rule, are punished. A person who steals or kills may get away unnoticed once, twice, or several times and enjoy the rewards of the crimes. With success and enjoyment comes the desire to do it again and again. One day, inevitably, the criminal is caught and punished by the courts. That is, unless this person ceases and desists from a life of crime, dies before being caught, or becomes so powerful that no one in society can touch him or her, as it was with Stalin, Ghengis Khan, or Jack the Ripper. In such cases, it's natural that we should expect heavenly retribution for such people.

You've probably heard the story from the Christian Bible about Final Judgment. The souls of the departed and the living on that day come before God and are separated like sheep and goats. The goats are sent to eternal punishment in the fires of Hell, while the sheep move close to God and reside forever in eternal bliss. On that day there's gnashing of teeth and great crying and wailing from the condemned. The others laugh joyfully as they enter Paradise.

There are other views of Judgment. I visualize a situation where the soul is brought in contact with a loving and compassionate God who looks upon you as a devoted father sees a favorite son or daughter. You sit down together and have a chat and you report your experiences on Earth. There's the record, discussed earlier, on holographic compact disc, and you have replays of some actions. It will be like reviews of a game with your coach or trainer. Together you locate the errors in your play and get ready for the next game. Or, the situation is one of an astronaut returning to Mission Control from the moon. There is a thorough debriefing and preparation for the next flight.

Now, what happens to bad people? Do they get their comeuppance? They get what they deserve. Those people gravitate to a different deity and spiritual universe. You may want to call this place the House of Evil and Punishment. I call it a fitting place for those who have sought it all their lives on Earth. The ruthless fellow who believes "might makes right" and "the end justifies the means" goes there. Also, the soldiers end up there—those who did atrocities because they were ordered to do them.

The person who said, "My country, right or wrong," will direct his spiritual steps to this universe. The captain of industry who said, "My business is to show profits and increase shareholder value, not to look after the rainforest," will jet to Hell. Are these people evil? Was the Soviet Union an evil empire or simply a way of running a nation with a supreme state over the people, which looked after their jobs, health, housing, and security? To these people, Hell is their Heaven, and they're quite familiar with the grounds and the cruel way of dealing with people.

These souls are content in Hell, quite at home. There are no devils torturing humans. They are all of them the same breed. It's like an army. The general disciplines the colonel, the colonel disciplines the captain, the captain disciplines the lieutenant, the lieutenant the sergeant, and the sergeant the private. They all know their place and accept punishment as their due, because this is how this universe operates—not with love but with duty and discipline. Cruelty and brutality are the means of motivating people. Fear rules supreme.

In Hell, law and order prevails everywhere, except in certain places and times dedicated to the recreation of the damned souls. Those places are like Bedlam. Screaming and yelling, acid rock music, things being thrown here and there, a mixed-up mess of stuff, over which souls float in complete relaxation from their enforced rigid order. People throw trash everywhere, paint graffiti on walls, drive as they please, yell at each other for no reason, let cockroaches and other pests feed in the leftover foods, and people generally do as they choose to themselves and their fellows. So the people in Hell happily torture each other and thus advance the cause of their universe.

Good people, on the other hand, who have led virtuous lives, guiltless and free of compulsion, rise up to Heaven like white birds to the sky when they die. They go to a place where the air is sweet with the smell of gorgeous flowers and gentle rains keep the people cool and refreshed. Lovely music caresses the ears. You sit down in the company of your good friends and relatives and tell stories from your lives on Earth. Nearby are the kindly saints and spirits, gone there before you, always ready to bring you comfort and joy.

You are rewarded with perfect joy for your kindly deeds and for resisting evil temptations on Earth, while the all-pervading presence of the Great Spirit floats around you, enfolding your soul in perfect harmony and bliss. People in Heaven do what they do out of love and compassion, not coercion. God's purpose is to test good people in this life in order to shape and perfect souls for residence in Heaven and also for future expeditions to other material worlds and the further improvement of characters. Is there a Purgatory? That's unnecessary. No one is perfect upon departing this life, except a handful of souls like those of the Christ and of the Buddha.

7. Heaven, Hell, and Purgatory Are Ajar for Us

I will now give you my vision of Heaven, Hell, and Purgatory, as best as I can conjure one up at present. It's not like that of Socrates, Jesus, Dante, or Mohammed. I've given brief glimpses of what I see before in this treatise, and I'll continue along the same lines. A clear view of what follows this life is an essential ingredient to any religious consciousness and moral conduct.

We know that the universe expands, the galaxies moving away from each other, as space stretches out and out. That's not so bad, although communications among galaxies are likely made more difficult. Eventually though, many scientists believe, the primeval force that began the expansion is overcome by gravity, and contraction will occur, followed by a Big Crunch. Everything that was created during the expansion is reduced to pure energy in the original, concentrated fireball. Time comes to an end again. This is the Indian vision of Lord Shiva, creator and destroyer of worlds.

According to Cambridge physicist Stephen Hawking, a theoretical cosmologist of considerable reputation, in his book *A Brief History of Time*, the origin of the Big Bang is not a point but a four-dimensional surface. The implication is that the boundary conditions of the universal equation are such that an infinite number of different kinds of expansions occur, resulting in every conceivable type of universe in form and content. It's like tossing a coin with an infinite number of surfaces, tossing it an infinite number of times: every possible sequence of heads and tails materializes. Every type of universe follows its trajectory to Big Bang and then Crunch. An infinite number of universes coexist and are concentric in the fabric of matter and energy.

A living entity such as God, who is by definition eternal, would clearly need to escape the Big Crunch to survive the end of time together with his Heaven and the program packages of his creatures. Let me return to a notion I brought up earlier. On Earth, plants take up minerals and light energy and produce carbon-based living matter, which is later consumed by more complex organisms that can move and think but do not have the power of chlorophyll to convert solar energy into organic materials.

Let's imagine an organism, fortuitously formed in an early universe, when matter is closer together, that retains or acquires this trick with chlorophyll, but which is a rational, communicating entity. With abundant energy and materials close by in this early universe, this superorganism grows exponentially, both in size and intelligence as it faces the task of survival in the expansion of galactic space. Inevitably, it perceives the Big Crunch as the ultimate threat.

With its size and powers, it takes control of the racing galaxies and consumes all their matter. This Being, thereby, freezes up all matter and energy into one stupendous, super-conducting crystal ball in the form of a molecular computer. The Super Being extricates itself from the perennial process of birth and death of the worlds—the Bang and Crunch. Such a system of organization, with the energies of an entire universe at its command, would be an all-powerful God. In this universe, Heaven, coexisting with ours, God is immanent on Earth and everywhere present. Only a thin veil separates us from the Spirit World.

Now this Supreme Being, God, is outside time and space. Time, as we know it, doesn't exist in God's frozen, crystallized universe. Time begins with the Bang and disappears with the Crunch, and these processes don't exist in Heaven. There's no space-time cone of observation. All events are constantly observed. Everything that exists in this universe is eternal and unchanging. The second law of thermodynamics regarding entropy does not operate. Nothing decays or disintegrates. No matter or energy is lost. All forces of nature are in perfect balance and harmony. Peace and contentment pervade all. To me, that such a God exists, and has always existed, and is the prime cause of everything is no more incredible than the existence of our own expanding universe with spinning galaxies, stars, and planets.

You can imagine that such a God would be bothered by loneliness, marring a perfect state of being. He and She would want some action and excitement, such as God experienced when evolving. Thus, God could find alternate worlds in the process of evolution and on those worlds implant program packages in His and Her own image, which take over advanced bodies, such as the apes. Thus, we evolved from apes and were created by God.

Our bodies are material and transient, but our spirits are eternal and return to the Creator, as most religious mystics teach us. God would not want to interfere unduly in other universes, as this would upset the random processes essential to testing evolving forms of life. That would be acting like the casino operator that tilts the wheel of fortune. It would make the game both dishonest and uninteresting. Do you like to play a game when the outcome is certain?

What do you think about the game in Hell? On Earth, two processes lead to the evolution of more complex advanced beings: cooperation and symbiosis on the one hand, predation and parasitism on the other. Mitochondria in all our body cells are said to have been originally parasites.

Nature on Earth is a vast web of interdependent species. Even as a predator, such as a lion, kills its prey, it contributes to the health of the herd through culling. Viruses, bacteria, and parasites also do the same by eliminating the unfit members and populations of animals or plants. So the universe of Hell may have evolved from a Nature replete with such evil, while Heaven emerged from cooperating entities.

In human societies, the basic forms of government control are democracy, mostly endowed with freedom, and dictatorship, mostly imbued with compulsion, whether that is called kingship, tyranny, oligarchy, fascism, or communism. As portrayed in the *Star Wars* films, the emperor rules absolutely as opposed to the federation of planets, spearheaded by the rebels. So, while Heaven may have evolved from a society based on love and respect for other living beings, Hell came about from some form of tyranny. There, an absolute ruler dictates to his minions, who dictate to their minions. It's a top-down hierarchy based on decree and discipline enforced by means of punishment. The Romans survived this way very well for fifteen hundred years and contributed much to the world despite their callousness and cruelty. They had their culture too, mostly borrowed from the Greeks. But the Romans were superb administrators, statesmen, generals, and engineers, building roads, aqueducts, and buildings, many of them still standing. They built both institutions and infrastructure to last for many generations, and Hell was built the same way.

As for Purgatory, that's our world.

On this world, with a clear view of Heaven and Hell as presented in your mind, you can arrange your life and your goals according to your desires. Perhaps Heaven doesn't appeal to you, and you prefer to follow the path to Hell, as tyrants, terrorists, and criminals are doing every day. Visions of the next world are guides to behavior, and such visions are matters of taste, as religions also are.

8. The Relaxation Response: A Road to Recreation

Recreation means building again. We have indicated before that revelations by mystics, even by minor ones such as I am, have their source in a mental process called meditation. This process begins with a state of mind that has been called "the relaxation response," by Herbert Benson, MD. This is a psycho-biological process, which we apparently share with animals but with somewhat different results. We're interested in this because the relaxation response may lead to the meditative state of consciousness. Meditation, if you manage it properly, is a creative process, which can bring you new knowledge, spiritual as well as secular.

The process of relaxation begins by finding a quiet place where you can be undisturbed. You relax by keeping still or moving, alone or in suitable company, with your eyes closed or open. Commonly, you sit comfortably on the floor or on a chair and focus on something rhythmic, such as your breathing, in and out. You tense your muscles for a moment and then allow them to relax. Your trainer can help with a soothing voice, and so can peaceful and low-pitched music. You repeat some short phrase or sentence over and over, called a mantra. After the tension and mind chatter, which is normally with us, quiets down, you experience certain physiological effects that have health benefits. Blood pressure goes lower, muscle pains disappear or decrease, any anxiety and stress are relieved, and you feel better.

Benson and other researchers have found that the brain's alpha waves, which arise in deep concentration, increase in intensity and oxygen consumption, respiratory rate, heart rate, blood pressure, and muscle tension all tend to decrease. The parasympathetic system, connected to rest and recovery, is stimulated, and the sympathetic nervous system, associated with action and effort, becomes less active. The relaxation response has been called the opposite of the fight-or-flight reaction of animals. When we face a threat, our heart rate and blood pressure go up, hormones flood our system, and blood sugar and cholesterol levels rise to provide emergency power. If you work daily in a crisis environment, these body measurements may get stuck at a high level; your doctor will likely prescribe you medications for the reduction of your blood pressure, sugar, and cholesterol. But Benson and other medical scientists have shown that deep relaxation, practiced daily, can be an effective treatment without the use of drugs.

We are interested now, however, in the state of consciousness that may occur with deep relaxation. Once experienced, it's easily identified. You have an all-pervasive awareness of your body and its environment. Peace and quiet settle in. Time seems still. If there is pain, it's felt intensely, but it can be borne more easily. You hear the wall clock clicking, the cries of distant birds or children, the beating of your heart. Psychologically, the valve to the subconscious mind begins to open up, and information moves more freely in and out of it.

You dream with images, sounds, and smells, even while fully awake. You are in a trance, in a state of hypnosis, fully open to suggestions from the outside, whether good, bad, or disastrous. Your innermost being is exposed to psychological influence and danger. It's why the information gate to your inner self is normally closed. The gate is the same protection as your lips, eyelids, anus, and vagina are for the body's interior organs.

You can elicit the relaxation response by sitting quietly and counting as you breathe out from one to four. Inflate your lungs slowly, from the abdominal area to the top, pause, breathe out from the top down, counting, pause, and begin again. After a while, couple your deep breathing with a mantra. Benson suggests using the secular word "One." I use Kyrie Eleison, Greek for "Lord, Have Pity." With some practice, you'll begin to experience peace and quiet.

The gate will be open, and you begin meditating or contemplating. You'll be open to suggestions and programming from yourself or others. You'll eventually, with much practice, also start receiving direct messages from the subconscious and beyond. This is all a very natural function for humans, which our hectic lives have suppressed. Keep in mind, though, that relaxation and meditation are not recommended while driving or handling dangerous equipment. Also, you don't want to be in a trance while your boss is talking to you.

As you progress in your skill, you will find relaxation in many situations and for different reasons. You may use the response to guide yourself to sleep in the night or to wake yourself up in the morning without the aid of coffee. That is, after relaxation, you may suggest to your subconscious mind to aid you in sleeping or to keep you alert and awake. You may suggest to your buried mind to stir up a state of enthusiasm and excitement or tranquility and ease. Speakers and actors use it before they have to stand in front of an audience. Athletes and fighters often prepare themselves for a contest by means of suggestions to the subconscious. For more practical guidance in such areas, there are numerous books available, such as Maxwell Maltz's *Psycho-cybernetics,* Zilbergeld and Lazarus's *Mind Power,* and Henry Silva's *Mind Control.*

You may already have been using trance techniques without knowing what you were doing. Many people come to this practice in church or temple through prayer. My mother, a fervent devotee of the Madonna, often fell into a trance in prayer. She came to amazing insights, even in her years of senility in her nineties. How much more can you or I do while still in our prime! But before we go on, here's another word of caution, which you don't get from the books on mind control.

When in meditation, opening the gate to your subconscious, you need to be careful about the exposure of your innermost being. It's not a good idea to be hypnotized by television or false evangelical speakers. Much of the programming is for the purpose of selling you worthless, sometimes harmful, stuff and ideas. Don't relax with people you can't trust completely. If you practice meditation with a guru, be sure your guide is harmless. You cannot always trust the voices and instructions you get in a trance. The source could be God or Satan. Examine instructions received with your reason, another gift from God.

9. Meditation, Contemplation, and Hypnosis Work

We now come to one of the core topics of this treatise. The source of much spiritual knowledge, as well as misinformation, is the mental process of meditation, a practice brought to a high level of skill in ancient India, thousands of years ago. Other ancient peoples have cultivated the practice, the Egyptians, Greeks, Hebrews, Chinese—almost all cultures—but in India, more effort was put into this discipline than anywhere else in the world. If you're seeking spiritual knowledge and answers to the burning questions of your existence, practice meditation and its sister states of contemplation and hypnosis.

These techniques have been applied to extraordinary uses, such as the work of the fakirs, who can control their heartbeat, metabolism, and other autonomic functions of the body for the purpose of religious showmanship. Even cobras are hypnotized by flute music in bazaars and festivals. I'm not an expert in meditation. I simply have some ideas about the subject that may be new. I practice meditation on a regular basis, and on a few occasions, I've approached what's called enlightenment. Relaxation leads to meditation, which leads to an awakening of the inner mind or an integration of the conscious and subconscious parts of our being. Hypnosis arises when suggestions are made to the subconscious by a psychiatrist, hypnotist, advertiser, or the subject when in a receptive state. Suggestions can't be forced on you if you're unwilling to accept them, but when you're relaxed, they can be quite insidious.

Most people think of meditation as sitting cross-legged on the floor or mat like a Buddha, arms outstretched and hands resting on the knees with thumb and index finger touching. Forget about that. Meditation can happen in many different ways, active and passive. You can meditate lying down flat on your back on a bed or grass. But that can lead you to sleep, which is very different from meditation, or you can meditate while walking, jogging, running, swimming, hang-gliding, skydiving, making love, eating, urinating, dancing, skiing, surfing, harvesting grains, fishing, or singing with company or alone. Such activities are rhythmic, repetitive, peaceful, pleasant, and habitual. The gate to the subconscious slowly swings open when you do consciously what is usually automatic, such as breathing. When you do what is usually a conscious act, like saying a prayer, over and over, in a relaxed and easygoing manner, rhythmically, until it's so groovy you do it without thinking, then you enter the meditative state. A conscious activity has become automatic, and you have produced the relaxation response.

For example, let's do an eating meditation. Quite often we eat without awareness, which certainly takes away from our pleasure and may lead to over-eating. Look at your food closely; pick it up and sniff it. Take a nibble, like cats often do with strange food, and taste it thoroughly. Take a bigger bite and chew it well. Keep it in your mouth mixing it with saliva, until it is completely liquid and flows down your throat. Feel the fluid settling down cozily in your stomach and being engulfed with gastric juices. It continues down to your gut to be pleasantly assimilated and to energize your whole being. Now you imagine other animals eating together with you. Chickens pick up corn kernels and raise their heads to swallow. A cow munches contentedly nearby on the grass. Goats nibble on chaparral. All of Nature absorbs nutrition and energy with you as you pick up food, chew, and swallow. You're one with the world, happy in your body.

That is meditation. Now, contemplation is concentrating your attention on a single object or idea. In the East, the lotus flower is commonly used in contemplation and represents the many folds of reality and spiritual truth. It's extensively used as a religious symbol. Contemplation is a form of meditation. Remember that we live in a holographic universe, where every object, however tiny, is connected to the rest of creation and holds clues to its mysteries.

When a scientist is studying a particular phenomenon in an experimental setting, he or she is practicing contemplation. The scientist is also contemplating when concentrating on a specific idea, such as a law of nature or a mathematical formula. Answers come to scientific and mathematical questions from deep within the subconscious, and sometimes, these are scientific breakthroughs. A musical composer does something similar as he or she focuses on a melody or rhythm to express sentiments. The notes appear from somewhere, and sometimes they have the finality of perfection.

Occasionally, a rare individual in deep meditation apparently makes contact with a gate to another place beyond the subconscious mind. Consciousness is flooded with fantastic energies. The whole body of such a person is bathed in a pure, mystical light, an awe-inspiring aura. People saw that in the Buddha after his great awakening. Nausicaa saw such a light bathing the naked Ulysses, shipwrecked on her island, and realized he was a king. Heroes with great charisma display this overpowering quality and nothing can stand in their way when they aim for a goal. The hero—Jesus, Mohammad, Theseus, Hercules, Edison, Churchill, and Roosevelt—is possessed of absolute self-confidence. The hero's purpose is firm and fixed, and he or she possesses the power to achieve it. Thus the hero with a thousand faces succeeds and creates legends that live forever. To the hero and to the rest of us, information from the material, exterior universe reaches us through our senses: sight, sound, smell, taste, and touch. These are the gates to our body and what comes in is experienced by the conscious mind.

In deep meditation, after much diligent practice, a gate also opens to the vast subconscious; beyond the subconscious, a portal leads to the infinite inner cosmos, the spiritual universe. Well-hidden is the last portal in the depths of the subconscious, opening only for those with immense courage, strength, training and talent.

10. God and Satan: Servers in the Spiritual Internet

On the internet, you connect your computer to bigger and faster machines that store more data and programs than your computer and handle communications with other computers using devices called routers. Celestial server computers, each with spiritual WEB sites, are far more sophisticated than the systems we have today on Earth. God's servers are not simple hardware devices but vast crystal structures operating with light and the ultimate speed of electromagnetic radiation. Moreover, Heavenly servers possess feelings: components for love, compassion, and other emotions beyond our ken.

On Earth, people are becoming increasingly interconnected with telephones, fax machines, mails, and the internet. Distance barriers are dropping away and so are the costs of communicating. Workers everywhere that participate in a project are closer still with personal contacts and other meetings. Today, the entire civilized world is really one gigantic information processing system with cooperative production of objects of programs. Software engineers in India are cranking out code for companies in Silicon Valley. Twenty companies in tiny Finland formed an international cellular behemoth known as Nokia. Nokia also employs low-cost Indian engineers, sometimes relocated to Finland.

This is peer-to-peer computing in fact, where the information processing capabilities of highly trained people all over the world share in the solution of technical problems. Currently, Intel Corporation is researching peer-to-peer computing for the next decade. Unused resources of memory and central processing in personal computers would be turned over to the internet for extensive parallel processing of major problem solutions. Instead of one stupendous supercomputer, millions of smaller, personal machines around the world would work together to execute very extensive data transformations. Major problems would be solved piecemeal, as airliners, space shuttles, and other complex systems are designed today by thousands of engineers scattered all over the world, but particularly Europe, America, Japan, China, and India.

Such distributed data processing is going on today on the Spiritual Internet by untold billions of intelligent beings throughout the universe. As you download music, programs, and data from a server's web site to your personal computer, so your soul is downloaded from God, or Satan, to your primate body. Then, upon death, as we theorized earlier, your soul is uploaded to Heaven, minus memory data. Memory data may be saved somewhere for future reference but are not sent back down with your soul's next assignment, so that you arrive on Earth fresh and eager to learn anew with novel experiences and experiments.

What is it exactly that is saved in Heaven or Hell and recycled? It's your personality, consciousness, your self, what you call "I." Where does this thing reside? It's in the brain, with billions of neurons working together. Could it be that a single brain cell holds consciousness? That's unlikely. Personality carries out many functions beyond the capabilities of a single cell, although the cell may hold a rudimentary awareness, as in a one-cell organism.

Sir John Eccles, the famed British biologist, searched all his life for the seat of consciousness. It was not in any one place in the brain, and he was not able to locate it. There are centers for pleasure, pain, memory transfer, sleep, etc., and they can be stimulated into activity by electrical probes. As a graduate student at Caltech, in Roger Sperry's psychobiology class, I implanted such probes into cat brains and was able to put the cat to sleep at will or excite it into rage or panic in the presence of a mouse. But that's not the totality of consciousness. The higher center is where most of us live.

Consciousness, then, is a function of many specialized neurons in close communication—working together for survival, service, and experience. Whole colonies of animals of some species, such as ants, bees, and birds, appear to live and function like a single organism. Jesus spoke of himself as the body of his Church and told his disciples that he would be there whenever a group of them would gather together in his name.

Early human tribes were communal, and food was shared by all after the hunt or gathering. Young warrior males and strong mature leaders would defend against intruders and attackers. Some of the warrior males would sacrifice themselves instinctively to protect the tribe. Such tendencies still persist in modern closed societies, such as the Japanese. A collective consciousness rules such a society, similar to the collective of the brain cells. This is dramatized in *Star Trek's* Borg episodes, but the Borg people are mechanistic and unemotional.

Borg society, with its rigid structure, total obedience to the will of the collective, and lack of compassion for individuals, is properly sinister and inhuman in the show. The Borgs are images from Hell because that's how Satan operates that universe, with absolute tyranny and heartlessness but high efficiency. The Borg society is like a modern, antiseptic, perfectly ordered factory operating with the single objective of assimilating others and turning out more and more machines. Feelings, tenderness, love, or respect for the integrity of individuals are excised from the Borg. Everyone is a replaceable part, a cog in the system, and looks and acts very much like everyone else. Uniqueness and special, endearing characteristics are not allowed. Any Borg is easily disposable, like a Bic razor. The Borg society sustains and is sustained by Server Satan.

God, however, is like a mother and a father to all who hear His and Her voice. In His and Her hands, we're held, and Jesus, with other prophets, saves our souls, even as accidents, diseases, old age, and murder demolish our bodies. To be with Him and Her, we only need to maintain contact through meditation and prayer. The God connection will preserve us though we walk in the valley of death. Where's the God connection in the brain? Is it a transmitter-receiver to the Ideal Universe? Will we ever locate this brain structure, this modem to God? There may be a gene in the human race, implanted there one hundred thousand years ago, that controls the growth of the God modem in the brain.

This gene may be located and identified sometime during the detailed analysis of the human genome findings. Then we'll have proof of the existence of the Supreme Being. The Supreme Being is made up of you and me and all living forms in the universe, connected together by means of the Spiritual Internet, a variety of servers providing different forms of entertainment and information.

Heavenly servers are not cold and unfeeling machines like those of our internet; they are living entities feeling, loving, and caring for all creation together with God. The servers are the spirits of saints and other gentle spirits and they intercede for us in Heaven when we need them and deserve their help.

7

GOD LIKES SEX

My sister Alice has been married to her husband George for fifty-two years. Like all couples who stay together for many years, they've had some turbulent times, but they held to their marriage vows, being tolerant towards each other's foibles, building up the bonds of marriage as they went along with children and grandchildren. I expect they'll go to Heaven together after death as promised by the Bible or some other good place. It is said happy marriages are made in heaven; I suppose, miserable ones in hell. George and Alice are happy: always together, holding hands, looking after each other.

I was the best man at their wedding. After the wedding ceremony, I joked to George, who was my friend, "You're in a trap, George." He laughed, but now he often reminds me of that joke. I was twenty then; perhaps marriage seemed to me to be a trap, but he was thirty-one, ready for a family. He knew happiness, Heaven, was being in the arms of his beloved. Male and female belong together in our species because they are interwoven in Nature.

1. Yin and Yang Gave Birth to the Universe

The ancient Chinese sages rightfully gave a central role to the concept of sex, yin and yang, in their scheme of things. Yin is the female principal, and Yang is the male. The Chinese saw this duality throughout Nature as a fundamental principle. The mystical philosopher Laotse spoke of the strength of the female, passive resistance, in overcoming the male, aggressive action. Regarding the origin of the universe, he wrote, "It is a problem that defies the mind and language of man . . . the great yin is majestically silent; the great yang is impressively active. Majestic silence comes from heaven, and impressive activity comes from the earth. When the two meet and merge, all things are formed." God loves sex because we see it everywhere for reproduction, growth, and diversification in nature, God's creation.

Biologically, sexual reproduction allows for a mixing of genes from two different sources and an acceleration of evolution through natural selection of the fittest combinations. There is asexual reproduction in organisms, but it's restricted to less complex forms and in many species, such as snails, it's periodically followed by sexual reproduction. Spiritually and in physics, forms in nature are based on a combination of opposites.

Thus we have positive and negative electricity and magnetism, matter and antimatter, light and darkness, good and evil, growth and decay, mountains and valleys birth and death, rise and fall, noise and silence, etc.

Walt Whitman wrote in his selection of poems *Children of Adam*, "Ages and ages returning at intervals, undestroyed, wandering, immortal, lusty, phallic, with the potent original loins, perfectly sweet."

Biologist Desmond Morris demystified sex in his best-selling work *The Naked Ape*. Much wonder and mystery, however, remains in the union of man and woman. When the sexual act is right, there's a change of consciousness from the normal, followed by an experience similar to the bliss of deep and perfect meditation. You feel complete and no longer lonely. You feel at peace with yourself and the world. It's like a form of religious ecstasy or rapture.

In sexual union and reproduction, one joins the long procession of living things from the earliest organisms billions of years ago to the unlimited future on Earth and perhaps to the stars. *Per aspera ad astra*: through hardship to the stars. One becomes a part of the sea of life by contributing to it and achieves a form of immortality through the perpetuation of the codes in the genes, which also hold the scriptures given to us in DNA. The commandments in the DNA are preserved far better than on stone, safer from deluge, earthquake, asteroid impacts, and storms, to be passed on to whatever succeeds our species.

It's true what Bertrand Russell wrote in *An Outline of Philosophy*:

The actions of all living things are such as tend to biological survival, i.e. to leaving of a numerous progeny. Living matter has the chemical peculiarity of being self-perpetuating, and of conferring its own chemical composition upon other matter composed of the right elements. We may regard the whole of evolution as flowing from this chemical imperialism of living matter.[1]

Humankind is only the last example. Humankind transforms the surface of the globe, taking in matter from minerals, plants, and other animals to manufacture billions of human bodies.

Russell continues, "Perhaps intelligence is reaching the point where it can conceive worthier ends, concerned with the quality rather than the quantity of human life. But as yet such intelligence is confined to a few, and does not control the great movements of human affairs."[2] Indeed few are those to whom life is a spiritual process with higher ends than mere reproduction. The average healthy male may have as many as ten thousand ejaculations of sperm in his lifetime, and in America produces 2.1 children.

A Brahman bull, by comparison, may be the sire of 50,000 calves with the aid of artificial insemination. Without evoking memories of Nazi nonsense, would it not improve our race to encourage our best men and women, whatever their skin pigmentation, tribal affiliation, or religion, to contribute more genes to posterity? Why should serial

---

1. Bertrand Russell, *An Outline of Philosophy* (New York: Routledge, 2009), 115.
2. Russell, *An Outline of Philosophy*, 43.

polygamy be the only honest and legal means for a successful man to produce more offspring? Christian ethics may be a detriment to quality reproduction compared to ancient Hebrew, Hindu, and Muslim customs. But let's not give up our progress in women's rights. If polygamy is re-instituted, it should be coupled with legal polyandry. And a woman should have the right to choose the sire of her offspring, whether he's the spouse or not.

Better still, for the evolution of the quality of life, we might forego children until we're dead. Then the living can decide who should contribute to the gene pool with their frozen sperm and eggs and by how much. Currently, much of human reproduction is the result of carelessness during sex. Quite often children are not planned at all to come to a nurturing family structure. They sprout like wild seeds when the rhythm method, the pill, or prophylactics fail.

It's far better for society if worthy people would donate their ova and spermatozoa for the next generation. Such couples, gay or straight, would be those who had raised adopted children with care and love and were good grandparents, too, before passing on. Donors to the gene pool would be those who established records of having conducted their lives well, with attention to health, character, and intelligence.

We ask no less today from people we employ for ordinary business or government jobs. Should we not do the same for the people who parent our next generation? Sexual union between the sexes can then be truly devoted to composing the harmony of parents. Such couples can offer sexual love to God like a prayer with full awareness, in meditation.

For few things indicate the presence of a Great Evil Spirit stalking the Earth than the treatment given to the sexual act by so many people. This "act divine," as Walt Whitman put it, the means for producing new life, is debased in curses, in commerce as prostitution and pornography, and in conflicts as rape. Pregnant women are violated, and their bellies cut open in the name of "religion." Drunken or drugged women engage in sex with random men and later resort to abortion or welfare existence. Out of compassion, society supports their numerous children and the children of their daughters.

The alternative of abortion, often called family planning, is no less evil. When does life begin if not at conception? If we kill the fetus, when do we stop killing? We know that in the final months of pregnancy, the infant is able to kick in the mother's uterus; it's aware and can be influenced by good music and talk. If we kill babies, can we not justify the killing of old, disabled, or sick people on the same grounds? Can we not justify suicide? The killing is someone's choice. But the choice should be up to society, not any individual, parent or other relative. Better still, leave life or death decisions to God.

God loves life, so he loves sex. He brings new beings to the world, mixing genes for variety and growth, beauty and health. Yin and yang, male and female, unite in Nature and in our species to produce different forms and recreate the world anew.

2. The Earth Mother Makes the World Bearable

Inspired by my own excellent mother, I respect mothers and motherhood. Mothers bear us, bring us to life, and make our lives bearable when they live—and as long as we live with the memories we have of them.

Before the Madonna was revealed to us and stirred our enthusiasm, there was an Earth Mother. She was worshipped in many cultures in the ancient world and in the Mediterranean region she was sculpted in buxom and round-bottom figurines, looking much like a pregnant lady or a South African bush-woman. Later, Hera emerged as the formal wife of Zeus, who wore a shapelier figure than the Earth Mother and represented the female aspect of God, the force in Nature that promotes life.

Early Christians, the worshipers of the One God, scorned polytheism. But God has many aspects or representations. The Holy Mother of the Hindus is one. Another was Aphrodite or Venus, worshiped as the spirit of sexual attraction, *eros* in Greek, as compared to *agape*, brotherly or sisterly love. Eros was also the name of Aphrodite's son, the cupid with bow and arrow. Aphrodite inspired passionate love between man and woman or other combinations. In the Greco-Roman world there was also Bacchus, God of wine and celebrations.

With the arrival of new wines, there were feasts known as the bacchanalia that often became drunken orgies. Not unlike our own carnivals, these occasions allowed people to get together in a freer spirit and, dropping their customary inhibitions, to exalt in their union with the god. Spouses could forgive each other's infidelities with other people for a short while before returning to the ways of fidelity. It's what people do today in swingers' clubs, but usually, participants end up in divorce court.

It's fitting to remember that in ancient times and primitive cultures, exuberance in sexual matters was common. Without much in the way of contraceptives, sex represented fertility, growth, and the horn of plenty with the fruits of agriculture, which produced most of the goods consumed. Phallic worship was common; huge penises were paraded in public celebrations. The phallus was a symbol of potency and power.

Small societies of ancient times were constantly in peril from stronger or more aggressive neighbors. If a tribe was defeated, it was common for all the males and everyone else to be butchered by the victors, except the young and attractive females. Or else, the young and strong were taken as slaves to work for the rest of their lives in the homes, fields, and factories of the prevailing tribe. Even during the golden age of Athens, slaves did much of the work. In ancient Sparta, the slaves outnumbered the citizens, and all male citizens from the age of ten lived in army training camps to suppress the slaves during numerous revolts and to defend Sparta from other city-states.

In ancient times, sanitation was nearly non-existent, open sewers being the norm. Thus, periodic disease epidemics decimated the population of a city, such as the plague that struck the Athenians during the Peloponnesian War with Sparta, which contributed to the defeat of the Athenians. Hence, fertility was very important to the survival of the tribe. With high infant mortality, large numbers of offspring were mandatory.

Frequent, productive sex was desired in order for the tribe to flourish amidst enemies. Constant warfare kept the numbers of men small. The strongest survivors recruited women slaves and concubines to replenish the population. Fertility rites were a frequent feature of ancient societies. Sexual union was a prayer to God because continued existence depended on it.

In the dialogues of Socrates, Plato mentions this common belief of ancient Greeks: man and woman were once a single being, which the gods split up into two parts. Ever since then, man and woman have searched for each other to be united again into one whole entity. It's why we feel complete and at peace with our beloved. This is the basis for our notions of romance. There's a person in the world, so it's theorized, that matches our sexuality and our personality. That person is our ideal mate, and once found and connected, that person becomes one with us for this life and, Christians say, for all eternity. It's a tall order.

I recall, however, many real cases and some fictional ones that support the theory of romance. Remember *The Graduate* ending with Dustin Hoffman on the bus with Katherine Ross? After creating an outrageous scene at her wedding with another man, he runs off with her on the bus, sitting next to her with a look of total contentment. Have you seen the film *Sleepless in Seattle* with Meg Ryan and Tom Hanks? There was magic in their encounter and union. Less well publicized was the film *She's So Lovely* with Sean and Robin Penn. After a ten-year marriage to actor John Travolta's character and three children, she leaves her lovely home to rejoin her first husband, just released from a mental institution. He was her true love, poor and crummy as he was.

It is possible that such unions of two kindred souls are made in Heaven, and they return there upon death. We don't understand well the nature of sexuality. There's more to it than biology.

Why are there so many older couples who love and cherish each other long after childbearing? Why are there so many romances and marriages between superannuated people who have no chance at procreation? I've known passionate love myself two or three times in my life, but unfortunately, all these episodes ended in breakups. I would like to know why this happened and how I can recapture the magic again and keep it forever.

Passionate love frequently leads to marriage, marriage to children, and a wife becomes a mother. Bringing new human life into the world is a blessing and a miracle; a new soul is created, or an old one is brought back to bodily existence. A mother bears the baby close to her heart, her blood and spirit flows into its body, nourishing its flesh and mind. No one is quite as beautiful as you, my mother; may you rest forever in God's bosom as I rested in yours.

3. Why the Madonna and Virgin Birth Inspire Us

The Madonna, or Divine Mother, has inspired more great art than any idea other than Jesus on the cross or the meditating Buddha. She's important because so many people connect with her spirit. My beloved mother had a close relationship with the Madonna, which sustained her during the darkest nights of senility. She often woke me up as she prayed to "the mother of all mothers," quite loudly because she was hard of hearing. Her faith and devotion to this deity made it possible for her to get through the night. The Madonna is our ideal of infinite kindness, compassion, and tender pity.

The Divine Mother is a representation or aspect of God. In the Hebrew tradition, God was very patriarchal, an elderly man with an imposing beard, loving, but often harsh in His disciplinary actions towards His people. Early Christians introduced the Madonna as a revival, I think, of the Earth Mother of ancient times. She was the bearer of life, being the mother of Jesus, kind, compassionate, and silent. In the Holy Bible, she has very little to say, except to inform her son at a wedding reception that the hosts are out of wine, and could he do something please—like turning water into wine. According to St. Luke, at the beginning of the story, she also complains to the angel as to how she is to bear the child Jesus when she's a virgin.

The early Christian Fathers declared that Mary was a virgin when she conceived Jesus by means of the Holy Spirit. Mary was perhaps as much of a virgin as Queen Elizabeth I of England. But purity was associated with virginity in those days before prophylactics and the bacterial theory of venereal disease. Not that impregnating a virgin with superior DNA would be more than child's play for a superpower like God. As for transmuting water into wine or producing loaves and fishes to feed multitudes out of energy fields, have you not seen *Star Trek*'s synthesizer machine on television? With the help of a very advanced civilization, Jesus could perform all kinds of miracles to amaze the people of his age.

In the end, Jesus was crucified at the hands of the Romans and hostile Hebrews in order to perform his greatest miracle: his own revival. But his mother first had to bury him—a picture so beautifully represented by Michelangelo in his sculpture *La Pietà* at St. Peter's, the Vatican, Rome. The mother holding baby Jesus was tenderly represented in Raphael's *Madonna*. With deep compassion and pity, she held his body in death. I remember my own mother holding me as a child and caressing me. Those were the moments in my entire life when I felt perfectly safe and content. So a female God, as proposed by feminists today, will do just fine for me.

Female or male, a God occupying an entire universe has all facets of sexuality under control, including gay preferences and all seven sexes necessary for reproduction on earth. Did I say seven? That's the view of the Tralfalmadorians in Kurt Vonnegut Jr.'s *Slaughterhouse Five*. Let's see. There are men who love men. There are women who love women, men who love both and women who love both. Moreover, there are those who are neutral, and the routine male and female sexes. That makes seven sexes, and even if there were forty-seven, God would contain them all. Just how, according to this theory, all seven are involved in reproduction isn't clear to me, but I'm working on that.

Coming back to the Madonna, she's much admired by both Catholic and Orthodox Christians, and she receives considerable respect from Mohammed in the Quran as the mother of Jesus. Is she saint or goddess? Many believe that she performs miracles from Heaven and is kind and compassionate to all Christians. The Byzantines held her up as the defender of their empire against the barbarian infidels, and their victories against attackers were often attributed to her.

These were echoes of Athena as the defender of the Athenian Greeks against the Persians. The Athenians rebuilt their Acropolis in her honor, including the Parthenon, meaning the virgin's house, and Pheidias sculpted a giant statue of the goddess covered with gold and ivory. Athena, you may recall, carried a spear and shield, wore a helmet, and was a warrior woman, aloof from sexual interests, pure in her virginal wisdom.

A virgin was pure, the ancients thought, because she was unused and innocent of sexual lust. What's not used is not likely to be damaged, infected, or defiled. Innocence is also associated with emptiness and nothingness, conditions that existed prior to the creation of the world. The universe was borne from the void, where there was nothing, not even space.

So Mary, pure and innocent, gave birth to Jesus, the essence of divine knowledge, the vessel of God's message on Earth. As such, she was the creative force of the world, the yin, patient and loving, an immense fertile valley, versus the masculine, the yang, the male God's aggression and periodic destruction. She creates the stars and planets, and He explodes them into supernovas in order to produce materials for the next generation of planets with heavier, more potent elements. This is pure imagery that may not make sense to you, but it does to some people.

In the overused, eroded, exhausted Mediterranean lands, fertility is much to be desired. Here the Madonna is put on the highest pedestal. It's part of a culture where men award extraordinary respect to mother, sister, and daughter. Men divide women sharply between good, chaste ones and those who are not; the latter are equated with whores. Crimes of passion may occur sometimes, where a father, brother, or son kills a man to avenge the dishonor of a female relative. *Mama mia* means a lot to an Italian, and so does *Mi madre* to a Spaniard, and *Metera* mou to a Greek. It's "Mother of God" in the context of religion.

In pop culture today, we have the superstar Madonna of song and dance, not a virginal type in spite of her great beauty and charm. Her manners and morals are not those of the pure Mediterranean female either and represent the acute materialism of our common culture.

A sexy female superstar is the opposite of our ideal Madonna, an ideal of complete tenderness, love, and devotion to her child. A woman following the Madonna as her model is a superstar to her family, devoted to her husband, children, relatives, and community; fame, diamonds, wealth, and pleasures all mean nothing to her compared to her duty and love for her family.

4. Most People Go the Way of All Flesh

We'll examine here the implications of sexual existence in a "mortal coil" and the future of this existence in the next world. The title of this section refers to our destiny on Earth: to be born, seek mates for childbearing, and then, by accident, disease, murder, suicide, or, if all these fail, by old age, go to our death. It's also the title of the classic novel by Samuel Butler. And yet, as in Butler's novel, some of us have this constant longing for something of value beyond the normal ken of pleasure, survival, and reproduction. We look for values that are eternal and transcending, which we sometimes find in artistic and religious pursuits. Such a value is what I seek in writing down these thoughts at a time of life when most men seek repose, relief from labor, and diversion. I warn you what I produce are unusual offerings. I'm like a blackberry bush. If you want to taste my sweet and sour fruit, you'll have to deal with my barbs. If you're like most people, your body too will go the way of all flesh from birth to marriage with offspring, and finally dissolution, while your spirit escapes free.

In the meantime, we're winged insects in a variety of traps, thwarting our escape, and sex is one of the stickiest in the whole of life. We're trapped in a body that's constantly urged by Nature to seek compatible companions and mate. Even when our choice would be to be free of this pleasure and burden, we're, most of us, inexorably led to the trap.

Sherwood Anderson, in "Winesburg, Ohio," tells the poignant story of Hal Winters, a farmhand who got a young girl in trouble. He asks an older friend, Ray Pearson, "Well, old daddy, come, advise me. I've got Nell in trouble. What do you say? Shall I marry and settle down? Shall I put myself into the harness to be worn out like an old horse?"[3] Ray couldn't answer because he had lived the trap in his own marriage and shut out adventure, travel, and wonder. Ray threw off his torn overcoat and began to run in the fields outside town. "As he ran, he shouted a protest against his life, against all life, against everything that makes life ugly."[4] He rushes to find his friend and tell him not to tie himself down, but Hal Winters has already made up his mind. He says laughing, "I want to marry her. I want to settle down and have kids."[5] Ray Pearson laughs also and, as his friend walks away, says, "It's just as well. Whatever I told him would have been a lie."[6]

Marriage and family may be a trap, or it may be only a labyrinth, a meditation exercise that has a solution and an exit out to a better world. Hindus and Buddhists believe that the life cycle of birth, suffering, and death repeats innumerable times until one has perfected one's soul for entry into Nirvana. And how does one perfect one's spirit except through the trials of life? Moreover, what trial is more severe than falling in love, laboring to make a marriage work, and raising children? You can turn your back on attachments and seek liberation in a life of chastity, but I wonder what's easier to do. Live with chastity or the vows of marriage?

Hermann Hesse, in his novel *Siddhartha*, takes up the tale of a young man's denial of the flesh and his abandonment to the way of the flesh later in his life. Hesse's hero, Siddhartha, a contemporary of the Buddha and with the same name, follows Buddha's life course in reverse. While the Buddha, a prince at birth born to luxury and ease, grows up, marries, and has a son, Hesse's Siddhartha was the son of a priest, a Brahmin, raised with a strict religious education and training.

Very young, Siddhartha determines to become an ascetic, a *Samana*

---

3. Sherwood Anderson, *Winesburg, Ohio: A Norton Critical Edition*, ed. Marc Dudley (New York: W.W. Norton & Company, 2016), 43.
4. Anderson, *Winesburg, Ohio*, 43.
5. Anderson, *Winesburg, Ohio*, 152.
6. Anderson, *Winesburg, Ohio*, 161.

in the forest, against his father's wishes. He spends many years in training, advancing his mental skills, but isn't satisfied with the answers he finds in the forest, even after talking with the most enlightened of men, the Buddha himself. Later he meets a beautiful courtesan who teaches him the ways of the flesh. With his meditative mental skills, he enters the profession of trading to amass a fortune.

As old age approaches, Siddhartha is disgusted with the excesses of his lifestyle and his thickening body. In the meantime, his mistress, threatened by her biological clock, produces a son for Siddhartha. But Siddhartha abandons his life again to wander the forests as a Samana, never satisfied with any answers but always filled with questions.

This was also true of the Buddha who denied knowing very much, just as did Socrates in Greece about the same time in history. However, the Buddha believed he had a way of alleviating mental suffering from frustration, just as a physician knows cures for diseases without knowing how they work. It's a simple formula expressed as the four noble truths and the eightfold path.

To avoid frustration and anguish, desire nothing selfishly, or next to nothing, and detach yourself from earthly desires such as love, sex, and marriage. Don a saffron robe, shave your head, and eat one vegetarian meal at noon. The Buddha's message is freedom from the way of all flesh through detachment from desire and devotion to God. It's a renunciation of worldly goods in the search for spiritual values. The Buddha spreads the gospel, as Jesus also teaches: to find your life, you must lose your life.

Losing your life means that you ignore the pleasures of the flesh and material possessions; flesh will go the way of all flesh after birth, marriage, children, grandchildren, and back to the earth, while your spirit remains, escaping free. Escaping free is good, but perhaps you are a true hero or heroine, not by renouncing flesh and family but by cheerfully shouldering the burdens of love and caring. You attach yourself to family, spouse, children, parents, brothers, and sisters; you don't walk away from your relatives to escape responsibility in a monastery. Perhaps flesh is a trap for us as the cocoon is a trap for the caterpillar. I will examine denial of the flesh and senses when I come to the matter of asceticism. Meanwhile, consider whether acceptance of birth, love, marriage, and parenthood may not also be a way of liberation and growth, if taken with the right attitude. As someone has joked, "Life is a test; it's only a test."[7] In case of panic, please tune in to the cosmic frequency for further instructions.

5. Do Fasting and Chastity Purify Our Spirits?

We deal here with two of the chief sensual pleasures and preoccupations of mankind and all animals: food and sex. We also consider their avoidance in fasting and chastity. The sense of sight is in our species the one that provides us with maximum information. But taste, smell, and touch can supply us with maximum pleasure, especially in food and sex. It's not surprising then that ascetics, who are interested in the denial of the senses, stress so much the control of their appetite for food and the denial of sexual contact. Some moderation of these animal urges is also good for you and me to preserve health and well-being. Moreover, if you have the capacity and training, you abstain from sex and food to purify body and soul from deadly toxins.

Well, now let's see how fasting and chastity aid or thwart our efforts to link up with Divine Intelligence. Much of the credit for the celibacy traditions of the Christian Church goes to the early Christian philosopher Saint Augustine. In his *Confessions*, he admits to sexual indulgence in his youth, but in later life, he gave all that up and became a bishop. The Catholic Church today still maintains the celibacy tradition for priests, while the Orthodox Church supports marriage and family for priests up to the rank of bishop. If one is to rise to that level of the hierarchy, he's expected to be unmarried and rely on nephews and nieces to continue his family line.

When we're hungry, though, we're apt to think of food more intensely than when we're adequately fed, and when denied sex, we constantly dream of it. Sexual drive is normally distributed. Some

---

7. Jack Kornfield, *A Path with Heart: A Guide Through the Perils and Promises of Spiritual Life* (New York: Bantam Books, 1993), 215.

people have a very low sex drive, and for them, abstinence is no hardship. Those at the other extreme of the curve, if they happen to catch religion and want to be priests or bishops in the old churches, those poor souls are destined to be sorely tempted and side-tracked from the ways of chastity.

Tempted and caught, someone who overindulges in food or sex is not on the road to sainthood. A fat person doesn't, as a rule, appear spiritual. In the East, a fat sitting Buddha is common in statues and paintings, but it's unlikely he was fat in life. In many individuals, the denial of sex leads to the abuse of food. Friar John of Robin Hood fame is a case in point. Many monks and priests end up obese because of much food and wine. Food in excess draws us to the life of the earth, frequently putting us into the earth prematurely.

On the other hand, people who use nourishment sparingly present appealingly thin figures like in the paintings of El Greco. His figures don't have thick, sensual lips and ruddy cheeks. According to most artists, venal and low types of mankind carry such features. Santa Claus is an exception among saints, who are thin as skeletons and quickly end up as such due to sacrifice and martyrdom.

Consider that noblemen and noblewomen have traditionally been slender, tall, high-brow, and agile, as opposed to peasant types: short, squat, chubby, coarse-featured, slow in mind and body, short-legged, devoted to crude pleasures, and close to the Earth.

C.S. Lewis idealized spiritual types of people in *Perelandra*. They were extremely tall and slender creatures, over ten feet tall, evolved in the lighter gravity of Venus. You may recall that Mahatma Gandhi, India's political saint, was very thin, due to his nature, much walking, as well as frequent fasting to promote his causes.

I take the view, though, that eating and lovemaking can both be paths to spiritual growth if practiced in a special way, as tools for deep meditation. We see some of this view in the religious paintings and sculptures of Hinduism. As mentioned earlier, Hindus believe that food is holy. Living creatures give their lives so that we may live, and we, in the end, become food for other creatures unless cremated. Thus, food should be eaten slowly with great respect, never wasted, and with deep concentration on its flavor, texture, and aroma, and used as a vehicle for meditation. As for sexual love, India's holy sculptures and paintings always amaze Christian Westerners with their frank sensuality. A favorite subject is Lord Krishna embracing his nude or nearly nude consort, Shakti, in intimate contact.

The ancient Greeks and Romans also lacked customary Christian restraint in matters of food and sex, although Hippocrates, the father of medicine, recommended moderation in the consumption of both. In the pottery paintings, sculptures, and mosaics that we have unearthed, Greco-Roman culture was free in expressing the enjoyment of wine, food, and sex in all forms. Satyr, with his immense penis, was a common subject, which today, in reproductions, amuses and scandalizes tourists in Greek shops.

Fasting, however, has an ancient tradition as a meditation tool. The Buddha is said to have fasted very strenuously for years and reduced himself almost to a pile of bones, but his goal of Nirvana remained unattainable. Then a kind lady took pity on him and fed him a string of delicious snacks. He recovered from his weakness and, very determined, sat under a sacred fig tree for a whole night in deep concentration until he finally realized enlightenment and awakening. The lesson in this story: it's useful to fast, cleansing the body and mind for a period of time, but not to the point of physical weakness. You need strength and vigor to carry on any difficult task, meditation being one of the toughest jobs around.

Jesus also is said to have fasted forty days and nights during which he was severely tempted by Satan in his meditations. But he emerged from the ordeal strong and pure in thought, ready to begin his mission. What happens during such a lengthy fast to the body and mind? Blood sugar drops, and one becomes lightheaded for a while. Then blood sugar stabilizes as the body begins to feed on stored reserves of fat. Metabolism slows down, and the mind smolders in dampened energy fields. Visions and hallucinations may occur, especially as one meditates deeply. Dead or weak body cells are scavenged, and the debris of their combustion is excreted. When fat reserves are low, muscle tissue is put on the fire and one becomes emaciated and drawn. Powerful energies are released in a last-ditch effort at survival to prepare the body for the hunt. Since such an outlet is denied, these energies can be directed to the task of seeking God in the subconscious mind.

Abstaining from food for many days cleans out your digestive system, drinking plenty of water flushes out poisons accumulated in your body, vitalizing your organs and clearing your brain, and abstaining from sex allows you to forget it for a while and to occupy your mind with matters of the spirit. The sexual drive seeks other channels to release its forces, and if you properly direct it, you can achieve a breakthrough, reaching the spirit world. Sublimation of the basic drives for food and sex, therefore, may contribute to a higher purpose than mere survival and reproduction: contact with God.

6. Romance Can Bring You Closer to God

Sex, as a crude sensual activity, takes away from spiritual growth, while romance leads you closer to God. Every thought, activity, or experience you choose to do either detracts or adds to the quality of your soul. The process begins with a simple idea or impulse in your mind. The idea stimulates your feelings and emotions, stirring you into corresponding actions. The idea of romance gives birth to a spiritual process, leading you closer to your source, the Cosmic Mind.

Some thoughts and actions are experimental. We engage in them to discover things and to learn, and if we're astute, we back off from these adventures after we know enough. Examples are seen in young people trying once or twice a drug or a lover and then turning away from the experience. But when we repeat a behavior again and again, we acquire a habitual response and suffer benefits or damages depending on the activity. We're no longer experimenting. In the long run, we become what we think and do habitually. If drinking is our habit, we become drunks; if we indulge in much exercise, we turn to hunks. Later, we become that which we do easily and unconsciously, such as a perfect skater or liar.

Now as to sex, there are many varieties of this most popular idea and experience. Most mammals, including primates with the exception of man, are led to engage in sex on a seasonal basis with the female's estrus cycle. The female becomes ready to be fertilized, emits odors, and engages in behaviors signaling her mating readiness to the males in her territory who compete for her favors. After a number of sexual encounters with the same or several males, the female ceases to be receptive, and sexual activity ends in her case until the birth of offspring. Some human females seem to follow this pattern, even in marriage, but most do not. Developments have occurred in our species that have changed the sexual makeup of the female and her behavior. As the maturation of the offspring required more and more years, because of the developing brain, the female evolved to attract and hold male attention and affection for periods longer than a season.

In fact, female sexuality now mimics the male sexual characteristics. The clitoris is a small replica of the penis without the urethra. The female's hormonal cycles have adapted so that she's practically always ready for sexual activity just as the male. And her overall sexual response is far more pronounced than in animals, involving orgasms just like the male's, with sperm-free ejaculations, of course. Simultaneously, human females evolved the hymen that makes initial intercourse somewhat difficult, encouraging the acquisition of a more considerate and patient mate.

Thus a couple may bond to each other with habitual pleasures and stay together for the protection of the children. This sexual experience, although vastly expanded compared to animal behavior, still has one function: reproduction and the care of offspring. It's a biological function and has no spiritual value unless it leads to the birth and nurturing of new and improved souls.

The growth of societies, cultures, and conventions has brought about other uses for sex, which largely depart from Nature's ways. One is commercial sex, which may be practiced in the streets or in the home. With the invention of money and constantly expanding power, sexual favors could be exchanged, not for pleasure received or a desire for parenthood, but for what money can buy: quite a lot today with all the fancy services and products available.

Another variant of "civilized" sex is based on convention and cultural needs. People maintain a marriage and an intimate relationship because success in society demands it, relatives insist on it, or it's simply the easiest thing to do under certain circumstances. These ways of sex debase one's spirit and lead to places other than Heaven. It's not surprising that about half of prostitutes are addicted to drugs and lead a miserable existence under the thumb of a pimp.

In the Old Testament of the Hebrew religious tradition, such uses of sex were condemned as fornication, except within the context of conventional marriage. Fornication included homosexual acts. Religious authorities punished such deviant behavior with death by stoning. The object was to rid society of the evil doers and maintain the purity and strength of the tribe. In those days, aggressive neighbors quickly attacked a weakened tribe and enslaved or slaughtered them.

Marriage was holy and numerous offspring were desired, as many of them died in infancy. Clearly a strong relationship between a husband and his wives was desirable. A woman was, to an extent chattel, property or commodity, traded from father to groom and used by the husband for pleasure and children without much regard to how she felt—a social aberration leading to all kinds of evil, similar to prostitution.

In spite of these horrors of sexual behavior, romance flourished at the same time and great legends emerged about beautiful love affairs. Delilah betrayed Samson, it's true, but there was the wonderful story of Orpheus and Euridice from ancient Greece. He went to Hades, the underworld, in search of her and reclaimed her from Pluto, the god of death. There was also the tale of two male friends (gay lovers?), Damon and Pheidias, each ready to sacrifice his life for his beloved.

In the Middle Ages, there was Tristan and Isolde of northerly climes. Also, the legend of the Flying Dutchman, a ghost condemned to sail forever on the high seas unless a woman out of love would sacrifice herself for him. Knights, whatever other mayhem they may have done, were supposed to pay allegiance to a fine lady of good breeding and gentle manners, joust in her honor, to death sometimes, and fight valiant battles in her name.

Sir Walter Scot's knights come to mind, with Ivanhoe worshipping the blonde noblewoman while secretly desiring the brunette Jewess, immortalized by Elizabeth Taylor on the silver screen. Cervantes wittily exploited, in his tale of Don Quixote and his Dulcinea, the ideal romance of a knight with his lady.

You don't need to be a knight to be noble and offer romance to your lady rather than crude sex. With romance, you idealize the passion into a vision of purity and goodness, and you set aside selfish desires for the sake of your beloved. There may not be a better connection to God than this. We'll go next into the matter with our investigation of Zen sex, or Tantric love.

7. Zen Sex is Pure Love

We'll now enter the realm of spiritual sex, known also as Tantric love in East Indian culture. Zen sex is an art form created to please the loved one as well as the lover with its excellence of technique and execution. But our interest is in appraising such sex as a pathway or link to God and to a full awakening of the spirit. One key element of spiritual sex is love and affection. You engage in it to express devotion to the person you love. The shell of the ego breaks down in the process, and your soul merges with the soul of your beloved. When both partners experience this, it's a complete act. They feel not like separate people but like one living entity. It's very similar to what mystics call union with God. The lovers share the pure joy of being together, and their state of consciousness transports them to a world of eternal values.

This is lovemaking as a meditative practice. One moves slowly and surely as in a deep trance. The animal urgency and violence of vulgar sex are absent. I'm referring to a pure act which is the opposite of the "f**k of the century," as shown in the movie *Basic Instinct*, with Sharon Stone and Michael Douglas. Consummation of the act in orgasm is not important. It comes when it comes, but it can be delayed indefinitely. The process of caressing and hugging one's partner is what is sought, not the final result of ejaculation and burst of pleasure. It's not an act of procreation, although that adds to its intensity at certain times and in some circumstances. Such times occur when both man and woman desire to become the conduits to a new life. Otherwise, people of the opposite or the same sex may experience Zen love.

Sexual organs in such couplings perform a different function from their strict biological one. A penis has evolved to become a very efficient organ for the passing of spermatozoa to the female. And a vagina, with attendant inner and outer lips, is a perfect funnel for receiving the male seed. So, how do they lead to spiritual revelations? It happens in the same way as lips, tongue, throat, and teeth evolved for grasping and eating food, serving to offer up to God the divine songs of Puccini's *Madama Butterfly*.

Our hands, which our primate ancestors needed to grasp tree branches, can be an instrument of prayer for a great violinist like Gil Shihan. So can sexual organs transport us to a different dimension used with devotion and artistry. Also, hands, eyes, lips, arms, and, in fact, every part of our bodies may serve to enhance and embellish a mystical sexual act.

I'm not an expert on Zen sex, but I know it's true that the act may go on for many hours, as long as both partners want it so. This is possible with proper training. There was once in America a religious sect known as the Oneida community. Men practiced sex without ejaculation or faced ostracism. All the women in the community were shared, but due to the practice of male restraint, no children were desired or born. Eventually, the community collapsed due to lack of regeneration; what remains is the manufacture of silverware under the Oneida name.

Mormons had a different idea. Church leaders encouraged numerous children, and in the past, polygamy was permitted, making large families easier to achieve. Today, large families of five or six children are common among Mormons, even with one wife. The Church is growing this way—and by sending zealous missionaries all over the world.

In a missionary position or other engagements, Zen sex is an art form, and art has a different language from our rational thought. One can intimate the experience by employing another art form, such as poetry. Passages from Walt Whitman's poem "From Pent-up Aching Rivers" may illustrate this:

God Likes Sex

> Hark close and still what I now whisper to you,
> I love you, O you entirely possess me,
> O that you and I escape from the rest and go utterly off, free and lawless,
> Two hawks in the air, two fishes swimming in the sea
> Not more lawless than we;
> The furious storm through me careering, I passionately trembling,
> The oath of the inseparableness of two together
> of the woman that loves me
> and whom I love more than my life, that oath swearing,
> O I willingly stake all for you,
> O let me be lost if it must be so!"[8]

And later on in this poem, he writes:

> From the hour of shining stars and dropping dews,
> From the night a moment I emerging flitting out,
> Celebrate you act divine and you children prepared for
> And you stalwart loins.[9]

What is required in Zen sex is the concentration of attention on the act of loving. It's what Robert Heinlein, in his science fiction epic *Stranger in a Strange Land*, called "grokking." Total involvement in what you're doing so as to become one with your lover. In that novel, a young man was raised and trained by Martians to perform feats and miracles using

---

8. Walt Whitman, "From Pent-up Aching Rivers," *Leaves of Grass: 1891–92 Edition*, Whitman Archive, https://whitmanarchive.org/published/LG/1891/poems/54.
9. Walt Whitman, *Leaves of Grass*, ed. Sculley Bradley and Harold W. Blodgett (New York: W.W. Norton & Company, 1973), 193.

psychic powers and deep meditation. One of his feats was pleasing, at the same time, several beautiful young ladies with his perfect loving—and making them all pregnant before getting himself martyred at the hands of an angry mob.

Zen sex is union with your partner, not so much of bodies, but of the spirits. An act not just between you and your beloved but both of you as a unity linked with God. Jesus said to his disciples, before ascending to Heaven, "Whenever three or more of you meet in my name, there I shall be among you."[10] He could have said the same of two lovers who are joined with total devotion to each other. There with them, He is also, and the Holy Spirit descends, filling their moment together with the most pure light of Heaven.

8. Who Are the Dark-Eyed Virgins of Paradise?

The Persian poet Omar Khayyam wrote: "A loaf of bread, a jug of wine and thou, and wilderness is Paradise anow."[11] What's disguised here is that a woman is similar to a loaf of bread and wine, a male chauvinist viewpoint. Many visions of heaven place women in the role of consumption items for the enjoyment and comfort of men. The Quran of Islam states:

> But the true servants of God shall be well provided for, feasting on fruit, and honored in the gardens of delight. Reclining face to face upon soft couches, they shall be served with a goblet filled at a gushing fountain, white and delicious to those who drink it. It will neither dull their senses nor befuddle them. They shall sit with bashful, dark-eyed virgins, as chaste as the sheltered eggs of ostriches."[12]

---

10. Matthew 18:20 (NIV).
11. Omar Khayyam, *The Rubaiyat of Omar Khayyam: A Critical Edition*, trans. Edward FitzGerald, ed. Christopher Decker (Charlottesville: University of Virginia Press, 2008), 35.
12. Quran 37:41-49.

In other words, Heaven is where we shall drink delicious wine without getting inebriated or satiated, and men shall enjoy beautiful virgins without deflowering them. This is a vision of Paradise appealing to men and to women too if women want to be bashful virgins again in the next life. In God's house, there are many mansions, and perhaps there's one for macho men and coy women. Still, that's a man's heaven, and this is still a man's world, and I object to it because I feel women deserve better treatment; to advance from now on, humanity needs females as more than entertainers for men and as mothers.

Walt Whitman, a bisexual, expresses the feelings I have about women beautifully in his poem, "To the Garden the World." He writes:

To the Garden the world anew ascending...
By my side or back of me Eve following,
Or in front, and I following her just the same.[13]

But let's be fair to the Quran. There are passages such as these regarding Paradise: "They shall dwell in gardens watered by running streams ... wedded to chaste spouses, they shall abide there for ever."[14] The Quran also says, "Women are your fields: go then into your fields whence you please."[15] Similarly, in the Christian Bible, women are helpmates and support persons, seldom taking a central role. And according to Jesus, there is no marriage in Heaven with spouses as on Earth. In a Christian Paradise, people are neuters sexually.

In spite of what goes on with women's rights in America and the breakdown of the glass ceiling in business, professions, and government, in most of the world, the status of women is inferior to that of men. In China and India, female babies are still killed in the womb or after having been born. Even in Europe and Japan, most women are

---

13. Walt Whitman, *Leaves of Grass*, ed. Sculley Bradley and Harold W. Blodgett (New York: W.W. Norton & Company, 1973), 116.
14. Quran 4:57, 2:25.
15. Quran 2:223.

given an expensive higher education only to end up serving husband and children in the home, or as secretaries and assistants to men in business. You have a long way to go, baby.

The average woman is smaller, less muscular, and less aggressive than the average man. She has higher verbal ability than a male but less mathematical or mechanical skill. Few women achieve high honors in science, the arts, business, or government, but most live longer than men. Why have we not seen in history more great female prophets, apostles, or scientists? We have known a bountiful supply of female saints. The so-called inferiority of women, however, is open to question, as it is for dark-skinned people.

Given half a chance, women perform as well or better than men, except in athletics. If those in power deny the right to excel to a portion of the people, then that portion's inferiority becomes inevitable. Therefore, we must now question the theory that women have no souls worth praising and can't possess a linkage to God. We should challenge all the churches barring women from becoming ministers to change their practices. I question the theory that God is a male entity communicating with men only, that the hypothetical God gene is only attached to the male's Y chromosome, and that a woman can't talk to God directly but must do it with a male priest as an intermediary.

The case of Mary Baker Eddy, an American prophet of some stature who founded Christian Science, proves that women can be as insightful as men in spiritual matters and lead new religious movements quite ably. This can happen only in the United States and such nations where women are given some opportunities to make something great with their lives. However, the scarcity of women overachievers in the arts and sciences can be explained on biological grounds. Breakthroughs in any field require aggressiveness and the expenditure of prodigious amounts of energy. Women naturally conserve energy and other assets for the benefit of embryos and young children. Overly aggressive women, or big ones, are a turn-off for most men and do not find husbands easily. Aggressiveness in women puts offspring at risk.

As to the God connection, that can lead to extremely risky situations when it's activated. It may be that the God gene is present in women, but it's seldom triggered because of the dangers involved. A pregnant woman or mother of small children would jeopardize their lives if seized by God's madness. At best, she would be declared a witch, facing serious punishment by religious authorities for the sake of her own soul.

An older woman past child rearing might explore spirituality, especially as female hormones have subsided that predispose women to conservatism. Hence, the more common appearance of aged witches, rather than young and pretty ones who have better uses for men than burning at the stake.

This is a man's world still today, and whatever we think and do is colored by the situation. A successful woman, as a spiritual pathfinder or business executive, has to have the guts and ability to swim upstream like a salmon. Fortunately, women have more patience and ingenuity; they plan better than men and have a keen appreciation of all the vital details in a situation. In our technical civilization, brawn is worth less than brain; women are as well equipped with brains as men. Women will continue to advance, making major contributions to society in our country; they should not be excluded from key posts in religious affairs. In the Unitarian Church I attend, our woman minister does at least as well as her male partner.

In the past, visions of Heaven and the future of the world were seen and projected outward by men, mostly in the Holy Scriptures of all religions. We're in a vastly different world, and prospects for the future are dismal without contributions from the gentler sex. As they assume leadership roles in more nations, we are going to have more peace and charity than in the past and fewer wars and violent acts. When major female prophets emerge, religion will assume a much better character, with more understanding, gentleness, and compassion. Political and business affairs will go better too, as women assume more leadership positions in those arenas, exercising their natural tendencies of caring for people and devoting time to social values.

9. Open Polygamy and Polyandry for All the People

This is an issue we brought up earlier that needs to be re-examined in detail. That, in this country today, polygamy (or polyandry) is illegal is a patent and totally unnecessary infringement of society upon individual freedom. Of course, our concern in this volume is mainly with the spiritual implications of the one-wife and one-husband institution established on the basis of historical religious preference for Christianity in our country. One man to one woman is a convenient social arrangement, but not a moral imperative. If there's a message coming to us from another universe regarding matters of morality, it doesn't urge upon us the institution of monogamy.

It may be time to open up marriage to change. Complex marriages may become a nightmare for bureaucrats administering social security and other social services and for the courts deciding on parental responsibilities and inheritance; but our ideal of personal freedom demands we allow them. Same-sex marriages are being debated today, which, as a rule, offer no benefits to society. Complex marriages, such as polygamy or polyandry, could be beneficial to all concerned. As a start, children would benefit from having several parents responsible for them, both personally and financially. In polygamy, if one mother is at work pursuing a career, the others can be at home looking after the nursery. Several husbands would add needed extra income for a poor family.

In any case, most people would still opt for a monogamous marriage as they do in Islamic countries, although up to four wives are allowed by religion. In most countries, the constraints for monogamy are financial. Only wealthy men can afford more than one wife, and women have few opportunities to earn money themselves. Besides, people now like to imitate the European model of marriage.

In some African countries, such as Zimbabwe, polygamy is common, made practical by the work of multiple wives in the fields and marketplace. There are villages in China so poor, one man alone cannot support a wife and children. So, several men marry one woman and contribute their meager earnings to one family. In capitalistic areas of China and Taiwan today, wealthy men follow the age-old custom of taking concubines, either openly or secretly.

In America, with due deference to justice and women's equality, if polygamy is allowed, so must be polyandry. In ancient Israel, men of property often had more than one wife and numerous children, as told in the Old Testament. Women did not have the same privileges. Today, successful men in America and Europe practice serial polygamy. When the first wife gets old or boring, a younger one takes her place, and the first one is out. What else can a virile rich man do? Even if an arrangement could be made for the two wives to remain, our laws don't allow it.

In some cases, the man falls in love with another, usually younger woman, but he still loves the old wife and wants to keep his family together. The old wife may be willing to accept the new one and continue the marriage. But our social conventions make this arrangement impossible.

Another benefit of polygamy and polyandry is that they foster the production of offspring of higher quality. Successful men, like strong and healthy stags, give birth to more children, raising them well within the law. Beautiful and charming women, with many husbands looking after them, are able to devote themselves fully to bearing and rearing numerous children.

I also see some spiritual benefits to polygamy, which the Oneida community mentioned earlier recognized. Monogamous marriage eventually becomes boring in bed. There's not enough variety in sexual encounters unless the couple is extraordinarily creative in sexual activities. Inevitably, most couples get into extra-marital sex with its many dangers from communicable diseases, pressure on the marriage from other parties, and social disapproval. Multiple marriage partners would offer legitimate romantic adventures within a recognized and socially acceptable family structure.

Unacceptable is that much of marriage involves the selfish, narrow motive of possessiveness. "My wife" or "my husband" is often said with pride of ownership about someone who should also be a free man or woman. It's a form of slavery. Moreover, sooner or later, one or the other spouse will fall into the trap of jealousy, fear, and hatred. It's often the road to bitter divorce, recriminations, and loss of a complete family life, with the children bearing the major burden of the breakup. None of this is necessary, if the partners would not engage in the ownership of another human being, allowing other loves to enter their lives, provided they're legal and wholesome. With the right outlook, complex marriages would expand our lives and our consciousness, as was foreseen in the sixties but never realized in our institutions.

I don't suggest that family problems would disappear with complex marriages. I'm not sure polygamy or polyandry would solve the mating problem for most people. Quite the contrary, most people would freely choose romance and monogamy with one person. But what's wrong now is that monogamy is forced on everybody in our country. That's not necessary; it's not moral, and it's not right. Alternate marriage forms wouldn't damage anybody any more than conventional marriages. And people should have a choice of lifestyles, including gay relationships, without shame or fear.

Despite injunctions from the Old Testament, we should judge a relationship by its fruits, not with prejudice. Many perfectly legal heterosexual relationships are disastrously horrid, leading to wife and child abuse, as well as numerous extra-marital affairs by the partners who stay together, suffering their whole lives from doing so.

The message coming from Beyond is cryptic and difficult to interpret, but it doesn't include the moral dictum of one man for one woman in marriage. No one knows for sure what's right, not even the greatest prophets. Some have a vision clearer than others, but no one really knows the whole truth about morality. A few things we can believe with almost complete certainty. Freedom should be respected unless it causes harm to other people. Citizens should be allowed choices. Children should be loved and cherished. The strong in society should look after the welfare of the weaker members, not exploit them. Women continue, even in America, to be the weaker sex and ought to be protected still. Any marriage structures and laws should adhere to moral imperatives, not mere conventions.

10. Does the Soul Enter the Body at Conception?

We theorized earlier that, although Darwin's theory of evolution is most probably correct for the body, God also created man and woman and breathed into them a spiritual essence. The Biblical clay was actually the animal body, which took billions of years to evolve with natural selection, the survival of the fittest. But souls were first implanted in us more recently, perhaps a hundred thousand years ago when Homo sapiens appeared or ten thousand years ago when civilization began. A key question: When does the soul enter the body in the life of a human being? It does this at conception.

It follows we need to examine the sexual politics of abortion, a woman's choice in getting rid of an unwanted pregnancy. Is abortion the exclusive right of the woman who carries the child, or is it a mortal sin and crime, the same as killing an infant already born? Our society is debating this issue, with people being almost equally divided on one side or the other. At the same time, abortions are routinely carried out in many parts of the country when pregnancy is simply inconvenient to the woman.

The religious right of the Christian Coalition says that abortion should be a crime, while the feminist movement says it's a woman's right to choose, and society should not interfere. Religious extremists have bombed medical clinics, where abortions are done, killing medical doctors, but the massacre of babies in the womb continues unabated.

We can make many good arguments on both sides. Liberated women in this country are not about to give in to pressure and relinquish one of their hard-won freedoms. They feel that the whole argument is based on male dominance over women's bodies and the exploitation of the female with pregnancy and domestication. Politicians, it's argued, being mostly male, favor limiting women's choices.

What I write here will not change anybody's mind on the matter. But I hope to throw a new and different light on the issue. Let's look at some facts. Life doesn't begin at birth; you can see that in sonograms and x-rays: the baby in the womb is capable of much activity and feeling, especially in the last three months of pregnancy. It can't breathe or see, but it can hear; it responds to soothing sounds, love, and affection from the mother. When it's hurt, it writhes in agony, giving a silent scream.

On the other hand, our observation of Nature shows that it has little regard for new life. Nature produces seeds, eggs, and offspring in abundance, largely decimated before they mature. Predators enjoy munching on tender young bodies. The snake enters the gopher's nest and swallows the young while the mother runs away to save her own life. A leopard attacks the helpless calf, relishing the young flesh, just as we enjoy the suckling pig or lamb.

Before the arrival of modern medicine, women had numerous children in order to be left with just two or three after disease, accident, and famine had taken their toll. Also, before the arrival of legal abortion, women who couldn't afford to have the child or simply didn't want it would often go to dirty, unskilled practitioners to be rid of it or would attempt with needles and potions to do the act themselves. Many lost their lives or health, as well as the baby. Sometimes, among poor families burdened with too many children and no means of preventing pregnancies, parents resorted to infanticide. So, safe, hygienic, and nearly painless abortion under a doctor's care can be justified.

And yet, under careful scrutiny, the killing of the fetus is murder. New life begins at conception, not at birth. Consider all the premature babies that we save and cherish. Yes, often, the mother miscarries when the fetus is defective, or its environment in the womb is poor. That is an act of God or Nature. When a healthy baby is killed in the womb, those who perform the operation, or those who order it, are morally responsible for the evil done, even if it's somehow justified. The same responsibility applies to the killing of convicted criminals by society, as well as the taking of one's own life. Not even in self-defense or righteous war is killing morally excusable; it remains a cardinal sin. Killing of a living human being is abhorrent under any circumstances.

If we believe in the existence of spirits, then we must inevitably conclude the soul leaves the body at death and goes to Heaven or elsewhere. Similarly, when a baby is conceived, its soul descends from God and begins to guide its destiny and shape its mission on Earth. It's a sin for anyone to terminate that mission since no one but God knows what it is. The loss of the flesh is nothing. We know that will be destroyed sooner or later. The appalling aspect of killing is that a soul is sent back to the Creator without regard to its mission. Every child is born with some gift, some talent from God, which is his or her endowment at conception. It supplements the information packets from the parents' genes and combines with growth experiences in the family, school and workplace. Guided by the Holy Spirit, the child grows from weakness to strength and from ignorance to understanding.

If the soul enters a baby at conception, life's meaning for this new human being resides in the fulfillment of his or her destiny as ordained by God. To interfere with that destiny by killing the fetus is a horrid sin, which should be avoided by a moral being at all costs. It's vastly better to suffer the birth of a baby, even if it brings the parents much difficulty than terminate its life in the womb. Who knows whether that human life ended prematurely may be destined to become another Jesus, Mozart, Einstein, van Gogh, Madame Curie, or Tolstoy? Does the mother submitting to the abortion know the answer to this question, or does the doctor performing the D and C? The birth and death of human beings should be left to God or Nature alone. Certainly, no individual, or even a social organization, is mature and wise enough to make that decision.

8

CAN WE HAVE MORALITY WITHOUT RELIGION?

It was World War II. My aunt Lulu struggled to feed and clothe her family with her husband's small salary, while he used a sizable portion of it for his drinking and partying. Her youngest son, Demitri, did not talk much but always behaved well. He was a small, freckled redhead of nine years in 1944. His two older brothers kept on with their schools and games. I've often wondered why Demitri, with the same heredity and background as that of his brothers, was different. He realized his mother suffered; the family was short of money. What could a young boy do to help? Near his house, Mr. Maheras ran a grocery store. Demitri would visit the grocery often, pick up a broom and sweep, or run errands without asking for payment.

Maheras liked the boy's attitude and finally gave him a job. Demitri could have done as his older brothers and kept living as an ordinary boy. He could have begged in the streets as some children did then. Instead, he went to work. And he put every drachma he earned each week into the hands of his mother. Demitri never finished high school like the other children, but when he grew up, he became a clerk at the National Bank of Greece in Volos. He earned his high school diploma in night school and had a successful career with the bank. He married lovely Anna after many years of courtship; together they took care of Aunt Lulu until her death in her nineties from extreme osteoporosis.

Now, all people in Volos who know Demitri like him and admire his happy marriage with three fine children. His father, a communist, and his mother, not a church member, had given him no religious instruction on moral behavior. Yet his steps were always guided without fail in the path of righteousness.

1. Social Consciousness Builds Morality

The moral imperative, much of religious thought, has to do with our relationships within a family and community: our social consciousness. The newborn baby is almost totally self-centered; it has to be so to survive because it depends on others completely. Later, a child normally learns to socialize with other children, having fun with others as well as fighting for his possessions and privileges. Parents usually face a stressful phase in a child's development during the teen years. That is, they often loathe their beloved child; in response, the teenager hates the parents. That's all very normal and proper according to Nature for growth to occur. The teenager is still dependent on parents more than ever, perhaps for emotional and financial support, but at the same time, wants his or her independence and peer group approval. The teen continues to be very self-centered but has an expanded consciousness to include close friends. The teenager's morality derives mostly from the peer group. Normally, after graduation from school and some years of job climbing, a person attains financial independence, falls in love, marries, and gives birth to children. Now, social awareness includes wife, children, and other relatives. In the final years of life, one may become the least self-centered, with expanding social consciousness to embrace all of society or even all of humanity. In some old people, however, the soul shrinks with concerns over illness or death, and social consciousness collapses within. These old people return to the self-centered attitudes of the teenage years, childhood, and then infancy, as they become too dependent again on others. If in youth you believed in religious ethics, now getting older, rely on the same social guidelines: keep active, work for others more each passing year, search for truth, the right way to live, and grow to avoid falling again into a helpless state.

Searching for the truth in morality and faith was Moses' purpose when he climbed up on Mount Sinai. The first four commandments on his tablets have to do with our God connection, the rest with social relationships. The commandments admonish us to have no other gods than Jehovah, worship no idols, make no idle use of His name, and have regular contact with Him on the Sabbath. None of this makes any sense if you don't believe that God exists. But God is simply the ideals of love, compassion, and perfection projected into the universe; it's imperative to respect the deity's orders, devoting a day each week to the cultivation of such ideals. Moreover, this way, we follow the dictates of our own social consciousness.

Other gods in the time of Moses were involved with human sacrifices, worship of stone images, and cruel power. An idol can be money, fame, lust, power, or any other vice. Moses urged us not to worship material, transient things but the eternal spiritual values of a true God. As for taking the Lord's name in vain, it's understandable that ringing up God for trivial or profane purposes could not be pleasing to Him. And the Sabbath, clearly a regular schedule of contact with such a mentor, is very helpful—your teacher, shrink, or personal trainer demands that too.

Considering now the other six commandments, they're necessary for the smooth and efficient operation of any society. Honoring father and mother implies that you listen and obey their admonitions, usually given to further your own life and to civilize your behavior towards others. Also, parents looked after in their old age stay around as valuable consultants and advisers to the younger generations. Since we all age—if we survive accident, illness, or foul play long enough—the children will someday be aged parents to be looked after in turn. Being loved and cared for will extend their life and make it better.

The command not to kill used to apply to members of one's own tribe or nation. People of other nations were, and are today, fair game and could be freely butchered in war. The command also did not apply to animals. In Biblical times, a crowd could stone, on the spot, perceived violators of strict religious laws if found guilty on the slimmest of evidence. Perhaps, the message from Beyond is simple and clear and means what it says. "Thou shalt not kill" is what echoes in my head, without qualifications. The intent of the Father is that we respect all life, as the Hindus believe, and avoid killing any living thing. Is it practical to take such an extreme ethical view; is it a good idea?

If we're forbidden to kill any living thing, what are we to eat? Since mana from heaven is a rare treat for us, we must seek other solutions. We can eat from the fruit of trees and plant the seeds in our dung, as animals do. We can trim some of the leaves or roots and not destroy the whole plant. That has advantages too. We can take some of the excess milk from cows, goats, sheep, yaks, and other mammals and spare their lives so they will keep feeding us. If we must cut down a tree, we should plant two or three in its place so at least one reaches maturity. Perhaps insects should not be sprayed with poisons but controlled by other natural, environmentally safe products.

All these actions have benefits for our own health and the viability of our environment. Medical science has shown that avoidance of animal flesh in our diet lowers cholesterol levels, extends our lives, and improves our dispositions. In the end, nothing matters more than the preservation of our natural habitat for our own species as well as our fellow creatures. Archeological excavations and historical data reveal innumerable civilizations that perished after the deterioration of their natural environment and the loss of resources, such as soil, plants, and animals. The people who created the magnificent cultures of Mesopotamia, Egypt, Greece, Rome, Middle America, and so many others grew complacent, neglecting good behavior toward each other and toward living things around them.

Growing older, take care of the world around you. Don't ever become complacent, self-satisfied, negligent of duty to your people, lazy, or self-indulgent: you risk sinking into helpless infancy again. The message from Beyond is clear: we humans need to keep working and striving for higher goals until our end. The message beamed at us is urging our species to cooperate, to look after each other, and not to fight, kill, or destroy. Lying, stealing another person's spouse, desiring another person's possessions—all these lead to conflict, bloodshed, and loss of cooperation. Earth's evolutionary forces dictate fighting for survival, killing the enemy, competition, and bloody struggle, but Heaven's message is altogether different. The refinement of our spirits demands other strategies and tactics. The emphasis should be on love, caring for those who are weaker than we are; also, caring for species of animals and plants in danger of extinction. The survival of the fittest isn't an obsolete concept; it hasn't ceased to function. But Heaven now dictates that we—smart, tough, and oh-so-ingenious humans—start looking after all of Earth's inhabitants, causing no danger to other species of life.

2. Is God Merciful and Compassionate?

In much of religious literature—Hebrew, Christian, Islamic, and Hindu—God is merciful and compassionate. For example, a common prayer in the Christian faith is "God have mercy on our souls, or God have mercy." In the Quran, the Recitation, each passage begins with the words, "In the Name of God, the Compassionate the Merciful." God, the Great Spirit of ideas, is perfectly just, wise, all-mighty, all-knowing, kind, and loving towards all his creatures. Yet, God often allows the innocent to suffer great misfortunes and agonies—an observation not fitting our image of God as powerfully compassionate and infinitely powerful.

People afflicted with extreme and undeserved misfortune feel wronged by God; they often become bitter. A cancer patient, suffering and failing, may ask, "Why do I have to face this horror? I've not been smoking; I've not abused my body any other way. I've been virtuous; knowingly I've wronged no one. I'm a believer in the Almighty and have faithfully observed the Sabbath and other commands. Is this my reward? How am I better off than the cruel, unjust, selfish people I see around me, walking in good health?"

The basic question is: Where's God's compassion and mercy when you're in extreme pain for disasters you didn't bring upon yourself? At the same time, we see in the world all manner of evil going on, which doesn't bring any of God's punishment on the wrongdoers. The Earth is damaged, and nature is trampled on by tyrants and warmongers, who continue in power after elected officials are voted out of office.

In the past, this planet has suffered mass extinction of species; today, many animals and plant species are being lost, and God doesn't seem to care enough about this damage to life. A large meteor will impact the Earth any millennium now, wiping out us humans, as one did to the dinosaurs. Looking at our own planetary system outside of Earth, we observe planets and satellites to be in utter desolation, hostile to life. With our telescopes and radio antennas, we see stars exploding, destroying their planets, possibly inhabited by advanced life forms. We see entire galaxies running into each other, causing havoc in their planetary systems. Where's the Divine Architect when these things happen?

Here on Earth, much anguish and bewilderment hits us when a loved one dies prematurely, such as a promising young person in an auto accident or from some rare disease. We do expect, painful as the loss may be, an older person to pass on, his or her life all played out, but what sense does it make when a child, husband, or wife is taken from us in the bud or prime of life with many useful years remaining? The obvious conclusion: this is a hostile or indifferent universe, ruled by no one except blind forces operating with total disregard for our pain and prospects as sentient beings.

Religious leaders and thinkers have stock answers you have heard before for these difficult questions. And I, being neither a devotee of religious dogma, nor hostile to Faith, prefer to explore the possibilities of analytical thought in search for answers. What atheists say is true: there's no God in our universe. Nobody really cares what happens to you and me outside of those who love us in this world. But what little scientific evidence we've collected so far is not all on the side of atheism or agnosticism. Science, in a few hundred years, has barely scratched the surface of reality. Much of what we've learned in the last one hundred years with the advance of particle physics actually refutes the notion of a purely materialistic universe. What remains to be studied: a wondrous place with many fantastic possibilities in it—even the possibility of God's existence.

First, as to pain of any sort, physical or mental, it's simply a warning from Nature that something is wrong. Pain is a signal that forces us to think and act in such a way as to avoid or minimize serious damage. It also focuses our attention on the hurt, so that the mind can help in healing. If you break a leg, the pain excruciating, walking on it is psychologically impossible, impossible *before* it becomes physically so, due to further damage. You stop walking on the leg, allowing it to heal.

If it were not for the severe pain, you would continue to walk, perhaps injuring your body irreparably. If you get cancer with early pains, you're lucky. Usually doctors can take out the tumor before it spreads. Pain prepares a pregnant woman for labor, preventing excessive activity during the last few months of childbearing. If pain persists, however, and nothing can be done about it, we get accustomed; it usually gets duller and more bearable. So it is also with the pain of losing a loved one. We don't forget them, but the suffering subsides. The pain of their loss fixes their presence in our minds; we keep them in our memories forever. And we care for, with more fervent love, those people we still have with us.

God is merciful because we don't suffer more than we can bear if we have enough Faith. God is also compassionate but doesn't interfere in our lives too much. We have to manage for ourselves. If you've raised children, you know this was true for your family. Let's return to our idea that life is a test. If so, God doesn't want to mess up the results of the test by putting a finger in it. If life is a game, what fun or interest would it have for God to stack the cards one way or another? Do you like to watch a play or show when you know the act is contrived?

Life is a mission. We get hints of our mission when what we're doing feels meaningful and good. I've the feeling now while writing to you. God, the Chief Executive, alone knows the full goal of the whole enterprise of your life. You're here to play your role, to carry out your small tasks or large, only as long as you're needed. Afterwards, you're relieved of your duties; you can go home.

Yes, God allows your agonies, but they will soon be over. How would you feel, going across the ocean in a small ship, beaten by waves, almost wrecked, and then you're recalled, with your mission completed or aborted? You would be relieved to abandon your wrecked boat and go home to rest. You obeyed orders: you did your very best, and you're happy, although you may be happier in the event of a successful outcome. Think of what Admiral Nelson said dying on his ship after fighting tyranny: "I regret only that I have one life to give to my country."[1] If Admiral Nelson would say such words upon dying, without any complaint, for king and country, could we not serve God and the Divine Mother and die as bravely as Nelson when fortune strikes us down? God's mercy and compassion are always with us. The ultimate disaster of death we fear so much, in the final analysis, is a laughing matter when we get to Heaven.

3. Purity of Soul Is Our Armor against Satan

The Buddha said that only the pure of soul could ascend to Nirvana. Pure and good are equivalent notions. Jesus was called by his followers good. He said to them, "Why do you call me good? Only God is good."[2] In much religious thought, purity and goodness are associated with unselfishness and love for all living things. That's certainly the case with Hindu, especially Buddhist thought. So, purity has to do with our social relationships and freedom from selfishness, malice, jealousy, and hatred towards others. Jesus said that we're not to be admitted into Heaven unless we approach as children: free of guile and evil intent. I say to you, be pure and naked like newborn babies, so that your purity may deliver you from the Evil One.

Such a premise for salvation from sin is worth examining. We know that meditation is a merging of the conscious and subconscious minds and sometimes a linking also with the Cosmic Mind. The Buddha said,

---

1. William Hull, *Memoirs of the American Revolution: So Far as It Related to the States of North and South Carolina and Georgia* (New York: Samuel Campbell, 1811), 51.
2. Mark 10:18 (NIV).

"We become what we think."[3] Thought processes and dominant feelings enter our inner world and guide our destiny through habitual actions. "As your desire is, so is your destiny,"[4] declared the Hindu Upanishads. The concentration of the mind on one thing, the generation of alpha brain waves, resonates every thought as a crystal transistor amplifies radio waves. Every defect of character, however, and every harmful emotion is also magnified. So, when we come to meditation with selfish motives, greed, hatred, and envy, those can wreak havoc on our journey to the spirit world. Base motives attract forces within, eventually sinking the spiritual traveler in the river separating us from the promised shore.

A few humans have traveled far to the other side before sinking. Remember the lives of some of history's greatest achievers and their ultimate ends. Each one was filled, early on in life, with a sense of power and personal destiny. Alexander the Great knew that when he inherited his father's throne in ancient Greece, he was meant to conquer all that was known then as the world; he nearly accomplished that goal, going as far as India to the east and North Africa to the south. Alexander led his own troops in battle, unstoppable in his charges against the enemy's center. Fear was obviously unknown to him; wounded while charging at the enemy numerous times, he didn't die in battle but from an infection, after bathing in a river. His mission ended prematurely, but the result of his conquests was the establishment of Greek thought and language in the ancient world, which eventually, with the framework of the Roman Empire, allowed the spread of Christianity.

Remember the star of Napoleon the Great, which rose in Europe in the nineteenth century. His military exploits astounded the world. The brilliant young Corsican captured fame and power with his military victories against France's enemies during the revolution, which had swept away the French king and France's nobility. Napoleon made use

---

3. Gautama Buddha, *The Dhammapada: The Sayings of the Buddha*, trans. Thomas Byrom (New York: Alfred A. Knopf, 1993), 1.
4. Brihadaranyaka Upanishad, *The Upanishads: Breath of the Eternal*, trans. Swami Prabhavananda and Frederick Manchester (New York: Signet Classics, 2002), 35.

of French patriotic fervor to seize the title of emperor, as he conquered most of Europe for France. He was totally convinced of his important destiny, his lucky star, and sure that he was guided on his path by a Supreme Power.

The pinnacle of Napoleon's success was the battle of Austerlitz, where he defeated the combined armies of the Austrian and Russian emperors. The defects in his character and thought were greed and selfishness. He betrayed the ideals of the French Revolution when he appointed himself emperor, while he made his undistinguished relatives kings and queens in his empire. In the end, his uncontrolled greed led to his attack on Russia with the Grand Army, leading to his defeat in the Russian winter, and his ignominious run to France, abandoning his troops to the enemy. Later, Waterloo sealed his fate. The point isn't that a real hero, like Admiral Nelson, is not to meet with death one day, but that in the hero's case what he or she achieved lives on in our culture and future.

A very similar fate to that of Napoleon befell Adolph Hitler a little more than a century later. Hitler brought under the rule of the Third Reich—for a thousand years as he said—most of continental Europe, only to be stopped by England and Russia. Hitler destroyed himself because of his defects of arrogance, hatred, and vanity. Hitler, too, was convinced of the existence of a guiding star that shaped his destiny and thought he was infallible in thought and deed, a superior individual picked by God to be The Leader. In self-confidence, Hitler was as great as Moses, but he was also like a flawed crystal that amplified cosmic waves of power negatively like all evil geniuses.

The Buddhist faith, which relies much on private meditation by the faithful, states in the Dhammapada: "Those who practice the teachings, overcoming all lust, hatred, and delusion, live with a pure mind in the highest wisdom."[5] Again in verse 94, "The saints . . . are pure like a lake without mud, and free from the cycle of birth and death."[6] Later on,

---

5. Gautama Buddha, *The Dhammapada: The Buddha's Path of Wisdom*, trans. Acharya Buddharakkhita (Kandy: Buddhist Publication Society, 1985), verse 21.
6. Gautama Buddha, *The Dhammapada: Verses and Stories*, trans. John Richards, Access to Insight (BCBS Edition, 1996), verse 95.

we're admonished in verse 236, "Become pure and innocent, and live in the world of light."[7] "But there is no impurity greater than ignorance."[8] I see these admonitions as urging us to deny our selfish desires as we bask in the power of the Cosmic Mind, prompting us to direct the immense energies placed at our disposal through contact with God, to higher purposes for the welfare of all living things.

It's what a great military leader, like George Washington, does at the end after achieving victory, when he refuses to become king, but turns his power over to the people. The billionaire, such as Andrew Carnegie, Henry Ford, or David Rockefeller, follows the same path near the end of his life when he sets up a foundation for charity to promote the arts or to preserve the natural environment. Pure-hearted leaders, when they conquer, like Churchill and Franklin D. Roosevelt in World War II, are magnanimous towards those defeated, allowing them to live freely and prosper, as they did for Japan and Germany. By comparison, Stalin, blinded by power, oppressed and exploited captured countries.

If you come to great power in your life, when making momentous choices, be an infant before God, pure, simple, and vulnerable. Dealing with your enemies, you can be magnanimous like Roosevelt or grasping like Stalin. God will not make your choices for you: God wants you to be a free agent, acting independently. Deliberate, be conscious of what you're doing, making careful choices with an open heart, walking in the path of sacred duty, the dharma of life.

4. Widows and Orphans Need Looking After

The Quran, in many passages, admonishes the faithful to care for widows and orphans and not to rob orphaned children of the father's estate. At a time when tribal warfare was common in Arabia, and many men died in their prime, clearly, there was a moral imperative to protect those left without a father. A tribe needs to protect women and

---

7. Gautama Buddha, *Verses and Stories*, verse 236.
8. Gautama Buddha, *The Dhammapada: The Buddha's Path of Wisdom*, trans. F. Max Müller (New York: Dover Publications, 2000), verse 243.

children, and this is also true for modern society. The cry when a boat is sinking is always "women and children first!" We observe such behaviors even in chimpanzee, baboon, and sea lion troops. As the troop advances, younger or secondary males are on the periphery, acting as early warning signals at the risk of their lives. The females and their young are encircled by them and in the center are the strong, dominant males, ready to charge in any direction to confront a leopard or other predator getting too close to the troop. Aunts and uncles in the troop look after any of the young offspring orphaned by predators or sickness. The weak, the sick, and the injured, however, are left to fend for themselves, usually becoming meals for predators. This behavior in animals makes for a healthier gene pool in the wild population. Among humans, however, the Holy Scriptures in East and West command that we care for the weak members of society: the sick, the lame, the old, or the handicapped, making survival easier for them.

Such a command is contrary to the biological necessity of culling, which has been observed to occur in herds. It's generally recognized today that the health and growth of a herd requires the regular removal of weak or defective individuals. People who husband animals have known this since ancient times. In the first place, the desirable animals in the herd are encouraged to breed; those not measuring up to the breeder's standards of quality are butchered.

Such methods have been applied to human societies also when power was in the hands of autocrats. In ancient Greece, the city-state of Sparta was famous for its tough treatment of the weak. Newborn infants were examined by a council of elders and, if found defective, were tossed into a canyon to die. Nearby, the more civilized Athenian citizens often practiced the exposure of defective infants to the cold to eliminate them from the population. This method is still used sometimes in the Orient today to get rid of unwanted female children. And let's not forget the victims of the Nazi era in Germany, when mental defectives were gassed to death together with Jews, anarchists, and communists. At the same time, Hitler ordered the propagation of so-called noble Aryan men by means of breeding camps for his troops with young women volunteers of the same type.

Such attempts to improve the human stock seem absurd, abhorrent, or stupid to us today. Hitler's selection methods would have excluded Einstein, Mendelssohn, Mozart, Buddha, the Hebrew Jesus, and innumerable great men and women because they lacked the Nordic adaptation to lack of sunlight. The conflict remains, however, between the demands of religion regarding the protection of the weak and the requirement of biological evolution for their removal. I want to analyze and resolve this paradox of the moral imperative and throw some light on the efforts to improve the human race.

No one with any sense and access to information can doubt that our bodies are the products of evolution over billions of years. Our bodies and brains have advanced because of the ruthless application by Nature of the law: the fittest survive and multiply, and the weak perish and stop their reproduction. We ignore this law at the risk of losing our viability as a species and degenerating physically in our civilized populations. Inevitably, the result will be that wilder, more savage human strains will overcome our more advanced societies, as the Barbarians did to the Greeks and Romans. It is imperative that enlightened populations promote eugenics, not through coercion and cruelty, but through education, moral training, and admonition. People with hereditary defects should see the wisdom of having fewer children. People with superior traits of health, character, and intelligence, no matter what their race, should be encouraged by our leadership to have larger families.

On the other hand, we have a moral obligation, laid down by the Holy Scriptures of practically every religion, to succor the unfortunate and weak. This moral paradox is resolved if we accept the theory, proposed earlier, that our bodies have evolved, but our souls have been created. When our fellows are suffering pain, hardship, and despair, our first objective is to provide comfort and relief to them. We can't let a hungry child starve because the parents were careless with contraception or improvident with finances.

When we offer compassion with help, we're not only saving the bodies of these poor people but also their souls. Cruelty breeds discontent, sprouting evil thoughts in those suffering. Kindness purifies the soul of the person receiving it as well as the person giving it. Consider the beautiful story of Jean Valjean, Victor Hugo's hero in *Les Miserables*. His heart changed forever towards virtue and love by means of the one kind act towards him by the Abbe, who forgave him for theft and gave him charity. Valjean lived the rest of his life caring for others and rose to become mayor of his town.

There is a moral imperative in the Scriptures to care for widows and orphans, the weak and unfortunate. First, treat pain and suffering, then see to their moral uplifting and improvement of their souls. Lastly, see to it that those who are congenitally defective and substandard are encouraged not to reproduce to excess. People who receive too much help from charity often become lazy and continue to indulge in their addictions and weaknesses. There are reasons why people are poor and stay poor. They lack enough intelligence, character, or health. Misfortune is never constant. The wheel of fortune is forever turning, lucky days succeeding unlucky ones in everyone's life. The perennial poor are those who don't have the capacity to seize good fortune when it comes their way. We should pity and help them, but not enable them to make more of their kind.

5. The Poor In Spirit Point to Humility As a Path

My allusion above is to the Sermon on the Mount by Jesus. He said, "Blessed are, the poor in spirit: for theirs is the kingdom of Heaven."[9] He was referring to the blessings of true humility. Laotse in China and other sages, many centuries before Christ, praised the virtues of humility. Heaven cannot be entered by the proud and arrogant. Remember the story in the Old Testament of the Tower of Babel? A long time ago, people had become so bloated with their accomplishments that they sought to build a tower to reach Heaven. It didn't work. People became so arrogant, so full of themselves, and so light-headed that they could no longer communicate. The tower eventually collapsed under its own weight, and that was God's will. The collapse of the World Trade Center

---

9. Matthew 5:3 (NIV).

towers, could that have been a similar warning? Yes, we've reached the heavens of space with our rocket ships and other technology today. But it's been accomplished after centuries of patient and humble study of natural laws, the practice of science. The advancement of science and any other difficult discipline requires that we put away our preconceptions together with our pride in our existing knowledge and humbly ask questions of Nature. In all phases of life, not pride but humility brings us closer to the Divine.

Humility was a key concept in the philosophy of Laotse and his greatest disciple, Zhuangzi, who used the analogy of water to praise humility as a central human virtue. "Water befits all things. It dwells in the lowly places that all disdain—wherein it comes near to the Tao."[10] This was a principal teaching and a recurrent theme in Asian philosophy, but not much admired in the arrogant, hero-worshiping West. Laotse touted that the wise person doesn't seek to be first in the world. It was wise to lie low and seek the lower levels, just like flowing water.

Laotse often praised the strength of the female, who passively may overcome the male. He was against strife, contention, and fighting for advantage. He praised meekness and non-resistance to evil. "Turn the other cheek" could have been his teaching. He knew that anger only provokes anger in return and one cannot overcome hatred with hatred.

While Confucius relied on reason and argument, Laotse was fond of intuition, another female trait. Intuitive knowledge comes from deep down in the subconscious mind, as opposed to logical thinking, which is a function of the conscious part of the brain. Laotse admired the spirit of the valley, a hollow place, like a woman's womb, which collects sediment and is fertile, as opposed to proud and bare masculine mountains. Idleness and leaving things alone were extolled because strife and hard work are not needed when Nature's laws are closely followed. He said, "Because the sage is able to forget his self, therefore his self is realized."[11] This was the way of the Buddha and of Christ.

---

10. Laotse, *Tao Te Ching*, trans. Stephen Mitchell (New York: Harper & Row, 1988), Chapter 8.
11. Laotse, *Tao Te Ching*, trans. Jonathan Star (New York: TarcherPerigee, 2001), Chapter 7.

The Buddha also taught humility and simplicity in one's living arrangements as a means to salvation—Nirvana. The only possessions needed for our way to the other shore are a robe, a pair of sandals, and a begging bowl. Then we can concentrate on what's really important. Any other possessions or attachments are distractions and detractions from the process of meditation and the search for Truth. "And the Truth shall set you free,"[12] as Jesus said. The Truth in Buddhism is the realization of the atman, one's individual self, as part of Brahma, the ultimate divine reality, and thus the intimate linking of one's soul to the Spirit of the Universe.

The Buddha and other prophets realized that the gates of Heaven are not to be entered by storming them. One needs to approach the Heavenly Judge with respect and awe. We honor an earthly judge as we approach his bench and humble ourselves before him and the majesty of society's law. How much more humble should we be in approaching God and His or Her universal laws?

With the utmost humility, that's how genuine scientists approach Nature in order to unravel her secrets. The scientist does not hesitate to get their hands dirty and get into the nitty-gritty of materials and equipment. He or she doesn't embrace theories as dogmas and doesn't fall in love with them. A good scientist works hard and patiently for many years or decades in pursuit of discovery and works with others, sharing his knowledge and his progress. Thus the edifice of modern science has been built, one or two bricks each year, one wall every century. Should not religious and moral knowledge also be constructed in the same way?

On the other hand, we have an opposing view from the elitists. Super-achievers are most often people with super-egos. A person with a strong ego is confident, fearless, and enterprising: all essential ingredients for the management of great projects. Generals, kings, princes, captains of industry and finance, entertainment stars, temperamental artists, prima donnas, and politicos all charge forward, stepping on toes or entire bodies to success and fame. Once they have attained riches,

---

12. John 8:32 (English Standard Version).

they surround themselves with admiring followers, live in luxurious mansions in exclusive areas, and puff themselves up way out of reach of us common folk.

Here's another paradox: success is usually to be found in an environment of fierce competition, which demands a measure of brutality and selfishness from those who would win favors from such a bitch goddess. At the very least, it appears that, if one is to pursue any great goal, one needs to be indifferent to the pain and concern of others and concentrate on his vision with single-minded effort. The Buddha himself abandoned his father, wife, and young son when he went to the forest to meditate as a hermit and pursue his quest for spiritual freedom. His legend stresses the fact that he gave up his princely throne but doesn't dwell much on the pain he brought upon his family by disappearing from their lives.

Moderation in all passions may be the proper course, especially in pride and ambition. A good dose of humility will get you through. Here's how to resolve the paradox of humility and pride, the moral dilemma it imposes on you. Undiluted humility may lead to diffidence and lack of effort while overweening pride is the downfall of many brilliant individuals. If you don't respect authority, you're likely to be crushed by those in power or Nature, but if you're too humble, you're not going to confront incompetence in authority, innovate, and overturn corrupt or outdated ideas. A very thin line is tread by prophets, such as Jesus, who deferred to Caesar, but not to the Pharisees. You overturn the tables of the moneychangers at the risk of your own crucifixion.

6. Peacemakers Are Children of God

In the Sermon on the Mount, Jesus said, "Blessed are the peacemakers: for they shall be called the children of God."[13] The moral imperative of the search for peace is one of our main links to Divine Intelligence. Peace is preached and proclaimed by nearly every leader in the world.

---

13. Matthew 5:9 (NIV).

Even Hitler declared that he only sought peace with justice for his people. So did Stalin. Protestants and Catholics in Northern Ireland declare for peace, and so do Palestinians and Israelis. Theodore Roosevelt said, "Talk softly, but carry a big stick."[14] Still, peacemakers, like UN Special Envoy Sérgio Vieira de Mello of Brazil, who was killed in Iraq, are indeed children of God, the offspring of a great idea.

If you want to be a peacemaker, be prepared: you will get shot. That is what happened to Anwar Sadat of Egypt after he made peace with Israel. Mahatma Gandhi and Martin Luther King Jr. confronted injustice with peaceful, non-violent means, and inevitably, they were gunned down. A peacemaker stands in the midst of people in conflict, a very hazardous area, and tries to keep them from killing each other. So violence falls on the peacekeeper. But he or she is doing God's bidding and is well received in Heaven after the destruction of the body.

That's why religions make so much of the importance of keeping the peace. There's inner peace, associated with the relaxation response or meditation. One is quiet within, and striving has ceased, leading to contentment and joy. And then there's social peace within the family or community when people put aside their differences and enjoy play, food, and drink together. There's also the peace of the cessation of tribal warfare where parents can raise their children without worry and gather in crops and animals with security and plenty. We have, however, evolved as warlike animals and enjoy a good battle. And in peacetime, we delight in sports and games, simulated warfare.

In our species—as with lions, wolves, and apes—the territorial imperative is supreme. Defend your land, which sustains you, and encroach on other people's lands as much as you can, testing weaknesses in your neighbors, so you can seize as much of their territory as possible. Man is a predatory animal, and his quarry is another man, on the other side of a river, mountain, or ocean. Social consciousness always revolves around "us" and "them." People are automatically polarized this way, and the battle lines are drawn. "They" speak a

---

14. Theodore Roosevelt, "Letter to Henry L. Sprague," *The Letters of Theodore Roosevelt*, ed. Elting E. Morison (Cambridge, MA: Harvard University Press, 1951), 5:242.

different tongue. "Their" skin color or facial features are different from those of your tribe. "They" are subhuman, alien, ugly, evil, dirty, and smelly. We hate their differences, and at the first opportunity, we attack them.

This is our evolutionary heritage. Skulls have been found in ancient sites with holes in them from which brains were sucked out. Captured enemies were routinely sacrificed at the altar. After a victorious battle, the enemy's settlement was burned, old people butchered, young women raped, and children taken away to be raised as slaves. What is peace but a time of preparation for the next war? Heroic legends speak of the glory of battle. There's no greater honor than to die for your people, sword in hand. Great warriors enter Valhalla and reside with the Gods. War is how lands are taken from other tribes and how empires are built, after neighbors are overwhelmed and humiliated. The weak are vanquished and eliminated from the species, and thus, there's advancement. Technology is improved, both for wartime and peacetime activities in competition with other people. Those prevail who are equipped with advanced tools for the production of goods and with weapons to kill the enemy more efficiently. Thus William the Conqueror seized England after the battle of Hastings was won because his men were on horses equipped with stirrups.

Yet, no one who has been in a real war retains any illusions about the glory of battle. It is bloody, painful, dirty, ugly, and miserable. Men cry in anguish as they fall. A battle is confusing and uncertain. It's *Guernica*, painted by Picasso. It's forever a bitter memory for those who survive. Any sensitive soul is filled with abhorrence and disgust. Like St. Francis of Assisi, many men abandon their ordinary lives and seek salvation from war memories as monks or vagrants.

War is very much in our past as a species, but it can no longer be in our future. There's a fortunate trend, wherever larger societies are formed, which include many more "us" and fewer "them." It's our destiny to free ourselves from the tyranny of warfare and seek our evolution in other ways. Games will continue, but they will be bloodless or nearly so. The trend is towards tolerance and justice becoming more widespread.

God's message tells us to accept all people on this planet as "us," no matter what their color, language, or features. It's God's purpose to unite us in one family of sentient beings and to build a peaceful world on this planet and beyond. We can continue to evolve for the better as a species through wise selection of the best genes in the planetary gene pool, accepting contributions from all races and all nations.

But the practical difficulties of peacemaking are horrendous. Hatreds between nations and religious groups date back hundreds or even thousands of years. This ancient bad blood will not ebb away very quickly. Many small wars will inevitably continue around the globe.

Our efforts should be centered on preventing a world war between major, industrialized nations. The advancement of international trade and economic cooperation should help a great deal in this. It's not profitable for a nation to attack trading partners because the economy suffers.

Another move should be to strengthen and gradually restructure our United Nations so that this forum of opinion becomes something closer to an international government.

As a rule, wars end when people unite under one government with justice for all. Union, both economic and political, is happening in Europe, and that's a very hopeful sign after so much bloodshed on that continent. But our ultimate end is a planetary union, which will include a military force and a real-world court, the decisions of which will be enforced uniformly on large nations and small. The remaining problems will be taken care of by police action, as in all civilized societies. That was the trend in the world until the US invasion of Iraq and the ensuing Muslim revolt, leading to the bombing of the UN Mission there and the killing of Special Envoy de Mello.

Peacemakers, children of God, make fine targets for terrorists, fanatics, and other workers of evil. Why does the Almighty permit their killing? It's not easy to fathom God's methods or intentions. Peace on this planet, however, is assuredly one of God's wishes for us. It will be a necessary step in the evolution of the human spirit and our preparation for travel to other planets, encounters with alien civilizations in the universe, and our continuing growth as a species. All life is one, and

God may simply be the collective of all sentient beings. The message is from the future.

7. Thou Shalt Not Steal; Thou Shalt Not Lie

Some of God's commandments, handed to us by Moses, deal with proper social behavior. The seventh commandment forbids adultery, a form of stealing, and so does the tenth one that admonishes against covetousness of another man's possessions. Interestingly enough, covetousness is a strong desire, a thought imbued with inordinate emotion, surely enough, likely to lead to stealing the of what a neighbor owns. Stealing and lying are still prevalent in our society, even at the highest levels of business and government: it's a measure of how uncivilized we still are. So stealing and lying continue to be primary vices to wash out of our spirits.

Remember the story of King David and Bathsheba? He saw her bathing on the roof of her house while her husband was away and desired her uncontrollably. According to legend, the great King David was the author of the beautiful psalms and a devout Jew. Yet he sent Bathsheba's husband to war to be killed and took the woman as a wife to give birth to King Solomon the wise.

There are many forms of stealing, all contrary to God's wishes for us. Envy and jealousy often lead to stealing, when with malicious gossip or unfair criticism, we rob somebody of their self-esteem. Few things destroy more surely a human spirit and body than the loss of self-worth. Robbing a young girl or boy of sexual innocence and purity with deceit and false promises is a horrid sin of stealing. The robber receives carnal pleasure at the expense of a young victim.

Tax fraud robs a community of needed resources and so does graft by officials or corporate agents. All fraud is a form of stealing, such as insurance, loans, sales, and welfare fraud. Let's not forget the widespread theft of intellectual property, both in this country and abroad, such as illegal copies of copyrighted material, patent and trade secret infringement, and plagiarizing. Resources are misallocated to those who don't deserve them and have not earned them.

Human society organizes and progresses largely based on the institution of property and ownership of items for consumption and production. Without the right of property, few individuals would strive to work, produce, and save things of value for themselves and their posterity. Stealing reduces this right and impedes social advancement. The result is that the movement of people towards a better world and the establishment of God's will on Earth get thwarted.

Sometimes, theft of resources is perpetrated by a government that has excessive power, even one that declares they are for society. Socialism may go too far and rob the productive members of society to reward those who are lazy or incompetent. A dictatorship or other authoritarian rule may tax people unduly to build up armaments and wage wars. That kind of taxation is stealing and is inevitably followed by the robbery of people's lives in battle. Dictators are Satan's instruments.

Jesus said, "The worker is worthy of his hire."[15] It's a dastardly sin to refuse to pay a worker fair wages so that they can take care of themselves and their family. Fair wages are based on the value of one's services to those able to pay for them in competition with other willing workers. When labor unions are organized to bar others from entering the work force of a company and then strike to obtain wage raises and benefits that they have not earned through higher productivity, that's stealing also.

Unfair union practices lead to inefficiencies in production and the bankruptcy of companies. Or, if companies will not compete, they pass on higher prices to consumers, causing inflation. If the government prints more money than is needed for commerce or allows credit to expand unduly, people are also robbed due to inflation. It's official counterfeiting. Then government takes in higher taxes based on inflated incomes and insult follows injury to the people. This is not the way to establishing the Kingdom of God in our world.

Another sin that impedes the harmonious operation of society is the habit of lying. In its extreme form, this monkey wrench to smooth

---

15. Luke 10:7 (NIV).

social functioning is castigated in the ninth commandment, "Thou shalt not bear false witness against thy neighbor."[16] Today, it's called perjury in court testimony, and it's common because penalties for it are not that severe.

We're all very aware of how damaging for family life is the practice of lying by one or more members. We all yell at our children when they resort to it. Marriages break up if one or both spouses lie to each other habitually. We lie to hide a weakness or transgression. We lie out of fear and cowardice. We falsify information to gain a temporary advantage at the expense of the priceless trust of our loved ones or associates. A strong, moral person doesn't need to do it.

In a larger social sphere, lying is common in commerce. False advertising, forbidden by law, is often practiced in the form of exaggeration, which makes it more difficult to prosecute. Companies lie in their financial reports. People tend to lie in difficult social situations. They lie in their resumes to get a position. People seeking a mate or sexual favors lie when dating and at parties. On the job, we often lie to superiors. We call in sick to the office when we're not and take advantage of sick leave. The end result is a loss of efficiency in operations and, when discovered, a loss of the trust that superiors have for us.

Our society, therefore, could use some improvement in fighting the vices of lying, cheating, and stealing. We even attempt sometimes to lie to God and hide our guilt in confession. That's lying to our inner Self, the most damaging practice of all. It's called delusion and self-deception. It leads to the decay and collapse of personality, rotting of the will, and loss of spiritual power. It's a sure pathway towards that universe known as Hell.

8. Heal the Sick and Injured

Healing the sick and making the lame whole is a common activity of religious practice. If that's not possible, you provide comfort or solace to those afflicted. Jesus is said to have performed many miracles during

---

16. Exodus 20:16 (NIV).

his pilgrimage walking around Palestine. He healed many of the sick, made the lame walk again, and drove out demons from those mentally deranged. Jesus even raised Lazarus from the grave. Some Evangelical preachers today pursuing the tradition of healing effect many real cures because, aided by a loving spirit, healing is natural, part of the endowment by God given to all creatures from plants to dogs to humans.

Atheists who witness these miracles in the name of Jesus Christ sometimes convert to the true faith. This tradition is well established in the East also, especially in India, the Empire of the Spirit. A holy man often makes his reputation with the cures that he accomplishes among the faithful. Sai Baba, in India, who has declared himself an avatar, reincarnation of God, is known for his miracles of healing among his devout followers. He's said to absorb the sickness into his own body and then dispose of it with the power of his magic.

We have an explanation for such miracles in the scientific community. We attribute them to the mind-body interaction, and they're called spontaneous remissions, not cures. That way, we have an explanation in place if the illness returns, as it happened to Nathan Pritikin, the diet and exercise guru, who had leukemia at forty and then succumbed to it at the age of seventy. As for myself, give me remission, I say, and let me live with it as long as possible. After all, life itself is a remission from sin. Nobody's life is actually saved by healing or medical intervention; it's only extended. Life extension is good. Let life be long so that I can experience a few more wondrous moments and get some worthwhile things accomplished.

Miracle healing is a good method for reaching the faithful to renew their faith and the unbelievers to convert to religion. After all, a seriously sick or injured person is highly susceptible to a message of hope. People resent having to abandon their earthly existence and move to the unknown. Sometimes, they get downright bitter about that. I remember that both my parents in their nineties, disabled and disgusted with life, still were clinging on to their mortal coil and hating to leave it to reach for the other side. Now here comes Jesus, or one of his clan, who says, "Have faith, and you'll get well. Stand up and walk.

Follow me and you'll have everlasting life."[17] It's hard not to accept such a message coming from a glowing face and bright eyes. It's no wonder that a whole branch of the Christian religion was built up around this matter of faith healing, called Christian Science by Mary Baker Eddy.

Do healing miracles actually happen? Can a holy man or woman bestow health through prayer, by touching and channeling God's compassionate energy to the patient? The answer to that depends on whether you believe that the healer and his subject possess a mysterious component of being, called spirit. If that's the source of animation in our bodies, then why would it not make us feel better and recover faster when our spirit is stimulated and it's vibrating with full intensity?

When we're very sick or injured and near death, we are close to God, Satan, or nothingness. Depending on what we visualize at the other end of the passage, we're appropriately conditioned. If we see joy, love, hope, compassion, and life ahead, then with such, we are infused. If we see torture, oppression, and desperation, we descend to these, and if nothingness is down our road, then we become apathetic, inert, unfeeling, and quickly slip to the ground.

No physician should administer to patients without keeping in mind the power of hope. Marvelous though they may be the tools of surgery and drugs, their effectiveness is made far greater when coupled with the potency of faith. A great surgeon, whom I met once in an accountant's waiting room, told me that when he operated, he felt that his hands were guided by a supreme power. He performed difficult and delicate operations without conscious thought, almost totally with the subconscious mind, as the rest of us drive or ride a bicycle, and the ultimate perfect result of the operation was not under his control, but under the direction of Someone Else. How's that different from what the miracle worker does in a revival tent? There were many years of scientific education and training behind the surgeon's performance that enabled him to affect material substances with precision, but the approach is the same.

---

17. John 5:8-9 (NIV).

Now, the Buddha took a different tack to the problem of suffering from illness and other hazards of life. The Buddha's message is that pain and suffering in the end are always unavoidable. The right mental attitude and discipline can promote better health through contact with Divine Mercy, but in the final analysis, one can accept the inevitable and prepare for the other shore by putting away his feeling of separateness and accepting universal life still thriving outside his separate ego.

One's mental tool is mainly the practice of right thinking and meditation, and the Buddha himself, in his final hours, found peace and freedom from pain through deep concentration in his inner self. The Buddha's countryman, Mahatma Gandhi, we're told, had an appendectomy without anesthesia, and avoided pain by meditating and withdrawing from his body during the operation. This isn't healing, but it's better than pain drugs that suppress vitality, especially when the patient can aid the surgeon in the operation.

Go out, then, and give cures and good health to yourself and others with the powers of your spirit. For God and Nature give life, withdraw life, or extend it. Healing power comes to you through your God connection; you can grow your healing art and project it to others more effectively by spiritually entering in prayer God's crystal domain of perpetual perfection and peace.

9. Good Works Pave the Way to Heaven

Part of the social consciousness of religion is the admonition by spiritual leaders for us to do good works while on Earth. What's the point of good works? Everything in the end decays, life comes to an end, even the whole planet is doomed when the sun becomes a red giant, and the universe as a whole is destined to total entropy and death due to the second law of thermodynamics. The answer is that good works are desirable because of what they accomplish in our spiritual growth and the spiritual salvation of our fellows that we help. Good works are better for you and your community than rapture and ecstasy with God in isolation from the world.

I understand why people are disheartened by the futility of

achieving anything of lasting value in this world. The author of Ecclesiastes in the Old Testament put this in a very memorable way: "Vanity, vanity, all is vanity."[18] This reminds me of the famous poem by Percy Bysshe Shelley: "My name is Ozymandias, King of Kings. Look upon my works ye mighty and despair."[19] Sometimes, we're filled with gloom, thinking that even our own children and grandchildren, whom we are to leave behind, too will, in turn, crumble into dust. Every material thing that we create will eventually decompose and disappear. Atoms and other particles puff out of existence once in a while, and the universe will go the same way. Should the conclusion then be "drink and be merry, because tomorrow we die"?

There's a thin veil, so thin we cannot even see it, that separates our universe from the eternal spirit world. Mystics are apparently able to see with their hearts through this veil to the next world, and they tell us that really nothing is lost because of this ideal world that exists beyond. Does a great opera, like Puccini's *Madama Butterfly*, end with the last notes? Is Shakespeare's *Hamlet* finished with the death of Hamlet and the last curtain? We enjoy the play every time we see it and look forward to more performances with new actors.

The world we live in is like a Lego toy. We pick up pieces and build structures, and after the game is done, our creations are admired for a while—then disassembled. Yet, something remains: the enjoyment of building and the learning we've accomplished. It's so with life as a whole. The monuments we build will crumble, but the experience of creation will remain with us in the next world.

The bodies we wear in this world have their counterparts in the ethereal world. Those bodies are eternal, but they're affected by what we do here. They become better or worse depending on our actions and our experiences on Earth. As discussed before, kindness and love, given and received, make us gentler and more Godlike, both in this world and the next. So do other good works. Andrew Carnegie labored

---

18. Ecclesiastes 1:2 (NIV).
19. Percy Bysshe Shelley, "Ozymandias," *Shelley's Poetry and Prose*, ed. Donald H. Reiman and Neil Fraistat (New York: Norton, 2002), 197-198.

his whole life in the steel business to amass this country's greatest fortune of his day.

Carnegie, founder of US Steel, and his team of steel experts achieved much in business. His stature was greatest, though, when he sold the business to J.P. Morgan & Co. and gave away ninety percent of his fortune to charity. He funded thousands of libraries, where young people could give themselves an education, as he had done as a young boy. He founded the great Carnegie-Mellon University in Pittsburgh and Carnegie Hall in New York City, a major venue for fine music.

There's a tradition of philanthropy in America, unequaled in any other country, and we should be very proud of it. In many countries, wealthy individuals tend to endow their children with perennial fortunes so their offspring may continue to live in splendor and idleness. We prefer to put our children to work to produce more riches, eventually to be given for the betterment of the world and our souls. Ford, Rockefeller, Hughes, and thousands of other rich men and women set up foundations to support worthy causes, such as medical research, protection of wildlife in the environment, and help for the poor. The walls in the lobbies of our hospitals are filled with the plaques of big and small donors. I, with my limited means, support the Nature Conservancy and Athens College, my old preparatory school in Greece, among other charities.

Today, high-technology tycoons, such as Bill Gates of Microsoft, are giving away billions of dollars to charity. And their contributions to our technological civilization have brought comfort, ease, and power to our lives. As miracle worker Thomas Edison changed the lives of our fathers by giving them the electric light, gramophone, and hundreds of other tools, so we're enriched today by computers, cell phones, pagers, the internet, and genetic engineering. With these inventions, we're moving rapidly on the information highway, and that's the path to the spirit world. Because what are spirits, if not packages of information, both computational and emotional?

And spirits need to express themselves in society with good works, not live in isolation. What is, moreover, purest and finest in our souls is put into great paintings, musical scores, poetry, and sculptures by artists and artisans, living forever in this world and the one beyond. Creations in the arts offer many examples of information windows with intellectual and emotional content. A fine work of art uplifts our spirits to Heaven and is as great a miracle as healing a sick person. It's no wonder that some of the most astonishing artworks around the world are inspired by religion. The Parthenon was a temple that housed the great statue of the Goddess Athena, covered with ivory and gold. Later we had the Sistine Chapel with Michelangelo's divine frescos. In China, India, Central America, and Egypt, the finest artworks were found in temples and other places of worship.

10. Listen and Pray to the Lord of Love

Jesus has been called "Love's pure light" and Krishna is worshiped as the Lord of Love. In the midst of our normal, everyday strife and struggle with other people in a competitive world, and when one of our periodic bloody conflicts with other nations is raging, we must wonder what love is all about. Jesus said, "Love thy neighbor as thyself"[20] and even, "Love your enemy."[21] How is it possible for anyone to love one's enemy? You begin this difficult process by first understanding your enemy, then appreciating that the enemy is a kindred human being, and lastly by forgiving your enemy for transgressions done to you.

I remember the treatment our Japanese and German enemies received from our press, the movies, and other propaganda media in World War II. These people were treated as ugly, evil, subhuman, and horrible. They were offered as objects of pure hatred. Our government found that it was of paramount importance that we hate the enemy thoroughly so that we would fight them with the utmost dedication and ferocity. How do we reconcile this official attitude with our Christian culture?

Let's look at love objectively. It's a mammalian emotion, a result of specific neural impulses in the brain. It's best exemplified in mother

---

20. Mark 12:31 (NIV).
21. Mark 5:44 (NIV).

love. Anyone watching a mother cat or dog licking and breast-feeding its young can sense the emotion at work. Later, the mammalian mother guides and trains the young and protects them from predators, sometimes even the male of the species. The pups or kits are charming and delightful, and the mother fondly gazes upon them as they play.

Some of the most blissful experiences in my life were in the arms of my mother, being caressed and cared for by her, and I'm sure they were blissful for her. Mother love has great survival value for mammals, and so do other kinds of love. Love is a product of evolution. There's love for brother or sister. That's very special also, and it's no wonder we're told by spiritual leaders to love our fellow human beings like brothers or sisters.

Christians from ancient times called each other brother or sister and so do our African American friends today. The love of a father is usually different from a mother's, imbued perhaps with more discipline and restraint, but it can run just as deep. I know my father loved his children dearly, although he seldom voiced his love.

Children love their parents in still a different way, mixed with devotion, dependence, and even resentment for that dependence. But with maturity, a child's love changes to a purer feeling, and if parents survive to become exceedingly old and dependent, the roles are reversed, and they, in turn, are loved and looked after like babies by devoted children.

In many cultures, family is the core of our being. Beyond family, we love our neighborhood or church, our town or village and the people in it, our nation, and finally all of humanity. Many people feel a deep love for Nature, tame and wild. People often love a pet as much as a human. Some people have an abiding and consuming love for this whole planet Earth, with its natural beauties and its great variety of living things, plants and animals. That includes love and admiration for the species that once existed and became extinct, the dodo and woolly mammoth, and those that are in danger of perishing today, the panda bear and the Siberian tiger.

Love is the primary emotion that makes everything more meaningful and romantic, full of the glow of spirit. Do you sometimes feel that your life has no meaning and is depressing? The breadth, depth, and intensity of joy you experience generally equal your love for people, places, things, and activities. Do you sometimes feel your heart is empty and dry? Put away your hatreds, angers, annoyances, and frustrations by laughing at them, for they bleed your life of its essence.

Songs, stories, movies, and artwork are all most moving when they deal with love. "I left My Heart in San Francisco." How about the movie *It Happened One Night* or *It's a Wonderful Life*, and more recently, *Life is Beautiful* with Roberto Benigni? How moving was the love of the father for his young son and the love of his wife for him! She voluntarily went to concentration camp to be with him, though she wasn't a Jew.

The psychologist Karen Battaglia built up a whole series of lectures and books on the sole subject of love. God is said to look upon us from Heaven with the love and compassion of a father. As we live, suffer, and struggle, that emotion from above washes over us and makes our pain tolerable and worthwhile. Why does God allow our agonies in spite of His and Her love for us? Why does an earthly father allow his son or daughter to mount a bicycle and fall again and again, scraping knees and hurting, until the art has been mastered? Yet, the father steps out and intervenes when it's necessary. And he's always there, consoling and advising.

Yes, love is an artifact of electrochemical impulses in the brain, but it's also a spiritual force. Its effect is to bind and unite living things together and to bring us closer to harmony with our natural environment. It has evolved as mammals have emerged, but it's also a God-given gift when Divine Intelligence intervened here on Earth and created our souls. Otherwise, why is there selfless and altruistic love that has no personal objective and no survival value for those who experience it?

Love is like the valence property in atoms that prompts them to form bonds and aggregate into molecules, which, in the case of carbon in organic chemistry, can be exceedingly large and complex. Love is a force that unites and allows relationships to grow. Tribes grow with love, justice, and peace and become nations and super-societies like the United States or the European Union.

This process begins when people understand, forgive, tolerate, and even love their enemy as Jesus taught. The overall trend in history is towards larger and larger organizations of people, brought together with better travel, trade, and faster communications. It's the intent of Divine Intelligence that we should put away our animosities, unite as one planetary entity, then move out into space ready to interact peacefully with alien cultures. The end result will be one universe of sentient beings, connected together in a crystal lattice of perennial tranquility, what we call Heaven.

9

HOW TO EXPLORE YOUR SUBCONSCIOUS MIND

My father, Elias, meditated often—I know now, remembering his behaviors. He had read the books of Émile Coué on self-hypnosis and self-improvement using affirmations. When he ate, he liked to close his eyes, chew well, and concentrate on his food. He listened to classical music whenever he had the opportunity, again with his eyes closed. After retirement at age fifty-three, he developed the habit of walking twice a day, rain or shine. While walking, he listened to the songs of birds, gazed at flowering plants, and discreetly admired beautiful young girls walking on the street. With each step, he would say silently, "I'm younger. I'm younger. I'm healthier. I'm healthier." With such self-suggestions, he quit smoking at an early age, and thereafter, he followed all the habits for good health which he knew.

While my mother meditated emotionally with prayers, my father followed the way of the intellect in his practice. He meditated more like Marcus Aurelius, Descartes, or Pascal, rather than St. Augustine. He was an agnostic or atheist, but his meditations kept him reasonably happy, calm, and content, except when my mother irritated him with her noisy and intrusive ways. He lived a very long life, dying free from any illness, when he decided it was time to go. In his inner explorations he never encountered the Divine Presence as my mother often did intuitively. Somehow, my father did not look deep enough inward or was wearing spiritual blinders because the link to God, our connection to Divine Intelligence, is inside us, in the deepest recesses of our subconscious mind. Remember, Jesus said heaven is within us.

1. Delve with Freud into the Subconscious

It's ironic that Sigmund Freud, one of history's best-known atheists, was a pioneer investigator of the inner world of humans who studied the route leading us to God. Freud and the Vienna school of psychotherapy he founded are not so fashionable today because of the availability of inexpensive brain medicines and group therapy. In the thirties and forties, the wealthy indulged in three-year treatments on the couch with Freud's medical disciples. Novelists then penned adventures in the subconscious mind, and Hollywood made smash movies with scripts on Freudian themes: id, libido, superego, dream interpretation, and childhood trauma. Freud and his colleagues were medical doctors interested in treating mental illness and other aberrant behaviors with what they believed were scientific methods. In their practice, they faced anxiety, hysteria, depression, and schizophrenia. Their desire to treat mental illness shaped their perceptions of the subconscious mind and cast a negative aspect on perfectly normal and powerful processes. In their explorations, they did not search for a connection to God and the bliss of the unitive state, but for the relief of mental suffering as did the Buddha, but with different methods. It's often helpful to delve into the subconscious mind for both purposes: to find God and to cure our mental funk.

Psychotherapy did heal people, albeit slowly. As opposed to religious practitioners who accompanied their cures with mumbo-jumbo, therapists treated their patients with a rational and modest attitude. Instead of demons being driven out, it was some damaging subconscious implant from childhood, a trauma, or a bad "engram," as Scientology's analyst-guru L. Ron Hubbard would put it. The subconscious was thoroughly examined by Freud, and all sorts of dirty linens were brought out to light from down deep, having to do with sexual desires for close relatives, to be washed in the light of the post-Victorian world.

Sigmund Freud, who can't be accused of excessive optimism, in *A General Introduction to Psychoanalysis*, gave his prognosis to an analysis patient as follows: "No doubt fate would find it easier than I to relieve you of your illness. But you will be able to convince yourself that much will be gained if we succeed in transforming your hysterical misery into common unhappiness."[1]

In those days, hysteria was a common complaint, especially among frustrated and oppressed women, and caused serious psychosomatic disabilities. I'm sure the prolonged attention these women received from bearded analysts helped them a great deal. Psychoanalysts healed mainly by having the patient relax on a couch and by a variety of hypnotic techniques, putting the subject in a trance and enlarging the opening to the subconscious mind.

Moreover, the analyst mediated an exploration of the patient's long-repressed memories in the subconscious, where injuries to the ego might still fester. As the subject recounted experiences with a stream of associated images and ideas, he or she brought up bitter feelings to be aired in the conscious mind and to be rationally discussed with the analyst. Rational thinking quiets emotional turbulence. And stream-of-consciousness thinking is not unlike the bubble method of meditation —to be discussed later.

Today, hypnosis is called the relaxation response. We know that this mental state, which is the antipode of the fight-or-flight mindset, is beneficial to health if it's practiced on a regular basis. Lawrence LeShan, in *How to Meditate,* made astute connections between psychotherapy and meditation. LeShan was a psychiatrist as well as a teacher of meditation, and his little book *How to Meditate* is considered an authoritative text on the subject for a lay reader. He sought the integration of psychotherapy and meditation. Both procedures have as a

---

1. Sigmund Freud and Josef Breuer, *Studies on Hysteria*, trans. and ed. James Strachey (New York: Basic Books, 2000), 202.

goal personality growth and integration, but their approaches are different.

The psychiatrist primarily emphasizes the content of an emotional problem, such as anxiety, working to reorganize its meaning and symbolic representation in more healthful ways in the patient's mind. On the other hand, the teacher of meditation, as a guru and spiritual guide, is concerned about strengthening the structure of the sick personality. Then, the guru hopes mental content will automatically be rearranged along healthier and more positive lines so the patient can function better.

Other psychiatrists have also seen the similarities between modern psychotherapy and ancient meditative healing. Sheldon B. Kopp, in *Guru: Metaphors from a Psychotherapist,* compares the psychiatrist to the shaman, zaddik, witch doctor, and religious healer of other cultures. Kopp points out that there was considerable wisdom, power, and effectiveness in the hands and teachings of such gurus. With the myths and stories told by these masters of the human psyche, and the legends connected with their lives, resides immense healing potential, some of it beyond the ken of today's medical science.

A myth is a spoken expression of basic struggles, joys, and ambiguities, while a dream is a silent inner voice and, according to Erich Fromm, "less reasonable and decent but . . . also more intelligent, wiser and capable of better judgment."[2] Remember Joseph in ancient Egypt and the Pharaoh's puzzling dreams about the seven fat cows? Dreams require an analyst or a seer to interpret. They may not throw much light on future events, but they have much to show regarding our hidden anxieties, hopes, and desires because their origin is the subconscious mind, unleashed in sleep or trance.

Dream interpretation and other psychoanalytic techniques are powerful tools both for healing psychic wounds and searching for the Divine. When you evaluate psychotherapy or spiritual healing, remember that no one is perfectly sane or totally mad at all times. Even

---

2. Erich Fromm, *The Forgotten Language: An Introduction to the Understanding of Dreams, Fairy Tales, and Myths* (New York: Open Road Media, 2013), 39.

a raving lunatic locked away in isolation has moments of mental clarity. Similarly, occasionally a hardened criminal has feelings of tenderness and love for someone. The rest of us, outside and loose, go about our lives rife with irrational fears and sick impulses. We're free to be in society because we contain our crazy notions inside our skulls acceptably well—most of the time. Therefore, we can all profit from the healing methods of psychotherapy and meditation, practicing preventive medicine for our minds, as we do for our bodies with physical checkups and vaccines.

2. Let Us Revisit the Relaxation Response

In this section, we're concerned with the physiological changes that occur when we enter a trance state of mind, facts that are clearly observed and recorded with EEG machines and other scientific instruments. We're not dealing here with speculations and religious theories but with hard facts about human physiology, metabolism, and neural function. A well-known source for this material is the work of Herbert Benson, MD, and his colleagues at the Thorndyke Memorial Laboratory and Beth Israel Hospital in Boston. Dr. Benson's book *The Relaxation Response* has numerous references to scientific articles on the physiological changes during trances, such as the type promoted by Maharishi Mahesh Yogi as Transcendental Meditation. Whatever the method used to induce it, medical science has shown that the relaxation response is beneficial to the health of people under excessive stress—almost everyone today.

To understand the relaxation response, it helps to look at its opposite mental and physiological state, known as the fight-or-flight response. During our long evolutionary history (probably going back to the early mammals of a hundred million years ago), our ancestors found ways to quickly adapt to the changing roles of being prey or predator. When you're prey, you flee and hide; when predator, you attack and try to kill.

Conflicts also occur with equals, often with members of the same species in competitions for food, mates, or territory. In all these situations, injury is possible, and you need to muster energy and speed promptly. The epinephrine glands pump adrenaline into your blood, and your metabolism rises rapidly. Blood pressure, cholesterol, and blood sugar increase, and coagulants thicken the blood to slow down bleeding from injuries. Your breathing becomes quick and shallow—you're hyperventilating. You're alert, tense, and on edge: you're under stress. Your sympathetic nervous system is strongly activated as you experience fear, aggressiveness, hatred, or panic.

Such a response to an emergency has survival value. In a natural setting and at a young age, you get into this mode of fighting or running and get out of danger. When the crisis is over, there's a quick return to normalcy. Nerves settle down. Blood pressure and respiration drop, and the body recovers from its temporary stress. Energy reserves recover. Health problems, however, emerge from the fight-or-flight response when it's repeatedly aroused in your mature years and physiological reactions remain stuck at a high level.

This often happens to modern humans in a crowded city, a busy work environment, or a chaotic home. Return to the normal state becomes more difficult as one grows older and cannot adapt as quickly. The result might be chronic hypertension with high cholesterol and blood sugar. Often, arteriosclerosis follows, leading to heart attacks and strokes.

You counteract the bad effects of stress using the relaxation response. Find a quiet place to rest and achieve a comfortable position. Relax and become passive. Inhale deeply and slowly from the diaphragm and hold your breath briefly before inhaling or exhaling. Repeat a word or phrase to yourself in a rhythmic fashion. Counting your breaths to four or ten and then over again may be helpful. If you subscribe to a religious tradition, you may want to repeat a phrase from your particular faith. After a few minutes of this practice, you'll achieve a peaceful mental state and the desired physiological response. It will take longer if the upheaval you faced was major. Many people do this exercise before they start a working day as a preventive measure for stressful situations they're likely to face.

It's also beneficial to relax this way at the end of a hard day at the office or home. It's best to do this regimen away from your stress-producing environment, such as in a park or on the beach. A passive attitude is very helpful, but mechanical and habitual actions, such as walking, biking, lifting weights, etc., performed without effort, can be part of the relaxation routine.

Dr. Benson goes into considerable detail in his book discussing the physiological benefits of the relaxation response. A very important benefit is the drop in blood pressure to normal levels. High blood pressure is dangerous, especially as we age and arteries lose some of their resilience and strength. Benson provides evidence that with regular meditation practice, even with chronic high blood pressure, we can return it to a normal level. Now occasional stress will cause excursions of the blood pressure to a less dangerous level. But you get more benefits. We know from the studies of Dr. Hans Selye and his colleagues that many illnesses are caused by excessive or persistent stress. It weakens the immune system and thus makes us susceptible to contagious agents of illness. Thus, sufficient stress reduction through meditation prevents many diseases.

Like sleep, another hypometabolic state, meditation allows one to use less of the body's reserves of energy and other resources. There's less oxygen consumption also, much less than in sleep, but it's not due to human hibernation because body temperature doesn't drop as it does in hibernating animals. Alpha waves of the brain increase in intensity and frequency during meditation, but don't do so in sleep. So the term hypnosis for such a state is not fitting. Meditation also reduces the blood lactate level, often associated with anxiety and neurosis. Thus, the net effect of the regular practice of relaxation is the restoration of the body's normal state and long-term health. But there are psychological and spiritual benefits as well.

Under a state of stress, in the grip of the fight-or-flight response, you tend to experience hostility or fear. This can lead to aggressive actions or abrupt escapes from responsibility. Problems are compounded when you consume stimulants, such as coffee, cigarettes, tea, or cocaine. Inhibition-releasing substances, such as alcohol, are well known to get people into trouble in stressful situations.

You may enter a black mood and become mean to loved ones, or worse, towards perceived enemies. Your contact with religion and Divine Intelligence is broken. All sorts of violent and destructive actions are possible at such a time. You're likely to counter any word you hear that's colored with animosity with your own intense hostility.

No matter what your problem is, you seize on a solution faster after going into a relaxed state of mind and soul for a while. When you enter the relaxation response, you quiet your mind, and you experience peace and kindness. You find a resolution to your conflict, harming no one, especially yourself. God's peace is easier to achieve when you're calm and in control of your spirit. You're at the beginning of contact with the Divine Source of life.

3. Hypnotic Trances Can Lead to Greatness or Gloom

Some people believe that hypnosis, from the Greek word *hypnos* for sleep, is a different mental state from that of meditation. No so. It would be uneconomical for Nature to have two such processes available in the brain. Hypnosis is simply meditation you achieve guided by someone else, such as a trained hypnotist. Self-hypnosis, the meditation you do on your own, can accomplish great deeds or bring disaster for yourself and others, depending on your skill level and purity of purpose.

In hypnosis guided by others, there is stage hypnosis for show purposes, the hypnosis conducted by a psychiatrist for therapeutic reasons, and the phenomenon of crowd control exercised by great orators and leaders, such as Alexander, Napoleon, Peter of Russia, Hitler, and practically every charismatic person. Such power may be put to good or evil use and that depends on the motivation of the leader and the quality of the audience: how well educated, trained, and indoctrinated they are.

Lawrence LeShan points out that the physiological condition in hypnosis is that suggested to you by the hypnotist. He refers to the brain's alpha waves, blood pressure, oxygen consumption, respiration, etc. This is not surprising, but it doesn't prove that hypnosis is a different thing from meditation. You enter the meditative state through a process of relaxation and concentration on one thing at a time. When you're in a trance, suggestions may come into play from a variety of sources, including a hypnotist. Although the initial physiological state is indeed as described by Dr. Herbert Benson, what follows depends on the course of the meditation. The hypnotist, demagogue, charismatic leader, teacher, or therapist first wins your confidence and trust. He or she puts you in a relaxed and receptive mental set. Nothing can be done unless you're willing to cooperate. Before you can be hypnotized, you have to be willing. The hypnotist must ask for your help in a nice way and allow you to say yes or no to the request for cooperation; your freedom can't be infringed upon.

The hypnotist may use a variety of visual, auditory, or even tactile stimuli to put you in a receptive condition. Friendly and rhythmic gestures are often used together with a deep, sexy, or soothing voice. The hypnotist may use, when appropriate, caresses, handshakes, shoulder holds, hugs, pats, or the classic swinging pocket watch. Have you observed in historical newsreels Hitler's or Mussolini's hand gestures when orating? To us today, the gestures seem ridiculous, but they did their job then to rouse the public. The voice tones are different in the beginning of a speech than later on. The orator begins in a soothing manner with a placating attitude. So began Shakespeare's Mark Antony in his oration at Caesar's funeral: "Friends, Romans, countrymen, lend me your ears. I've come to bury Caesar, not to praise him."[3] The audience was persuaded to relax and open up, and then he proceeded with his real message and purpose.

After the trance is in place, then the suggestions begin. For suggestions to work, the speaker builds rapport with the audience and changes their consciousness to a receptive state. Hypnosis may occur in many situations. Here are some examples: You make suggestions to your inner mind: self-hypnosis. A psychiatrist giving psychotherapy guides a patient through the minefields of childhood traumas. A merchant makes a sales pitch to a prospect to move a product. A

---

3. William Shakespeare, *Julius Caesar*, ed. Barbara A. Mowat and Paul Werstine (New York: Simon & Schuster, 2009), 3:2.

general issues a rousing call to his soldiers to fight bravely. A hypnotist puts on an act on stage for laughs or astonishment. An athletics coach gives a pep talk to his team to try harder and win a coming game. In all these cases, people are moved by subconscious powers to perform almost beyond their abilities and achieve extra-ordinary results. Soldiers in battle charge forward without regard for their lives, bent on defeating the enemy. Not only kamikaze pilots but also American soldiers sacrificed themselves with patriotic fervor when the occasion demanded it in battle—they were in a hypnotic state of mind.

A maniac possesses the strength of several people and can overcome obstacles that are not surmountable by individuals in an ordinary state of consciousness. This is because the madman has focused all his faculties on one idea or objective and proceeds to achieve it without regard for his personal comfort, safety, or use of resources. Enter the al-Qaeda terrorist. Pain, his or her own, and that of innocent people, even children, means nothing to the terrorist, and neither does blood, damage, or danger of dying. The Vikings went into frenzies like that in battle and were called berserkers. They were formidable warriors, feared in all of Europe. Terrorists today perform the same way.

On the other side of the world, faith in Chinese medicine leads a patient to experience healing from acupuncture, which is also used in place of anesthesia in major surgery. The actions of the doctor in placing the needles lead the patient to a receptive, trance-like state, and pain becomes tolerable. It's what happens to women in labor with the Lamaze method. Special hormones secreted during labor, the support of the husband and doctor nearby, and breathing meditations, allow childbearing pains to be endured without general anesthesia.

Colors, patterns, odors, and music, especially from drums and other rhythmical instruments, can play a big role in hypnosis. The Nazi barbed cross, the swastika, was a powerful emotional symbol reaching the subconscious. Red flags and banners, torches, and parades of uniformed soldiers roused the public and induced exuberance.

The drums and fifes of the Scots excite advancing columns to fight without fear of losing life or limb. How many times in battle a nation's flag is picked up by man after man as the standard bearer each time is shot dead to the ground! The story is told of a Greek guard in 1941, who, in the face of the invading Nazi armies, jumped from the edge of the Acropolis with Greece's blue-and-white flag draped around his body. That was an admirably heroic deed or a piece of nonsense, depending on your point of view. But with great skill in hypnosis, you can achieve heroic deeds or cause much mayhem. Suggestions in hypnosis can be positive or negative, constructive or destructive. A suicidal person walks to death in a state of self-hypnosis, and we can lead him or her away from destruction using proper suggestions. Murder is often the result of self-hypnosis gone wrong. Many criminals confess they're led by an irresistible voice to perform their heinous acts. Hypnosis may be the reason behind the expression "the Devil made me do it!"

4. How to Be Enthusiastic Like a Gifted Genius

A gifted or talented person is one whom God has blessed with a special and uncommon ability to perform some wonderful service to mankind. That person is inspired to cultivate this ability, grow it, and express it fully by absorbing the spirit of God and finding an outlet in God's ways. The word "talent" comes from the Biblical story of Jesus about the three servants who each received a talent coin from their master before he went on a journey. What each did with his talent is a lesson for all of us because we all receive a gift from God upon birth, and it's the purpose of life to put that gift to good use for our benefit and for others. What is the connection of this matter to meditation? Your special gift is embedded deep in your subconscious mind, and to cultivate it, you need to enter there and grow it to full bloom.

When a person shows great native ability in doing something, we say that he or she possesses genius in that expertise. Saying that does not explain anything about this amazing phenomenon. Genius is a Latin word meaning guiding spirit. There was the belief that each person was born with both a good and an evil genius that influenced one's destiny, like a tutor from God. Even today, people often resort to mysticism to explain such rare and tremendous abilities because science cannot supply much light. Everyone has heard about Mozart's extraordinary skills at playing a variety of instruments with virtuosity and at composing perfect musical scores with ease and certainty.

Such was also the style of Napoleon and Alexander the Great, who led their armies brilliantly and won many victories against superior forces at a very young age. They both ruled over vast empires before they reached the age of thirty-five. Vincent van Gogh painted masterpieces, and Percy Bysshe Shelley penned immortal poems at a very young age. Jesus taught the world's now-dominant faith before he was thirty-five also. None of these people lived long lives. They blazed like supernovas for a brief period.

George Patton, the famous World War II general, lived until his sixties and died from an automobile accident. He loved to do battle as a tank commander and was totally unafraid of death, as portrayed in the Oscar-winning film *Patton*. He believed that he had lived many lives in the past as a warrior. He was as natural in military command as Felix Mendelssohn was in music or Babe Ruth in baseball. The poet John Keats called his own skill "something given to me."[4]

Louis "Satchmo" Armstrong believed God gave him his ability with the trumpet to make people happy and forget their troubles. He felt that he and the Angel Gabriel would make great music together in Heaven. In our time, Wynton Marsalis plays an equally marvelous trumpet, both jazz and classical. I find the clarity and joyfulness of his music totally captivating. Pick up the CD of Marsalis playing Haydn's trumpet concerto and listen.

As for myself, I jump into philosophical discussions just like a frog into a pond. Philosophy is the creative solution of human problems of a general and fundamental nature. I had some experience with creative work as an engineer, scientist, and businessman. As a student, I learned early in my career how to solve challenging assignments and test problems. There was a time when I would be stumped by a difficult question and get bogged down. Later, I picked up the habit of first examining the tough problems very intensely and then moving on to

---

4. John Keats, *The Letters of John Keats*, ed. Maurice Buxton Forman (Oxford: Oxford University Press, 2011), 183.

the simple questions that I could do from acquired knowledge. Afterwards, I would return to the unsolved problems; usually the answers would pop up in my mind.

While I was busy with routine matters, my subconscious mind was cranking out the answers I needed. After all, the subconscious is the central processing unit of the brain with most of its power. The conscious mind acts as the front-end or input-output unit in charge of awareness of the outside world, and it focuses attention properly. Later on in my life, I applied the same approach to other difficulties. I would pose a leading question to myself regarding any dilemma and then wait a while for the answer to emerge. If that didn't work, I would ask a different question. As Jesus said, "Ask and you shall be answered; knock and the door will be opened."[5]

People who've learned to use the subconscious mind in creative work possess a tremendous advantage, no matter what their field of endeavor. There's a connection to the spirit world or ideal universe deep in your subconscious, and you can reach that and link up. Then there's no limit to your potential to achieve anything. And faith is the key to this linkage. It's true that with faith, and some earth moving equipment, you can move mountains.

We've seen evidence of this in the works of great men, whatever their fields of endeavor. High intelligence helps a lot. So do energy and good health. Character is also very important, but you achieve great deeds with guidance from a Higher Source. The accomplishments of the fictional hero Forrest Gump come to mind. He was an idiot, but his character was sound, and God's grace was with him always. He won military honors, wealth, and success while others much smarter than he failed.

The mechanisms involved in great and inspired work are not well understood and are difficult for most people to implement. We know that much effort must be made to achieve the desired result, but then one needs to relax and let the Muse come. The revelation of a good idea

---

5. Matthew 7:7-8 (NIV).

may hit one in the shower or during a walk after many days of unfruitful toil. Much perspiration usually precedes inspiration.

To inspire yourself, enter your subconscious mind and search there deeply for the creative seed you need. To produce works of genius, follow your dreams as Walt Disney advised. Quite often, like the case of the mathematician Henri Poincaré or the organic chemist Friedrich Kekulé, the solution appears during sleep as a dream. Kekulé dreamed of a snake biting its tail—the structure of benzene. Illumination may be very gradual and slow or it may strike one suddenly, like lightning. The emotion upon finding an important truth can be very intense. One may be driven to run out into the streets screaming, "Eureka!" like Archimedes when he discovered his famous principle regarding bodies immersed in water. Be prepared for the great excitement of discovery, and hold on to your stack.

5. Cross over the Razor's Edge Without Getting Cut

Here is an issue raised rarely in meditation classes, books, articles, and lectures: what are the dangers and risks of meditation? The ancient sages of India compared inner mind travel to movement on a razor's edge. This image was exploited by Somerset Maugham in his novel *The Razor's Edge* about a young American who travels to India and delves into the mysteries and dangers of deep meditative practice. In the end, he gives up the customary pursuit of riches and fancy women, common in the roaring twenties, for a job as a detached cab driver in New York City. Other characters in the novel proceed to the catastrophe and disillusionment of the stock market crash of 1929 and the depression that follows. To avoid the razor's edge in mysticism, you'll need to understand well the process of meditation and get the required training in its use.

Let's examine the process of meditation. It's a gradual opening of the information valve in the brain that allows the integration of its conscious and subconscious parts. This valve or channel is normally tightly closed for good reasons, as explained earlier. The internal mechanisms of the mind must be protected, just as your gastrointestinal tract, lungs, and other organs are secured by your mouth, nose, vagina, urethra and anus. It's not good for dirt, dust, germs, and other harmful substances to come into your body or for foul waste products to be excreted at inappropriate times. These openings become operational when needed and are normally closed at other times. It's the same with information packages processed by the brain. Everyone has become familiar with computer viruses these days. Similar viruses can infect the human mind. The subconscious is vulnerable.

Here's the razor passage from the Upanishads:

Get up! Wake up! Seek the guidance of an
Illumined teacher and realize the Self.
Sharp like a razor's edge, the sages say,
Is the path, difficult to traverse.[6]

The passage is from a religious dialogue between an aspiring young searcher, Nachiketa, and his spiritual teacher, Yama, the king of death. Death is the ultimate horror that the vast majority of us fear most deeply. For animals, the danger of death is quick and immediate. It arrives, or it goes away like a puff. But humans know death is inevitable and will eventually take them and their loved ones in youth or old age, ready or not. On the tree of knowledge, the forbidden truth wasn't sex —animals know sex—but the thought of death. We ceased to be simple animals when we realized the future moment of our own extinction.

The monsters from the Freudian id, the source of instincts, are fears of death—for ourselves and for those we love. When lost alone in the jungles of the subconscious, what dreams may come so horrendous that may uproot one's reason? Hence, the value of a good spiritual guide or guru when one is practicing meditation. Common teachers of meditation like to talk about the benefits of the relaxation response. That's good, but relaxation is only the beginning of the process.

Deep meditation has been compared to climbing a steep and high

---

6. Eknath Easwaran, trans., *The Upanishads* (Tomales, CA: Nilgiri Press, 2007), 126-127.

mountain. At the top are the rewards of Heaven: bliss and tranquility with a grand view of the world below. But think of the dangers of deep ravines and slippery ice, avalanches, and bitter cold. That's what the mystic has to face every day he sits down to meditate deeply.

Like the mountaineer, the trained mystic uses his pitons, hooks, and the slender rope of faith. Sturdy and trusted companions are useful, and an experienced guide is indispensable for first climbers. It's very rare that a person survives the ascent alone to a major peak. Jesus and Mohammed were two such individuals, and they were not known to have had guides in their quest. What of all the multitudes of solitary ascetics who have tried it? Quite often, they became insane to a lesser or greater extent.

Then there are the temptations of Satan, the Great Tempter. With the flow of information in and out of the subconscious, the mind expands; psychic energy and intensity are enhanced. In a trance, you feel able to accomplish anything you desire. Control over your inner mind can empower you in dealings with other people. You're tempted to take advantage of others and use deception, pressure, or crime to succeed. Illusions, visions, and hallucinations plague you in a trance.

You experience psychic powers: the paranormal seems normal in this state of consciousness. In a trance, you sometimes feel you're capable of telepathy, telekinesis, and astral travel. I've experienced such things, and I've refused the temptation of using them. I'm neither Jesus fasting in the desert nor Goethe's Heinrich Faust or Oscar Wilde's Dorian Gray.

Sometimes, the danger is in the bliss, joy, or rapture of religious experience. You may be seduced by the pleasures of the deep quiet and the effect it has on others, known as charisma. The novice may wallow in these satisfactions and not want to go further to real liberation, enlightenment, salvation, and knowledge of God: the true goals of meditation.

Train yourself well then in meditation, and steer away from the razor's edge. In a trance, you don't perceive reality, the external world, as in a normal alert state. Inner visions and other sensations are mixed up with sensory input and often confused with what is actually happening in the outside world. Delusion is not uncommon. This is the road to mental derailment if, as a spiritual traveler, you're not properly coached and guided. In this so-called dreamless sleep, you don't want to be doing anything that requires full, conscious attention, such as operating a car, plane, or other dangerous equipment or pushing a baby stroller. Remember also that meditation amplifies the quirks of your personality. It brings out hidden aspects of the ego normally hidden from your consciousness, and if these are ugly, when they come out, your spirit can suffer a tremendous shock. Fears of insanity, of losing one's hold on reality, of being lost in the void may drive you over the razor's edge.

6. How to Reach Deeper Levels of Meditation

Buddhists speak of the four levels of meditation, *dhyana* in Sanskrit, that their master reached in his practice: the fourth level being Nirvana, enlightenment, satori in Zen Buddhism, or union with Brahman the Godhead. These levels can be described as deeper into the subconscious or higher to the supra-conscious, depending on one's viewpoint. We know that the subconscious mind is vast and complex. To connect with God, you must reach the deepest levels of the subconscious mind safely.

Freud, as we have seen, described parts of the subconscious with explanations of the id, libido, ego, and superego, all of them residing in the living tissue of the brain, which most scientists believe today is the seat of consciousness. Eastern philosopher-gurus, on the other hand, take the view that the source of consciousness is the Godhead, and the brain is simply a medium of communication with our world. The brain becomes active and responds to sense impressions from the material world for the survival of the body. When survival issues are not at stake or are set aside temporarily, then you're relaxed and may withdraw consciousness from the senses in order to concentrate on the inner self. That is the relaxation response and the first dhyana.

You now live more in the inside world than the outside. The perennial struggle for existence, worry for tomorrow, over jobs, business, children, health, and enemies has been temporarily halted. Relief and relaxation bring a sense of peace and joy. Your body is calm, and your mind is beginning to concentrate on the Divine and away from selfish desires. There are many benefits to reaching just this first level for the individual.

We have discussed the gains for health earlier. But you're also better equipped after such a session to deal with problems in a more detached and cool manner. You approach the world again with a freshness of attitude and renewed energy. Yet thought is still diffuse at the first level, and the mind is active with a multitude of ideas connected with living and this world. Before you can move to the second dhyana, the Buddhists say you must make the mind "one-pointed" or achieve the "right attention."

Now, thoughts drop away like yellow-red leaves from a tree. The mind becomes empty except for one central idea: the search for the Divine Presence. You enter the unitive state, free of any thought. We've mentioned earlier the concept of an information valve to the subconscious. There are several such valves that open to different chambers of mind. Some of them even lead to the most primitive and automatic functions of the brain, such as control of the heartbeat and metabolic rate, which are normally outside our control for reasons of safety. Some East Indian fakirs, however, can control such functions and survive burial in a coffin by putting themselves in hibernation. If you're new at meditating, you're advised not to fool around with such valves inside your inner mind.

The essence of the second level is concentration on one thing and further withdrawal from the demands of the senses. The object of concentration can be the image of a flower, like the lotus, Christ on the cross, the Madonna with child, or some other symbol of deep significance for you. In this mental state, distractions that can break the course of meditation become more distant and are less likely to intrude. Most people will not reach this level even after many years of practice.

It's no wonder that the task causes many seekers to abandon family and society and move into isolation as hermits or join a monastery in the company of others with the same goal. Eventually, you may reach the ability to put away selfish motives and be aware only of the whole sea of living entities. Awareness is very intense, and thought has almost come to a stop. Stillness and quiet prevail. Every motion is slow and deliberate; there are no quick, automatic responses to stimuli—you're at the threshold of a new existence.

With continued concentration on the inner mind, the third dhyana is reached even beyond birth to an original state of consciousness, filled with the most pure and clear joy. Thoughts stop completely, and you experience what Zen masters call "no-mind." In Sanskrit it's called *bodhi* and lasts only for a moment, but it's of great intensity and magic, so that all of life's other experiences pale by comparison. It's the feeling of rapture. You feel so close to all creation that with one more step, you'll be one with the universe. Time stops, and it seems that there's no further to go in your search, but this is not the end of the process.

Efforts in meditation, the opening of more barriers as you search deeper into the subconscious mind, can lead one, after many months or years, to the fourth dhyana, where the connection with God is located and all the energies and powers available to Him and Her. At this point, your conditioned responses to life are all burned out and remain in the background.

The experience of unity is repeated over and over and becomes established. But at this level, compulsive desires may be amplified a thousand times. There's grave danger ahead. You may seek power and dominance with this knowledge and be thrown to regions of evil. Yet, if you have the strength to resist temptation and seek the light, you find Nirvana, never to be completely deprived of it afterwards. This is your original Self, at the source of creation.

At this deepest level of the subconscious, you can safely and securely connect with God. You have achieved perfection in the ideal universe of God by being in intimate contact with Ultimate Reality. You need nothing more to experience, and if you're like most seekers, this is sufficient. For those like Buddha or Christ, it's not enough. Their hearts are filled with compassion for their fellow creatures, suffering the slings and arrows of outrageous fortune, not knowing how to escape. Great mystics are compelled by irresistible inner forces to return to the world and give a helping hand to the poor creatures who can't see the light; to bring comfort and salvation to those without the strength to reach Nirvana, the other shore, unaided.

7. Use Different Types of Meditation to Advantage

I've spoken of the meditative experience and of techniques for achieving it. I'll now go into more detail regarding the different methods of meditative practice. Keep in mind, however, that the path to salvation is very unique for each individual. You may receive guidance and comfort on the way from those more skilled and experienced, but you have to walk the way on your own feet and reach whatever summit is possible using passes and ridges of your own discovery. There are many sources on meditation methods: two good ones are Lawrence LeShan's *How to Meditate* and Ram Dass's *Journey of Awakening*. LeShan is academic in nature; Ram Dass, inspirational. Many meditation techniques appear silly. As LeShan points out, they're like pumping iron, jogging, or doing pushups to build muscle and fitness. They're repetitive, monotonous, and tiresome. But they build serene emotions and sharpen the intellect. An increased ability to concentrate on one thing intensely turns your mind into a mental laser boring into any problem and resolving it.

Directed concentration is one key to unlocking the doors to the subconscious mind and its powers. What other keys are there? We're now concerned about what lies beyond the relaxation response that we analyzed earlier. Putting yourself in a passive attitude, letting go of the fight-or-flight mental set, and concentrating on a mantra are good in the beginning. Breathing control and counting are also helpful to put yourself in a trance. With sufficient practice and experience with relaxation, you can achieve a trance almost instantaneously using a cue, for example, crossing two fingers, as suggested by Henry Silva in *Mind Control*. Remember, the cue works after some practice. Taking a relaxed position in a habitual meditation place and crossing the forefinger with the thumb. You may then proceed to deeper probing.

What means may be used to open deeper information channels?

LeShan proposes the path of the emotions, mainly love and devotion for God, saints, gurus, or friends of merit; that of the intellect, cultivated in Habad Hasidism; and the route of the body or action, such as the Sufi dancing, archery, weaving, Tai Chi and Hatha Yoga. We spoke earlier of romance, almost as a religious emotion, separate from physical contact, such as Don Quixote's for Dulcinea. For some people, love for their work, their country, or their family leads them to the Divine Source in deep concentration.

Approaching basic truths with the intellect may appear to be a contradiction since inspiration is basically unfathomable and inexpressible. Yet it was a great deal of help to me in my search, and it is so to the Habad Hasidim. Habad is an acronym of the Hebrew words for wisdom, intelligence, and knowledge. Without undue arrogance regarding my intellect, these are the qualities I have always sought to possess. I like to begin with a firm foundation of reason in my path and go as far as I can with that. I was very impressed by the lecture of Arnold Schrödinger, the Austrian physicist, "What is Life" and his discussion of entropy and negentropy. Where the path of intellect cannot take me further, I rely on emotional approaches, and if again I get stuck, I give vent to action, especially dancing.

Most societies employ dancing for religious purposes, particularly in Asia, Africa, and Native America. Some Christian sects have prohibited this activity on the grounds it leads to pagan licentiousness, which it may do, judging from some rock festivals. But it's simply an expression of human feelings, and as such, it can be directed towards God or other entities. Dancing may go on for hours among American Indians or African voodoo practitioners until some individuals are totally exhausted and enter a trance state. They have been entered by spirits, which now control their actions and words.

Other types of meditation are said to be structured or unstructured; also, they are of the outer, inner, or middle way. For example, breath counting, mantra, and the lotus meditations are structured because they're precisely defined and organized. In the East, the lotus flower with one thousand petals symbolizes the idea that everything is connected in the universe. Nothing is really separate. One visualizes the petals with the center being one main object or event to be contemplated. Then the petals are examined one by one as other related events. One thousand is just a large number, and it can actually be infinite. This is also an outer meditation because we're visualizing something on the outside of us.

There is a meditation called "Who am I?" that is structured and of the inner way. As an answer, most people give their name. But you proceed by saying, "No, that's not the real me." And ask again, "Who am I?" You might say, I am the person born on such a date, such a place, from those parents. And again, you deny that as the real you by saying, "But these are only memories I have." You continue in this way until you have stripped yourself down to the atman, the innermost self, connected with God.

We are involved in an unstructured meditation when we choose an object, problem, or relationship and actively explore it and our feelings towards it. You are free to choose a subject that has meaning for you, and you stay with that for a week or two, for twenty minutes every day. After a while, you'll come to an understanding of the subject that will make an impact on you or get the answer to your problem. It will help clarify your life, your dreams, and goals.

A very gentle but powerful meditation to connect with God is what the Byzantine mystics called hesychast or sweet repose. Today it's more often called the "safe harbor" approach. In a relaxed state, with your eyes closed, you allow yourself to drift towards "home" in your mind, the safest place you can imagine, where you can be calm and content without anything at all threatening your peace.

You're now concentrating on this one thing: finding "home." Your mind becomes an instrument of enormously penetrating light power, searching for the answer to the riddle of existence in the fog of the subconscious. As you drift, you imagine that this home or safe harbor is sending you a beacon signal to guide you, and you glide towards it slowly and surely. You feel the signal—you don't hear it or see it—like a guiding presence that eventually allows you to find your goal. Once there, everything feels perfectly right, like your mother's bosom when you were a baby. You're finally home, where you belong, whence you started, where you always wanted to be after your adventures on Earth.

8. Follow the Drug Path at Your Peril.

We will investigate here the drug path used to acquire Heaven by serious searchers such as Aldous Huxley, Timothy Leary, Ram Dass, Carlos Castaneda, and many others—artists, musicians, psychologists, philosophers, shamans, and holy men. We'll not be concerned with people who use drugs for recreation or escape from their unhappiness but with the spiritual mountain climbers who have looked for aid and a shortcut with the help of drugs. Be safe, and don't look for shortcuts to God. Drugs will not make your way to Heaven easier; you have to explore and work hard through desert land to find the path to the springs and streams of true existence.

Ram Dass, a Harvard psychology professor under the name Richard Alpert in the early 1960s, together with Timothy Leary, is quite frank about his drug use in his book *Journey of Awakening*. He once experimented with LSD and other psychedelics for enlightenment, finally ending up in the Himalayas in India at the feet of a guru. He came to understand that he would have to approach his inner being directly to find a lasting answer. He found meditation to be the best way to do this.

I've never used hard drugs for recreation or spiritual searches, and I'm not going to suggest that you do now. Remember, though, that we all use legal drugs every day quite casually. Most of us begin the day with one or more cups of coffee or tea to stimulate our nervous systems for work or play.

Caffeine is addictive and has some undesirable side effects. So is nicotine for those who smoke or chew tobacco. Sugar is not generally considered a drug and is used extensively in packaged foods and sweets, but it is, in the way it affects our blood sugar levels and in its addictive power.

The high feeling you get from a piece of cake is from sugar and refined flour, which are nearly sugars. And let's not forget the legal chemical for recreation and mood enhancement par excellence: alcohol. We also use medical drugs to alleviate pain and other conditions with or without a doctor's prescription, although there are side effects, which are often serious. Why not then use drugs when they aid in self-discovery and spiritual enhancement if side effects are considered?

My first objection to drugs is that they are sometimes illegal. As a rule, I like to obey the laws of my country. Secondly, I'm deeply concerned about acquiring an addiction. I smoked for ten years, and it required ten years of unrelenting effort on my part to quit the nicotine habit.

Finally, I believe that any drug use is like a crutch, which aids for a while but, in the long run, inhibits healing and growth. The gates of Heaven cannot be stormed with chemicals. It's too easy. Once briefly inside, the drug user is unprepared for dealing with the high energies, feelings, and challenges of spiritual existence. It's like going to the moon with a rocket but not having a space suit to get out and walk on the surface.

On the other hand, some societies have used chemical means to train for spiritual awakening with some success. With much delicacy and literary artistry, Carlos Castaneda documents such activities in his books about the teachings of Don Juan, a Yaqui Indian shaman or sorcerer. Jimsonweed, peyote, and hallucinogenic mushrooms are used by Don Juan and his circle of disciples for religious purposes. Users receive preparation and support. Some members of the circle don't engage in drug use and instead serve those who do and look after them in case of a bad trip.

Eating the plants is done in a serious ceremonial manner as a group activity, not as a joyride. It's done infrequently, not all the time, but as a special occasion. The plants are used like medicines to achieve certain spiritual results. The shaman and other experienced members of the group guide the faithful users along the way.

In his book of Don Juan's teachings, *A Separate Reality*, Castaneda makes the point that our everyday perceptions of the world are only one of many possible descriptions of reality and the judicious use of psychedelics and wise sorcery may open for us other worlds. This is an enticing prospect. Certainly, it's true that adventuresome and free-thinking people are likely to explore unusual means to further their understanding and their creativity. Many famous artists and writers have used drugs in their efforts to be more novel and enterprising in their work. Arthur Conan Doyle, creator of Sherlock Homes, experimented with drugs.

Rock musicians are proverbially addicted to chemical aids. But this is not for me. Evidence from biochemistry suggests mammalian brains use substances, such as endorphins, that result in natural highs. The danger from artificial devices is that they may be overused, becoming habitual tools for pleasure rather than mind expansion, and they pose health hazards. Moreover, as Ram Dass points out, the user is tempted to seek quick results rather than earn his or her rewards the old-fashioned way, by working for them.

Castaneda's Don Juan explores the notion of "stopping the world." This is similar to the Buddhist idea of slowing down time, internally, through a concentrated effort of emptying the mind of habitual thoughts. It amounts to training yourself to be more deliberate in thought and action and avoid falling into the common patterns of conditioned responses, automatic behaviors or habits.

Unfortunately, psychoactive drugs are easy to use and lead to bad habits. What we need is to try new approaches to problems and search wide spaces for solutions outside social mores. From the time we make our entry into the world, our family and society inexorably force us to behave, react, and think in "acceptable" ways that suit their needs and their customs. Much of this training is pleasant, functional, and beneficial. A great deal of it is simply detritus. Henry Thoreau realized this and went off to his pond-dwelling at Walden to meditate and escape conventions. He promised himself he would live in a deliberate way, free from compulsions and conditioned behavior. He was very unique and non-conforming by nature. Some people need to be jogged out of their set mental states when they stagnate, and drugs or electroshock may do that. Regular and disciplined meditation, however, is far more effective in the long run for the release of hang-ups and usually without unpleasant side effects.

9. How to Survive and Thrive on the Forbidden Planet

Forbidden Planet is a Hollywood movie of the sixties starring Leslie Nielsen, about a mad scientist and a planet where monster dreams from the primitive part of the subconscious mind, the id, take physical form by means of alien synthesizing equipment. The deep recesses of the subconscious are indeed like a forbidden world, where ugly fears, rages, and desires lurk in the abysmal darkness. These are primal instincts, established long ago in our evolution before civilized behavior became the norm. Penetrating to such depths in meditation, you risk confrontation with forces that may lead to murder or self-destruction.

The problem is that as you meditate and withdraw from the senses, you abandon the lifeline to the physical world outside; you may be lost in the inner wilderness, experiencing disorientation and panic. If that happens while you're in the primal sector of the subconscious, you're likely to be overcome by animal urges and fears.

Cultural memories of fierce predators, elusive prey, and hated antagonists chase away reason and stability. Thus, you could approach savage and insane territory. If you're not very skilled in meditation, well-guided, and in possession of a stable personality, it's best not to navigate such waters and sail away to safer seas.

Consider the vast expanses of the subconscious. There are many places to visit and more to avoid in this inner universe. Be guided by the conscious will and thought, as the Upanishads put it, at least in the beginning of your journeys. Later you may risk using the "no-mind" approach of some Zen schools. When you become sure of the current you are riding, you can drift to the right destination by emptying your mind and allowing your spirit to float to the Divine Center. Are you sure of the purity of your motives and basic character? Few people qualify for sainthood. The danger always exists that you'll gravitate to the Evil One.

As you progress in your explorations, you'll often encounter sensations, images, and feelings that are startling and new to you. Hallucinations and illusions, called *makyo* by Zen masters, will come to haunt you, pleasantly or painfully. It doesn't matter whether the makyo are ecstatic or nightmarish. They should be set aside as unimportant at best to your spiritual development, and at worst, these are serious hindrances and distractions to growth.

You may get visions from your own particular religious background. Catholics and Orthodox Christians may see the Virgin Mary in full splendor and light. Jews may encounter Moses or King David. You may hear celestial harps or smell delightful aromas. All these are defensive actions by your subconscious mind to thwart your entry to vital sites.

Many spiritual travelers report experiences with powerful vital energies. They're convinced of the existence of mystical centers in their bodies, called *chakras* and *kundalini* in the Indian mystical tradition. In China, people are well aware of the vital force *chi* that travels the meridians of the body, energy channels along the length of the body.

Chinese medicine people believe that when these channels are blocked due to a disturbance of the body's balance, illness follows; but the flow of chi along the meridians may be released by means of acupressure or acupuncture. Modern science has yet to find a rational explanation for these matters. Such phenomena are subjective and possess no objective validity at present. The best we can say about them is that they are experiences limited to the inner world and can be useful in treating the subconscious mind of dysfunctional tendencies.

A major danger in mind explorations while in the altered state of consciousness of a trance is the loss of contact with customary thinking: the attitudes and mores of one's society and familiar logical procedures. A person in meditation may not be able to communicate with friends and relatives in a reassuring way; one lives in a very personal world. Innovative ideas and daring leaps of the imagination are possible now, but so are huge faux pas of reasoning.

One may be carried away too easily by the emotions and bright images of a different reality and assume that events in inner space can be directly projected outside. If the dreamer maintains sanity and properly organizes these experiences to apply rationally to the outside world, much creative potential is released. Acting out these fantasies prematurely, however, leaves the road wide open to the booby hatch or worse.

Worse than the madhouse is what the misguided spirit traveler may do to one's society and to the world. Murder, arson, destruction, and war, even, if the evil mystic assumes leadership, as happened with Adolph Hitler. I can imagine Hitler's meditations as he languished in prison after his failed Munich Putsch. He furiously scribbled his venomous treatise to be published as *Mein Kampf* (My Struggle). In this, he not only outlined his Nazi doctrines but also provided a detailed plan for his future exploits, which he proceeded to implement when he was in power as the dictatorial chancellor of Germany.

I can't help but wonder from where the inspiration came to people like Hitler, Kemal Ataturk, Slobodan Milosevic, Sadam Hussein, and Osama bin Laden. I would like to know the source of such crimes against humanity: the genocide of Jews in Europe, Greeks and Armenians in Turkey, Muslim Slavs in Yugoslavia, Kurds in Iraq, and Americans in the World Trade Center.

Such powerful but flawed minds penetrated deep into their subconscious and grasped forces allowing them to wreak evils on their fellow human beings. My heart grieves deeply when I think of such acts, and I sometimes come to the notion that there's indeed a great evil spirit, known as Satan, promoting such mayhem on our planet. The Christian novelist C.S. Lewis called the Earth a "silent planet" because he visualized it sometimes as a place of isolation from the glory of the heavens and other civilized planets. In spite of much beauty on its surface, the Earth may be a place of quarantine for those carrying the horrid germs of evil. Or perhaps, it's a penal colony and a forbidden planet itself. A penal colony for spirits infected by Satan, where a few souls are rehabilitated and returned to their true home with God, while others are sent back here death after death to serve their sentences and hope for redemption.

10. Coming Home to God

In this final section on meditation, we'll explore the idea of union with Divinity, the goal of the spiritual search, what has been called by people who practice this art as "coming home." The feelings that are experienced when contact with God is made are profound peace, harmony, tranquility, and perfect security. Nothing may happen in this life or the next that needs to distress us. In this state of consciousness, everything has an explanation that cannot be explained in words, and this world is the best of all possible worlds, a notion satirized by Voltaire in *Candide*. It's like coming home at last after a long absence.

In the words of Ram Dass, in this moment of unity "the universe appears fresh; it is seen through innocent eyes. It all begins anew."[7] It is the moment of creation and at once the moment of fulfillment; it is, in fact, a timeless experience. Above all, one senses the presence of a powerful and benign Being, permeating one's consciousness with total compassion and understanding. The same feelings are reported by people who've had a near death experience.

Such images may only be a great illusion, as Sigmund Freud put it. Or they may have real meaning. If a human being does possess an imperishable soul derived from God or some powerful process in the universe, is it not natural that it enters the body upon conception and leaves it upon death to return to its Maker? Is it not also natural that in deep meditation, as you explore the origin of your consciousness, the self, you encounter the connection to God and enter, to an extent, into Self, the Creator's mind. "The eye with which God looks at me is the eye with which I look at God,"[8] said Eckhart. This is a two-way channel of communication.

As you meditate deeply, your spirit must be pure, clean, healthy, and free of viruses, or it will not be permitted to make contact with Heaven. One must be guided in the search of God by motives that are

---

7. Ram Dass, *Journey of Awakening: A Meditator's Guidebook* (New York: Bantam Books, 1990), 46.
8. Meister Eckhart, *The Complete Mystical Works of Meister Eckhart*, trans. and ed. Maurice O'C. Walshe (New York: Crossroad Publishing Company, 2009), 298.

good and unselfish. In effect, those who enter Nirvana must first give up the self and its attachments to the material world—pleasure, vanity, ambition, greed, jealousy, hatred, power, and other vices—in order to merge with the Self. This is called Self-realization in the Hindu faith.

So, while it seems unlikely that anyone will ever be able to prove the existence of God with scientific arguments, He and She may be experienced internally through profound meditation. After all, that is how we gain knowledge, through direct experience. There is no cause to believe that an introspective experience is any less valid than a sensory one. After all, the senses often lead us astray, and things seen with the eyes are often illusory.

In the writings and sayings of the great mystics, such as Moses, Jesus, Mohammad, St. Augustine, Meister Eckhart, St. John of the Cross, Krishnamurti, and Rumi, we get a sense of the presence of God. That's, perhaps, because these people made contact of the most intimate sort with God in their thoughts and their lives, or they were somewhat insane, thinking that they did. The real test is not the source of findings, internal or external, but the consensus of other bright minds and the test of ideas against observations over a period of time. That's exactly how experimental scientists validated Einstein's theories of the physical universe, contrary to common sense as they were.

Now, as to the methods of approaching God in meditation, you begin with caution. It's easy to fall into traps and makyo, as stated earlier. Detachment from worldly things and withdrawal from the senses is helpful. Selfish desire must be given up, according to the Buddha. You kill the ego first, according to Sufi masters, and then there's little to stop your union with God. But asceticism should not be carried to extremes. It's not wise to deprive yourself of necessary nutrition, rest, and energy because meditating is hard work, even if you're sitting down while doing it.

Placing yourself in a trance, through the relaxation response, you call the name of God in a mantra, repeatedly: "Rama Rama, Hare Hare, Krishna Krishna, Hare Hare," or some other such appellation. Now you contemplate and feel intensely the qualities of God, most of all His and Her immense love and compassion for all creatures. As you do this, you forget that God usually refrains from exercising His and Her infinite power and wisdom in rescuing humanity and other living things from their misery and suffering; and that, as a rule, God allows them to solve their own problems if they can, and if not, to perish. Instead, you pray for the rare privilege of Grace, for a miracle, for guidance in the labyrinth of the subconscious.

With images of the great saints and mystics in your heart, you allow your consciousness to drift to the Source, slowing down your mind and senses until there's a complete stop to your train of thought. Now time stands still. You've arrived at your destination, and you're one with the Creator, as Moses, Jesus, Mohammad, Buddha, and Laotse were before you:

"Oh, Israel, the Lord, Our God is one."
"Our Father, who art in Heaven."
"Allahu Akbar."
"Imperishable is the Lord of Love."

Thus you have achieved enlightenment, satori, Nirvana, and the "unitive" state. Or have you? Where are you exactly in this state of consciousness? Are you in a higher reality or out of your mind?

These inner explorations of God and your celestial home can only be validated by your return to the everyday world of the senses and to sound wide-awake reasoning. The objects you bring up from your deep dives into the subconscious should be scrutinized in the bright light of the sun. Have you got pearls and other treasures in your hands or toxic trash and slimy poisons? With a fully alert mind, you consult with your best friends and the brightest minds to determine whether your findings are good and useful. You look for the fruits of your prophecies. Doing otherwise may lead to the ways of evil, as followed by Jim Jones, David Koresh, Hitler, and Napoleon.

A good connection with God in meditation should lead to better science; also, good science, operating in the physical world with mathematics and experimentation, should lead to better religion. These two methods of knowing need not be in opposition unless one or the other becomes false. Truth should reign in both worlds of reason and intuition.

Come home to God walking upright, head up, after an absence of a lifetime on Earth, the leg of scientific reason working with the leg of religious intuition. Depriving scientific actions of religion leads people to spiritual desiccation, indifference, and the wholesale destruction of life. The epitome of such a course was the invention and exploitation of atomic energy in war and the preparation for war. Religion without science leads to fanaticism, ignorance, and aberration of mind, such as in Europe during the Dark Ages and now in many areas of the Muslim crescent. Good people were burned as witches, and brilliant minds, such as that of Galileo, were thwarted from doing their best work. Whatever marvelous and enthralling vistas you may enter while meditating, keep your hold on reason and objectivity.

10

FINDING YOUR COSMIC CONNECTION

When my older brother George was fifteen, he lost his faith in God, including all the other religious beliefs our mother and the priests had taught us. My father, very ethical but an agnostic, never said anything to us for or against religion. In Greece, ninety-five percent of the population is baptized, married, and buried by the Orthodox Church. It has been like a second state in the country since the Roman emperor Constantine embraced Christianity. The priests wore long beards, top hats, and black robes. Like the other little boys, I ran to kiss the priest's hand in the street when I encountered one and to get his blessing.

My brother talked to me about his doubts late at night, keeping me awake until I could not keep my eyes open anymore. "The priests lie to us," he would say. "There's no God. Christ was just a man who insulted the authorities and got punished according to the laws of his country." I protested: "But we do have souls, which live after death, don't we?" "Sorry, my friend," my brother would say. "When you're dead, you're dead and go nowhere; you become nothing, what you were before you were born." I was disturbed about this fate for my ego and became determined to seek out in my life the truth about the matter. I now conclude this book with my best thoughts on the big questions of God's existence and the soul's immortality. My conception of God, an idea innate in humans and projected on the universe, is based on findings from meditation and, more recently, from scientific cosmology. Now I'll retrace, detail, and develop some notions proposed earlier in this study.

One such notion is God's body as a universe-size crystal, grown molecule by molecule, layer after layer from the basic materials of the universe, like a silicon or germanium semiconductor—not artificially in a clean room but spontaneously in the vacuum of space. This crystallization may be happening in our own universe, resulting in a perfect habitat for God at some time in the future, or it may have happened in an alternate universe that coexists with ours.

1. An Evolving God and Heaven Watch over Us

Since the magnifying glass, people have marveled at the beauty of snowflakes—water droplets crystallized into ice with a variety of intricate patterns. I remember as a child being amazed by such magic on the window glass as snowflakes settled on it and disappointed when the ice jewels melted from the heat of the house. Diamonds, the hardest and most durable thing on Earth, are also carbon crystals. DNA, with its double helix form, is a carbon crystal of a different sort—flexible and adaptable. X-ray crystallography was instrumental in revealing DNA structure, as so thrillingly told by James Watson, the American on the Cambridge team that modeled DNA, in his book *The Double Helix*. DNA chromosomes have evolved to split and grow again into a new whole, using raw molecules from their environment, thus providing reproduction for living things. God may be growing in our universe or in some other universe and evolving from simpler living forms.

With the use of energy from the sun and Earth's interior, living forms have converted much of the material on the surface of the planet into organic mass. If this miraculous process of photosynthesis can be duplicated in factories, more and more material from Earth and other planets can be converted to living tissue—and thinking brains. The sun can be encircled by artificial planetoid cities that capture most of its energy and turn it into more living things. Moreover, planetary energy may be tapped by means of deep wells.

Energy can also be generated through fusion reactions using hydrogen, the most plentiful element in the universe, the fuel of stars. Spaceship colonies may thus be powered for travel between star systems and galaxies. With populations doubling every few years in such habitations, it's easy to calculate that in a few million years, much of our solar system, then our galaxy, and finally, much of the universe may be converted to an interconnected living and thinking entity.

Perhaps the ultimate form of this future entity will not be human but more like an organic computer, made up of trillions of units, communicating through an internet system, capable of very advanced and intricate thought processes. The brain is a similar collection of interconnected neurons, stimulating each other to activity through axons and dendrites. Now, we know electronic processes generate no friction and incur no damage to parts at a temperature near absolute zero. Such temperatures are freely available in space. Therefore, an intelligent computer system would operate forever and have an infinite existence, such as attributed to God. But the threat to that kind of life still would remain from an ever-expanding universe.

With the fabric of space pulling the galaxies further apart at an accelerating speed from Einstein's "negative force" or collapsing through gravity back to the original pinpoint discontinuity of creation, the end of the cosmos would inevitably come. Our super intelligent, infinitely wise, and all-powerful entity may have found a solution by absorbing all matter into its fabric of existence, a universe-size crystal containing all the pulsating energies required for eternal life.

Let's try to fathom such a Being. It has had unlimited time to organize itself, its program, and its hardware to the point of perfection for optimal functioning. After that was done, there was no further need for change and improvement; therefore, this satisfies the requirement that God, the universal operating system, and Heaven, the cosmic hardware, both are indeed unchanging and eternal. God is not, as many mystics claim, the ideal universe. It's the ideal living, feeling, and thinking program operating it. God is like the melody emanating from a Stradivarius violin or a Steinway piano: not the notes alone but the emotion in the playing of the instrument. He or She is like the reading of the lovely phrases of a poem, not just the words. This explains why artists and other creative workers are so close to God: God is the source of their inspiration.

With absolute peace, tranquility, and security from damaging change, God might still want more. He might want the company and affection of beings similar to Him or Her, who would be less than perfect and, therefore, more unpredictable and interesting. As a wealthy old person living in a splendid mansion with all the comforts of existence might want the love of pets and grandchildren on occasion, so God wanted to have us. So He and She created us through the evolution of Earth's soil, from lowly bacteria and such to our primate ancestors in the forests of Africa.

In the end, with Homo sapiens, God breathed spirit into true humans, and our race started to become somewhat civilized. With the aid of God's creative imagination, we domesticated animals and plants and gained relative security from famine so that we could devote some of our energy to culture. The great civilizations of China, India, Egypt, and Mesopotamia came into being. Then appeared the great flowering of the mind and spirit with the ancient Greeks, which, suppressed for a thousand years after Barbarian onslaughts, re-emerged in Spain with Arab Moors and in Italy's Renaissance.

Why did we have the Dark Ages after civilization reached such peaks with the Greeks and Romans? A Cosmic God, such as I have described, would not want to interfere unduly in our affairs and the life of our planet. God, compassionate but not controlling, would allow us the freedom to grow in our own way and would be amused by our quirks and irregularities. God would feel sympathy and concern for our occasional downfalls, plights, and injustices inflicted by evildoers, and occasional atrocities seen on Earth, such as the death of innocent children in tribal warfare.

God, with the capacity to gather up the spirits of the lost to an ample bosom and comfort them after death, would not want to interfere too often and mix in our frays to save those threatened on Earth of losing their paltry bodies. God would want to allow us to shape our destinies with the help of our own experiences and develop as a species in our own unique way, as long as we didn't mess things up too badly.

God, having grown and evolved from living entities like us and having experienced mortality once in its isolated units, would be like a wise parent, allowing a child to play, to find joy or hurt to some extent as part of learning, but preventing the child from running into traffic. God would not intervene except to stop total catastrophe, and perhaps not even then.

2. This Oscillating Universe Gave Rise to God

The fate of the universe is intimately tied to the concept of God and our relationship with Him and Her. In all major religious traditions, God is known as the Creator of the universe, the great designer of the game of existence, laying down its statistics of operation and fundamental rules. According to the Taoists, God grows the world continuously rather than building it from the beginning to full completion.

In Greek thought, God was known as the *Demiurge*, like Brahma, the Godhead, from whose thought or meditation emanates all we perceive. I've no pretensions as a cosmologist. I'm fascinated by astronomy and by speculations regarding the growth of the cosmos and its end. I like the scope of cosmology, dealing with the tiniest particles and the largest galaxies.

The theory of the oscillating universe, which expands from nothingness to nearly infinite space and then contracts back to nothingness, intrigues me. It ties in well with the Socratic and Hindu thought of the eternal cycles of the world, like the seasons, birth and death, creation, and destruction. I know that may not be the case in fact. The universe may expand forever at an accelerating speed under the influence of dark energy. However, that doesn't seem likely to me. We know that most of the matter in the universe is invisible black holes and such and may eventually exert sufficient gravity to pull everything back together again. Also, space may not be capable of stretching to any size. If space has elasticity, it could start compressing things again.

Another consideration comes from the science of quantum mechanics.

In quantum mechanics, material bodies have a dual nature, such as particles and waves. For example, light scatters like particles, called photons, and like electromagnetic waves. Larger bodies have shorter wavelengths; that's why an electron microscope is more penetrating than one based on light. Your body and mine are waves and can be beamed to other locations, given the equipment on board the USS *Enterprise* of *Star Trek* fame. Earth and the sun move around as heavenly objects and also as waves of energy. Why not, then, the whole universe? Yes, the entire cosmos is, according to this approach, one huge ball of oscillating energy, rising in intensity to a maximum level and then subsiding to almost nothing—unless it was frozen into a controlled crystal by the action of a living God, or Satan.

A quantum universe, which admits all possible developments, is essential to our concept of the existence of God. In an infinite waveform made up of universes, there's bound to be one period of oscillation that produces a perfect harmony of events leading to life and its growth. Our particular universe is a very unique one in this respect, although it's by no means a perfect one. Most of the equations describing the world in physics include a constant, such as Boltzmann's constant (k) in thermodynamics, the gravity constant (g) in gravitation theory, and hundreds of others. Scientists have stated that if any of these physical constants were outside a certain optimal range, the universe would not hang together, and life would not be possible. Consider Earth. It's just the right distance from the sun, possesses the right combination of gases in its atmosphere, and has just the right geology—all of these factors, and many others, being absolutely necessary for the emergence, evolution, and perpetuation of life.

Was this coincidental or according to the design of a Super Being? Either explanation is possible. With an infinite number of universes, our particular type was bound to come up. It's like poker: once in many thousands of deals, a player will get a royal flush, or perhaps a card mechanic produces this special flush with the skill of his hands.

In an oscillating universe wave, any imaginable structure is possible, the most perfect one being Heaven or the God universe, but also Hell, Satan's world. Both of them are crystals, but they operate under very different principles, and both of them are eternal because a vast intelligence controls every event in each place.

As we've stated before, Heaven is a place of love and cooperation, while Hell is the domain of hatred and compulsion. Since Heaven and Hell coexist with our universe, both are immanent in ours. Thus God and Satan are present throughout our universe, as claimed by theologians. We are separated from these and the other worlds of the oscillation by a thin veil of probability. One toss of the coin and we have crossed over to another dimension on another planet, to other people, to a different existence.

Oscillations, or cycles, are seen everywhere in nature. They are described by Fourier mathematics and manipulated as easily as algebraic expressions using the Laplace transform. This math is a basic tool of electrical engineers and physicists. The oscilloscope, the electronic engineer's most important equipment, displays waveforms on a cathode ray tube, CRT, similar to your computer monitor. Artistic oscillations of airwaves result in beautiful music: they are called standing waves in the language of physics. Mystics talk of vibrations, such as the Hindu OM or AUM sound, which is the sound of the living universe. Laser light is a coherent energy wave of a single frequency, which has great penetrating power and can cut through steel as a hot knife cuts through butter. At Jericho, the walls tumbled down at the sound of the powerful Hebrew trumpets.

What we call colors are simple reflections from objects at certain wavelengths of light. Reds have lower frequencies, while blues have higher. Yellows and greens are in between, as is seen in a rainbow. Ultraviolet and infrared radiations can't be seen by humans. Ultraviolet energy has the highest penetration and burns your skin when the sky is overcast. Infrared is used effectively in night vision binoculars as it's reflected well by objects. The reflections are converted to frequencies we can see.

God, the ultimate light of the cosmos, is growing, creating, and perfecting us and the world continuously; He-She did not complete the world in one of His working weeks, as originally thought by ancient Hebrews. As we progressed, so did all our faculties, such as our voice. From guttural sounds to express anger, love, or pain, our vocal cords changed and tuned to produce a standing wave of great precision. High notes of great intensity can shatter champagne glasses due to their penetrating frequencies. But also the voice of a trained and talented singer, the finest musical instrument, produces oscillations, reaching into the deepest recesses of our heart, moving us to experience ecstasy and rapture, like those of a holy person in sacred meditation and Nirvana.

3. Travel in the Fourth Dimension

The fourth dimension we are going to talk about here is not that of time but the dimension along which the oscillating universe extends. If you can travel along this dimension, using the meditation techniques of the Buddha, Socrates, or Dante, you may visit with your mind other universes much different from ours, including Heaven and Hell. The practice of Eckankar in the East is one approach to such adventures. With developed skills in meditation, you can travel along the fourth dimension.

Physical travel to parallel universes is a common theme in science fiction books and movies. A scientist, or sometimes an amateur engineer, develops a machine that enables such travel. If that's possible, then the traveler may also visit proximate earthy planets in the past and in the future.

Traveling in the fourth dimension with one's body may be impossible. True, some tasks are not achievable, but it's not creative to judge beforehand which ones. Consider flight by humans. Dreamers and visionaries imagined this adventure many centuries ago, as far back as Daedalus and his son Icarus. Da Vinci designed flying machines in Renaissance Italy, and around the turn of the last century, many brave men flew various flying contraptions with some success, even before the Wright brothers. And yet, all along, most people thought objects heavier than air could not fly unless equipped with wings by God or Nature.

Most people also thought space travel was impossible. Few people believed men would walk on the moon as early as 1969. Science fiction placed such achievements well into the twenty-first century. On the other hand, Arthur C. Clark, one of the deans of science fiction, imagined human habitats on the moon in the year 2001, which did not happen in our universe.

The future is difficult to decipher. The ancient Greeks had a saying: "The future is invisible." So, travel in the fourth dimension may be closer than we think. It may be going on at the present time by some people. Perhaps every time we make a critical decision, we move to a different universe. What we decide makes all the difference, as in Robert Frost's famous poem "The Road Not Taken."

> I shall be telling this with a sigh
> Somewhere ages and ages hence:
> Two roads diverged in a wood, and I-
> I took the one less traveled by,
> And that has made all the difference.[1]

Decisions make all the difference in how the universe unfolds. There's cause and effect in our world. Determinism has its points; fatalism, kismet, may be a valid point of view. I'm inclined, however, to believe in the power of our will and the grace of God. Mixed in with the inexorable progressions of cause and effect, which make life predictable, there's also randomness, giving birth to unexpected events, even miracles.

I see the universe as a random branching process, a stochastic

---

1. Robert Frost, "The Road Not Taken," *The Road Not Taken: A Selection of Robert Frost's Poems*, ed. Louis Untermeyer (New York: Henry Holt and Company, 2019), 15.

machine. From the tiniest particle to the largest galaxy cluster, events are not totally predictable, meaning they can never be completely determined, even with computers of immense power. Thus multiple universes emerge randomly and by means of decisions made by sentient beings.

In the beginning, the universe was a singularity, not a dimensionless point, but a surface, as postulated by Stephen Hawking in *A Brief History of Time*. Initial conditions can be different, giving rise to a variety of different universes. Terminal conditions also differ, so that each universe, which emerged from the Big Bang, may have a different fate. What we experience is a trajectory of events based on the initial and final conditions, but the passage of our consciousness, and even of our physical bodies, may be possible from one trajectory to another one.

Such explanations are best described with the mathematics of differential equations, such as Schrödinger's particle-wave expression, which I can't assume you know. Electromagnetic theory is also an elegant description of propagating events, so beautifully formulated by Maxwell, which again may be outside your experience. Simply put, what actually happens depends on initial conditions only but also the present state of things, which becomes an initial condition for the next stage of development. With deep thought and deliberate action, we may be able to control the outcome for the next stage and thus become masters of our fate, in effect entering a better universe more suited to our ideals.

Moreover, it's possible that communication channels exist between our universe and others, such as Heaven, Hell, and places in-between that might be called Purgatory—probably a good name for our own world. If that's the case, then great souls in religious meditation can reach God and Heaven and, from there, get insights into a variety of possible worlds. The intimacy of this experience may have caused Jesus to say to his followers, "I am not of this world."[2] After his death and resurrection, he disappeared again, as so many others have done,

---

2. John 8:23 (NIV).

through a mystical door to another dimension of being. Like Mohammed and the Buddha, he was a traveler in the fourth dimension.

How is travel in the fourth dimension accomplished? By raising our consciousness above the constraints of ordinary time and space; as the sage of Bhagavad Gita wrote, "By the exercise of the intelligent will."[3] Some philosophers dispute the existence of the will on the basis of causality and determinism. For me, the will is simply defined as that function of the mind that permits one to do what is logically necessary despite pain or pleasure. There may be an organ for the will in the brain, or the will is a more generalized function of the frontal lobe.

You can travel along the time dimension with your intelligent will and imagination. If you can, like a yogi, slow down your mind in meditation, time freezes up for you; it's possible then to be totally deliberate in action, making those decisions necessary for travel to other worlds. I believe great scientists, inventors, and artists possess this faculty, and they're able to produce the creations that transform our cosmos. Thomas Edison, Alexander Graham Bell, Einstein, van Gogh, and Madame Curie traveled elsewhere and, with their discoveries, brought the rest of us along to a different universe.

4. Going beyond Space and Time

One attribute of God is that He or She is eternal; that is, He or She is not bound by the constraints of space and time, with which we mortals have to contend in our brief lives. Well, gods in all places and times have been considered immortal and very powerful. The Greek gods were over ten feet tall in the popular imagination; although they could be wounded, they healed quickly and always recovered from any damage to their bodies. These gods were capable of very rapid, almost instantaneous, movement through space, at what "Star Trekkers" might

---

3. A. C. Bhaktivedanta Swami Prabhupāda, trans. and comm., *Bhagavad-gītā As It Is*, (Los Angeles: Bhaktivedanta Book Trust, 1972), 3.42.

call today "warp speed." Thus, the gods were timeless, not constrained by space, and they were more permanent than gold.

Time is linked with motion. Can there be time if there is no movement of anything or everything moves at the speed of light? We've learned, from Einstein and corroborating experiments, that time slows down as the speed of light is approached. An atomic clock was placed on a satellite in recent years, proving the slowdown to be true.

Now, earth-orbiting speeds are not anywhere close to the velocity of light, 186,000 miles per second, but after many orbits, the atomic clock registered a delay compared to a clock on Earth. Well, the earth, sun, and galaxy are also in motion, so all clock readings are distorted relative to a clock placed motionless at the center of the universe, where the Big Bang began. But the center is everywhere, which presents a paradox.

Let's leave this paradox aside for the moment and consider the fact that recent cosmological evidence indicates the universe is expanding at an accelerating speed. It's conceivable then that eventually, galaxies will acquire something close to the speed of light, and all clocks everywhere will slow down their ticking, time stretching out interminably. This hypothesis has also been applied to spaceships traveling at near-light velocities, with crew and passengers hardly aging at all and returning to Earth to find their families dead, except for great-grandchildren. Einstein's theories state that no physical object with any mass may attain the speed of light. But if dark energy is pushing galaxies to higher speeds, it may eventually convert them into pure energy without mass, and then time would stop completely everywhere.

Coming back to the God concept, if God is a Being of pure light, as the angels are, God is outside of time, as no clock would register motion and the passage of time. In any case, our suggestion is for a Heaven as an entire crystalline universe, with God in residence as a vast photon program, with sentient probes, such as us humans, in every conceivable universe at all times in all stages of evolution. Such a Being would be omniscient and omnipotent.

This Being would be perfect in simplicity, being one crystal being. A crystal is perfect, having no entropy or disorder; everything is in its place, and there is a place for everything. And it's unchanging because any change would detract from its perfection. All these are qualities of God, as numerous mystics have told us.

Mystical and profound meditation masters also report this quality of timelessness in their experience of rapture. So do true lovers in their moment of ecstasy. Obviously, for us humans on Earth, timelessness is a subjective phenomenon: as soon as we return to normal consciousness, we are again operating in normal time. An explanation for the sense of time stopping may lie with the event of contact with God. As we approach the Divine Presence in prayer or meditation, we get a sense of His consciousness. And if union with God actually happens, we may become immersed in his eternal existence.

In union with God, the passage of time ceases to have meaning. When the spirit of the mystic returns to his or her body after such a trip, he or she feels born again. This may be what happens when one is born to a new body. It could be the experience of God's grace when a sinner repents truly, is baptized, and changes in character and destiny.

Intimate contact with God, however, can blow your mind. It's what happened to Moses at the burning bush. This prince of Egypt was happy with his new wife, sheep, and goats until he got the message to save a clan of Hebrew slaves from the pharaoh. Similarly, Mohammed was happy driving caravans of camels to Syria and beyond until one night in the desert the angel of God commanded him, "Recite."

And Jesus, coming out of the desert and being baptized by St. John, saw the Holy Spirit like a dove and heard the voice of God: "This is my beloved Son, in whom I am well pleased."[4] These men, and others like Saul of Tarsus, known as St. Paul, may have had psychotic episodes, but they founded world religions and have shaped the course of mankind by uniting diverse populations far better than any empire.

That's because as the prophet's contact with the Divine Being is made, temporal considerations—personal safety, gratification, and survival—recede in importance. The prophet's vision is much larger, encompassing all humanity and going far into the future. As Martin Luther King, Jr. said, in one of his last speeches before being assassi-

---

4. Matthew 3:17 (NIV).

nated, "I have been to the mountain top. I would like to live a long life like anyone else. Longevity has its merits. But this is not important. I want to do God's work."[5] Thus selfish desires ebb in the heart, the soul becoming fixed on the ideals preserved for all eternity in God's crystal mansion.

Like the ancient Greek gods, our One God is timeless, beyond ordinary space; we share in this existence when our ideas take us to Heaven. This day has little meaning except as a decision point, a springboard to a better universe. This year, even this century, is but a short interval for the prophet. Even the five billion years remaining to Earth and the sun pass like an instant in God's eyes.

5. Linking up with Infinite Intelligence

Infinite Intelligence is a word for the Divine Entity preferred by the inspired teacher of success and happiness, Napoleon Hill. In his books and lectures, he occasionally refers to such a source for much of his wisdom. Hill's best-known work is *Think and Grow Rich*. This man from rural Appalachia had many followers and imitators, but none has approached his fire and sincerity. He talked with the accents of an illiterate country hick, but his ideas were pure gold. Hill claimed Andrew Carnegie as his mentor and the man who gave him the assignment to research and write about the best methods for succeeding in business and other endeavors. He also received introductions from Carnegie to other wealthy men, such as Henry Ford, resulting in interviews and discussions with these men. Napoleon Hill, however, attributed his best ideas to a certain presence looking over his shoulder as he was writing and a Mind to which he drew close in his daily meditations that lasted an average of three hours. Napoleon Hill clearly specifies the means to be used for contact with God: prayer. You ask God for what you desire

---

5. Martin Luther King Jr., *A Call to Conscience: The Landmark Speeches of Dr. Martin Luther King, Jr.*, ed. Clayborne Carson and Kris Shepard (New York: IPM in Association with Warner Books, 2001), 202-203.

with the greatest fervor and intensity you can muster, and you ask repeatedly until you're answered.

When a facsimile machine or computer is ordered to contact another machine, it issues that familiar tone that pierces your ears. It will repeat the call many times until there's a response from the other end of the transmission. "Mayday, Mayday" goes out from distressed ships or planes. The operator does not stop calling until a rescuer appears or the ship goes down. The male frog belts out its song all night until a female appears, and so does the male cricket. What message does the wolf howl at the moon? What's the meaning in the song of a pod of whales? These are prayers to the Divine Source of all life.

In ancient times, people sacrificed as they prayed. Usually, the victim was an animal. The ancient Greeks offered the entrails and blood to the gods. They rightly believed the Gods preferred these body parts. They ate the rest. In other cultures and pre-classical Greece, priests often sacrificed a human to appease the gods, as Agamemnon sacrificed his daughter Iphigenia to quiet the seas from Poseidon's anger for the crossing of the Aegean to Troy. The Mayans cut the heart out of the human sacrifice, a young warrior captured from the enemy as a rule, and the priest held up the still beating heart for all to see.

A sacrifice can be anything that you value greatly or your people value, and you give it up for your prayer to be answered. It's really a commitment. You are dedicating yourself this way to the pursuit of the goal. The message enters the subconscious mind after many repetitions and finds the link to Infinite Intelligence.

A sincere and firm promise to God may accompany a prayer. When I was in the middle of writing this book, I had an episode of acute gastritis that tortured me for many days, and I could not work. I made a solemn promise that I would dedicate myself to finishing this volume and avoid distractions and other pursuits. I begged for healing. God's grace, or my doctor's strong antacid prescription, quickly took away the pain, and I've been laboring well on this project ever since. Conclusion is near. I think you can expect from me, in the end, a strong commitment to Faith of some sort, with qualifications.

I'm reminded again of Michelangelo's Sistine Chapel painting of God and Adam reaching out to each other. Adam is reclining on the ground naked and stretches out his hand and finger toward the Heavens, where God, the image of an imposing older man, beautifully attired and with a magnificent beard, inclines his hand and finger to Adam. There's a gap between the fingers, like the synapse between neurons in the brain. The gap must be bridged before contact can be made. Our investigation here has to do with this bridging.

Concentration of the mind in meditation with prayer is the key to the divine portal. A powerful technique for prayer is visualization. An excellent little book on this subject is Shakti Gawain's *Creative Visualization*.

God wants to help us, but not too much. And He or She doesn't want to infringe upon our personal freedom of choice. We need to make up our own minds as to what we want and visualize it clearly. Then God will provide what is necessary for success, whatever that may be in our minds. That's the theory. As Napoleon Hill points out, "Be careful what you wish for,"[6] for it's likely to come true, and it may be the wrong thing. The genie in the bottle must be handled with great care.

Still, Shakti Gawain writes, "Every moment of your life is infinitely creative, and the universe is endlessly bountiful. Just put forth a clear enough request, and everything your heart desires must come to you."[7] Is this naïve and exaggerated? Perhaps, but the method works up to a point. A clear and definite purpose is necessary for success, and a strong desire for its achievement is critically helpful. The subconscious mind, the inner universe, or God, to some people, will not respond otherwise.

Action and effort follow a strong desire for something clearly perceived. That frame of mind also influences other people to cooperate or overcomes their objections and obstructions. When a person

---

6. Napoleon Hill, *Outwitting the Devil: The Secret to Freedom and Success*, ed. Sharon Lechter (New York: Sterling, 2011), 86.
7. Shakti Gawain, *Creative Visualization: Use the Power of Your Imagination to Create What You Want in Your Life* (Novato, CA: New World Library, 2002), 25.

or society has established a strong link with infinite intelligence, few obstacles will stand in the way.

When you link up with Infinite Intelligence, be sure you have the right connection; when you ask for something repeatedly from God, be careful of what you wish. Hitler and his Nazis were sure of their destiny and the rightness of their actions in founding the one-thousand-year Reich. But they were in the wrong. When we direct our prayers to Heaven, where do they go exactly? It's the quality of our deepest desires that determines the ultimate linkage. "As you sow, so you shall reap,"[8] according to Jesus. As you think and feel in meditation, so shall the linkage to the spirit world be. Because evil spirits abound in the world beyond, but there's only one Lord of Love.

6. Mysticism and Reason Can Work Together

I now come to the million-dollar question: can faith and reason be reconciled? Is it possible for a man of logic to be an ardent follower of some religious set of doctrines and still abide by the dictates of reason and scientific objectivity? Many scientists who believe in God and His commandments would respond with a "Yes!" They divide their minds into compartments: an innocent, childlike, ignorant, believing section and an objective, intelligent, open-minded, skeptical part. There is a place in our minds for rational faith.

The Nobel prize-winning philosopher Lord Bertrand Russell, who had a strict religious upbringing, later rejected Christianity and castigated unreasoning faith in two brilliant essays, "Mysticism and Logic" and "Why I am not a Christian."

Russell doesn't waffle in his position. He believes mysticism is bunk. But he can't do without faith altogether. He makes a statement in favor of enlightened humanism. He was actually a passionate advocate for peace and the preservation of human life together with Nature as a whole. He was jailed for his antiwar activities both during World War I and the Viet Nam conflict. He was in favor of fighting Hitler in World

---

8. Galatians 6:7 (NIV)

War II, especially after the Soviet Union was attacked. He considered Hitler a quintessentially evil personality that had to be fought. Was all this rational? Ultimately, he had to rely on his feelings and intuition for any of his social actions, as the rest of us must do.

As a teenager, I was in full agreement with Russell's atheistic opinions. Now, I am not so sure. There are indications that a wise and compassionate Entity rules over the universe. It's just very hard for our limited brains to fathom His or Her ways.

Can a dog understand what his master is thinking? No, but the dog can sense the master's feelings and intentions. So can we sense God's love for us, and we understand His or Her wishes that we serve by obeying the laws laid down. There's a clear message in all the Scriptures: God is served best when we look after our fellow humans and other creatures as the keepers of life and nature.

Having said these positive things about religion, I must also state that there has been so much nonsense and absurdity connected with the practice of most faiths that I continue to be sympathetic towards those that reject the whole gamut of dogmatic opinions about God and His or Her ways. I'm still searching for a methodology to sift through religious teachings from the world over to extract a few gems of truth regarding morals and destinies.

I'm still seeking personal inspiration in deciphering messages from the subconscious spirit gate so I can place confidence in them, as I do in scientific findings. I'm not thrilled by dogmas such as the Holy Trinity: The Father, the Son, and the Holy Ghost. Christians adhere to this belief, but Mohammed taught there's only one God, who doesn't require a son, but only a prophet once in a while to transmit fresh messages to us. Muslims have their own unfounded beliefs, I'm sure.

I object to people asserting that they know something is true without sufficient evidence. I hate fervent believers who charge at their neighbors, yelling, "infidels!" I loathe religious authorities who burn heretics. I despise moral majorities who want to impose their own ideas of what's right and wrong on other members of society.

There's a place in life for rational faith. Here are my guidelines. Accept spiritual findings with a grain of salt. Employ any religious belief as a working hypothesis, not as an absolute truth. I choose to believe there is a just and loving God. I like the idea of a wise guiding hand in Nature and in the lives of people, and I find it useful.

But I know I could be mistaken in this assumption and those that don't agree with me are free to go their way unmolested, as long as they leave me undisturbed in my pursuits. I like the idea of an afterlife—a part of me imperishable and eternal, which will fly to another existence after my body dies.

I fervently, but not dogmatically, cherish and admire my body, believing that it's priceless, a temple for my spirit to be maintained and put to good use for as long as possible. I value people, knowing each one is unique and potentially useful to society and Nature, and I enjoy being with people of all sorts. Also, I don't think that criminals are evil but only mistaken, misguided, or deranged, and they can be reformed and put on the right path with proper treatment to help others and not do damage.

If many of my beliefs are Christian, it's because I was raised as such or because these preferences are more workable and useful. I'm open, however, to differing opinions, and I'll not impose my ideas on others. Religion is much like art. There are fashions and different tastes in the arts as in religion.

Can you assert that Rembrandt was a true artist and his style should be followed, while van Gogh was a flake and his paintings should be burned? Well, the Nazis and the communists thought so. Our choice of artistic expression depends on our particular sensibilities, which change and cannot be universal for all. We naturally object to someone who wants us to like what he or she likes and doesn't allow us to follow our inclinations.

Our reason tells us to respect the beliefs of other people, though they may appear irrational to us. We should draw the line to new religious ideas only when they hurt others. If the zealot annoys us in public places, we can annoy him or her back, but please, let's not jail or kill an innocent believer. Let's laugh at the innocuous fanatic's foibles if the antics appear so to us, but let's not burn the fanatic in a gas chamber.

7. God Follows the Non-Interference Principle

The *Star Trek* sagas have popularized the notion that an advanced civilization should not interfere in the evolution of other societies when their spaceships land on other planets. Local societies and cultures should be free to follow their own course of development, even if apparent errors and injustices occur in such societies. Each planet inhabited by intelligent beings should be free to shape its unique character and style without an outside disturbance from the star travelers. To get the story going, though, in every episode where this non-interference directive is mentioned, the Captain and crew of the Starship are forced into a conflict with the absolute nature of the directive by their desire to help innocent victims. God follows the non-interference principle more strictly.

You might say that the directive in *Star Trek* stories was put into the script in order to be violated for the purpose of dramatic interest. Yet, it still makes sense in the real universe we live in to protect different infant cultures from being violated and overrun by superior force, as were many native civilizations by European expansion overseas during the so-called Age of Enlightenment. The Conquistadores devastated outstanding Mayan and Aztec cultures in Central America, as well as that of the formidable Incas in Peru.

Now, most religious people are frequently praying that God step in and straighten things out that have gone wrong in their society or their lives. Others complain that God "allows" horrible things to happen to innocent people. A child is dying from leukemia, and devout parents wonder why. How could Almighty God permit the death of their beloved child? What sort of heavenly justice is this? This is where the non-interference directive comes in.

We on Earth need to sort out these disasters for ourselves, almost in all cases. Very rarely, there's a miracle attributed to Divine Providence. God's grace descends upon the scene, and things go right when there was almost no hope. It's perhaps Nature's quantum mechanical display or God's compassion that overrules the non-interference principle.

After all, the God that mystics encounter in deep meditations may not be the Biblical God but a super-intelligent and vastly powerful alien being who loves all living entities in the universe, including our own misguided species.

In my inner travels, that's the Being that I've encountered. It's possible that this Being created our Earth and our heavens from the debris and desolation of the early solar system. He and She richly endowed our planet with the water and other compounds necessary for the evolution of life and watched over the web of organisms as it progressed to more complex and advanced systems. In the end, He and She selected one species of pre-human ape and breathed His or Her spirit into it. Homo sapiens, our ancestors, took up the business of worshipping the divine and creating civilizations.

If God is our Father and Mother in Heaven, God possesses some of the characteristics of all parents raising sons and daughters. Any serious parent will, upon reflection, appreciate the non-interference directive. You cannot control your child's life too much and expect proper growth to occur. An adult child requires that a parent mess with his or her life even less. It's best (I know, having raised two daughters) that you stay away unless total disaster is approaching.

Let young people make their own mistakes, not yours, provided they are not fatal, and thus they suffer and learn. That's how I learned to behave in my own life. If you have a young child, let it play as it wishes as long as it doesn't smash your grandmother's china or run out to play in traffic. God, as a vastly more powerful and comprehensive parent, may stay invisible, inaudible, and untouchable almost constantly.

If interference occurs in the life of a living entity, it grows in the ways of the caregiver and not in a unique and interesting way. A bonsai pine may be an art form, but it's not the plant that would have grown in nature. A housecat is very different from a bobcat. A dog is nothing like a wolf. Which is nobler? An apple that we eat is not like the wild variety. It has less resistance to disease and drought. We're not the slaves of God in spite of what Christian tradition suggests. God doesn't want us to be pets but true inheritors. We shall inherit the Kingdom of God because we possess the divine spark, small as it may be, and to that extent, we're gods with the freedom to choose good or evil, creating worlds of our own.

Here's another personal view. In my inner explorations, I have encountered a Benign Being of vast power and wisdom with a spirit, which was a brother of my own. The Spirit was both distant and intimate and knew my most secret thoughts and desires. I asked this Supreme Being that upon my death, to be allowed to remain on my beloved Earth and not be taken away to another world. He promised to let my spirit soar over the land and sea of this beautiful planet, over mountains and down green valleys. Here I shall be content forever, talking to the birds and animals, watching lush trees and grasses glow green, passing over my people, maturing gentle and kind and thriving in all countries, all cultures of the Earth.

God will not interfere with Earth's evolution, and I was asked to promise one thing to God in return. I am not to interfere also when spirit or talk or even whisper to the people of Earth, except in their dreams. Nonsense, you say? You may be right. However, I find joy in these images. And, perhaps, I will be allowed, on very rare occasions, to perform a subtle miracle and save something or someone of value.

8. We Are Spiritual Senders and Receivers

We'll get a little technical in this section, but don't panic, it won't get too hairy. In my graduate university work, I researched computers, communications, and controls, an area of study known as cybernetics in some circles. At the California Institute of Technology, I applied this approach to biosystems analysis and the process of perception. My training in technology has been broad and interdisciplinary, almost philosophical, rather than narrowly focused on a job category. I naturally jump over mental barriers and divisions to common concepts. I'll now explain how each one of us is potentially a spiritual transmitter and receiver.

Consider the case of entropy, a quantity involved in the second law of thermodynamics. Entropy is a measure of the disorder in a system. The second law states that a system, left to its own operation, tends to greater disorder, and its elements become uniformly distributed. On the basis of this law, some scientists have speculated that, eventually, the entire universe will reach that state and cease to function.

Yet, living things go contrary to this tendency. They possess "negative entropy" or "negentropy," according to Erwin Schrödinger in his book *What is Life?* Life builds order in the world and counteracts physical disorder. Now, entropy may be a physical quantity, but it's also a measure of information according to Claude Shannon's definition. Shannon, of Bell Labs, is generally considered one of the founders of modern information theory. This is one discipline where physical entities merge with mental or spiritual matters.

I've believed for a long time that information theory and its offspring, known as pattern recognition, hold the keys to understanding the mind and its connection with physical reality. Pattern recognition, by man or machine, is the process of organizing raw data into categories and appropriate responses. It's the beginning of intelligence. I did my PhD work at the University of Southern California in this field and its application to machine reading of handwriting.

What Shannon stated was that a proper measure of information is the degree of uncertainty in a message. That is, if there's nothing new in a message sent by the sender or transmitter, the receiver obtains no information, and energy might as well be saved by not sending the message at all. Quantitatively, this is expressed as the natural logarithm of the probability of an outcome, times the same probability, summed up over all possible outcomes, taken with a negative sign, since a probability is at most one and its logarithm negative or zero. Zero results in the case of minimum entropy of a certain event. That also possesses no information.

Outcomes are events of interest to us, which are random and unpredictable, as exemplified in gambling and other games. A very uncertain or improbable outcome delivers a large component of the information transmitted: it's the punch we get from a surprise. Impossible events, however, are excluded from this calculation, as the logarithm of zero is undefined (or infinite). As the system that sends the message increases in complexity, we get more information. Thus, the entropy or information of a coin toss is 0.346; of a die, it's 1.78; and that of a deck of fifty-two playing cards is 3.95.

What does all this have to do with God and our connection to Him? God's Heaven is one and is an integrated crystal with no parts, unchanging and eternal, according to earlier theories developed here. Thus, Heaven's entropy is zero, possessing no randomness and existing in perfect order, since God, Heaven's operating system, is perfect.

Messages from God, however, are very uncertain and incomplete. They reveal to us a little bit of The Truth at a time, only as much as we're able to understand and put into practice. Let's not forget the hypothesis that there's more than one sender from the spirit universe, giving us conflicting and contradictory information. We still have the ancient enigma of distinguishing instructions from God as opposed to those from Satan.

It appears that God is like a diamond, of one piece and very clear. But God has many facets, and the reflections we get from all the facets are infinite in number. What we perceive in meditation is surprising and illuminating, holding much information for us receivers, while for God, what He or She sends to us is known.

Let's look at this question another way. Every object in the world has a characteristic signature, what scientists call a specific spectrum of electromagnetic frequencies. The spectrum of our sun is characteristic, and so it is of the moon and every heavenly body. The EEG emanating from each human brain clearly identifies the individual, as much as the fingerprints, retina, voice, or genes. Such signatures can be imitated but not duplicated. They are fake van Gogh paintings, but careful examination reveals them for what they are. It's the same with God and the messages He or She is sending. Once they're truly recognized, they can't be confused with any other transmissions from other sources.

We know for sure that susceptible people, such as holy men and other mystics, receive information from sources outside their immediate experience and environment. The source is probably the subconscious mind in the receiver's body or from an outside transmitter-sender, which could be the Biblical God, a powerful alien intelligence, or some sort of tribal consciousness, made up of the minds in society, somehow connecting together. The messages are coded and require interpretation. They're also fuzzy, ambiguous, and uncertain.

Many of us mortals are followers and believers in such holy men and prophets. Their voices speak with certainty and unshakable conviction. That's one characteristic that makes them so persuasive and charismatic. But our favorite leader and prophet could be wrong or misguided. It's foolhardy and frivolous for him or her to be so certain about a vision that could be misleading.

The rest of us also are potential receivers and transmitters of God's message; it's foolish and dangerous to be blind, passive, and devoted followers when we can judge what is right for ourselves with God's light. Using our own minds, we'll avoid going over the precipice to disaster, as the German people and the Japanese did in World War II. It's best to be skeptical of leaders and cautious about the validity of their message, even if it means a loss of enthusiasm and drive. At least with skepticism, we don't hurt anyone.

9. Does God Need Us Humans?

If God is so powerful, wise, and immortal, why does He and She bother with us? Why should such a great Being be interested in creatures as small and miserable as humans? Nature on this planet certainly has little or no regard for any single life or even any species that crawls on the surface or swims in the seas. God cares for us because God needs us.

What makes God want to give the slightest attention to the suffering of a single human being? What makes us important and valuable to Him and Her? Why would a totally wise and content God care about praise, sacrificial offerings, or even devotion from beings as weak and foolish as we are?

Let's tackle these questions one at a time in a positive or negative way, as reason dictates. First of all, if God, as defined by religious scriptures, doesn't exist, He or She is then a product of our imaginations fired by subconscious fears and desires. God did not create humans, but rather humans have created God. If this is the case, God certainly has a great need for us to embellish and promote His or Her image. We come back here to the thesis of God as a powerful idea. Ideas originate in human minds. Humans are part of Nature. Therefore, God and Heaven grow and spread as a natural evolution of living things.

At some point in time, far into the future, God's Kingdom is established throughout the universe, and echoes from that temple reach back to us and prove the reality of God. This is similar to the event of Emperor Constantine's setting up of the Christian religion as the state faith of the Roman Empire or the introduction of the Orthodox Church in Russia by the czar. Official recognition makes an idea become a fact of life for all. That applies to religion as it does to political notions and economic systems, such as democracy, communism, nationalism, or socialism.

Now, let us consider the business of praising and glorifying God. It's true that human rulers and people of high status usually expect praise and esteem from their people: Excellency, Serene Highness, Lordship, Honor, Mighty Ruler, Holiness, and many such outrageous appellations are common in the company of the highly positioned. These types of address are offered with kneeling, bowing, and scraping in front of the Lord. The mighty are placed on high thrones, lavishly dressed in splendid robes and colorful clothing, and wear precious jewels, crowns, and other ornaments. There are some exceptions, such as the case of Mahatma Gandhi, who humbled himself extensively and wore the clothing of low-caste peasants when he assumed his mantle of holiness. Does God care for such stuff?

In prayers, we say, Almighty God, Hallowed be Thy Name, Thy Kingdom come, Glory, Glory Hallelujah, and many such encomiums. We sing hymns in praise of the Lord. We praise Him or Her for His or Her compassion and pity, for His or Her love and kindness, for His or Her might as Lord of the Hosts. For practical considerations, an earthly ruler may want his or her power and prestige enhanced among their own people and with foreigners by means of splendid titles, high seats, and deference.

Also, among a pantheon of many deities, godly jealousies and competitions would prompt praise. But a being with unlimited power, as the one and only God, clearly has no need of such. He or She is likely to be impassive to our praises, outcries, or curses, like a rock. His or Her concern would be with our doing the right thing in any dilemma we face, and He or She would not give in to our begging because we heap praises on Him or Her.

But does God care about our love for Him or Her? "Love Thy God" is the first commandment of the Hebrew God of Moses. What does it mean to love God? How do you love someone you cannot see, touch, or talk to? We love what we enjoy and what we cherish. We love what is of value to us and what is vital to our survival. We love those to whom we are bonded and connected, such as family and friends, community and country.

God can be such a person if we are able to sense His or Her presence and His or Her love for us. Why does God love us? Does a father love his children? Does a mother love her babies that she carried in her body and nurtured through infancy? God is father and mother to us, his or her special creatures, made in the image of His and Her spirit.

Does a father in his full prime and power need his children? Not really, not in any material way. A father needs to have his children do well, advance in their lives, and be responsible and self-sufficient. So, I think God's need of us has to do with our nations, societies, and our one species. So He or She does want and need to have every unique and individual soul of us grow fully and realize our true worth in our personal lives by actualizing our special gifts, our shining talents.

Does God have any need of us? Does a gardener have need of her garden? She goes around the gravel path to her roses and clips a few dead branches, digs out some weeds and pours some water into the roots with fertilizer. She stands up and gazes at the gorgeous blossoms. She cuts a few perfect ones to bring a bouquet to her home. So God gathers a few precious souls to His or Her bosom before their lives are played out with old and withered bodies.

Does a farmer need his wheat field or cornfield? He cultivates the field for his winter table and gathers the crop for the threshing floor. He keeps away pests and irrigates the soil as necessary. So does God gather our souls during the harvest of the Last Day, and good crops are saved, while spoiled seed is tossed aside. The good souls are needed for the nourishment of Heaven so that boredom and stagnation are kept at bay in God's mansions.

Does a shepherd need his sheep? He would be without an occupation if they were lost. He guides them onto green pastures. They shall not want. The shepherd loves and needs his flock, as a musician needs his violin, piano, or guitar. He carries the newborn lamb on his back so it doesn't fall behind the herd and get lost. He looks after the sick and the lame, giving medicine to the one and putting a splint on the other. The shepherd, with his sheep dogs and his staff, protects the sheep from wild animals and thieves. So does God guide us through our lives in this world and protect us from danger, as much as advisable, until the stable is reached, where we'll be safe all night long.

10. Let Us Recapture Our God Connection

We're here to provide a final answer to the question: is there anything real to this matter of communications with an Infinite Intelligence? Religion powers people to pursue great goals in all societies. It leads us to work, save, sacrifice, strive, and achieve beyond any reasonable personal wants. Religion, faith in God, and contact with Divine Intelligence are then of great value in our lives as individuals, families, and societies.

Persons geared towards business, such as Carnegie, Ford, Rockefeller, Getty, and Gates, accumulate vast riches during their lifetimes, only to give most of them away to charity, the arts, and the sciences. People with no money, such as Mother Theresa and Albert Schweitzer, devote their lives to the poor. On a grander scale, a little fellow with dynamite energies named Saul was inspired by Jesus on the way to Damascus and spread the Christian doctrine of sacrifice and resurrection throughout the Roman Empire. The Empire fought back and tried to squelch the new faith, but it was eventually taken over by Christianity.

Later, in the sixth century AD, a camel driver who was prone to meditate under the starry skies of the desert began to recite religious poems of great beauty and power about the One God. He united the Arabian Peninsula under his banner, and Islam spread west, east, and north with wars of conquest for the new faith.

Those killed in these wars to spread Islam were martyrs, destined for Heaven, and many still perish in Palestine in defense of the faith, strapped to bombs. God has always demanded sacrifices, going back to pagan times. Among the ancient Greeks and Romans, the ancient Egyptians, the Incas, Mayans, and Aztecs there were sacrifices of animals, sheep, goats, and cattle.

The Hebrews also sacrificed, and Abraham came close to shedding the blood of Isaac.

Sometimes there were human sacrifices, even children. Usually, slaves or battle captives were cut open at the altar; sometimes, that was the fate of a king, a beautiful maiden, or a young man victorious in sports. When disasters plagued the tribe, the gods had to be propitiated with blood. The skies, the stars, and the planets were carefully studied to determine the will of the gods.

What was the source of these notions about the sacrificing of present life and the persistent belief in an inevitable afterlife? Is the God idea a great illusion drawn from disturbances in the subconscious mind? Illusion or not, it's a grand concept. It's a majestic image that gives much meaning to lives, really trivial and short.

I feel the body I possess is like a candle burning to light the way for other spirits. This is the sacrifice demanded by God, not the slaughtering of innocent animals or human victims. Like many people, I've had the experience of contact with God on several occasions in my life. I may have been in delusion, but I don't think so now. There's a radiant thumb-size being in my heart, and there's one in yours, if you are able to concentrate well enough. This is not an easy task, and there are many pitfalls along the way, perhaps even mental derangement.

I think I've received some valid messages from a powerful and compassionate Being in my inner explorations: Life is to be cherished, loved, and prolonged. Every hour, every minute of living, is a precious jewel to be guarded and spent wisely. Great pleasures and other satisfactions are fine along the way, but hedonism is not the goal. Neither is the avoidance of pain, even anguish, if these are necessary for achievement.

What is achievement? What is worthwhile? That's different for each one of us, but some values are common to all of us. We need to preserve our lives; otherwise, we can't make use of them. We need to preserve our families and communities for the same reason.

Above all, our duty is to preserve the living Earth, with all creatures on it, for with the Earth lies the future of the next five billion years and evolution yet to come. It's better for our species to die out than for Earth to be destroyed completely because of our activities on it.

The directive to be kind and respectful towards all living things is another message. As God is compassionate towards us, it's fitting that we be so towards others. No being is unworthy if it contributes even a little to the advancement of life. Even strange alien creatures are all right and acceptable to me if they're not hostile.

Those who are aggressive and dangerous are to be avoided and contained, not fought and killed. Evil is to be disarmed and made impotent, as it's impossible to extinguish it. Evil is an idea, as is charity, and ideas are immortal, so they can't be eradicated. For example, drug use can't be eliminated, and the war on drugs can't be won. There will always be poverty.

As Jesus said, "You will always have the poor."[9] That doesn't mean that you can't help some of those who are addicted or some of the poor. It means that you accept poverty, disease, conflict, and disasters as part of the human condition and don't despair. Things are all right in Heaven. Here on Earth, we're on testing ground, where souls are tempered and proven for a higher existence.

These are the thoughts that emanate from my connection with God. Does the connection really exist? It seems to me that it does. Why not try it for yourself? Begin with a sincere and persistent effort at meditation. Come back to the question of God's existence in a year's time. I cannot prove directly and rationally any of the premises regarding God and His or Her commandments. I have assumed a

---

9. Matthew 26:11 (NIV).

working hypothesis that there's a kind and understanding but largely non-interfering God.

An afterlife follows the end of bodily existence. This afterlife is a fitting continuation of what we're doing with our current opportunities. The body I now operate is of little value, but it's priceless as long as I'm putting it to good use for its mission on Earth. This working hypothesis is useful to me in my daily living and has done me no harm.

My personal connection with God, real or imagined, has been a boon for my life and for those who depend on me. I'm at peace with myself, and I don't fear anything. Accidents, injury, pain, disease, misfortune, aging, death, none of these calamities disturb my dreams or my waking moments. Every human being is agreeable to me and I'm content with myself. I'm thankful to God, the Ideal Being, existing in my mind.

ADDITIONAL ESSAYS

1

LIFE AFTER DEATH

Belief in an afterlife is prevalent in all societies and cultures; the soul or spirit (consciousness and identity) continues after the dissolution of the body. Also prevalent is the belief in a Great Spirit, God, from which our souls derive and to which they go after death, perhaps to be sent again on another mission in a material body. Many philosophers, among them Socrates and Descartes, declared that spirit or mind, an immaterial and eternal component of humans, is a separate entity from the physical body it occupies. If so, we can have life after death, a life in which identity and consciousness continue.

Of course, the opinions of many people and great philosophers are not evidence for the existence of the afterlife. But we cannot ignore these opinions. They do lend a measure of support for the notion of an afterlife. We do count the votes of the population to make social decisions, and we must pay attention to the sayings of a man like Socrates, one of humankind's finest teachers, and to the writings of Descartes, who made fundamental contributions to modern mathematics and science.

Religious thinkers like Descartes, Spinoza, Jesus, Mohammad, Laotse, and Buddha all taught that the body dies but the soul lives on in another place, another time, in a different body, or in the domain of God.

We know that the body and the brain decompose after death into their constituent elements. Consciousness resides in the brain, as we can see when someone gets pistol-whipped. Consciousness and identity almost disappear when the brain partly shuts down in sleep. How can the body become alive again unless time reverses direction? It appears that the notion of life after death violates Aristotelian logic: A is B or A is not B; both statements cannot be true. But this reasoning is allowed in modern logic and quantum theory.

We may not now know of a process for the transfer of consciousness and identity, but such a process may exist in a universe with eleven dimensions, dark matter, and dark energy. We have come up with dark matter and energy in order to make observations fit the laws of motion and gravity as laid down by Newton and Einstein. Nature does not dictate any laws; we make up the laws as we go to predict outcomes and gain some control over events.

We cannot detect spirits with any of our scientific instruments, but also, we cannot detect dark matter and energy. We judge that dark matter exists because of the way stars rotate in galaxies and that dark energy exists because of the acceleration in the expansion of the universe; that is, we derive the existence of these things from their effects, which we observe. We can conclude the same about invisible spirits and God; they cause phenomena we can see.

Modern physics tells us that nothing is really lost in the world but simply changes form or place. Matter changes into energy, as in the sun, and energy can change into matter elsewhere, even in the Large Hadron Collider. Similarly, the spirit leaves the body but is not lost from the universe.

Yet, nobody has ever seen or otherwise detected spirits except those who imagine things as real, those who create illusions, sometimes honestly, mostly deceitfully. After three centuries of investigation, modern science has not found any clear evidence for the afterlife. We know of no process that transfers consciousness and a person's memories to another body or to a hypothetical heaven.

Modern science has its limitations. We observe that events in the universe happen in cycles: the sun sets in the West, but it rises again in the East; summer is followed by winter, and winter is followed by another summer. Consciousness and identity appear with birth, and they reappear after death. Not all events in nature, however, are cyclical. The sun will not rise one day after five billion years but will grow into a red giant and engulf the Earth.

Nature has larger cycles that we cannot observe within our own space-time continuum; one such cycle may allow for rebirth. Consider child prodigies in the arts and sciences, born with extraordinary abilities. We cannot attribute genius to genes or memes if a genius did not inherit them; we must look for another cause. The spirits of great geniuses may have entered these children. Operational abilities, not specific memories, are transferred to another existence after death. We don't recognize those who have returned from the dead because they lack specific memories from previous lives and because they inhabit bodies that look quite different.

All of us, not only prodigies, are born with some prior knowledge of the world, which implies that the soul brought this knowledge to the present. On the other hand, evolutionary biologists, such as Richard Dawkins, say that any prior information that we possess comes to us from our evolutionary past as our ancestors survived various challenges, information which is now in our genes and transfers to the brain when these genes are activated by triggers. Dawkins says that inborn operational abilities in child prodigies and idiot savants come about from rare combinations of genes and atavistic behaviors inherited from ancestors.

Science is a method for dealing with physical phenomena, doing experiments, observing, and measuring events outside our minds; spirits are inside our minds and cannot be measured. We do not perceive spirits with our five skin senses, but people and animals can experience spirits using a psychic connection. When people have established a connection with the other world through prayer and meditation, they can communicate with other spirits.

People in deep meditation, especially great mystics, sense the presence of an immensely wise, powerful, and compassionate entity—God. That is the unitary experience. The existence of God is indirectly supported by the achievements of those who contact God. These feats are beyond the normal abilities of a human being, such as the accomplishments of Saint Paul, Mohammad, or Joseph Smith of the Mormons.

It is also true that sensing and speaking with God or lesser spirits is common among mentally ill people suffering from delusions. If God is wise, all-powerful, and compassionate, why is our world replete with evil, anguish, and the random destruction of innocents?

God is all-powerful in the spiritual domain of Heaven. On Earth, God influences events through faithful creatures who serve the purpose of bringing life, peace, and joy to all. Satan rules in the spiritual domain of Hell and operates on Earth through evil bodily creatures to cause suffering and destroy good works.

Evolved as free agents, humans can choose good or evil. God hides any direct evidence of the existence of spirits, so we may choose freely to believe or reject religious messages, not through fear of punishment for our sins, but through our love of righteousness.

Does the fear of death make people believe that they will continue to exist after death in Heaven or in another body? People don't believe in the afterlife because they fear death; instead, they deny the afterlife for fear of punishment for their sins since nearly all are sinful rather than righteous.

Sinful or righteous, people have had near-death experiences well documented for large numbers of subjects. Subjects recall floating above their clinically dead bodies and entering tunnels with a bright light at the end, which emanates peace and joy. Those patients who felt sinful have had visions of Hell. Are these accounts trustworthy? We get these stories from drugged patients in surgery, dreams and images as the subjects emerge from their ordeal. Each experience is private and located in a patient's brain; it cannot be corroborated by others. Similarities in the accounts are due to a common religious upbringing.

But what can we say about paranormal phenomena? Serious and unbiased investigators have verified that humans possess abilities such as telepathy, telekinesis, clairvoyance, precognition, and medium skills. These abilities indicate that the universe is more complex and subtle than our science today reveals, allowing for the survival of personality after biological death.

In most cases, mediums and other paranormal practitioners are deluded individuals or fakers working tricks for money. The results most mediums produce have repeatedly been debunked, shown to be fabricated illusions, like the reported miracles of saints and prophets, offered up for consumption to the credulous.

The teachings of great mystics, however, are in a different category. We cannot set aside the sayings of Pythagoras, Socrates, Confucius, Jesus, Mohammed, and the Buddha, which have captivated the minds of humans around the world. In their meditations, the mystics experienced a separate reality from ordinary experience. Humans are capable of transcendental visions; we may even have a "God" gene to enable us for mystical insights.

Important philosophers and mystics may have believed in the immortality of the spirit, but their opinions are not objective evidence. Quite often, mystical experiences are worthless products of minds deranged by long fasting, psychoactive rituals, mushrooms, herbs, and other ingested toxic substances.

Whatever the cause of mysticism, is the existence of a soul necessary for the survival of living things in addition to the perpetuation of their genes and memes? Atheists claim that living bodies evolved naturally from material processes, which we will eventually duplicate in our laboratories. Organisms store energy that allows them to move, acquire fresh energy from their environment, replenish their stores, and duplicate their form or species.

Still, living objects have a quality not found in non-living matter. This quality is the force of life, or spirit, which allows them to move with a will and to experience consciousness and identity. The notions of the afterlife and God can be especially useful for our existence. Granted that many cheats and fanatics apply the afterlife idea wrongly, with this belief, we tend to honor our bodies as temples of spirits and treat our fellow creatures kindly. What is useful deep down has a strong connection with what is true; otherwise, it would not work.

Particularly appealing is the Hindu and Buddhist belief in reincarnation. We have innumerable opportunities to be reborn to a new life, adopt different behaviors, and perfect ourselves for Nirvana.

If the soul and God did not exist, we would have to invent them. Descartes regarded these notions as axioms, self-evident truths. We can use axioms and definitions to design theorems and theories for practical living, provided our theories don't directly contradict scientific findings. If theories don't work well enough, we modify our axioms and our theories to fit the situation and be successful.

Certainly, we encounter the souls of the departed in their works: writings, music, poetry, paintings, sculptures, scientific findings, and mathematics—everything men and women create in their lifetimes. The spirit of the creator is imprinted in the creation, and that spirit deeply influences the minds of the living to advance their own consciousness. The spirit of Thomas Edison lives in the lights that surround us, and the spirit of Jesus Christ guides our steps whether we recognize his divinity or not.

More importantly, our spirit and our God inspire us with ideals of beauty, perfection, and eternal truth, which transport us from a humdrum existence to sublime experiences and the creation of a world that matches our finest dreams.

2

LEVER AND LOGIC: MASTERING THE UNIVERSE

How can one be master of the universe without being God? God does not master the universe. He or She allows the universe to evolve with chaos and self-organization on its own. As humans, we use logic, our reasoning faculty with symbolic language, our machines, and our social structures to become masters of the Earth to a greater degree each passing year since the Dark Ages. We may master the universe eventually with logic, our mathematics, and our devices, if we don't destroy ourselves with our conflicts. Our mastery will not continue for long unless we first learn to master our own minds.

We are, to a large extent, masters of the Earth but not very kind masters. If we use our reasoning properly, we protect the Earth and its creatures from harm, and we stop warring against each other. We can use our great powers to prevent damage to the Earth from disasters such as meteors, volcanoes, tsunamis, and pestilence with all the tools at our disposal, tools that inventive minds have given us over the generations.

One such tool was the simple lever that can move large boulders. Archimedes worked out the principle of the lever mathematically. The force applied at the long arm over the fulcrum is multiplied by the ratio of the long arm over the short arm. Archimedes declared: "Give me a place to stand, and I will move the Earth."[1]

All other devices we have developed, from the wheel to the supercomputer, with our logic and mathematics and our dealings with materials and energies, are really extensions of the lever principle—mind over the physical world.

Now, as a human individual, not a society, you can acquire mastery first by learning to control your own mind, always doing what is logical, like the fictional Mr. Spock of *Star Trek*.

No, you don't need to deny your feelings and strong emotions. Do not allow feelings, however, to throw you into mental disorder. You always look to what is profitable, beneficial, and benevolent in your thinking and behavior.

With mastery of your own mind comes a gradual mastery of what you can control in your environment, just as the first human learned to control fear and handle fire, later learning to domesticate plants and animals for a reliable food supply, mastering famine.

What you cannot master in the world, you are ready to accept as is, bringing calm to your heart, so the universe remains congenial and peaceful. You will not be disturbed by anything.

No matter what disasters befall you in the world, with firm logic, you can say courageously with poet William Ernest Henley, "Out of the night that covers me, Black as the pit from pole to pole, I thank whatever gods may be For my unconquerable soul."[2]

Mastery is dominion over something with great skill and knowledge in exercising that power. The universe is reflected in your mind, at first, the only place where you may exercise dominion; therefore, you master the image in your mind or not.

If you can master the image of the world in your mind, you may acquire the ability to project that image as you want it modified to make it real in the external world.

---

1. T. L. Heath, ed., *The Works of Archimedes* (New York: Dover Publications, 2002), xix.
2. William Ernest Henley, "Invictus," *The Penguin Book of Victorian Verse*, ed. Daniel Karlin (London: Penguin Books, 1997), 564.

Logic, combined with mathematics, is the most powerful tool for shaping our minds and the universe as far as we can control it. Logic or reason is based on an exhaustive search of all possibilities, analyzed from truth tables and a few undeniable axioms. Rules follow to make the analysis easier.

Aristotle was the first to organize logical principles, but people have used logic informally ever since they began to think with symbolic language.

I have no desire to control the universe with my mastery but only to live in it well, benefiting myself and my fellow creatures. Only in that sense do I wish to be a master. Let the universe run its course, just as God lets it.

When I look at the world, I see perfection even where there appears to be chaos and evil; my object is to make use of that perfection for good. I am satisfied with the result, whatever the outcome.

Even a failure is something I endure with equanimity because every failure teaches me something of value.

The main value of logic is that it enables me to look at the universe objectively, as an impartial observer, even in situations when I face disaster and death for myself or those I love. I look at events with detachment, like a free spirit above the tumult.

With strong logic, I can stand above the fray of life, looking calmly at whatever happens. That is mastery too, even if I cannot control the situation. How do I try to accomplish such detachment?

"Know thyself" was a Greek aphorism inscribed in the Temple of Apollo at Delphi. When you truly know logic, you know the best part of your mind; you possess the mind of Homo sapiens people like you who acquired the use of symbols in communication and used the symbols or language to think more effectively.

Logical axioms or clear truths evolved together with our brains in dealing with the world as humans to master the environment. That is why we accept an axiom as true without doubt, such as not (A and not A); a thing cannot be and not be. Well, maybe it can, but that would not be an effective tool of thought ordinarily, except in Buddhist circles.

In ancient Egypt, the Luxor Temple had the proverb, "Man, know thyself, and you are going to know the gods."[3] The proverb implies that as a human, you have an element of the divine in you, an element that you enable when you look within deep enough. Hence comes mastery of the universe, a mastery to you and me and to humankind.

It's no wonder that persons who discovered their inner god and subsequently became kings or emperors often came to think that they were gods until, of course, in the end, they died—sometimes ascending to Heaven, according to the legends.

Gods are generally considered to be benign to humankind, wanting us to live, be happy and productive, helping if we do what we're told by the prophets. But godlike humans with great charisma and ability frequently do evil things, even when they are logical.

Logic does not dictate values; the things we want changed in the universe with our powers of induction and deduction. Logic is only a set of tools. Our feelings determine our goals and the energies we put into our endeavors.

You can expect that logic, the intellect, when active, tends to moderate your emotional responses to a situation. When you're upset, solve a mathematical problem, count birds in the sky, listen to Bach, you'll calm down.

Conversely, when your feelings are strong and rampant, the intellect tends to shut down, and you're unable to use logic well. To be the master of your universe, you need to balance your feelings with your intellect and never, never let go of logic.

---

3. Peter Cajander, *Fragments of Reality: Daily Entries of Lived Life* (Helsinki: Cajander Publishing, 2006), 109.

3

DOES THE LAW OF CONSERVATION OF INFORMATION HAVE IMPLICATIONS FOR IMMORTALITY?

In Search of Meaning

We have known since Sir Isaac Newton in the seventeenth century that momentum is conserved in a moving object. That is one of Newton's laws of motion. An object keeps moving at the same velocity unless something interferes with its motion. Science has also shown since the eighteenth century that energy in a closed system is never lost but conserved; energy may change form, but it remains constant. That applies to the universe if the universe is a closed system. Sixty-seven percent of the total energy in the universe is dark energy. In the twentieth century, Einstein and others proved that matter is equivalent to energy; so, matter may change to free energy and energy into matter, but the total remains constant.

Also, in the twentieth century, with the advent of quantum mechanics, science established that information as a total entity is never lost but remains constant. This law led to the paradox of black holes, which appears to have been resolved recently. Information destroyed when a black hole absorbs a body goes to the black hole's event horizon. How does the law of conservation of information relate to immortality? We, as individual entities, are bundles of information contained in our genes, memes, and what each one of us discovers. If so, then we are conserved as information after the end of the living body. We continue to live in our creative products, including our descendants. That may not be enough of immortality if you are religious, but it is something of value.

I understand that the law of information conservation was established for quantum mechanics with the "no-hiding" theorem and other such statements. Information is never lost and moves to the subspace of the environment. The New Age scientist Rupert Sheldrake calls this subspace a spiritual ether, which transfers information to related beings.

You may say now that the quantum world is not the same as the macroscopic world in which we humans live. Billiard balls do not obey quantum mechanics. But they do, although it is hard to detect their quantum or probabilistic behavior. Quantum phenomena were first studied with photons or light. Then we found electrons also followed quantum rules and we developed the electron microscope. Later, we learned that protons and neutrons also had a quantum nature, as well as atoms and, lately, molecules with up to 2,000 atoms. Billiard balls, you, and I also are quantum objects but with a much higher frequency or shorter wavelength of oscillation than atoms. We contain information in our bodies and minds, and we project that information to the outside world with our creations.

What, however, is information? It is a quantity in structures or patterns that have symmetry and organization. An example is music versus noise. Music is made up of organized sounds, standing waves with regular shapes. Noise is jagged and random. The musical works of great composers, such as Beethoven and Mozart, have this quality. So does the work of fine painters, such as da Vinci or van Gogh. Their creations are imperishable, immortal.

In past ages, artists with paint, marble, walls, notes, and movement followed rules of symmetry, such as you find in geometrical figures and other mathematical objects. Clearly, even a simple line drawing holds more information than a scrawl. Mathematical figures and other symmetrical objects were thought by Plato and other idealist philosophers to be perfect and eternal, coming to us from a timeless and imperishable world, or Heaven, if you like.

At Plato's Academy, a sign over the door proclaimed: "Let no one enter here who is ignorant of geometry." Indeed, we have no knowledge of what the source is of these mathematical patterns which we use so much in science and in technology. Do they come to us, these patterns, from Sheldrake's psychic ether medium? Certainly, if the information in these patterns is conserved, then they give us a glimpse of eternity. Moreover, to the extent we entertain such patterns in our minds or perhaps create them, we, too, participate in immortality.

The universe appears to obey rules of symmetry, which led us to conceive the existence of certain particles before we detected them in the lab, such as antiparticles, among them the positron, an electron with a positive charge. Time itself shows symmetries between the past and the future. The organization of the universe prompted Einstein to say that he wanted to know the mind of God.

Still, we have a contradiction in scientific thinking that we need to resolve. The second law of thermodynamics, amply demonstrated in the lab and outside the lab, states that a closed system always tends to greater disorder or entropy. Of course, that must be because the states of disorder in a system are far more numerous than the states of order. Yet, order exists, and it appears, or it is created somehow, sometimes by humans. Well, the law of entropy was derived for dynamic and moving systems of many particles, not for crystals or other fixed forms, such as the eternal forms of Plato. DNA, which holds our genetic information transmitted through the generations, is a carbon chain crystal and has persisted for billions of years in Earth's living systems.

In fact, living things can create negative entropy, or negentropy, according to Nobel Prize quantum physicist Irwin Schrodinger in his little book *What is Life?*

In conclusion, let me re-iterate. Information in a quantum system is not lost but transfers to the environment of the system. All physical systems are quantum, although that may not be apparent in the behavior of large, macroscopic objects because of very high frequencies of random vibration.

In theory, at least, information that is transferred to the environment can be retrieved to reconstruct the system. We know, for example, that we can reconstruct an organism that has become extinct from a DNA sample we have found in the fossil record.

We reconstruct ancient artifacts from the ruins of past civilizations. The Acropolis with the Parthenon in Greece has been reconstructed partly in numerous buildings in Europe and America. We have reconstructions of ancient Pompei, which was destroyed by Vesuvius and buried in ash. The same is true for diggings in the Cretan palace of Knossos and the ruins of Santorini Island in the Aegean Sea.

We also can access genetic information that tells us much about our origins. The DNA of Native Americans tells us much about their arrival from Asia to the American continent about fifteen thousand years ago. So, perhaps nothing is lost, not even you and I, and we are preserved in some form in our environment to be reconstructed someday.

Vista, California
March 2023

4

CAN SCIENCE BE A GUIDE TO MORALS?

Religion has been the source of moral guidance. Now, some philosophers, such as Richard Dawkins, Dan Dennett, and Sam Harris, deny the existence of God and a good role for religion in ethics; these philosophers, like Bertrand Russell before them, propose that we can establish morality with science rather than religion. Can scientists play the role of ethical teachers? Yes, scientists can throw light on some moral questions, but the scientific method was not devised for that purpose, and it will do poorly in giving us guidelines on how to behave toward ourselves and our fellow humans, as well as other living things.

The founders of modern science in seventeenth-century Europe, men such as Francis Bacon and René Descartes, were Christians who did not doubt God and the Scriptures, the Old and New Testaments. If you have faith in scripture, you just follow its commands without questioning. Bacon and Descartes wanted a reliable method for finding out what was clearly true in nature, what *is*, rather than what *ought* to be, as religious skeptic David Hume put it a century later in the Age of Enlightenment. We would have to modify the scientific method to enable it to tackle ethical issues. It would be a mistake to do so because ethical or value considerations detract from the objective attitude of science, which has proven very useful in investigations, in effect mixing religion in the pursuit of what is true.

Religious ethicists, like Moses, the Buddha, Jesus, and Mohammad, claimed that God revealed to them moral guidelines that people should follow. God carved the Ten Commandments on stone with heavenly fire. God commanded Mohammad to recite, to be the voice for the teachings of Islam. In deep meditation, the Buddha and Jesus discovered moral dicta inspired by Heaven. Followers of these prophets don't need to puzzle as to how they behave. Followers have their ethics laid out for them, like food from a master chef.

The rest of us are condemned to agonize about what is the right thing to do or the wrong thing to avoid.

We may turn to philosophers for their opinions, which do not have the authority of religious proclamations. Socrates, as expressed by his student Plato in the dialogues, taught self-examination, respect and service to one's country, and seeking the truth and other virtues. Most philosophers have given their version of ethics or virtuous behavior, including Aristotle in his Nicomachean ethics books, which expound on his basic concept of *eudaimonia*, or well-being and happiness of persons, our reason for living.

The cynic philosophers, such as Diogenes, dwelt on the values of simple living, in imitation of the dog. Epicurus proposed hedonism, the pursuit of pleasure in the company of good friends. The stoics, among them the slave Epictetus and the Roman emperor Marcus Aurelius, believed in being content and tranquil no matter what misfortunes fate might bring.

Spinoza wrote an interesting treatise on ethics, setting out his arguments in terms of corollaries, lemmas, and theorems, like mathematics. Kant wrote on ethics, and Bertrand Russell penned a little book, *The Conquest of Happiness,* on the value of work, family, effort, and resignation. Nietzsche held the view that the *ubermensch*, or the superior man, was entitled to setting his own ethics in achieving his life purpose, with all others serving him as a people serve their emperor.

Essentially, philosophers express their personal feelings about what is the best way to live. They don't provide an objective foundation for ethics. If you like a philosophy, say stoicism, you live accordingly.

Alternatively, you may follow the sentiments of prominent literary persons, such as Fyodor Dostoyevsky, Franz Kafka, George Orwell, or Aldous Huxley. Why follow one thinker's sentiments rather than another's? Again, you end up adopting what you feel deep down. As the old sophists declared, man is the measure of all things, and we end up in a chaotic world of values.

Of all mental disciplines, the scientific method has been most effective in dispelling chaos and enabling technology to cure many unhappy conditions for mankind, such as disease, poverty, famine, and powerlessness in the face of natural disasters. Where religious teachings have failed, some scientists want to step in and offer solutions to moral issues.

Bertrand Russell was not a scientist but a philosopher, logician, and mathematician who admired science and doubted religion. He lectured on "Why I Am Not a Christian," a polemic against the faith that he was taught as a child and abandoned in favor of science, logic, and free thinking.

Russell taught that religion had done more harm than good with dogmas and the persecution of those who did not choose to abide by the prevalent faith of society. Yet, Russell admired many Christian virtues, such as kindness, generosity, compassion, and love of mankind. With his ardent efforts to prevent war, cruelty, and injustice, Russell fought for humanity, although he denied the existence of God and the afterlife.

In our time, philosopher and cognitive scientist Sam Harris has shown the same passion for humanity and against religious authorities, particularly the Muslim faith, which he castigates for all manner of evil —unjustifiably.

Harris bases his ethical theory on what adds to human well-being and what improves living conditions: what causes pain, unhappiness, and damage to humans is bad or evil and is to be avoided. That sounds good, but we must specify who's well-being we're talking about. Is it the well-being of masters or of slaves? The ancient Spartans in Greece enjoyed power at the expense of helots, who were horribly oppressed, and the same situation existed in the United States, with plantation owners enjoying opulence and splendor from the sweat of African slaves. Interestingly, these slave owners were generally religious and taught their slaves to be good Christians.

Still, attacks on religion by Harris, Richard Dawkins, and philosopher Dan Dennett are unjustifiable because all major religions admonish us to be compassionate, generous, and forgiving, kind to widows and orphans and to all those unfortunate people who suffer through no fault of their own. That some religious people turn to cruelty and violence is not a reason for blaming the entire religious community.

Overall, the major religions have contributed to the betterment of mankind and the world at large, particularly the Christian religion, which has so strongly fostered love among all humans, and Hinduism, which extends that love to animals. Buddhism, an outgrowth of Hinduism, is particularly commendable in its teachings of love for all sentient beings and the alleviation of suffering with compassionate meditation.

Militant atheists blame religion for many bad events, but they should only blame fanaticism or extremism. The Dark Ages have unjustly been blamed on the spread of the Christian religion. Ignorant invaders from Northern Europe destroyed Greco-Roman culture in the West. Monks in monasteries preserved some of the ancient literature, arts, and sciences, and the Greco-Roman Byzantine empire in the East also saved much until the fall of Constantinople in 1453. Many scholars in Constantinople escaped to the West with their manuscripts to help kindle the Renaissance in art and scientific endeavors.

Science can throw much light on the human condition, especially psychology, sociology, and anthropology. We're social animals, more like wolves than bears, and as such, we tend to love our relatives and our tribe.

A scientist, however, does good work when thinking objectively about what is, not about what one wants to be. Yes, a scientist may be motivated by curiosity, a sense of wonder at the marvels of nature, the desire to help others with discoveries, to earn a salary, or to get a grant; it's okay to be subjective in this way. In doing research, however, the scientist must consider only what is the case in nature, not how nature *should* be.

Therefore, we cannot expect science to provide us with a value system. How do we get one, then? We get our ethics through introspection, looking inward into our own psyche, which has evolved along with our bodies. We are going through an evolution of consciousness, which began many years back with the emergence of culture out of savagery.

We no longer feel that enslaving other people or beating women and children is acceptable behavior because they are not strong. We don't sacrifice children or even animals to the gods.

Religious prophets may get messages from a cosmic source about the right way to behave, but all of us can tap the source to some degree if it exists. The message is often filled with static, or simply, it is misunderstood by us or our prophets, but it appears to be coming in continuously and is changing our societies.

Listen to the inner message carefully; consult your favorite prophet, philosopher, literary artist, or even visual or auditory artist such as Mozart, and draw your own conclusions about what is right. Always, however, reserve some doubt about your ethical opinions. You could be wrong, so be humble and continue listening, thinking, and feeling deeply.

5

GOD IS THE GREAT INVESTOR (AND WARREN BUFFET IS HIS PROPHET)

God is Great, says the Quran, and Mohammad is His Prophet. At the beginning of each passage in the Quran, God is also declared to be compassionate and merciful. God is the creator of the world and of humans and will be their judge on Resurrection Day. The Hebrew scriptures give similar attributes to God, who is also wrathful on occasion when His chosen people misbehave: fornicating unlawfully, worshiping idols, and neglecting to pray to Him; then God allows famine, war, pestilence, and enslavement to fall upon His people. The Christian Bible, which plagiarized the Torah in the Old Testament, speaks of all these qualities of God, who is also our Father, especially the Father of the Son, of the same substance as God, all-powerful, all-knowing, everywhere present in the universe. He feels pity for people on occasion, forgiving their sins and intervening with a miracle or two to cure them of deadly diseases or other ills. I say God is a great investor, and Warren Buffet is His prophet.

Pray to God, the Great Investor, and honor His prophet, Warren Buffet.

Why is God an investor, and Warren Buffet His prophet? The prophet, we know and hear, and then, through the prophet, we learn about God Investor Almighty. We know Warren Buffet as "the Oracle of

God Is the Great Investor (And Warren Buffet is His Prophet)

Omaha" among investors, in 2008 the world's richest man, having surpassed Bill Gates of Microsoft Corporation.

Bill Gates founded and managed Microsoft, growing it to become one of the most valuable corporations in the United States and the world. Buffet bought his company Berkshire-Hathaway, a textile company, converting it into an investment corporation. He has bought major positions (large chunks of stock) in traditional corporations, such as Coca-Cola, See's Candies, and Geico Insurance, holding the stock and exerting some influence on the companies by appointing directors. He holds stocks for many years, usually not getting involved in company management. Occasionally, if one of his companies flounders, he places a management team to run the company until it is on the right track.

Warren Buffet invests in companies he judges to be more valuable —having the potential to earn higher profits—than other investors recognize. He does not like to speculate, generally avoiding "hot" stocks in high technology. He has a following of devotees, like any bona fide prophet, who throw their chips on the same bets he has made. Nobody quite matches his performance.

Warren Buffet is God's prophet because he has a vision of supporting men and women with his money, i.e., any resources money can buy, people capable of turning a profit in their operations, enriching their community and the world. He pledges to donate 90 percent of his estate to charity; in the meantime, he holds on to his money to keep growing it for the sake of charity when he is gone. Buffet has the best of both worlds, present and promised. I follow him, clutching my money tightly, enjoying it in life until the government, charity, and heirs take it after my body is certified dead, then seeking my reward in the next world.

Prophet Buffet preaches investing in sound companies, companies with effective management teams, marketable products, continued prospects for profits, valuable assets, and low ticker prices. Investors listen carefully to him, but most of them chase after the idols of greed, quick appreciation, and speculative profits. The true and faithful zealots prosper with Buffet, holding their shares of Berkshire-Hathaway close to their hearts at about $100,000 each.

Pay close attention to the words and deeds of Warren Buffet, the prophet, if you want to be among the chosen few who can own stocks each at a six-figure price. His sermons are of traditional economics, not momentum strategies of going with the crowd; make Paul Anthony Samuelson's *Economics: An Introductory Analysis* your bible and pick your daily prayer from the *Wall Street Journal*.

With the help and guidance of the Great Investor, Warren Buffet performs an occasional miracle, saving from bankruptcy a desperate company, with proper intervention in the company's affairs; otherwise, he watches over his investments from afar and above in Omaha, Nebraska. Every few years, the prophet will shift his investment from a non-performing company to one with better prospects, but as a rule, he is loyal to his chosen people. Buffet's chosen people must play by the rules and laws of the country and of business to deserve his loyal support and compassion. When the people err in one of his companies, he and his God do not persecute, punish, or condemn, except by withdrawing investments.

God, the Investor, is Great; wise beyond our comprehension are He and His prophet, Warren Buffet.

Leave not the bulk of your estate to heirs, Buffet preaches; leave it to worthy causes doing good works, avoiding inheritance taxes. Invest most of your earnings and re-invest appreciated assets, trading up to avoid capital gains taxes. Life is short, but not for well-managed and well-positioned corporations like Coca-Cola or Geico Insurance. Own stocks in corporations with unlimited life spans.

Like Mary Poppins, Warren Buffet is very nearly perfect, at least as an investor. His God is the ideal of perfection in investment know-how, as He is our ideal for other attributes: wisdom, knowledge, kindness, and power.

What we sense about God is an entity like Nature, laying down laws, rules, or regularities in the phenomena we observe, regularities such as gravitation, electromagnetism, relativity, evolution, or justice. Make use of the laws of Nature or God; you are more likely to succeed, flourish, and survive. Ignore the rules; you are not going to be around for long as a living person or an investor. Democritus, 600 BC, spoke of necessity and chance ruling the world. The laws are necessary, but chance is behind the scenes, churning events. Even the most regular phenomena possess random elements. Who expected venerable Citigroup to lose billions in mortgage securities? As an investor, you face risk; the greater the apparent risk, the larger the profit potential because risk scares off others, afraid of it more than you are. You can take calculated risks, as Warren Buffet does, to succeed more often than timid people in investments.

God likes to play dice with the universe, to misquote Einstein on quantum mechanics.

Why so? God-Nature challenges every living thing to change, evolve, and get better; He gives us all random testing, even investors—especially with investors—because He is the ideal Great Investor. We face the unexpected, even the bizarre, outcome in our investments at irregular intervals. The business cycle puzzles us, with a recession starting the moment our head is turned away from the economy or a big boom in assets and profits when we are on a long vacation. Thus, God-Nature promotes and distills our spirits, separating the sheep from the goats: those who are to continue His works from those cast aside to oblivion.

Some people believe God arranges events to determine our fate; others say Nature is a blind force, acting on its own, with no regard for us, favorable or unkind. Certainly, God is a passive investor in the universe, in our own lives, and in our societies, letting chips fall where they may, allowing us the freedom to succeed or fail; on rare occasions, He appears to intervene in our affairs, performing a small or large miracle that we do not expect from blind chance. Is that not how life emerged on our planet billions of years ago?

Science explains the phenomena we observe through the actions of natural laws without Divine Intervention. A few events we encounter are puzzling for science and reason. Such is the appearance every century or so of a gifted person, talented with skills, imagination, and creativity of fantastic proportions: Democritus, Archimedes, da Vinci,

Galileo, Newton, Shakespeare, Gauss, Beethoven, Einstein, and such, luminaries who guide our progress to the future. A rare combination of genes explains such phenomena for some commentators; for others, such innovators and creators are miracles of God.

By and large, God applies the *Star Trek* principle of non-intervention on our planet. We are free agents to determine our own fate, good, bad, or indifferent. Like Warren Buffet, God is an investor allowing us, the managers of our world, to make decisions freely and take credit or blame for our mistakes. If we manage poorly, we simply lose out on resources to carry on with our lives.

We should take this lesson to heart in considering the use of Earth's resources; they are finite, and spoilable. When the forests are gone from the face of our lands, their cool comfort does not come back readily; when the ozone layer is depleted, when with excess CO_2 planetary warming has run away; when the oceans, land, and air are polluted; our blue-white planet will not be as hospitable and profitable for humans or other living things. Then without recrimination or wrath, God invests His resources in a different planet, with better managers of operations than Homo sapiens.

6

ON CHARITY AND RUTHLESSNESS

Americans subscribe to charity in a variety of ways, helping the poor and hungry with soup kitchens, clothing, and other care. We donate to hospitals and libraries, to orphans and the disabled, as private individuals, as members of our church, and as governments. We have a welfare system for the poor and unfortunate supported by our taxes, a safety net for the unemployed and unemployable, single mothers, and their fatherless children. We offer free schooling for twelve grades, and our taxes or donations subsidize colleges and universities to educate the people in general knowledge and specific professions or trades. To a large extent, our charitable attitudes are derived from the Judeo-Christian-Muslim tradition. But going further back, charity has its roots in tribal affiliations, looking after the unfortunate in the clan. Societies have existed, however, in which ruthlessness, not charity, was prevalent toward weak members.

Most recently, the Nazis in Germany ran a ruthless society from 1933 to their defeat in 1945. In ancient Greece, Sparta was a society that treated all members harshly to shape men into warriors and women into strong mothers of warriors. Spartans were especially harsh on their large population of helots or slaves who worked in the fields and the trades. Nietzsche was a philosopher who espoused such attitudes in favor of outstanding men versus the common mass of mankind, and he declared Christianity to be the ethos of slaves. Although my heart pulls me toward compassion for my fellow human beings and for animals who suffer, I find considerable merit in the philosophy of ruthlessness. I tend to practice ruthlessness mainly on myself, not feeling sorry for me no matter what awful things happen to me and to work on getting tough in difficult circumstances, avoiding as much as I can seeking help from others. I inherited such an attitude probably from my mother who was always kind and tender toward other people but, like a saint, strict on herself. People who are kindly behave kindly, and those who tend to be ruthless behave ruthlessly.

The Nazis put to death in concentration camps not only Jews, whom they judged to be subhuman, but also mentally handicapped people, communists, and gypsies in a eugenic effort to cleanse the German Aryan population of inferior inherited characteristics. Eugenics got a bad reputation with the Nazi experiments because the Nazi's basic assumption that certain ethnic groups were inferior humans but Aryans were superior was false. Biologists know, however, that herds need to be culled to be strong and healthy, and predators in the wild perform the function of culling herds by eating the weak members of the herd as a rule. That's why wolves were brought back to Yellowstone National Park.

If a herd is approached by predators, the adults may circle around to protect the young with their size and horns, and the weak members also get protected. Predators try to stampede the herd so that each member is running to save its life, and those who cannot run fast enough are taken by the predators and will thus no longer contribute to the gene pool.

We humans, during our evolution, have developed such powerful tools and weapons, as well as social structures, that we no longer have large cats or crocodiles preying on us to cull our groups. The natural degradation in our gene pool has produced many unfit human beings with defects, which individuals are a burden on society and cause the deterioration of its overall health. We still have with us, however, tiny predators such as parasitic bacteria and viruses. These predators do the culling now to some degree and they adapt to counter our antibiotics and our vaccines. Periodically, these micro-organisms cause plagues and pestilence, which is not necessarily bad for the race, although cruel and ruthless in the extreme to individuals and families. Populations recover quickly after enough people have developed immunity, and these stronger people reproduce more successfully.

Another way the group gene pool improves is when males fight each other for females; the strong males get to do most of the reproduction. Primates do that also, and humans (according to DNA studies) reproduced the same way until they settled down to agriculture with pieces of land for each couple and their children. Human societies changed with agriculture and monogamy. Cooperation among males became more important than competition. Females acquired more status and their motherly influence changed ethics toward the weak or disadvantaged members.

Warfare continued with other tribes and men were killed defending the group. The tribe had to look after the widows and orphans. Specialized trades emerged and it turned out that even a weak or handicapped male could be a very skilled worker benefiting society. A society that looks after every one of its members has greater cohesion and fellowship, so in difficult times, people are more apt to work together to overcome problems.

On the other hand, groups which compete with other groups are likely to perform better. Consider athletic teams and business organizations. In a free-market economy companies compete fiercely for sales with other companies in the same product; the result is that the customer is better served than in a communist or socialist country; the customer has a far greater choice of better products in a capitalistic economy.

Our species has certainly developed greater abilities through ruthless competition among ethnic groups, bloody and destructive as that competition may have been on occasion with warfare. Such competition did not necessarily result in the survival of the fittest, but at least it promoted the genes of those more capable. The business of ruthlessness in such competition eliminated those actors who could not compete effectively in war or trade. This process of human evolution of human groups through competition is continuing today. It is bound to advance mankind unless it goes to the extreme of a world war with nuclear weapons or other means of mass destruction.

7

HOW TO BE AN ANGEL

You want to be an angel, my friend? Angels are beings of the spirit and imagination, messengers from Heaven, sent to bring us divine messages and guidance in times of crisis, catalysts for change. Seen only in dreams, angels are invisible, weightless, subtle, and impenetrable to all our scientific probes and to all our senses, except our sixth sense, but they can be mental and emotional entities also—like the myriad powerful ideas from calculus to cognitive therapy fertile human minds have devised, to be used as needed for our purpose.

Let us begin by assuming our purpose as angels is to see people lead better lives: lives free of addiction, such as alcoholism, overeating and obesity, kleptomania, drug addiction, smoking, filthiness and messiness, rudeness and aggressiveness, obsessive gambling, shopping and borrowing, hoarding, overworking, and numerous other sins of commission and omission. We want to bring the people we love from the edge of destruction and despair to lives full of health, vigor, joy, and usefulness. Normally, we cannot bring grown people to change their habits, but if we can help them change, how do we seek our purpose?

Certainly, we want to change people using no force, no punishment, no intimidation, no coercion, no pressure, no dominance, no cruelty, no violence, no chains, and no big stick. Such tools for persuading people may have worked in the Dark Ages, but they are the tools of demons, not angels.

I am not saying such tools don't work today. They work well for the Marines who build boys into men—and also for such leaders as Hitler, Mussolini, and Stalin. A dictator can mold public opinion, discipline dissidents, and shape lives into productive units for purposes of the State. People in prisons are rehabilitated, sometimes. Clinics strictly controlling addicts and their environment may change destructive ways permanently. Large corporations run training camps to reconstruct failing managers under threat of dismissal. Military academies and preparatory schools have been noted for their successes in molding young lives with harsh discipline, such as the fictional Welton School in *Dead Poets Society*. It has been said that the British Empire of old was run by the graduates of Eton and other such boarding schools. Religious cults, monasteries, communes, and salvation charities have taken derelicts and turned them into functioning human beings to promote a doctrine.

Such is not our purpose. Subtly, indirectly, invisibly, gently, passively without action, like angels, we guide those we love for their own good. We do not want to intervene actively in lives unless it's necessary.

We don't want to use any overt or strong actions or words; not dictating, we allow people to act on their own initiative. Think of how God, that all-powerful idea, approaches us. Many people doubt God exists—so invisible and impervious to our sense and senses God is. Let us be as impassive as God then. To be otherwise would render those we love less free to create their own destiny.

Destinies are mangled by authors who teach how to win friends and influence people for personal gain; that is the easy way to power, which we don't want to follow in our mission. We seek no personal gain. We have come to own all we want and need for our own happiness and now desire to bring some of the fruits we gathered on our road to others.

Most people begin an angelic existence as parents, looking after the fruits of their loins. Parents do just fine, usually, until their children are grown—then they often mess up (the parents, not the children). Now, parents love their children as well as ever, but at this stage of life, they wax critical about most of what their offspring do: they try to control the actions of their children as they did when their children were small. No wonder teenagers are often so rebellious. Criticism is out. Forget criticism for children or any person you want to influence for good. Criticize, and you are only asking for resistance to anything you suggest.

Never criticize, scold, or reprimand workers also, those you supervise; workers are not your slaves, as children are not your property. Workers and children own themselves and deserve their share of dignity. Your spouse needs respect too, weaker than you though she or he may be. The constant bickering of some couples as they seek to change each other leads nowhere except to divorce or worse. Praise your spouse, or your house may fall on you and crush you; don't complain and criticize. You chose to tie your life to this person freely, knowing the character residing therein; character alters very rarely after the age of five. Before you weld yourself with someone, expect that they will not get rid of the habits you dislike but rather will grow them deeper, higher, and thornier because that's how it goes nearly always. If you can live with this prospect, go ahead, weld and satisfy your desire to wed.

The Hindu Upanishads say, "As your deepest desire is, so is your character; as your character is, so is your destiny."[1] Sometimes, character will change for the better, given a very intense and persistent desire for the needed change. But before we can use desire to motivate, our loved ones need to realize they have a serious problem damaging their lives. As it goes in many stories, the hero comes to realize he has been too proud, like Mr. Darcy in Jane Austen's *Pride and Prejudice*; the heroine comes to realize, like Scarlett O'Hara in Margaret Mitchell's *Gone with the Wind*, she has been foolishly in love with the wrong man and had spurned her true mate. Similarly, the prodigal son comes

---

1. Eknath Easwaran, ed., *The Upanishads*, (Tomales, CA: Nilgiri Press, 2007), 127.

home to his father after losing all his patrimony, ending up living in a pig sty, where he becomes aware of the error of his ways.

The realization of a character fault by our loved one may come on its own one day, or more often after a major crisis and shock to the system, such as a deadly illness or other great loss. Thus, we come to the scene on a hospital bed when the wrongdoer awakens after a terrific accident, which leads to the confession of guilt. Alternately, the loved one looks over us as we lie dying and is led to the realization of sin.

If we want to spare our loved ones and ourselves from such a dangerous crisis, how do we go about awakening to the realization of error and change in habits? We may use any of several methods, none of them guaranteed to succeed, known in cognitive psychology as intervention.

First, in intervening, we may guide our loved one to confront a crisis less dangerous than the one that will inevitably follow from bad behavior. Like a doctor inoculating a patient, we induce a challenging crisis for our person, which must be met only by shaking off bad behavior. A change of place or country with a new environment may do the trick, such as it happened to Mr. Micawber, the perennial debtor waiting for something to turn up, in Charles Dickens's *David Copperfield*, shipped from debtors' prison in London to Australia; there he prospered.

Second, pick a person to confront the addict in a heart-to-heart talk to shock loose the needed realization of sin. This person must be someone whom the addict loves, respects, trusts, and admires most in the world, a close friend, family member, physician, minister, or other professional. Unless you are such a person, don't attempt confrontation yourself. You are very likely to elicit an antagonistic response.

Third, in some successful situations, the family and close friends get together for the confrontation, as they did for Betty Ford, the American President's wife, who drank to excess. They begin by expressing their love and affection for the errant member; then, they confront the miscreant with the full import of the character flaw. Now, the loved one must acknowledge guilt and seek help; otherwise, no further progress can be made, and there will be no intense desire to change.

Normally, people do not change, behaving as their genes and early environment dictate they should behave; you can get hoarse telling them what's right to do without any result on their behavior. Nearly no one has a free will to do what reason dictates. But after our family confrontation with the wrongdoer, should we never criticize? What about the erring children, the students making mistakes in their assignments, and the employees causing damage to your operation with faulty decisions? Consider this first: are you sure your ways are the right ways and theirs wrong?

We are sure the ways of our enemy are wrong. What do we do when we are attacked? We defend ourselves: that is the moral and legal rule. We need, however, to make sure we are in the right. Jesus said, "Love your enemy."[2] Such advice may be hard for us to follow. Remember, though, we are not talking about enemies here but loved ones who may cause damage to themselves or others. Therefore, if you clearly see serious damage coming, you will prevent it in every possible way, but don't waste your time and energy pointing out faults.

Fault finding is a highly ineffective technique for influencing others. You think you are helping the object of your attention, but the object thinks you are hateful and hates you back. Unless you enjoy being hated and being ineffectual, don't speak to anyone about anyone's defects because, almost certainly, word will get back to the party you criticize. Speak only of a person's good points, which you can honestly discover; no person is devoid of all merit.

Look hard for something your student, child, friend, or employee is doing right and point to that. This way, you'll reinforce good behavior; bad behavior, given no attention from you, will tend to extinction. Teach by example, engaging in the right behavior in similar circumstances without bragging or lording over the person you want to influence. Teach by going through the same right action over and over in different ways, making your action into a model easy to follow. Teach by feeling enthusiastic, moving vigorously in the proper course for success. Say very little, as words in such circumstances have few uses

---

2. Matthew 5:44 (NIV).

and tend to annoy. Influence by just existing in your special world of adjustment and contentment and let the spirit of your philosophy be absorbed by osmosis.

Influence people like a lighthouse in the stormy dark, quietly shining over the rocks. Be there to guide others, like Polaris in clear skies, distantly shedding your few precious beams to those lost on seas of old.

Those who are lost and not seeing the light need help too. Prodded by thorny genes, impelled by early dark voices, they walk with nasty habits of self-destruction. They are unable to change their ways except rarely in the white heat of a deep desire for something better. After some years of burrowing, habits have the strength of iron. Only in the blast furnace of a powerful desire for a new life will old habits meltdown and allow for a different form of movement.

We can blow on the tiniest spark of desire for a better life with praise, rewards, and encouragement until it blooms into a great flame for self-renewal. If we have the means, we may offer prizes, such as the one for manned flight a century ago. A sweet smile of approval is often enough for small changes in the right direction.

It is enough for us to glow with love for the good life to spark the same love in others.

For the spark to ignite the engine of change for growth, we need to reach into the vast subconscious mind where the bulk of our memories and habits are ingrained. We reach the subconscious through meditation or hypnosis. When we meditate, we enter a state of consciousness known as a trance or deep relaxation without sleep; when we hypnotize others, we put them in a trance. With hypnosis or meditation, a trance is a state of high awareness and alertness, not sleepiness.

In a trance, the channel of information between the conscious and subconscious mind is opened; it is normally blocked for the protection of the self. We may now influence the subconscious mind with our thoughts, accessing data and feelings deep in our mind ordinarily hidden from us. In a trance, what we suggest is absorbed more readily and converted to fitting action.

The subconscious absorbs suggestions best when they are offered subliminally, without the conscious mind interfering with the transfer of information. In relaxation, when the mind is quiet, it does not get critical and screen the intrusion of something new. New ideas are uncomfortable to us; they disturb our habitual equilibrium and we resist accepting them. Persuade subliminally by relaxing and distracting with something innocuous and familiar while submitting your suggestions. Don't feel you are doing something unacceptable.

Expert hypnotists will tell you that despite all the drama on stage, people voluntarily hypnotize themselves. We cannot hypnotize people if they don't want to cooperate. Some cooperate readily; others are more difficult. The charmer does not impose power; the power is granted by the subject, who retains freedom of action. Therefore, if we wish to influence by hypnotizing, we first establish rapport with our subject. We earn the subject's trust—trust, faith, attachment, as much as feasible. Begin by acquiring rapport before giving instructions.

Be specific in your instructions to the subconscious of the subject. For example, say, "Eat more fruits and vegetables," not, "Eat healthy foods." Be specific and use repetition with some variations of your instruction to avoid sounding boring. Say, "Tomorrow for breakfast, eat a juicy orange." "Upon rising tomorrow, munch on an apple instead of drinking coffee." Continue such repetitions for at least twenty minutes after entering a trance, focusing on a single training objective.

Focus is essential to effective meditation. Buddhists call it single-mindedness. Your attention becomes like a laser light, burning deep where it touches. Don't scatter your mental energies; concentrate your light on a single spot to get an effect.

Concentrate and intensify your feelings. You will not achieve change with a laid-back attitude. Stir up the deepest emotions that can strongly move the will.

The person you change in this way for a better life may be the one you love or your own self.

8

ON QUALITY

People talk and write about quality often in casual terms. Oh, this clothing is of excellent quality, or these shoes are shoddy. Shoddy products fall apart quickly with customary use, but high-quality things are more enduring. Around the world, even in the East, with all its trade barriers, people pay more money to own an MBZ or BMW automobile. German engineering has panache or verve; it's almost a synonym for quality. A German automobile is a status symbol; wealthy and successful persons often own it—and those who aspire to wealth want it too. Other people, some of them wealthy but thrifty, just want what's cheapest if it works. Such persons were my brother George and brother-in-law George.

My tastes in products and services are somewhere between the luxury seekers and the cheapskates. I want things cheap but also effective. So, I buy used cars and other products of high quality—whatever that is we'll examine—but still effective in their uses. That means, for me, owning used products that I buy and keep for a long time at the cost of care and maintenance. For example, I own a 1995 Lincoln Continental, a marvelous gas guzzler in excellent condition now with a new transmission. What approach is best? What does quality mean after all? Quality has a deep meaning besides the casual one, a meaning worth

On Quality

exploring. Quality is a value, such as love, compassion, hope, or peace, worth pursuing to the utmost by you, me, and every human being because it is a divine gift to us mortals.

Quality is a characteristic we achieve with the relentless pursuit of perfection, as the Toyota Motor Corporation slogan proclaims. Every year, Toyota engineering designers try to come up with improvements in their cars, especially their luxury division, Lexus, to make the cars better, even a little bit, and these improvements, small or large, accumulate over the years like interest compounded on deposits, a philosophy of manufacturing known in Japan as *kaizen*. Kaizen had its beginnings in Japan after WWII, and it was partly influenced by American quality management teachers—previously, Japanese products were famous for being cheap and shoddy.

To get an understanding of kaizen, it helps to know some ideas of Zen Buddhism. Siddhartha Gautama taught Buddhist ideas around 500 BEC in India. The religious element in Buddhism was the Hindu notion of reincarnation. Gautama taught people how to end the cycle of birth and death by reaching Nirvana, or union with God, through right thoughts, works, and meditation. Otherwise, Buddhism was a philosophy, not unlike Stoicism, which showed the means to reduce or eliminate the sufferings of life by putting away all selfish desires, such as the pursuit of wealth, fame, or power. From India, Buddhist teaching spread to Southeast Asia and China and from there to Japan, where it was refined into Zen.

A Zen story tells of the craftsman-artist who wanted to make the perfect cane. So, he went into the forest over and over to find the right wood; then he shaped and carved many pieces of wood to get the cane just right. Many years went by while the artist worked at his task to create the highest quality cane ever made, but he didn't notice the passage of time; time had stopped for him as he sought perfection with continuous improvement.

In an industrial setting, with kaizen, all persons on the job contribute their best efforts to the production, from top management to the person packing the product for shipment. And they continue these efforts year after year after year. That's how you can get high quality in a product. German workers do something similar in their factories, which I'm told are spotlessly clean and very well organized. At one time, German products were of poor quality compared to English ones. The Germans got their own idea of kaizen.

So let's talk about the metaphysics of quality, as explained by Robert M. Pirsig in his philosophical novel *Zen and the Art of Motorcycle Maintenance*, a strange little book that Pirsig sent to a slew of publishers who almost universally rejected it. Finally, after publication, the book sold over five million copies. The narrator, Pirsig himself, presumably, rides on a motorcycle with his son Chris from Minnesota to California. On the way, the narrator takes care of mechanical problems with the motorcycle and tells the story of a man he calls Phaedrus (after Plato), again Pirsig, who becomes so obsessed with defining quality that he goes mad because he's unable to pin down the definition.

Let's go on without going mad, if possible. Pirsig finally describes the undefinable essence of quality as the process of "Thou art that" or *Tat Tvam Asi* in Sanskrit, the process of being one with the object you create, not separate from it. Everything you think you are and everything you perceive are undivided. That is the Tao of the Chinese philosopher Laotse. The metaphysics of quality examines what exists as good or what was *arete* for the ancient Greeks.

Arete, virtue, for the Greeks, was different for different persons or things. A man possessed arete when he was courageous and strong in battle, while a woman possessed virtue in being gentle and caring. A thing was good if it performed its intended function well, such as a horse that would run well or carry a load easily.

Today, we would declare a car that runs well, a Mercedes or Lexus, a good car, and a car of high quality. These cars also look good: sleek, shiny, and curvy. Aha, now we're going into difficult territory with the aesthetics of things, what is beautiful or pleasant in what is also a thing of quality.

When we taste drink or food that we like, we say it's good. Is it good to taste or good for our bodies? We examine the function of drink or food, and we must first determine whether what we taste performs the function of nourishing our bodies in the best possible way. Oenophiles go through bottles of wine and experience subtle differences in taste that you and I cannot perceive. It is the same with paintings or musical pieces. Some persons will pay eighty million dollars to possess a van Gogh painting. A bottle of wine may cost a thousand dollars, worth the money for the oenophile, if affordable to the oenophile, but is it worth that much to you? What is the function of such wine outside of giving pleasure?

Quality depends on a person's value system. If you value pleasure highly and you appreciate wine, you pay a high price for what you want; I don't. Quality is what best fits the person or situation. As Pirsig points out, it's a matter of a romantic versus a technical approach to life. You can ride a Harley-Davidson motorcycle because you enjoy its looks and power, calling a mechanic to fix it—or you can get your hands dirty and repair it yourself because the motorcycle is you. You can run to a doctor for anything that ails your body, or you can use prevention, therapy, and meditation because you and your body are one, not different things in the dualist Cartesian sense of mind and body or matter.

We possess as humans mind, body, and spirit. Things of the spirit are not material, and we cannot deal with them using the laws of physics, which explain well how matter behaves, less well how the body (biological systems) function, and cannot explain at all how spirit does things, how things are in the universe of ideas and feelings. The aesthetics of products and services fall in the category of spiritual values. We have been learning now for some years how to appreciate these values in industrial products, such as cars.

With Henry Ford's Model T car, you got a gawky, horseless carriage in black. Typewriters, adding machines, washers, televisions, etc., all were in black or white. Shapes of products were irregular and awkward, like the body of a teenager. Then came modern industrial designers, such as French American Raymond Loewy in the forties, "The Man Who Shaped America." These designers put some beauty in common household products and even some commercial machines, like railroad locomotives. More recently, Steve Jobs imbued his company, Apple Computers, with a culture of style from the shape and color of the equipment to the appearance of the type fonts. Apple iPhones still maintain such a culture.

The kind of culture and style you choose depends on your character, education, and social background. What kind of life you seek determines your taste in things; some people seek comfort, others pine for luxury, even ostentation. Still, others want adventure, even hardship, in pursuit of lofty goals, a Teddy Roosevelt kind of life. The styles of these people are rough, not tending to the fine arts.

Then you have the disciplines of mathematics, science, and technology, which deal with quantity, structure, space, change, and materials, not with quality or value. To most people, these studies are dry and impersonal, not having much to do with the spiritual life in themselves. Yet, the objects of these occupations often seem to the best practitioners replete with beauty, mystery, and romance. Werner von Braun was a consummate engineer but longed to fly rockets to the moon; building the V2 rocket for Hitler was, for von Braun, a prelude to the Saturn V rocket he designed for the moon landings.

When I studied the equations of Clerk Maxwell for electromagnetism in vector form, I found them very attractive. Interestingly, these equations were the springboard to field and quantum theory, so important in electronics and communications, as well as in the understanding of particle physics. It appears a paradox that mathematicians and scientists experience the thrill of beauty in their work, such beauty as it caused Albert Einstein to declare that he sought to understand the mind of God in his research.

We don't have a paradox with mathematicians, scientists, and engineers. Their materials are not spiritual, but researchers are so; they need to be spiritual to spin their webs, to create using imagination and inspiration.

Creative people tend to be obsessed with their tasks, constantly striving for perfection, but perfection implies increasing costs in labor pains and money. The costs increase exponentially as you approach perfection. So, we stop the creative process, at least for a time, put out the product and try to recover our costs.

A long time ago, as a transmission engineer for Pacific Telephone, I learned we could not hope to switch 100 percent of the telephone calls all the time; the cost of the equipment to be put in operation would have been prohibitive. We aimed for 95 percent successful switching. At very high traffic times, when a disaster occurs, the switching system fails. If your cell phone company drops your call, you've been talking for too long; let somebody else have a chance to connect.

You cannot connect with everybody when making a product. You can customize your product for a given group of people and make it as perfect as you can for that group. Composing country music to please the high-brow classics devotees is a futile effort.

Appealing to the low brow people or the high-brow ones, it's always worthwhile to aim for perfection, for excellence, whatever the product may be. Aiming for perfection is good discipline and makes you a better person. In any case, your product should be user-friendly; it should appeal to your customers. For example, fine literature is great, but pulp fiction should also seek perfection for its audience to succeed. Excellence is worthwhile, as declared by the private prep school in the film *Dead Poets Society*.

People who seek perfection belong to an aristocracy of mind, whatever their field. These are the people of quality, nobility, and pure blood. Such was Leonardo da Vinci of Renaissance Italy, who's said to have spent interminable hours perfecting his *Mona Lisa, La Gioconda*. Persons of enduring virtue, holy men and women, the saints who adhere to their lofty visions, they are people of quality.

Perfection is a notion from the ideal world, which is the real one according to Plato, and what we see ordinarily in our humdrum lives are simply shadows on the wall of our cave, cast from the heavenly objects outside in the light, messages from an alternate universe of peace and harmony, God's universe. We find an expression of the ideal world in our best arts, objects imbued with beauty, whether they are paintings, sculptures, melodies, dishes, perfumes, poems, stories, or mathematical expressions. Perfection is impossible but it's approachable—given enough time.

9

MIND OVER MATTER

When we speak about mind over matter, what do we mean? What is mind, and what is matter? Is our body part of the material world that mind can control to an extent? Bertrand Russell, the philosopher, joked about this issue. "What is matter? No matter. What is mind? Never mind."[1] Most of us associate mind with our ability to operate on the materials that surround us, such as stones, earth, water, air, and our own bodies—although our bodies are living sister cell colonies, each cell possessing consciousness and much different from inert materials.

In New Age thinking, we are body, mind, and spirit. Spirit or soul is associated with our feelings rather than our intellectual activities. African Americans like to talk of their favorite foods as soul foods, such foods that are comforting to them when eaten and associated with their heritage and culture, such as grits. In this essay, I will be writing about the effect of mind, our critical thinking, and of spirit or will in shaping the world around us, including the body, for our satisfaction, health, and performance. I will also tackle basic methods for achieving this

---

1. Thomas Hood, "A Short Cut to Metaphysics," *The Poetical Works of Thomas Hood*, ed. Thomas Hood Jr. (Cambridge: Cambridge University Press, 2011), 148.

effect, known as the *placebo* effect. I will also consider the opposite effect, called *nocebo*, which causes illness in the body and havoc in our surroundings.

Does our spirit bring about these good or bad outcomes depending on the kind of spirit we entertain? I accept that our thinking mind and our brain, along with other body cells, can do that. I am not so sure of the immortality of this spirit, as discussed in religious circles. Such a spirit is hypothetical. I would like to focus on scientific or objective findings when considering placebo and nocebo.

We can control, to a degree, our bodies and the world outside our skins. We affect events outside with our organs of movement, including our tongue and hands. Stephen Hawking did much good scientific work in his paralysis using special translation tools with those body parts he could move. Yuri Geller, in the television shows of the seventies, bent spoons and other metal objects directly with his mind and will using psychokinesis—perhaps. No, not perhaps. These paranormal feats of psychokinesis by Geller and other performers were proven to be tricks of magic and did not withstand the rigor of scientific investigation.

We rule in the world with our powers of reason extended out with our means of expression, including our limbs. If you want to bend a spoon, grab it with both hands and bend. That action is true psychokinesis. If you are attacked by a bully, form a fist and defend yourself—unless the bully is bigger than you. You are exercising your power of the will, your mind over matter. Your mind—will, pneuma, prana, or chi—is the life energy that shapes the world to your ideals by means of your bodily organs that your mind can control. Philosophers call this property of living things intentionality, an agent causing a first cause, not by being a link in a chain of causes.

The intentionality or purposefulness of living things is associated with consciousness. Scientists, such as Sir John Eccles, Nobel Laureate for his work with neurons, have searched for the seat of consciousness in the brain. This search made sense because when you suffer a serious concussion, you lose consciousness and become inert, unable to continue the fight. You also lose consciousness and mindfulness under an anesthetic on the operating table or after much alcohol guzzling. Scientists have not found out so far what in an anesthetic causes loss of consciousness or how, but it has a useful effect for surgeons. We also lose consciousness and our mind partially when asleep. But we may dream, usually nonsensical events. Some people also lose their minds and consciousness by going bonkers. The seat of consciousness in the brain has not so far been located, although some researchers place it in the reticular formation, the brain stem. The brain stem is a primitive part of the brain, which may lead us to conclude that the more primitive you are, the more conscious you become. Civilization dulls the senses.

Still, we associate the mind with reason, a human development in evolution, clearly a more advanced state of mind with greater consciousness, giving us far more capabilities than those possessed by other animals. But we share consciousness with other animals, even plants, as far as we can judge from their purposeful behavior, especially the behavior of our beloved pets.

We can say that the mind or consciousness is an emergent property of the billions of brain cells, or neurons, perhaps of all the trillions of body cells, connected and working together. It is important to remember this situation as we go along with our investigation of mind over matter.

It is also possible that the mind or consciousness is a transmission to our body, a receiver, from a transmitter somewhere in the universe, a conjecture posed by the New Age scientist-philosopher Rupert Sheldrake and other outlier thinkers. The body is a mechanical-electrical-biochemical machine powered by energy derived from the sun, known as free energy, which you must earn, but it is a machine that behaves very differently from other machines that we have. The body possesses an undetected ingredient, called *élan vital* by philosophers Henri Bergson, Martin Heidegger, and others, a creative force for change, growth, and adaptation. Such a force could explain how the mind or consciousness, together with the organ of the will, can heal the machinery of the body, enhance its performance, and, through the body, exert control over the inanimate things of the world. Scientists reluctantly accept that the mind can affect body healing, but they call that healing the placebo effect to avoid being embarrassed by appearing religious.

Healing and performance can be greatly enhanced with a positive or constructive mental attitude, including the emotions, the placebo effect if you prefer, a theme taken up to extremes by popular motivational writers, such as Tony Robbins (*Awake the Giant Within*), and Deepak Chopra (*Ageless Body, Timeless Mind*). Then we have the nocebo effect from negative or destructive thinking, which can lead to autoimmune disorders, such as arthritis, disorders diagnosed today by some fashionable physicians. Most physicians do not bother with placebo or nocebo and stick to writing prescriptions or ordering surgeries instead of encouraging patients to take up therapy with meditation and yoga because relaxation and stretching do not have to cost any money and do not require billing Medicare. A few doctors practice bad voodoo treatments with unnecessary surgeries and treatments, but they are properly licensed by the State. My mother, who was religious, one day wandered into a Christian Science reading room and read much of Mary Baker Eddy's profound text *Science and Health with Key to the Scriptures*, which has sold millions of copies.

My mother was deeply impressed by Eddy's conviction that Mind was the only thing that exists, not matter or body, so we can put away all bodily ills by using the Christian scriptures to effect. Thereafter, my mother refused to see doctors or even dentists and kept her teeth in old age by brushing regularly and eating unripe fruit. But in old age, when she became ill, she would not let me take her to the doctor, and if I dared to take her to the clinic, she would scream and walk out. She lived to the age of ninety-two.

Norman Cousins, a writer for the *New York Post* who contracted spondylitis and heart disease, also applied mind to healing, primarily through humor and laughter. When he became ill, he watched Marx Brothers shows for hours on end until he could not bear the silliness anymore. He was at least partially healed and lived thirty-five more years to age seventy-five. In the meantime, he produced the 1979 bestselling book *Anatomy of an Illness*.

The human immune system gets a boost from relaxation and

reduced stress produced with play and laughter. Even the body's T-cells that fight cancer cells and viral invaders are produced in larger numbers through relaxation and stress relief. Unrelieved stress causes the production of the hormones cortisol and adrenalin, useful for a brief fight, but which long-term have a negative effect, creating the nocebo proliferation of illnesses. Long live hypochondria!

My own method for asserting my mind over matter and body is to emulate Tony the Tiger, the cartoon character who pushes frosted cornflakes to kids: "They're Grrreat!" Except I say, "I feel Grrreat!"

10

BLESSED BE THE STRESSED

When the talk is about stress ("Oh, I'm so stressed today"), I remember the executive monkey from my college Psychology 101 course. In 1958, Dr. Joseph V. Brady gave electric shocks to two hapless monkeys; one could depress a lever and stop the shock, and the other had no lever (no control) but received the same amount of shock because it was yoked to the executive monkey. Both got stomach ulcers, but the executive monkey had more ulcers and frequently died. Twenty-three of the executives died in the original experiment. I remember the pictures in my textbook of the sad monkeys in their restraints, tears coming to my eyes.

In 1971, Dr. Jay Weiss got the same effect by stressing rats. In his experiments, the executive rat suffered more when its responses to pressing a bar after a signal of an impending shock were frequent; the executive rat suffered the worst ulcerations when negative feedback was applied, that is, with its response to the signal causing shock instead of preventing it. That is no way to treat close relatives of ours like rats just for the sake of science, but the findings were useful because they apply to humans.

Findings by Dr. Hans Selye of McGill University, Canada, and other researchers show that excessive stress, especially of long duration without relief, known as chronic stress, causes a host of illnesses, such as high blood pressure, severe headaches, heart disease, cancer, diabetes, depression, as well as stomach ulcers. Continued severe stress in war drives many soldiers to depression and suicide. Researchers estimate that chronic stress causes or aggravates as many as 80 percent of human disease.

Should we then avoid stress altogether and turn ourselves into vegetables? Well, vegetables get stressed too from lack of water, sunlight, or rock music. No, stress also is how organisms, under the right circumstances, adapt, grow and get stronger. Avoid the stress of exercise, and your muscles, tendons, and bones atrophy. Birds with wings tied for a while cease to be able to fly. Astronauts had bone loss and weakness from the lack of gravity until they started exercising in space. Great athletes suffer extreme stress to break world records.

Hercules battled the Hydra and other savage creatures; he tackled impossible tasks until he walked up Mount Olympus to live with the gods. Friedrich Nietzsche's superman was not born that way; he became super with immense effort. Think of Jesus on the cross. Crucifixion was an ingenious Roman form of execution for traitors and criminals that killed and tortured with splendid effect on the criminal and bystanders. (The old English custom of disembowelment and dismemberment while the criminal was alive equals the Roman feat.) One does not survive disembowelment and dismemberment, but Jesus survived crucifixion and arose from the cenotaph to preach again to his intimate circle, then left the land of Israel not to return. He survived thanks to his godlike response to the pain, hunger, thirst, and humiliation of being nailed hands and feet on a wooden cross after a mocking trial, beatings, and a crown of thorns. His disciples, Paul, Thomas, Judas, and the others, dazzled by his appearance after the crucifixion, fervently believed in the divinity of Jesus and carried on with his gospel, tortured and killed in their turn, making themselves martyrs and saints. Verily I say to you, *blessed be the stressed, for they shall master Heaven and Earth.*

11

THE PRICE OF MASTERY

To master, you pay a price. The price is a risk to health or even to life. After a splendid concert, a lady approached Isaac Stern and gushed: Oh, Mr. Stern, I would give my life to play the violin like you do. The master responded: Madam, I have.

A master baboon, an alpha, has more stress than a beta baboon and may get coronary disease if he remains an alpha for long, suffering attacks from those who want his position and best access to females in estrus. The worst position is that of a junior or submissive male forced on the periphery of the baboon troop foraging on open ground. Predators, such as a leopard, will often snap up one of these males. The females are in the center of the troop with their babies, surrounded by three dominant males. The peripheral male sounds the alarm and the dominant males run to face the predator jointly, baring their large canines, but junior may have become dinner. Becoming someone's dinner is an acutely stressful experience.

We have a similar situation in our business world where top executives suffer ulcers, heart disease, and cancers (think of Steve Jobs of Apple and his pancreatic cancer) more often than others in exchange for their position, money, a trophy wife, and mistresses. Great athletes and entertainers achieve fame, fortune, and awards at the risk of becoming addicted or suffering serious injuries in the field (think of Tiger Woods and his sexual addiction). Jim Fixx, runner and writer of "The Complete Runner," died aged 52 during his daily run from a heart attack. Three of his coronary arteries were blocked with atherosclerosis. Even sexual athletes sometimes die doing their thing, like Pietro Aretino, bisexual inventor of literary pornography, satirist, and poet in Renaissance Italy. President Bill Clinton (with heart disease) was wise not to have sex with that woman. At the bottom of the social ladder, however, things are worse. Blue-collar workers and the under-employed are more likely to smoke, get obese, drink to excess, and die young like the peripheral baboons, meat for corporations.

Moderate versus Great Effort

Is there no middle ground? Yes, you can be a beta or gamma, moderately successful—if you're satisfied with a moderate share of the mating. Strive, but not to such excess to injure yourself.

Still, great feats seem to demand great efforts and risks. Think of the explorers of the poles or the climbers of Mount Everest. Many lost their lives aiming for their goals, or at least toes and noses. Can I suggest a way to strive for the top without risking grave injury or death? Yes, I can. It's called a helical climb, like the climb of a car or a train going up a high mountain. The stress of effort should be followed by relaxation and recovery of equal intensity and duration. Following the recovery of bodily or mental resources, you pick up the effort with greater intensity than before, but if you don't have the energy for that, you back off because you have not recovered sufficiently. Perhaps you have reached a plateau, when you should try a different kind of training rather than persistence to a break. Maybe you have reached your limit, not being a god, and need to give up, but you'll never know your limit unless you have stressed yourself towards your limit.

The Price of Mastery

Finding our limits

Many factors limit our ability to withstand stress, create, and grow: our native genes, our lifelong experience, our ability to connect with spiritual resources, and our capacity to laugh at obstacles and failures on the way to our objective.

Finding the limits of strength in materials to stress was what we studied in the laboratory of engineering school. We defined stress as the force per square inch applied on, for example, a block of concrete. We increased this force with a hydraulic press until the block collapsed due to compressive stress; that was the limit for that material, a useful number if you're designing columns for buildings or bridge pylons. We also pulled on steel rods or cables; they stretched due to tensile stress, but after the force went up enough, they broke. We also had torsional tests with similar results. Most objects that we pulled on became longer. Elongation under stress is called *strain* and is proportional to the intensity of the force applied. Some objects that we stressed, like springs, returned to nearly their original shape, a response called hysteresis. But once broken, the material never returned to its original shape by itself—interesting. Even if the material does not break suddenly due to excessive force, it will fatigue and crack when stressed for a long time, such as an airplane wing vibrating in turbulence, its crystal structure changing, developing tiny cracks, and finally collapsing—more interesting.

Compare the above results to stressing muscles. When you lift weights sufficiently heavy or for long enough, your muscles develop tiny tears. After a day or so, given rest and good nutrition, the muscles repair themselves and become stronger—most interesting. Clearly, living things differ in some fundamental way from inanimate objects. Even large cuts in muscles heal after weeks or months with some sewing and stitching. Tendons and bones require more time to heal, and nerves almost never heal.

We normally don't damage tissues in people, but we train children, athletes and soldiers by gradually stressing their bodies and minds up to some limit we think is safe and profitable for growth.

Training for growth

We have at our disposal in training many types of stresses, which are due to different causes, called stressors. Stressors can be physical, such as toxic chemicals, caffeine, nicotine, cocaine, heroin, alcohol, cortisol, adrenaline, heat, cold, dehydration, hunger, pain, sleep deprivation, tiredness, radiation (including sunlight), smoke, dust, alcohol, bacteria and viruses, insect bites, or snake venom (used for training by American Indian shamans, or holy men).

Exercise is often said to be relaxing and stress relieving. It's likely to be so if we do it gently as a meditative practice, such as tai chi and qigong, or we do it for fun; it's stressful if we compete with others or with ourselves to win and break records. Stress reduction, in any case, comes in when we rest after the exercise. A guideline I follow is to rest physically for one hour after exercising for one hour. Mental or psychological effort also requires a commensurate period of rest and relaxation for our nervous system (when we get our most creative ideas).

Psychological stressors are just as numerous, from within ourselves and from without: any rapid change in life, divorce, marriage, death, birth, insecurity, having to learn new behaviors, loss of job, new employment, retirement, graduation, boredom, excitement, horror stories, competitive games (chess, backgammon, Warcraft), frustration, disappointment, depression, fear, anger, jealousy, envy, pride, greed, work, idleness, offending enemies or friends, demanding bosses, freeway jams, warfare, poverty, wealth, politics, business, beggars, solicitors, fundraisers, sullen-sniveling-screaming children, nagging or feuding spouse, conflict of any sort, deadlines—I can go on forever with the list, all stressors subject to raising blood pressure or laughter, depending on your reactions.

Deadlines can often lead to stress, but it's stress that motivates some people to act. I know people who wait for a deadline to come close to build up their internal energy for meeting the deadline. Use stressors cautiously in training yourself or others, never reaching dangerous levels and allowing for relaxation and recovery.

Some institutions, army, navy, air force, law and medical schools,

The Price of Mastery

and sports teams, frequently and intentionally put young people through dangerous levels of stress. The intent is to weed out incompetents and select the toughest and best candidates. In the film *An Officer and a Gentleman*, the character of Richard Gere goes through naval academy training, nearly breaking down but persisting and surviving because he has nowhere else to go. Medical interns suffer similarly, some of them breaking down mentally and committing suicide, as depicted in the television series *Grey's Anatomy*. Law schools routinely weed out 50 percent of the students in the first year with tough courses and assignments, sometimes impossible ones. In the one semester of law school I attended, I often found the relevant pages in reference books torn out, and I could not complete the assignment. I never had that problem in engineering school. Care to comment?

Stress is a different problem for individuals such as you and me, our children or loved ones, than for groups or populations. Leaders can tolerate losses in the group they command, relying on those who survive for success and victory. Generals send young people to training camps or battles, fully aware that they will lose some of them through breakdowns, backdowns, escapes, or even deaths. Those who remain in the line will be stronger and will fight on, win, and breed a tougher generation to come. Or perhaps the quitters will do the breeding while those who persist die in battle.

At least in hospitals, that is how populations of super bacteria are bred, such as Staphylococcus aureus. Hospital officials are overly prejudiced against bacteria, cleaning, scrubbing, disinfecting, and using antibiotics liberally, causing bacteria populations to adapt and change through natural selection until they become super tough and dangerous. If you want to stay healthy, stay away from hospitals.

If you want a healthy body, you need healthy body cells. Our bodies are complex cultures of single cells, much like bacteria. We are evolved colonies of cells that have differentiated to cooperate better and be more effective to survive. When we discipline our individual body cells through proper living, we strengthen the body and boost the immune system. Say to your body cells, "No pain; no gain." One way to do that is to keep nourishment to the minimum, with an occasional fast. Weak cells die, and the stronger ones reproduce body tissues. Stressing your body with calorie deprivation makes you healthier if you take in necessary nutrients but no more food. Trees that are given such tough treatment with little water produce the tastiest fruits. Such a procedure is sometimes called *eustress*, good stress.

Good stress allows for full recovery of the organism and further strengthening. We get a cycle of tension and then relaxation. The "stress of life" is not all bad as it seems to some people. Yes, when we face danger, a major challenge, our muscles tense up, our heart rate and blood pressure go up, adrenaline and cortisol hormones surge, blood thickens, and cholesterol and blood sugar rise; all of these and other changes get us ready to fight or flee. It's an old evolutionary response we share with our animal relatives, but it doesn't work well in the constraints of a modern world because we're not allowed to express ourselves by hitting or running. We suffer from bottled-up energies and feelings, leaving us with the options of crying (not for men) or turning the situation into a joke and laughing.

Once we have relaxed well enough, one way or another, after stress, after we have escaped danger, won, lost, given up, or withdrawn to sleep or elsewhere, our bodies return to normal and repair themselves. Calm and peace return to our minds, and our souls are refreshed and rebuilt —sometimes better than before the emergency.

In Japanese boot camps for managers, trainees are stressed with yells and rough talk. They wear ribbons of shame on their foreheads with inscriptions of their failures, as in a story about Japanese and American auto workers, tellingly depicted in the 1986 Ron Howard film *Gung Ho*. How effective are such treatments of young people? Some subjects will rebel and quit; others will submit to the treatment. Those who quit will not change their behaviors; those who submit may change under intense pressure. I know of no other way to change. Sweet talking, which is my choice, doesn't cut it.

Changing behavior

Change of behavior involves learning which occurs in the nervous system made up of nerve cells or neurons. Existing neurons adapt to change; even fresh young neurons appear in the brain, adapting more effectively. I mentioned earlier that nervous tissue heals only rarely from damage. For almost a hundred years, scientists believed we were born with about 100 billion neurons, never to have any more, but only to lose some every day because of aging, shock, and toxins, such as alcohol. In 1999, Elizabeth Gould and Charles Gross at Princeton showed that in marmoset and macaque monkeys, a continuous stream of fresh neurons migrated from the center of the brain to the cerebral cortex and became integrated by connecting with existing neurons. Other scientists confirmed the finding. Fred Gage of the Salk Institute in La Jolla showed that such neuronal regeneration in the human hippocampus is related to the degree of cognitive challenge. Use it or lose it.

But don't use it too much. Excessive or unrelieved stress can have the opposite effect on the hippocampus, causing the death of neurons and Alzheimer's disease. Stressed is best up to a point allowing a return to a body-mind equilibrium, or homeostasis.

It is often difficult for anyone to determine and set the right limit point for stress. IN 1888, Friedrich Nietzsche wrote, "What does not kill me, makes me stronger."[1] He was being a German romantic and exaggerating. Short of killing ourselves, trying too hard may damage our bodies or minds beyond repair. Extend yourself a little at a time, allowing your resources to recover completely before further extending your limits.

---

1. Friedrich Nietzsche, *Twilight of the Idols*, trans. Duncan Large (Oxford: Oxford University Press, 1998), 33.

The cause of stress illness

What causes illness is not stress itself, if reasonably limited in intensity; not letting go of effort after a time to allow for healing to occur—that causes heart disease, cancer, ulcers, depression, and even death. To stimulate growth, the struggle and pain must be controlled in intensity, duration, and frequency, with no permanent damage to the body or mind. Match the recovery to the struggle in intensity, duration, and frequency, and approach your limits in these parameters safely, just as a weightlifter progresses in raising weights to avoid an overload and injury to muscles, bones, or nerves. In exercising for a target, work slowly, fully aware of your ideal form, closing your eyes if necessary, warm up, breathe deeply, get a full range of motion, and strive for balance in using all muscles—or other resources. Before starting up again, cool down and relax.

Stress damages when not followed by relief, when it's excessive, when it comes on suddenly with no warning and no time to warm up, and when it stops abruptly, without a cool down or winding down of your system.

Andy Potts, star triathlete, does more than warm up or cool down. While running, biking, or swimming, he constantly monitors his heart rate and energy output. He remotely stores his body's response to stress in a computer for analysis, setting up a feedback loop for his efforts. He looks for a heartbeat of 165 for peak performance, then an adequate recovery at 140 beats per minute and an energy output of 410 watts. (For training, not peak performance, a steady pulse rate of about 80 percent of the peak is sought.) The trainer subjects Potts to a careful dose of punishment, reflecting the athlete's response to stress, pushing Potts to near exhaustion, and generating data for the next day's exercise plan; that's the feedback loop.

The feedback loop for growth

The feedback loop works best when recovery includes relaxation and meditation. Meditation is not lethargy, although we usually do it sitting or lying still. Body and mind function best when relaxed, after a struggle phase, to achieve whatever goals, athletic or others, you want to achieve. Meditation is awareness of everything that is happening to us, physically, emotionally (worry, upset, anger), and spiritually, in our connection with the life force. Breathe deeply, focusing on the here and now. Awareness, in turn, increases our control of resources inside and outside of ourselves. Quiet your mind in relaxation and take full notice of the effects of the stress you're under, making changes in your behavior before illness or accident strikes.

While some people make themselves ill, injured, or dead with overstress, some of us avoid any significant effort and stress if we can, often extending that attitude to others they can influence. When I exercised together with my daughter Alia and she would get flushed and sweaty, her mother would worry about her and stop her. Flushing and sweating are natural responses to vigorous movement and heat, the body's adjustment to these stressors. Most people today turn on the air conditioning as soon as they feel a little uncomfortable with heat or cold, weakening the body's ability to handle these stressors. I admire the Tibetan monks who wrap themselves in frozen blankets for part of their training or lie on lake ice until they melt it, bringing blood to their skin with mental discipline.

The attitude of some of us is: Always follow the easiest (not the best) way out of a difficult situation. I'll do all I can to avoid a problem instead of solving it. Let somebody else handle a nasty, dirty, smelly case. If I can't avoid a challenge, I won't fight. I'll cry, sleep, drink, smoke, play, watch television, read pulp fiction, or eat pizza and ice cream. Let relatives or welfare take care of my needs. If nobody comes to save me from trouble, I'll kill myself. Oh, death, the ultimate escape.

In his meditations, John Donne wrote, "Any man's death diminishes me, because I am involved with mankind."[2] I, too, am diminished by any living entity's death, suffering, or stagnation; that's why I write, cope with challenges, and teach others the tools of coping.

---

2. John Donne, *Devotions upon Emergent Occasions and Death's Duel*, ed. Anthony Raspa (Montreal & Kingston: McGill-Queen's University Press, 1975), 108.

"No man is an island, entire of itself; every man is a piece of the continent, a part of the main,"[3] John Donne also wrote. We are social animals, but not like insects. We evolved in troops or tribal units over millions of years for security, comfort, and reproduction. Being alone, physically or mentally, is stressful because it's dangerous or at least uncomfortable. People need people to feel secure, to love, and to be happy. A sense of isolation from others can be devastating.

Involuntary or forced isolation is different from chosen solitude. Moses on Mount Sinai, Jesus and Mohammed in the desert, and Buddha in the forest found solitude from the tumult of crowds and the constant business of life to reflect, meditate, relax, and communicate with God, then returned to the people to teach their message. Here's my message, such as I, too, have gathered in solitude.

Solitude and isolation

We may feel isolated, but the life force field permeates the universe like gravity inside of us and outside of us, connecting us all. After all, we are parts of this physical universe ourselves. Why do we then often feel isolated from a Higher Force, from our inner self in the subconscious, and from each other, loathing, disgusted, and even hating others or ourselves? Why does a sense of isolation lead many people to great distress and stress, causing ill health, accidents, and slow or instant suicide (sometimes homicide)? As theologians say, what separates us from the infinite compassion of God? As psychologists say, what is keeping us from reaching the gold or coal of our subconscious, which I believe is 95 percent of our brainpower? As humanists say, what is keeping us from speaking freely, truly, and peacefully to our fellow humans and listening to them attentively? What is doing that are barriers, walls, diaphragms, sphincters, valves in between heaven, the subconscious, and the social worlds, existing from birth for our protection and survival, barriers fortified, raised, hardened, closed tight to avoid rejection, pain, danger, fear, exposure.

---

3. Donne, *Devotions*, 108.

To relieve the stress of isolation, we need to loosen up these barriers gently and cautiously, with soothing, loving oils and massage, groping inside and outside of us until contact is made again fully, as in psychoanalysis, religious confession, or plain relaxation with meditation. In the end, we may have an epiphany, a sudden self-realization of our potential, or a gradual healing of our spirit (and body) from the stress of isolation.

Let me show you a picture. The vast space of the life force or universal mind is a sphere, touching the sphere of your subconscious mind, attached to the smaller sphere of your focusing conscious mind, sensing other sentient beings and the sphere of the physical universe. Two information valves or sphincters block or allow information and feelings to be channeled between the first three spheres. (Clearly, your skin, with sense-organ specialized skin cells, is the valve between the conscious mind sphere and the physical sphere of the universe, the eyelids separating you from light radiations.) When you open up to experience the love of the life force or another human being, you may be thwarted, rejected, disappointed, or hurt because of your own failings or those of others; the sphincters tighten up, closing the channels, insulating you from pain and isolating you at the same time. Isolation can become chronic, perpetual, lasting for years or a lifetime, exacting huge costs on your health, happiness, and overall effectiveness.

You're doing fine if, on occasion, you isolate yourself from others, from your subconscious, even from the searing energy of the life force, to protect your body and mind and survive the moment.

Acute stress, chronic stress

When you're experiencing acute stress—you'll get over it with rest, relaxation, and recreation, rebuilding your integrity of mind until your next foray. Your sympathetic nervous system is stimulated into action—your blood pressure goes up temporarily, your hormones surge, and your muscles tense up, but these return to normal (or you die) when you relax and your parasympathetic nervous system takes over (after the crisis is the time of greatest risk of depression, damage or death). In chronic or habitual stress, however, your vital fluids and energies get stuck at an unsustainable level, causing continuous damage that cannot be repaired by your body's or the mind's homeostatic mechanisms of recovery. Your parasympathetic system doesn't get a chance to do its work. Push, push, push! You're a spring that has been stretched beyond hysteresis. Chronic stress is itself a big danger, and many of us are habituated to it, suffering illness until this stress is subdued or until we're dead. Chronic stress has no benefits; it's a dead end.

How do you know whether you're suffering from chronic stress? Is your blood pressure up constantly? It may be due to a salt intake that is too high for your metabolism, to renal (kidney) failure, or other causes. Quite often, chronic stress is the cause of it. Is your resting pulse rate high? Do you get frequent headaches? Is your blood sugar or cholesterol level above normal? Do you have insomnia? Do you feel habitually nervous, tense, jumpy, or anxious? Do you overeat or eat sugary, starchy, fatty foods? Do you have excess fat deposits in the waist, hips, or buttocks? Do you get skin rashes, have unexplained aches and pains in the neck, shoulders, and back especially, suffer from frequent infections, virus attacks, fatigue when you wake up, heartbeat irregularities (arrhythmia), low mood, gastric acid secretions, sluggishness, sadness, boredom, irritability, petty anger, loss of appetite, suicidal thoughts, panic attacks, inability to concentrate, or lack of joy in doing your everyday activities? Most likely, you're under chronic stress; you're in danger of a health breakdown.

How do many people treat symptoms of chronic stress? Not by treating the cause of it as they should, but by taking palliatives. When sluggish, they gulp more coffee, tea, coke, or other stimulants. When nervous or tense, they drink alcohol. When unable to sleep, they take tranquilizers. When sad, they escape into fantasy. When they have infections, they take antibiotics. When their stomach hurts from gastric secretions, they take antacids. For headaches, they take aspirin. When they're bored, they seek excitement in competitive games, adventure in horror movies, books, and video games, or pick fights with a spouse, relative, friend, acquaintance, server, co-worker, or boss. For aches, these people take painkillers or muscle relaxants. When nervous or irritable, they take tranquilizers. All these "cures" of the symptoms simply perpetuate the vicious cycle of chronic stress.

Before you can have the benefits of manageable acute stress, before the achievement of any great struggle, before reaching the happiness of inner peace, you need a real cure for chronic stress before it kills you. If isolation is the problem, reconnect. If the cause of your chronic stress is your spouse, relative, friend, or boss, distance yourself from them or change your relationship with them. If in the morning you don't want to lift an eyelid, let alone your body, without your Starbucks coffee before heading for traffic and work, change employment. You yell, "I need my job; I can't afford to quit!" Can you afford cancer, heart disease, arthritis, or a stroke? You say, "I have young children; I can't quit." Will your children be better off as orphans, raised by others? You have no other choice but to cure chronic stress for good, doing whatever it takes to do the job, or else you're doomed.

Healing from chronic stress

To heal thyself, you begin by focusing on your life source connection, to strengthen it, to clarify it, to tap its power to the fullest. No doubt, the life force exists, though it may not be as fatherly, motherly, or compassionate as some people believe. When you tap it, you naturally re-invigorate yourself, as a battery does when it's plugged in to recharge. The closer you are mentally, emotionally, and spiritually to the life force, the more powerfully the force will affect your adjustment to homeostatic equilibrium, healing, and growth.

After you have re-established contact with the force that created you and all life, come to terms with your inner self through introspection, meditation, yoga, and the help of a good psychoanalyst, airing out long-suppressed anger, guilt, and regret. Also, get close to friends and relatives who soothe your nerves, support you, and cherish you. Distance yourself from disturbing people. Quit all stimulants and depressants, and avoid all games, dramas, and "entertainments" that excite you unduly. If you are often glued to such entertainments, you have a cortisol addiction to kick; enjoy comedies instead. You can include most news stories in things to avoid. Find romance and intimacy if you can. Engage in gentle exercises and activities that interest you but don't stir up your competitive urges, such as yoga, tai chi, and qigong. Enjoy fine art: music (try Massenet's *Thais*), paintings, dancing, and cuisine. Follow a healthy diet with delicious food. Take liquid potassium, calcium, and magnesium supplements. Try regular massage sessions with a therapist or a massage chair. Chuck every worry you have been carrying around, keeping only suitable concerns. That's the treatment.

How long will it take for a full recovery from chronic stress? It has probably taken years for the syndrome to develop; it may take a long time for it to disappear. As I grappled with personal, family, and business problems over several decades, I developed chronic stress syndrome and, last year, coronary ischemia. I'm still treating my syndrome as I have prescribed to you, hoping to return soon to major challenges in a measured way, cortisol and adrenaline under control, with full recovery after each fight; that is, I hope to do so before I'm stopped in my tracks by the ultimate stressor of us all—aging.

After we have reached the steady equilibrium of body and mind in homeostasis, we can turn to the great blessings of stress, staying duly cautious not to overload ourselves and not to relapse back to chronic stress. Studies at Harvard and other institutions have shown that business executives placed under stress keep becoming increasingly more productive as the intensity of the stress and its duration increase—up to a point beyond which performance declines. What's that point of inflection in the upward curve? When do we know we must end the struggle for now and take our rest? When we can struggle no more, empty of all reserves of energy, the pain no longer bearable.

Herbert Benson, MD, the Harvard researcher of the relaxation response, shows us how to deal with great stress in his new study, "The Breakthrough Principle." Briefly, for our great struggles to be effective, we must follow them with deep relaxation and meditation in the stillness, tapping the wellsprings of our spirit and transforming ourselves into beings of a higher order.

Struggle and Transformation

Like a butterfly emerging from the cocoon it made as a caterpillar, after a long rest, we emerge transfigured and winged. Like Jesus in the grave, we stand up and ascend toward Heaven. *Blessed are the stressed who have not broken or given up too soon, for they master themselves first, then go on to master the ideal world before possessing the physical world.*

Why is it that challenges and torture turn some persons into sinners and some into saints? We often say the saint possesses the resource of a sturdy spirit. We don't know scientifically what the spirit is, but we can experience it when we see the magic of spirit in others or ourselves, and the mind is steady and quiet. If muscles can repair little tears from intense exercise, if broken bones can mend and grow whole, if newborn neurons can emerge in the brain to mend it, how much more resilient and capable must the spirit be—a thing so close to the source of life!

Some people emerge whole and noble from great trials because of their sturdy makeup or because of their attitude toward pain. Taking pains means doing good work. Christ, wounded and parched on the cross, transcended his human limitations, becoming more than an ordinary man in extreme agony. Recovering from his wounds and thirst in the coolness of the cenotaph, he emerged to complete his mission on Earth.

The prophet Mohammed sat in deep meditation outside his desert cave and looked up at the brilliant stars. Gabriel, an angel of God, appeared before him and commanded: "Recite!" The illiterate camel driver recited the immortal poems of the Quran, later memorized by his followers and written down as the Muslim scriptures. Inspiration and creative passion may follow a powerful struggle to overcome an obstacle if a person afterward allows for a period of tranquility and meditation.

Herbert Benson has shown with EEG recordings that the brain in deep meditation is calm overall, but some parts of it are in a state of high excitation. Benson calls this state of mind calm commotion. Could it be that in a calm-commotion state, our minds approach the divine source of all life, knowledge, and power?

You don't have to believe in the divine to make use of scientific findings regarding extreme stress and meditation, devotion, and prayer. Direct your prayer and devotion, if not to God, to your ideal, whatever that is: beauty, truth, justice, peace, creation, invention, perfection, wealth, power, happiness. Be well prepared to pay the price of the struggle phase in your transformation. You will not transform yourself, changing lifelong habits, without first engaging in a great struggle. Jesus said, "Whoever wants to be my disciple must deny themselves and take up their cross and follow me."[4] You can only transform your world into a better place after you have successfully changed yourself to the superhuman you visualize vividly. A fine human character is like a diamond formed from coal under immense pressure and heat in the bowels of the earth or a laboratory.

As a rule, you can expect human beings to remain as they are without changing their character. You *can* trust people, yourself included, to be themselves—good, bad, or indifferent in their behaviors according to their established habits. We're like robots, each one of us following our internal memory programs blindly, helplessly; freedom of the will is an illusion. We break the chain of causality in our lives only rarely, very rarely, miraculously, only under great pressure and stress well directed.

You achieve greatness in any endeavor by driving yourself to exhaustion, but not to a breakdown. Yes, you risk a catastrophic failure of body or mind; taking calculated risks is a part of exploration, growth, and breakthrough achievement. You follow such an effort with relaxation, living the present moment, not thinking of things past or future, in deep tranquility, absorbed in soothing music, in a beautiful natural setting, bathing peacefully in warm waters, or just sitting and meditating. You breathe deeply, letting *prana* or spirit inside. The ideas come then, the fantastic visions that will be realized, the solutions to big problems of design, science, art, philosophy, or religion. No block exists to your creativity. Artistic block is fear of failure, fear of losing your

---

4. Luke 9:23 (NIV).

capacity to create—fear and block cannot exist after you have been transformed by guided stress and relaxation.

Transformation from stress can work for societies as well as individuals. Economic hard times can stimulate creativity, toughness, and growth in new directions in people of courage and enterprise. The ancient Greeks emerged victorious from their battles against the invading Persians, producing a golden civilization. In America, the Great Depression gave rise to a rebirth of culture, prosperity, and dominance in the world because many leading people, such as Franklin D. Roosevelt, met great danger, hardship, pain, and disappointment with courage and ingenuity.

If superhumans are willing to take on their shoulders the burdens of the Earth, the world will keep progressing. When Atlas shrugs off his responsibilities, as Ayn Rand wrote, watch out for a new Dark Age to begin.

12

ON DEATH AND DENIAL

My older brother George, eighty-five, is depressed and thinks he's dying, although doctors have not found that he has a terminal illness. We live in the same house, and I take care of him as we have been close brothers throughout our lives, our wives having divorced us many years back. I tell my brother, don't think of death; think of life. Death is nothingness: you can do nothing with it. You can do something only when living, so think of life, even if you can do just one little thing, smile, or say a loving word to those dear to you.

Giving such advice to people at death's door is too easy. They know they're terminally ill or terminally old and are of no use to anybody; they feel they're a burden on their families or society. Every move they make may be painful. They're tired of being tortured in hospitals or nursing homes, stuck with needles, given medicines, and having their diapers changed. They're ready to welcome Dr. Kevorkian or at least the hospice people. What would you do or say in that situation? Would you summon up a smile and keep on living a while longer—or quit eating like my father Elias, his method of ending his life, very frail but not ill at age one hundred?

I tell myself that I will face death and dying without fear. I will accept the torments of a terminal state of life, and I will keep on working to the extent I'm able to work in that condition. Even if I cannot produce any useful output, I will remain there calm and content as an inspiration to those around me, much like a monument of stone or steel. Will I do that? The day when I shall be tested is coming close.

One day, we're born and cry from the pain of it, clearing our lungs to breathe. We slowly acquire functions: drinking, eating, getting rid of waste in diapers, later learning toilet control, smiling, laughing, grasping, throwing, feeding ourselves, learning to speak, read, write, and do arithmetic, on to high school, college, and work training. We love someone and parent children. Then we age, slowly losing function, and finally end up being fed and wearing diapers again if we survive long enough. Eventually, we lose the power to move, to remember, and to think; painfully again, we return to the condition from which we started—back to darkness.

As darkness is the absence of light, so is death the absence of life; it has no other substance, although depicted in imaginative drawings as a robed and hooded skeleton holding a scythe. To understand death we must, therefore, understand what a living entity is and what is consciousness and identity, the inner state of being associated with systems that live. At the most elementary level, a living object contains DNA, giant molecules holding instructions and controls for the production and operation of life, at least here on Earth. We don't know what sort of mechanisms life employs off the Earth. Inanimate objects are passive, lacking purpose and adaptability; living objects act on and transform passive objects to survive, grow, and multiply.

Those alive fear and resist death, the process of becoming an inanimate object, unless they're mentally ill or deluded. If human, customarily, they also deny that such a devastating event can happen to them or their loved ones. Yet, those who aspire to philosophy, loving wisdom, should accept death when inevitable with calmness and dignity, avoiding denial of death in its many forms, religious or secular. The prospect of death, which humans with reasoning, unlike other animals, can clearly expect, should be a mirror on our past and remaining years on Earth, giving us a compacted and vivid image of what we have done, inspiring us to pursue moral goals, based on our highest values, and stimulating us to live more meaningful and worthwhile days, down to our last one.

A successful TV series, *Run for Your Life*, with actor Ben Gazzara, portrayed a dying man who traveled and lived life to the fullest helping others.

It's easy to make statements about facing death with equanimity and a firm purpose to keep being useful and enjoying life, but it's hard to do that when your very own body and consciousness are at risk of disappearing; it's easier to shake with fear and loathing of losing you mortal coil. To understand death and life, the concept of consciousness is more important than DNA, chromosomes, and genes.

Consciousness is awareness of things through numerous sense organs, with sensations both internal and external. Consciousness relates to something. I'm aware of pain or pleasure; I'm aware of light, colors, and shapes. Then we have our voluntary reaction to these stimuli. I can imagine a machine possessing consciousness without DNA, unrelated to the evolution of organisms on Earth. If such an intelligent machine, perhaps not as intelligent as we are or far more intelligent than we are, is behaving in a purposeful, autonomous, and effective way for its survival, I must accept it as conscious for the same reasons I accept you as conscious when I meet you.

After all, the human body is a biological machine that has evolved over billions of years to perform certain functions and produce useful output. When it has worn out and no longer has any value, it's ready for recycling. I own a 1982 Mercedes 240D with 340,000 miles on the original engine and transmission. The car chugs along very well and gets me around town, albeit irritating those behind with its slow acceleration. I service it regularly and fix small breakdowns. The car is useful still and economical, an old friend of thirty years, but I don't expect it to go on forever. I just try to get more mileage and performance out of it, as I do out of my body; when no longer of any use, this machine can be recycled, and I can move on to the next thing, whatever it may be.

Some futuristic investigators are considering the prospect of transferring our consciousness, with our memories and our identity, to a smart machine, thus extending the span of our consciousness indefinitely.

For intelligent machines, humans, or amoebas, death means permanent loss of consciousness and dissolution. Loss of consciousness, when involuntary and unnatural, is a distressing and alarming event. We don't mind going to sleep when we're very tired at the end of the day. The unconsciousness of sleep after a long day's hard work is most welcome to us. We rise the next morning rested and refreshed, ready for new adventures and accomplishments. Eight hours have gone away like a moment's wink. But if we faint from loss of blood or some other shock, that's dangerous and important to ourselves and our doctors. Death is even more fearsome, not at all like losing consciousness from fatigue, excessive alcohol, or other drugs. That kind of state is forever, as far as we know.

Yet, the state of final death can be delayed indefinitely. Is a frozen body, like a frozen embryo, alive? Yes, if it can be revived after hibernation. The cryogenic movement has people dying from a terminal illness frozen in liquid nitrogen in the hope of reviving the body when medical science has discovered a cure.

Most people believe that even irreversible death, with the body's dissolution, is not the end of life. We are taught to believe that by our religion or philosophy. Such belief is based on the dichotomy of body and mind, or soul, well expounded by Rene Descartes, but also many others before him and after him. Socrates talked to his disciples about an afterlife for himself in a place with other thinkers, continuing his discussions on matters of importance. Plato, in the dialogue *Phaedo,* justifies the perpetuation of the spirit primarily based on natural cycles. Socrates calmly drank the hemlock in prison, refusing to escape and violate the laws of his country.

If we're not religious, we need to find other reasons for accepting death courageously and peacefully, even with a smile or a joke. We had no consciousness before we were born or a few months before that event. Our consciousness appears from nothing, and to nothing it goes upon death. Our entire universe also emerged from a singularity, or nothing, and is headed towards nothingness. Why be upset about either situation? Death is a natural process like birth, sex, parenting, and aging—nothing to be alarmed about.

It's harder, however, for most of us to accept the loss of loved ones. We go into deep grief and denial, "Oh, no, no, no!" Who has lost a child and taken that event with complete equanimity?

Then, some people seek out death in a variety of ways: engaging in dangerous sports, abusing their bodies with recreational drugs, or picking fights. The men of ISIS have declared that they love death as opposed to the rest of us who love life. They have decided to go to war with nations large and small until they have achieved their death with the promise of paradise. And they have no concern for their remains.

Most of us want to preserve the remains of our loved ones as long as possible, embalm, beautify, and put them in a fine casket and burial site. When the flesh has decomposed, the bones are relics. The remains possess no consciousness, obviously. The body is cold and pale. It has no heartbeat, no breath, and no brain waves. It quickly decomposes. Great people have built pyramids, monuments, and mausoleums for their dead bodies. The Viking chiefs burned their dead bodies in a boat, together with the chief's favorite woman, alive. Some East Indian Hindus practiced *sati*: the living wife burned on a pyre with the dead husband—but not the reverse. American Plains Indians put the body on a raised bed of sticks and let the buzzards consume it.

When a fallen warrior cannot be identified, we place the body in a tomb for the Unknown Soldier to honor the fighter's memory. In many societies, a hero who falls dead in battle cannot be allowed to be taken by the enemy. As in Homer's *Iliad*, brave comrades of the hero surround the body and protect it so it can be retrieved together with valuable weapons, and the body is later ceremonially burned or buried.

In some tribal societies, relatives of the dead person ate parts of the body ceremonially to honor the memory of the dead. Jesus offered bread and wine to his apostles at the Last Supper, symbolizing his flesh and blood as well as his spirit.

In some tribes, the custom was to eat parts, especially the heart, of a worthy enemy killed in battle to absorb his courage or wisdom.

Obviously, the dead body reverts to the elements one way or

another, having little to do with the person that once functioned inside it. My parents' bodies were cremated, and I took their ashes to my house in Greece, where they are buried at the foot of an olive tree in the yard. My own ashes will be there too soon enough.

We have ceremonies, rites, and rituals at the funeral of family members, friends, and public figures, not for their benefit but to assuage our own grief. The best way to dispose of the body is to put it six feet under the surface of the soil, in a simple pine box, or to cremate it. That is also economical; the money is better spent taking care of the living relatives who need help.

Jesus taught, "And whosoever liveth and believeth in me shall never die."[1] Other prophets in all religions have made similar promises to which people have attached themselves for hope and comfort. People say of a loved one who died that he or she has gone to a better place. How do they know that? Nobody knows. We just don't know, but it's all right; we're all headed that way sooner or later.

We don't like to say a loved one has died. He or she has passed on—across the river to the other side. That attitude is evasion and denial. We have no real evidence of any other side. After-death experiences are subjective and not available for scientific investigation. The declarations of prophets, mystics, and seers are handed to us without any proof of their validity. Believe and don't question. I do question, especially the perpetuation of consciousness and identity after the body's dissolution.

Yet, there may be a Universal Consciousness with which we merge, like John Donne's main. We may be part of that while our body is alive, an isolated part of it which, upon death, joins the Cosmic Self.

Do we return to a new body again after detaching from the Cosmic Self? Does transmigration of the soul happen? Not being a Hindu, I cannot answer that question positively. It's sheer speculation, perhaps denial of the inevitability of our own demise.

If we face the prospect of death, as we all do sooner or later, it is better to use that prospect to energize us, to encourage us to work harder and better, and achieve more in the life remaining, even if that is

---

1. John 11:26 (KJV).

only a few moments. We can say, like Goethe at the moment of his death, "Light, more light," shortly after completing his *Faust: Part II* poem, with this stanza:

> Turn, flames of love, once more
> Pure light reveal
> Those who their lives deplore
> Truth yet shall heal;
> Rescued, no more the thrall of evil cares,
> Soon with the All-in-All
> Bliss shall be theirs.[2]

---

2. Johann Wolfgang von Goethe, *Selected Poems*, trans. David Luke (New York: Penguin Classics, 2005), 210.

13

PRAXIS: THE ART OF VIRTUOUS ACTION

For thousands of years, in all cultures and all places, our ancestors have sought to find out what is virtue, good behavior, and how to attain it. Much of the search for goodness has been clothed in religious terms: the practice of piety and the avoidance of sin. The rest of the search and findings were philosophies in weighty volumes or the simple sayings of ordinary people known as folk wisdom. We have known for a long time what it takes to achieve a measure of peace, happiness, and a fruitful life for ourselves and our societies.

What we have lacked has been the will, the capacity to act with reason, carrying out what we know is the right course of action. We often ask ourselves when we mess up our lives, why or why do I do these bad things, and why don't I do this thing I know is the right thing to do for me and my fellows? For example, why do I smoke, drink too much alcohol, take this illegal drug, or sometimes hurt people I love? Why don't I work harder to succeed instead of wasting my time with trivial pursuits?

My answer is that we don't stop long enough to think as we pace our habitual dog run. We don't pause in our pursuit of comfort and pleasure. We don't listen to the source of our being. We don't deliberate, but rush ahead with what we have always been doing. We tend to react, distracted by others, friends, or adversaries, to do what we have been accustomed to doing with little conscious thought, planning, and foresight. For nearly all of us, the problem is not ignorance of how to act but the drive to act virtuously. How do we find the will to do what's right? I propose to you *praxis*, the art of virtuous action.

Praxis balances *ataraxia*, inner peace, coping well with whatever happens to us—a stoical stance. Ataraxia says whatever may befall me, I can handle it, even enjoy it, because my happiness is up to me. *Praxis*, by comparison, is action towards my goals; it's the application of theory to practice, the realization of plans, the fulfillment of dreams, and the contact with what religious people call God.

Parents, teachers, bosses, preachers, and all the gurus of success, from Napoleon Hill to Anthony Robbins, have lectured us on how to succeed. Now, you and l will search for the secret of *praxis* using our own peculiar reason and intuition. We're after that which connects-controls-couples what we desire and intend with what we actually cause to happen. We want to cause an effect, the same way gravity causes water to flow in a channel. We want a strong coupling of our purpose to our desired action so that action is free to flow in the channel of our intention without events or people interfering or blocking the flow.

Suppose, for example, we're fat and want to be lean, which is going from a given state A to a desired state B, the statement of any problem. We want to cause the effect of getting lean, which cannot be done overnight except with liposuction. We need to reduce this problem so it's subject to the inevitable laws of nature. We know that taking in more calories than we can burn adds fat to our bodies, and taking fewer calories reduces fat. We set up a calorie budget for each day, say 1400 calories; now we have reduced the problem to changing our behavior so that we stay within our calorie budget. Over time, we'll inevitably reach our desired lean state.

Wait, you say, changing our eating behavior, that's not so simple. Aye, there's the rub. How do we make this change in behavior inevitable? We do this by relying on an established behavior that is inevitable in all of us except in thieves. Don't we always pay for a meal at a restaurant? Put fourteen pennies in your left pocket when you wake up in the morning, each penny worth one hundred calories. When you eat, for each one hundred calories, put one penny in your right pocket. The right pocket is the restaurant's money; it doesn't belong to you until tomorrow morning when you will put the fourteen pennies back in your left pocket. When your left pocket is empty, you have no more money to spend on food today. You have effective control of your behavior on eating.

But what's to stop me from borrowing pennies and spending the borrowed money? Nothing will stop me except my will to succeed, to get lean. Yes, I depend on my will, about which thinkers debate whether it exists or not.

I say the will exists because I can feel it when it's on the same way I can feel anger, sadness, or love. When expressing my will, I may appear to others as stubborn, obstinate, and unreasonable—a bulldog. I'm like the English in 1941 facing the Nazis. I define the will as the emotion that moves me to do what's right, even when I'm alone, uncomfortable, pained, or terrified. It's the same emotion of the will that stops me from doing something pleasant, enticing, and even enthralling when it's not right or harmful to me or others. My will is tied to my moral sense, a strictly human trait, and it's my connection with the source of life and consciousness deep inside me and beyond.

If you are new to the will, it will be uncomfortable for you at first. Activating the will is stressful, producing tension and even anxiety. Preparing to act under the force of the will can even be painful, as it is when we make up a list of things to do, meet deadlines on the way to our goal, or face the necessity of changing our long-entrenched habits to succeed.

Life runs on fundamental habits, inherited or grown mostly by the age of five. Habits lead us to inevitable actions. You can be confident that people will behave according to their basic habits, their characters. People are predictable in what they do if you know their characters. Study a person's character well, and you'll know how that person will behave with a high degree of confidence. People, as a rule, don't change their habits, the good habits, the indifferent ones, or even the bad habits that they see as such. Only under great internal or external pressure will people change habits with great difficulty and slowly, if at all. Acting contrary to habit is uncomfortable, sometimes even painful, requiring much effort and concentration.

People don't like to stop, think, and concentrate on changing with life rushing on them as it does these days, demanding money and gratifications. They tend to avoid breaking long-held habits; they slip instead into old grooves, especially when they find pleasure in their actions. You can bet profitably that people will not change their ways.

Still, people need to change sometimes; it may even be a matter of life and death for some people to chuck a bad habit like smoking, for example. How do you change?

First, when a habitual routine is coming on, be on the alert and stop or hesitate before moving into it. Hesitate and become deliberate, choosing to recall your goals in life and decide if your habitual routine will help or hinder your goals. If your habitual action serves these goals best, then continue with it; otherwise, re-orient yourself like the captain of a ship checking the stars, compass, or GPS. Listen to your inner voice; if you cannot find a better way, then do nothing but meditate. Then deliberate. To deliberate means that you slow down your thinking, feeling, and action, slow down enough to move surely to the next step in what you want to do. It's like parking your car in a difficult space where you don't want to hit anything. You'll not move fast this way, but you'll do it right.

Second, you can change by strengthening your will, confronting temptation, letting the intellect engage in the struggle, and calling on the emotion of the will to counter the temptation. You can feel the emotion of the will stirring, stiffening like cold anger in your heart. If you're a smoker quitting your habit, you feel the cool anger of your will when you put out a cigarette you just lit. Once you have experienced the will, you can call it up as needed and nurture its growth. Each time you activate the will, you make it stronger. Each time you act with the will to counter a bigger temptation for pleasure or greater fear of pain, you make your will more potent.

Intellect alone is impotent; the emotion of the will links what you know must be done with what you actually do. Feel the rise of the will then when it's needed and let it run with full strength to change your behavior in critical times. When you have done this long enough, you will have extinguished a bad habit or reinforced a good one; thereafter, you'll run free in the right direction without effort under the force of habit. As Verdi might say, *la forza del destino* is the force of habit.

Third, you can change habitual behavior by blocking and channeling its flow before it occurs. For example, if, like me, you're prone to overeating, keep little food in your refrigerator and pantry; use a small plate, fork, and spoon; shop food less frequently; avoid restaurants, especially buffets, and engagements where the hostess serves food too lavishly; wear tight pants and belt; go to bed early to skip night eating; eat slowly, chewing thoroughly, setting your fork down after each bite until it's gone down your gullet; drink water one hour before sitting down to a meal; don't sit down to a meal, but grab a snack, and so forth. You can devise similar tactics for other habits you want to change. These tactics are cheating the will, but they work in the long run because a habit is a repetitive action, and if not repeated, it's bound to become extinguished. Similarly, you can set up channeling of desirable behavior, reinforcing a good habit. For example, if you want to get up earlier to attend to your duties, set a loud alarm earlier, out of reach unless you get up and out of bed.

We have found how to couple what we want to achieve with what we are doing, *praxis*, the exercise of the will, the force of life itself.

Now, let's think about life's purpose. Our purpose is to serve: to work and serve ourselves, our family, our community, our species, all species, Nature, God if you like. If we are children of a Creator, our purpose too is to create, work, build, design, produce new interesting patterns, and reduce the chaos and the disorder (entropy) in the world. Seeking pleasure, even happiness itself, is a lowly goal, unfit for us. Even less of a worthy goal is avoiding discomfort, pain, and even agony, if necessary, in doing our work. Not that we want to seek out pain, damaging our bodies, beating our backs with chains like religious zealots. We want instead to enjoy as best as we can whatever comes from doing our duty; that's fine and good. On our deathbeds, we shall accept the utmost pain and carry on with our work if possible.

In our work, we have primary goals: to achieve success in our chosen career, make enough money to provide food and shelter to ourselves, marry and raise a family, win and influence people enough for social acceptance or even fame, help cure the evils in the world, and promote justice. We need to observe a number of supporting goals also: to promote our good health and fitness, to keep learning new skills and knowledge needed as the world changes, to save money and property for our security and retirement, and to perform our civic duties, such as voting, tax payments, jury duties.

I want every year of my life, every day, every hour, every minute to be dedicated to my goals and actually be used to further these goals. How about rest and recreation? Some time should be given over to R & R, scheduled for that purpose as needed, and no more. When tired, rest; when rested, work. Needed fun for relaxation is helpful to a career; excess fun is damaging. What should I do about the arts—literature, drama, cinema, music, dance, painting, sculpture, and interior and exterior design? Art can enter every phase of life—work, family, society—because art is an emanation of the life force, invigorating everything we do. I would like to integrate art into my activities as much as possible, into my eating, exercising, traveling, sleeping, socializing, loving, and work. How about laughter, adventure, and spontaneity? I will allow for these also. Otherwise, life becomes boring, but I don't want the pursuit of trifles, pleasure, comfort, or happiness even, taking over my life, distracting me from my purpose.

Felicity follows function follows fulfillment. Fulfillment, my life's purpose, determines how I function, how I behave, and such behavior makes me happy, joyful, and serene.

I expect fulfillment in experiencing sensations and feelings, as well as thoughts in exploring this, our planet. I see myself as a robotic probe on Earth, my consciousness a transmission from another place, another dimension. My body is very valuable, a complex mechanism at my disposal to get around on the surface, much more sophisticated than the surveyor craft on Mars. But my body is not I. I belong elsewhere and will go there again to join my transmitter and be debriefed fully after my body has ceased to function. My body is like a candle holder with a burning light. As the candle is used up, the light goes out to infinity like all radiation. Seeing myself thus, I have set my goal while living here to learn as much as I can--skills, knowledge, wisdom, right behaviors—to explore the world, seeking adventure without terminating my body too soon, experiencing all the activities this body is capable of tackling: swimming, dancing, loving, singing, playing, laughing, knowing other human beings intimately, and accomplishing things of value to me and others.

Primarily, however, my goal in life is to think, with the sharpest reasoning my brain is capable of exercising, about the fundamental problems of existence and the universe--and to write down my answers to the big problems with the best art and artistry I can muster.

That is the purpose of my life. I hope my work is of value to other people. In any case, my efforts are valuable to me. What is the purpose of your life?

A definite major purpose in life, perhaps some secondary goals also, enables praxis, the control, the wheel and rudder in steering your body in turbulent seas. Your purpose must be concrete, definite, and well-defined. You cannot tie effective action to a vague, tenuous purpose. Your purpose must be vivid and foremost in your mind when planning and executing your actions. Repeating frequently to yourself and others, in writing and speech, what you want to accomplish reinforces your vision for the success you want. Detail your goal, embellish it, and picture it in your mind's eye often; it will help couple your goal to your daily activities, and you'll be less likely to be thwarted by adverse events and people.

The world around us is often turbulent, chancy, even mad. People fail us, contraptions fail us, nature fails us. We begin by exercising *ataraxia*, complete inner peace with a smile. We submit for a time to the will of all-powerful, compassionate, and wise Jupiter, Jehovah, or Allah. We accept momentarily whatever fate dumps on our heads; we resign, relax, and remain calm in the eye of the hurricane. We no longer feel pain, have no need of pleasure, and enter a state of perfect mental tranquility. That's *ataraxia*, taught by Epicurus, another concept taken up elsewhere. For now, we go the way of *praxis*, powerful action in the face of adversity. We want firm actions, day in, day out, hour in, hour out, to take us out of the storm to our port of call. Actions that inevitably follow from our intention, premise, or axiom, like a logical or mathematical argument, like the laws of physics: gravity, electromagnetism, and the nuclear forces.

Praxis is a method for controlling your time and life, directing your energies to succeed in your goals. Your day has twenty-four hours, eight hours or so of which are given to sleep and dreaming over which you have little control. You still have sixteen hours remaining for goal-driven actions. If you use your waking hours effectively, you'll find your sleep and dreams may also be productive in ideas. Working effectively each hour, you push towards your goals. What you may control is the push, the action you're able to take, not the result you want, although your aim is to hit your target.

In your daily schedule, do set up your target, but mainly plan your actions and later record what you actually did each hour. Stick to your planned schedule unless you find a good reason to change course; don't vacillate. At the end of the day, study how you have deviated from your planned actions and how to correct your behavior the next day. *Praxis* doesn't come at once without practice, like an epiphany; you perfect *praxis* gradually with constant and devoted training, like any other discipline. You may only control in the world what you feel, what you think, and what you do; the rest is up to the dice and toss of nature.

You can improve control of your behavior by rehearsing your planned actions enough times until what you're going to do is very vivid, certain, and real in your mind. Think of yourself as an actor preparing to go on stage to say your piece because "all the world's a stage, and all the men and women merely players."[1]

Unavoidably, some of the time, you'll be busy with necessary supportive actions: dressing, eating, exercising, resting, cleaning, and

---

1. William Shakespeare, *As You Like It*, ed. Barbara A. Mowat and Paul Werstine (New York: Simon & Schuster, 2009), 2:7:139-143.

nursing yourself. Enjoy what you can of these activities, but fit them in the interstices of your work schedule by making them brief. For example, eating is something we do too much; affluence leads us to overindulge. The adult human body requires few calories and nutrients in a few snacks: each day, sixty grams of protein, thirty grams of good fat, and thirty grams of fiber, with traces of vitamins, minerals, phytochemicals, and antioxidants, which you can best get from delicious vegetables and fruits with complex carbohydrates for clean energy. Any excess food goes to waste or body fat. We tend to eat too much and too fast. Less eating will give you, paradoxically, more energy—also better health and a longer life. Eat little, slowly, and enjoyably, focusing on fine, fresh food for ten minutes between work periods of fifty minutes, like a psychiatrist's hours. If the needed materials, like ready foods, are available at hand, you can fit most of your support activities between your fifty-minute productive sessions.

Begin your work on the hour and take a break for supporting activities ten minutes before the hour. Even exercise can be fitted into ten-minute sessions; the health benefits are the same as for longer exercise periods. Next to eating, we allow too much time for exercise if we are health conscious. Sweating in the gym for hours to lose weight is a waste of time. You can lose weight best by eating less. For bodybuilding, you need to work out more, but as for staying fit, three ten-minute sessions of exercise a day are sufficient if they include aerobics, weight training, and calisthenics for flexibility. You can set an egg timer to remind you of work and break intervals.

With regular breaks, you will have more productive work periods and more stamina to work hard till the end of the day.

You need to work hard each day to achieve important goals. *Praxis* is a discipline of feeling, thought and action, empowering you to work hard, enabling you to do what promotes your goals in life and to avoid what is harmful or wasteful of your time and other resources. Why do we often neglect the work we must do and indulge in actions that we should avoid? First, we seek pleasure for the sake of pleasure instead of utility. Second, we run away from necessary discomfort or pain. Third, we lapse into apathy, even depression, neglecting what we need.

Fourth, we submit to damaging habits, wasteful customs, addictions, and debilitating modes of behavior, such as overeating, smoking, gambling, drinking alcohol, shopping excessively, or fornicating indiscriminately.

Praxis will set you free from such chains of behavior and lead you to greener pastures because it is a belief system, a faith not necessarily tied to religion.

To achieve, you need to have faith in yourself, in nature, and in your ability to succeed in getting results you deem worthwhile. Motivational teachers have called this attitude positive thinking. Positive or constructive thinking and enthusiasm motivate us to move, exert ourselves, and achieve. Certainly, negative or downbeat thinking does the opposite, but it has its place in life too; it's conservative. When you practice negative thinking, you fall into a passive state, lethargy, inaction, sleep, conserving resources—sometimes your very life. That is the evolutionary advantage of feeling low, dejected, defeated, or depressed. Positive thinking, on the other hand, pushes you to expend resources liberally to get to your goal because you believe you can reach it, sometimes risking your money or your eye and limb. You may end up with irrational exuberance or mania. Your nervous system firing neurons, your glands secreting hormones, and your muscles contracting all act together with positive feedback into larger and larger swings to resonance, sometimes causing a complete breakdown.

Negative thinking and feedback are beneficial when breakdown threatens. Go then into *ataraxia* with laughter or at least a smile. It's all a game anyway to be enjoyed, this sporting life, acting on the stage of the world, having our exits and our entrances.

But while forging ahead with your daily goal-directed schedule, be prepared to counter distractions from your body, your negative mind, your bad old habits, your well-meaning friends and relatives, as well as those who mean to waste your time and damage your life. You'll be working intensely, doing much good work, when suddenly sleepiness will hit you, a friend will call to chat, or a salesperson will pounce on you. Be prepared to firmly resist these intrusions, pushing ahead with the things you have scheduled to do. This is the time to be stubborn, obstinate, pig-headed, projecting your powerful will.

If you want to accomplish anything extraordinary, you'll run into opposition; it's in the nature of the world. The world is jealous of achievers because most people are not. You'll need practice to defend your time and other resources from those friends or adversaries apt to waste them for their own aims or no aim at all. You have to possess the force of will to overcome the enemy, most of the enemy being within yourself, your lethargic, slothful self, demanding to be pampered, comforted, and pleased. The core of *praxis*, cold anger (*thymos,* I call it), drives you on; it's what they call in marketing circles aggressiveness. You're not hurting anybody, but you extend yourself, projecting your objective on your own actions and those of others. *Thymos* (aggressiveness or assertiveness) is that cool, calculating, controlled, enterprising push towards the goal, plainly seen in sports and business, but also energizing the arts, politics, professions, and sciences.

I'm not implying you should be devoting every hour of your day to your job except for necessary rest periods. You have other goals and interests besides your career: family, friends, and community interests. Give these interests their due—but no more if you want personal success.

The desire for personal success will lead you to exercise *praxis*, part of which is the right self-talk. What we think affects how we feel, and how we feel affects what we do. Psychologists say that cognition does not usually occur in an affective vacuum; that is, thinking is tied up with feelings. On the athletic field or in business meetings, you get a pep talk from the coach or the boss. As an independent performer, you need to give a pep talk to yourself: "I can do this." "I can handle it." "It's a piece of cake." "I'm going to win this." "I'm going to make it through this." Keep talking to yourself until you have built up enough drive inside to act unless it's time for conservation and negative talk: "I need a little rest now before I begin again." "Look out, you're over-extending yourself."

If a pep talk fails to motivate you rightly to solve your problem, if nothing works for a time, relax and fall back on humor and laughter with the aid of *ataraxia*. Counteracting *thymos*, humor is an easing up, spontaneous and frank, a play with friends or enemies you approach lightly, with laughter, the relaxing reflex letting go of tension and stress for a while until you recover your balance to press on again with *praxis*.

Praxis is mainly intentional living, tied to goals, not amusement, leading promptly to fitting and efficient action. It is not a casual and passive lifestyle directed by others, in which most people indulge, settling in mediocrity. Spiritually, *praxis* is the immediate and personal contact with the divine, a taste of the source guiding our destinies.

My lifestyle is a simple one as dictated by *praxis*, dedicated to purpose, integrity, conscience, ethical and frugal living in a village community, respect for the environment, mostly vegetarian eating, beneficence to all people and living things, and resistance to ostentation, commercial appetites, and excessive money making. Like you or any human being, occasionally, I'm assailed by doubts, anxiety, and even despair about my life, family, and the whole world. Then, I quickly respond with praxis, blocking such feelings and thoughts and substituting the mindset that leads me to thrive and help others. The human mind can entertain one powerful emotion at a time; therefore, I bring on *thymos*, banishing frustration, self-pity, fear, or despair.

When *praxis* with *thymos* is on, I know that every moment is a kernel of the future, my destiny, which must not be derailed by a foul mindset. As a rule, *thymos* transforms me to act with fortitude and enterprise. If in doubt about my next move, however, I stop and meditate, doing nothing, which is better than making the wrong move. I seek guidance in the silence of my spirit. I know that each moment, my actions should bring me closer to my goal, or else I pause and reset my mind. I may approach people I know who can influence me in the right direction or read a passage or two of wisdom from my favorite thinkers, Plato, Marcus Aurelius, St. Augustine, Descartes, and Russell.

Contact with good minds leads to good actions. I always seek to guide my steps with logic and sound reasoning, taking into account what I feel, but never to follow my emotions blindly. I program my actions towards my goal, visualizing each step in detail, in full color, rehearsing my movements enough times to completion, and then I stop again, listen, attend, and repeat the sequence of actions in my mind, never allowing distraction, until I'm satisfied my course is right, firm, and inevitable.

The core idea of *praxis* is self-discipline, a very different concept than discipline imposed on us by others. Self-discipline leads to true freedom of mind and such success in life as is possible for us mortals in an indifferent, often hostile world ruled as much by caprice as by law.

14

LIFE: IS IT A PHYSICAL SYSTEM, OR IS IT MORE?

Philosophers speak of physicalism, which states that everything is physical and everything else we know depends on physical properties, even consciousness and living. Yet, living things differ from inanimate things in that the living act upon other physical materials, using them inside cells to metabolize, grow, and reproduce. Of course, living things on Earth, based on carbon chains, are a subset of self-replicating systems, some species of which we can design. Physicalism is the general view of modern science; this essay will question this materialistic view of life.

To start, we all observe that what lives eventually and inevitably dies, stops acting, and decomposes into its component materials. Inanimate objects may wear out, but they don't decompose so dramatically.

Moreover, all organisms, including plants, have one or more cells with membranes. An organism without a membrane is a quasi-living thing and quasi-species, like viruses.

Viruses are quasi-living nuclei as they don't metabolize but exploit the resources of the host to replicate.

Living things with cells go back in time, surprisingly further back than six thousand years. The earliest life forms appeared on Earth about four billion years ago; all organisms are their descendants. Food for pessimists: more than 99 percent of all organisms that ever lived have become extinct. You should know that we have so far identified and cataloged less than 10 percent of existing species, well, most of the bigger ones.

We believe life formed under primeval conditions, in hot water pools filled with chemicals on Earth, or it came down from space on meteorites. Life from elsewhere only translates the problem of how life formed. Special conditions were necessary for life, as they were for diamonds, another concoction from carbon.

For many centuries, people believed that life could form spontaneously, given enough gunk. Louis Pasteur demonstrated conclusively that no spontaneous generation of life occurs, but it is the result of invisible-to-the-naked-eye micro-organisms. This was useful knowledge for brewers and yogurt makers.

When you culture living yogurt, you use the elements of life, the same as in the rest of nature: carbon, hydrogen, oxygen, nitrogen, etc. Carbon chains form large molecules, such as in DNA and RNA, which are amino acids or proteins. We have produced amino acids in the lab, but we have not assembled anything living so far. Why?

We should be able to produce a simple organism, or we should ask if anything is missing in our lab. Something, indeed, may be missing. From ancient times, thinkers have believed that life was imbued with spirit or a special energy. Even in our scientific world today, most people around the world (are they idiots?) believe spirits reside in living things.

On the other hand, most scientists deny the existence of spirit and relegate it to religion or superstition: cases in point are mesmerism (Mesmer), animal magnetism, Odic force (Reichenbach), and élan vital, or vital impetus (Henri Bergson).

In fact, most scientists believe that living systems can be examined and explained as other physical systems and that life follows the four established physical forces and their underlying particles.

Science generally follows the belief that those things exist only that can be sensed or measured by means of instruments and can be described by numbers, relations, and mathematics. I counter that clearly things exist that we cannot observe or measure, such as ideas or visions. Life and consciousness may be such things.

When it comes to life, many people think that health depends on spiritual or life energies: qi (chi), pneuma, prana, etc. Even scientists accept the placebo effect (20 percent average) in medical studies. In some outlier cases, the placebo can be as high as 80 percent of the result: the sugar pill really cures you if your belief in its efficacy and that of your health practitioner are strong enough. If a bunch of your friends and relatives are also praying fervently for you, you're more likely to be cured.

Friends praying or singing together make a sort of complex life form: minds joined with empathy, a social consciousness emerging. Life and consciousness are emergent effects of complex systems, such as our brain.

At the lowest level, if we assemble a living cell from components that we make, how do we activate it? How do we introduce the spark of life into it and get it going? Where does the life energy, the chi, come from, and how do we inject it into our assembly of amino acids?

Most scientists have discredited the theory of chi, vital impetus, the fifth force, or life energy, as they have done with Aristotle's theory of levity to explain gravity because the theory of life energy does not explain anything and does not help in predicting events.

Elan vital, the zoticon, the karmic particle, whatever name you want to give it, has not been detected yet. Neither has the graviton, which mediates gravity, but scientists believe it exists. Recently, gravity waves emanating from colliding black holes have been detected, as Einstein predicted.

The photon particle mediates electromagnetism, meaning it is the causal agent of EM waves through space, air, or liquids. As it moves at the speed of light, 186,000 miles per second, the photon vibrates, creating waves, somewhat like the man in the pool swimming and making waves.

The man in the water moves with a purpose and is aware. He's not being driven but is *driving*; he uses his arms and legs with a will. What is causing the man to do so? It could be a fifth particle of nature, which

Life: Is it a Physical System, or is it More?

I have named zoticon, hypothetical like the graviton until we can detect it.

In ancient Greek medical theory, the zoticon is an organ in the body that controls life energy, pneuma, breath, and spirit. When we die, our pneuma leaves the body for parts unknown. The Chinese of old had similar theories when they discussed chi, the life energy flowing through the body's meridian channels. (Google informs me that Zoticon is an Israeli company in therapeutics.)

The Jain religion of ancient India has proposed the theory of karmic particles, which transcend time and space and transmit some characteristics to human lives.

But when it comes to gravity waves, we detected them in 2016. We believe in the existence of gravity because of its effects according to Newton's and Einstein's mathematics. A mathematics of the life force is needed, and so are experimental designs to test the theory.

Many people believe a life force theory will come from an outgrowth of quantum mechanics, a field theory of living things permeating the universe. Is there a Light Force or a Dark Force?

The Dark Force is the absence of the Light. So far, we have not measured the life force field with our instruments, but we see its effects; we sense that the field is strongest where living things thrive and among people gathered with love, working, singing, and dancing.

Why not accept the existence of the life force from the effects it causes? We accept the existence of dark energy and dark matter because of the movement of galaxies.

It would help our understanding of life if we could synthesize it. Genetic engineering is the manipulation of genes inside the nucleus, not the production of life from inanimate materials.

All life has much in common. That should help our research. Consider that humans share 50 percent of our genes with bananas and 98 percent of our genes with chimpanzees.

The most fundamental characteristic of living things is, as physicists have discovered, that it is a thermodynamic engine using free energy, also known as negative entropy. What is that?

Free energy, or negative entropy, is produced by living systems, defying the second law of thermodynamics of increasing entropy or disorder in a closed system.

Also, living systems produce negative entropy in their environment by creating new objects. If life has a goal, that goal is to create order and beauty, enhancing consciousness.

We associate consciousness and identity with living entities, more so with humans and animals, although many people believe that plants are conscious and have feelings.

Humans possess consciousness, freedom of the will, and reason, or the capacity for these. With these faculties, when we exercise them, we can create a universe of love and light, beauty and order, good growth, and stability.

15

IS CONTEMPLATION THE ULTIMATE ACTIVITY OF A HUMAN?

The argument goes like this: reason is the highest human faculty, what distinguishes us from other animals. The exercise of reason or contemplation, therefore, is the highest and best use of our lives; that is, contemplation is the ultimate activity we can have as humans. Plato stated that contemplation may allow us to ascend to the Form of the Good, the highest good from which all other forms emanate. Other philosophers, closer to religion, praised contemplation or meditation as the way to *henosis* or union with God. I praise contemplation and meditation, but these practices without consequent beneficial actions are idle pastimes to avoid.

Contemplation is critical in solving problems. Auguste Rodin's *The Thinker* is impressive, a man sitting down with his head bent down resting on his hand, thinking deeply. Contemplation is accompanied by temporary immobility when a person is concentrating on the problem, focusing all attention on the details of the situation. The power of concentration is like that of an intense laser beam on an object we're examining. Without concentration, hard problems remain unsolved. Contemplation is attention directed outward to an object of high interest, a flower, a rock, a stream, or a planet, taking in every minute detail; it's not idle curiosity.

Meditation, or introspection, on the other hand, is attention directed inward to mental objects, such as mathematical concepts or other inner experiences, including mystical visions.

Both contemplation and meditation are active mental states, requiring alertness, awareness, and manipulation of symbols, images, sounds, emotions, and sentiments, but the actions they produce are internal, in our minds. These two practices are useful when they're directed by the will to concentrate on valuable ends, as the Bhagavad Gita states, resulting in constructive actions in the world. Some people feel their will is directed by God toward good deeds when they express their ideas in action; others feel the self, not the Self (God), is in charge.

Freedom of the will does not enter this picture. When you have choices to make, you have some freedom. Most people act habitually most of the time, doing the same things over and over; they have less freedom of the will. To change behavior to more effective patterns, we meditate, reach into the subconscious, and make changes in the subconscious because it controls our habitual behavior and also does most of the difficult problem-solving and creative work.

The conscious mind observes, directs, and focuses attention, but it's linear and lacks imagination. The subconscious is far greater than the conscious mind and works in non-linear and subtler ways. It's so powerful that ideas and images emerging from it are often attributed to divine inspiration and declared to be revelations from God. All the great prophets meditated in solitude, sometimes fasting to free the mind from mundane matters, as Jesus or Mohammed meditated in the desert or the Buddha in the forest. Then, the prophets returned to the world to teach and liberate others from the oppression of suffering the ills of flesh.

In deep meditation or contemplation, a person enters the state of consciousness called the relaxation response; one feels happy and free from worry, joyful like a saint in rapture after hours of prayer. Joy is not enough; it can become like heroin addiction. Meditation must lead to the discovery of some truth or solution to some problem, which we then express outwardly for our profit or the profit of our society. If that event does not follow, meditation and contemplation are a waste of time, dreaming without actualization—a waste of resources.

Great innovators and entrepreneurs are practical dreamers who put their ideas to the test in the outside world of affairs and business. People like Bill Gates, Steve Jobs, Jeff Bezos, and Elon Musk are national treasures; they lead talented people and investors to realize the visions these rare innovators have experienced in contemplation and meditation. Such leaders possess the ability to persist and not be discouraged by failures but to learn from their failures before taking another step forward to their goals. This is the quality of great leaders that makes them different from the rest of us.

A thin line separates impotent mysticism from creative imagination. Creative imagination is backed up with courage—a lack of fear that one will fail in what is attempted.

Much valuable work is initiated by intuition, ideas emerging from mystical experience; Pythagoras engaged in such work in mathematics, music, social activity, and nonsense, for example, denouncing bean eating.

Many scientific discoveries began with thought experiments, such as those of Democritus in ancient Greece and of Einstein early in the twentieth century. Murray Gell-Mann of the California Institute of Technology divined mathematically the existence of quarks making up the atomic nucleus, later shown to exist at the CERN supercollider. Now, physicists dream of vibrating strings as the ultimate entity in the microcosm and of many dimensions of space encompassing the multiverse; it's all just a play of fancy until experiments and observations show the existence of such things.

After contemplating and meditating with deep concentration, act and verify that possible ideas can be realized; any other attitude is wasteful of your valuable time. As an alternative, you can make theoretical proposals and let experimentalists or men of action carry out the verification of your notions, as did Einstein.

A thinker may be happy with the rewards of just contemplating nature and the soul, but when challenged by accusations of impotence, is capable of achievement and material success, like the ancient philosopher Thales of Miletus. That is the highest expression of humanity, being the thinker and the doer. What is the point of meditation without the rewards of that effort for oneself and for one's society? In the East, the emphasis was looking inward, or introspection, but in the West, we looked outward with our scientific and technological emphasis. Now, the East is catching up with the West and, in some ways, surpassing the West.

A global culture is emerging, along with the global economy, combining both inner and outer explorations, like the transcendentalism of Emerson, Whitman, and Thoreau in nineteenth-century America. We look outward, marveling at the splendors of the expanding universe of billions of galaxies, suns, cosmic clouds, quasars, and black holes, but we also find enlightenment within the splendor of our spirits. Futurists forecast a great life for our race—unless we destroy ourselves and our habitat on Earth by releasing and amplifying the monsters from the id, our primitive self.

We have in our minds an information valve between our conscious and subconscious, which valve opens in meditation and relaxation, allowing passage to monsters and other horrors and influences to flow in and out. That's a big problem with both meditation and contemplation when they are excessive and not interrupted by fitting action. Sales specialists and advertisers, for example, put us in a relaxed mood with entertainment first before they make a sales pitch, sometimes subliminally, to make us spend money on things we don't need or even things that harm us. Demagogues hypnotize us with gestures and emotional appeals to unreason, hatred, or fear before they lead us to disaster when in control. The lesson is: don't relax too much in the presence of predators.

A bigger danger is there for us if we hypothesize a second information valve between the subconscious mind and the universal mind, which mind may be either beneficial or harmful to us. This is the danger of mysticism, which draws us to extreme religious views, dangerous to ourselves and our fellow human beings. When delving into the subconscious mind, we need to be on guard for influences from cosmic sources, which are destructive and inhumane, influences coming through the inner information valve when we become too involved in meditation before testing the validity of our inspired ideas in the active world.

16

IS CONSCIOUSNESS AN ILLUSION?

Philosopher and neuroscientist Sam Harris wrote that the human will is an illusion in his book *Free Will*. We can conclude in that case that consciousness, which produces the will, must be an illusion too. Yet, consciousness seems to appear at birth or some months before birth, judging from the behavior of the infant or fetus. Then it expands, sometimes contracts, fades, rots, and, since consciousness is the process that enables us to will and accomplish deeds, it disappears at death because, after death, we see no further actions from a person except some growing of hair and nails. Well, something which appears and fades and eventually disappears is an illusion.

Daniel Dennett, philosopher and cognitive scientist, an atheist like Sam Harris, gave a TED talk on "The Illusion of Consciousness," with details on the physical basis of consciousness and the sense impressions of qualia, or subjective sensations. We associate consciousness with life. Is life also an illusion? Sigmund Freud called God an illusion. I disagree with these eminent philosophers. Consciousness is real for living things; the will exists, and maybe God, the universal consciousness, is in the world somewhere in some form we're still trying to decipher because many people are aware of the existence of God. They're conscious of God as a real entity, the source of all living things, a life-giving spring.

Religious people feel that they approach and contact God in prayer and meditation. Buddhists particularly stress meditation to reach nirvana—total peace and tranquility, freedom from suffering by forgoing selfish desires. But in the West and in Christian traditions, we attach more importance to good works to achieve holiness. Still, we have in the Eastern Orthodox Church the hesychast tradition of quieting the mind to increase our consciousness of the divine. It's like stopping and listening for a message in the wind.

We are more conscious when we experience an increased awareness through the five senses and our other senses inside the body of heat, pain, pressure, etc. Yet, when we meditate, we tend to shut our eyes to concentrate better and focus on our inner world, shutting out stimuli from outside our body. Some people even enter a water tank to exclude intrusive external stimuli and delve deeper into their feelings and thoughts. Thus, you elicit the relaxation response or, if you're religious, communion with God, which has important physical and psychological benefits.

Some individuals take this business of mind expansion through meditation to extremes, even taking drugs such as LSD and psychoactive mushrooms or engaging in repetitive chanting. According to the writings of Carlos Castaneda in the Yaqui way of knowledge of Don Juan, one reaches an alternate reality with the practices of the shaman and holy man. Such practices are said to alter and even expand consciousness, at some risk to health. Strong alcoholic drinks and coffees also alter consciousness: alcohol is a depressant and caffeine a stimulant, and you can combine the two in Irish coffee.

When we feel no pain or pleasure, when we experience no sensations, we are less alive, less conscious. A person who has no love, no empathy, and no compassion for others is closer to a dead state of being. A person who is callous and brutal, like a Nazi, is not a superior human being but someone less alive and less human.

The sensations of music and other art forms can cause consciousness expansion with no health hazards. Artists are deep sensualists, and they impart to us with their creations some of their deep feelings in response to sense impressions.

On the other hand, what happens to consciousness when sitting at a desk or standing on a factory floor doing repetitive tasks? What is the impact on consciousness when we watch idiotic movies or play video games and otherwise engage in vicarious living, even watching sports passively, unless we riot at the stadium? Our consciousness contracts—we become less aware—with popular entertainment, television shows, and monotonous music in the background, to which we seldom actually listen. We get no consciousness enhancement with these passive and dull activities. Doing nothing, we tend to doze off.

Sleep causes consciousness to largely disappear, except in dreams with REMs (rapid eye movements). Babies and old people sleep more because they do not retain nervous energy for long. We all need to sleep to recharge our brain batteries, but sleep is hardly a mental stage of high awareness; certainly, sleep is a disorderly state of awareness, a state dangerous when driving or operating machinery, as dangerous as operating equipment when you're in a meditative state, in the relaxation response.

"To sleep, perchance to dream"[1] is what we may hope to have with death, but death appears to cause a more permanent loss of consciousness. Dead persons don't awaken from their sleep—unless their name is Lazarus. RIP means rest in the peace of death, a euphemism, and even dreams do not appear in death since the brain has ceased functioning altogether.

Unlike Shakespeare's Hamlet, I don't dwell on death at all, finding life more interesting and challenging, focusing on full awareness of eating, working, playing, and loving. Focus increases awareness and conscious living—attention, attention, attention, as the Buddhists say. The Buddha means the Awakened One, awakened to the spiritual life. Much of what we do, however, is habitual, automatic, without

---

1. William Shakespeare, *Hamlet*, ed. Barbara A. Mowat and Paul Werstine (New York: Simon & Schuster, 2012), 3:1:66.

conscious awareness, particularly most work is tedious, lacking in the stimulation of the senses and vivid experience.

Follow the example of Henry David Thoreau then and go to your Walden Pond for a year or two, to front the necessities of life, and when it's time to die, to know that you have lived.

Find solitude somewhere, away from the distractions of boring people, chores, noise, obligations, real or imagined, thinking not of the past or future. Find yourself. Like Walt Whitman, stretch on the green grass and invite your soul, this mystery, which is you, by quieting the constant chatter in your mind. You may then reach a higher consciousness and contact the Cosmic Mind.

The mystery of consciousness is how, from inert physical matter, life and awareness emerge. How does the material become mental? Is it possible that soon we'll have an artificial intelligence system that will respond to questions just like a human, as in the Turing test? Will this machine be conscious? Well, if an AI machine or robot talks and behaves like a human, I'm prepared to accept it as conscious. I accept you as conscious for the same reason.

Throughout the universe, conscious beings exist, unlike us in appearance perhaps, but living and surviving; the universe is made up of the same elements and compounds, a plethora of planets surround stars, and stars exist in hundreds of billions in billions of galaxies. We may be in contact with these beings, some of them intelligent like us, through psychic channels, in which case aliens do not need to visit us for us to know their existence.

Closer to Earth, a psychological theory by Julian Jaynes, states that about 2,000 years ago, consciousness emerged when the intellect in humans connected with the emotional locus in the brain, as explained in the 1976 book *The Origin of Consciousness in the Breakdown of the Bicameral Mind*. When the intellect is very active, our emotional side is somewhat suppressed, and when we feel strong emotions, such as love, anger, or fear, the intellect functions less effectively. The frontal lobe, the neo-cortex, and the amygdala in the mammalian brain have complex interactions; sometimes, the interactions enhance the functioning of both brain centers, thinking causing more fear through the imagination and fear stimulating more intense thoughts and awareness of danger with hormonal secretions stimulating the nervous system.

Is your mind in the brain? Most scientists believe that consciousness originates in the brain as endogenous activity. It's possible, however, that consciousness and identity are transmissions, the brain being simply a receiver. When the brain disintegrates in death, we don't see any activity, but the broadcast continues.

It's likely that all living cells in the body participate in consciousness, not just neurons in the brain. Under a microscope, I can see one-celled organisms, like an amoeba, behaving with intention for survival, seizing nutrients, escaping dangers, and propagating—these organisms are conscious because of how they behave. Human consciousness is an emergent property of billions of cells in the body working together in synergism.

Some people would deny consciousness in animals because animals lack our brain and mind, but to me, a dog or cat, even a pig squealing at being butchered, these and all other animals have feelings and awareness, and animals deserve our compassion. Plants, too, are conscious, although they don't move much, with some exceptions, such as the Venus flytrap. Plants are made up of cells like we are and strive for survival in the face of hazards, competing for sunlight, moisture, or nutrients.

Some people, including Hindus, believe that consciousness permeates everything in nature, so even rocks, waters, and air possess awareness. Rupert Sheldrake, a philosopher and biologist, thinks that the sun and the galaxy are conscious, as are all self-organizing systems. That may be an extreme view because inanimate objects acted upon by living things don't behave like the living.

Living things are obviously different from other things, and if consciousness is an illusion, then life is an illusion, and so is the whole world. Plato's followers believe that the mind is real and the physical world is an illusion. I think, therefore, I exist, or *Cogito, ergo sum*, after Rene Descartes, I am the only entity that exists and all else revolves around me. Hello, solipsism, you're not for me. I see myself as simply a spark in God's mystic fire, as Ralph Waldo Emerson taught.

As written in the Upanishads of Hinduism, "I am the self, and God is the Self."[2]

As a self, I desire things, but not selfishly. I seek health consciousness, wealth, social, romantic Kama Sutra, power, and above all, God consciousness, the awareness that I am not ever alone but always part of the stream of life everywhere in the universe, a drop of precious water going down with the river to the sea or main, as described by John Donne.

---

2. Eknath Easwaran, ed., *The Upanishads* (Tomales, CA: Nilgiri Press, 2007), 52.

17

DEFEATING DEATH

Can we avoid dying and live forever? The quest for immortality has been with humans ever since they saw death occurring, and they realized they would die too one day. In ancient Mesopotamia, Gilgamesh saw his friend die and became apprehensive that he, too, would soon have the same end. The legend says Gilgamesh traveled all over the world in search of a cure for death; he found it, but jealous immortal gods snatched it away from him before he could use it. Ponce de Leon also searched for the fountain of youth in wild Florida but never found it. Yet, with modern science, we have a chance to cure aging and disease and to live indefinitely long lives, even to become immortal.

Most people want to live long to enjoy the pleasures of human existence or to avoid death out of fear. A few persons, however, in desperation or extreme pain, seek out death, an end to their troubles. "To be or not to be, that is the question: Whether 'tis nobler in the mind to suffer the slings and arrows of outrageous fortune, or take arms against a sea of troubles and by opposing end them."[1] I say how to live is the problem, not how to die.

First, to learn how to live, stretch your time on Earth, avoiding every conceivable way of dying. That is, life extension is the first step to a good life and possibly to immortality. Second, procreate because much of you is in your genes; your body is merely a host to the genes and a carrier to the future. Third, see to it that your best ideas and ideals are passed on to future generations because we are what we think.

Genes and ideas are fine, but they're not me as a person with my body, me as a conscious being, seeing flowers, thrilling to great music, making love. My brother-in-law, age ninety, who had his share of illnesses and accidents, likes to say we should get rid of our bodies: our bodies are too much trouble, subject to failure, and we should move our memories to a computer, which can be repaired indefinitely with ease. I doubt that our consciousness is just memories; transferring our awareness to a machine does not seem feasible to help you or me soon.

Another idea my brother-in-law proposed is cryonic suspension, about which he read in Robert Ettinger's best-selling book *The Prospect of Immortality*. Ettinger also founded the Cryonic Institute after becoming acutely aware of his own mortality at age forty-two. If you are about to die from an incurable disease or accident, the Institute will freeze your body or just your brain in liquid hydrogen and maintain it in suspension until medical science has advanced sufficiently to revive and restore it to health. Unfortunately, freezing causes a tremendous amount of damage to body cells. Future physicians would have to repair each individual cell; why should they go to that much trouble? Society can produce fresh human beings the old-fashioned way for all its needs.

Hope of medical miracles is persistent in our society. Did we not cure smallpox, leprosy, poliomyelitis, and so many diseases and breakdowns of the body? A friend of mine, at twenty-six, with a PhD in science, a professor at the California Institute of Technology, switched

---

1. William Shakespeare, *Hamlet*, ed. Barbara A. Mowat and Paul Werstine (New York: Simon & Schuster, 2012), 3:1:56-60.

to medicine after his father died suddenly at fifty-six. I was enrolled at Caltech myself in computers and biosystems Analysis, pursuing my own ideas for defeating death, the ultimate problem. I had grand plans for a life in search of vast knowledge, a life with a large family of my own making, and great riches, culminating in important contributions to the world. All those plans required longevity approaching immortality. I had read in 1966 I.J. Good's forecast of the advent of super-intelligent computers that would solve nearly any problem we might pose to them, even the problem of immortality. I.J. Good probably influenced Arthur C. Clark, physicist and science fiction writer, when Clark wrote *2001: A Space Odyssey*, with HAL, an intelligent computer on board a spaceship bound for Jupiter. Well, 2001 came and went, and we have not yet established colonies on the moon or designed a computer of even average human intelligence, although we have had much progress in computers, communications, and rocket science.

I still think we can eventually build a computer far more intelligent than any human through a process of evolving smarter and smarter machines, if we could only get to the first of the series. We are going to have to start by inventing machine pattern recognition, a human ability, not yet implemented in computers despite more than forty years of research going back to Frank Rosenblatt's perceptrons.

The cure for illness, accidental damage, and aging will sooner come from tissue replacement with stem cells. Organs from our own body's stem cells, not subject to rejection by the immune system, will replace damaged or aged parts of the body. The brain will have to be repaired with care so that we don't lose our consciousness and identity, injecting stem cells into the brain in measured numbers and arranging for their incorporation into the neural networks. This will be something like the immortality of the amoeba, replicating with mitosis and living indefinitely for as long as available nutrients and environmental factors allow.

What if we can replace damaged tissues? We would live longer, but eventually, death would overtake us through accident, murder, suicide, or war. We need to understand what death is—a difficult undertaking because we don't know what life is. Death is apparently like sleep: the eyes are closed, one doesn't move much, and one is helpless—consciousness is lost. When my dad was near death because he stopped eating, I was trying to feed him myself, and he kept saying, "I want to sleep. I'm tired; I want to sleep," although he had been sleeping quite a lot. He was tired of living and wanted to pass on. Poetically, we say loved ones are asleep in their graves, but we wake up from sleep rested, refreshed, and fully conscious. In death, people are in deep, deep sleep without an awakening. "To die, to sleep; to sleep, perchance to dream—aye, there's the rub: for in that sleep of death what dreams may come, when we have shuffled off this mortal coil."[2] No one really knows what dreams, if any, may come after death, and that's the rub.

We know the signs of death: breathing stops, the heart stands still, the body does not move ever again by itself, the skin gets pale, even gray, and coldness and rigor mortis stiffening set in. The brain does not broadcast EEG waves, and decomposition follows. The stench is an aphrodisiac for flies that swarm over the carcass, laying their eggs for maggots to consume the flesh. In the last stage of living, nobody ever experiences death; we only feel the dying: the pain, the surgery, the frantic efforts of physicians and nurses, and pre-operation and post-operation agony. This is the phenomenon of death, but what is the inner experience of death? Is it a blanking out of everything or a passage to another existence, as the prophets declare and religious people believe?

We read stories about people who experienced floating out of their bodies and hovering over doctors and nurses in surgery when these people nearly died or died for a moment or two; these stories are called near-death experiences and make interesting journalism. Some people near death also see a tunnel with an ineffable light at the end and sense a compassionate presence, presumably God. People under anesthesia and near death don't make reliable observers. Were they really at death's door when they had these experiences?

To understand what death really is, we must understand what life is

---

2. William Shakespeare, *Hamlet*, ed. Barbara A. Mowat and Paul Werstine (New York: Simon & Schuster, 2012), 3:1:64-68.

because death is the absence of life, like darkness is the absence of light, and evil is the absence of good. We say a dead body is lifeless, and that is a circular definition. What, then, is life? Erwin Schrödinger, Nobel prize-winning physicist, defined life as the process of creating negative entropy, building order out of chaos. In thermodynamics, entropy is a physical quantity that measures the degree of disorder in a closed system. The second law of thermodynamics says that all closed systems tend towards greater disorder—but life counteracts this law. Many generations of coral built the Great Barrier Reef in churning seas north of Australia, and generations of men and women constructed Chicago in the windy plains south of the Great Lakes. During life, the body, made of billions of cells or a single cell, creates negative entropy (negentropy, as Schrödinger called it). In contrast, after death, the body follows the natural law of entropy into decomposition.

Zombies are fictional characters; they violate the laws of nature and cannot exist. The life force moves living things in a purposeful way, a way in which material things cannot move. Life is the fifth force of nature, after gravity, electromagnetism, and the weak and strong nuclear forces, which bundle up energy in what we call physical mass. The zoticon particle mediates the life force, as the photon mediates electromagnetism, and the graviton, the force of gravity or gravitation. Physicists have not detected the graviton yet, but they are sure it exists because of the behavior of masses—and the zoticon exists because of the observed behavior of organisms.

Zoticon particles travel through space unseen at the speed of light; they enter any suitable structure of carbon, silicon, or any element that forms long chains of molecules and animate that structure. Living things must be abundant in the universe in a vast variety of forms. When a bodily structure fails and decay sets in, the life force leaves that body, and zoticons travel elsewhere to activate other structures. Sometimes, the life force leaves a body for no reason we can identify. I have seen identical plants or animals in the same area, fed the same, one sickening and dying as the spirit of life left, its sibling clinging on and growing, becoming more animated and stronger, but eventually, age or injury takes all away.

Key features of living structures are that they absorb materials (feed), grow, and replicate their forms. The life force holds the parts of a living structure together if the organism can function sufficiently well. Decay and decomposition follow quickly after the organism fails to function properly to feed, grow, and replicate. Then, the life field collapses, and zoticons beam away in the form of particles carrying consciousness to other spheres.

We associate death with permanent loss of consciousness. If we lose consciousness outside of sleep or controlled anesthesia, that's an emergency. Our body may shut down completely, or we may have a serious accident. Clearly, our brain is the locus of consciousness, and consciousness is strongly affected by injury to the brain, toxins, viruses, or high fever with inflammation. LSD was said to expand consciousness, but usually, the drug grossly distorts feelings and thoughts. It is an easy assumption to say that the destruction of the brain results in the total and permanent loss of awareness, but there is another possibility. Consciousness may not be an endogenous activity of the nervous system but a transmission to it. The brain acts as a receiver, bringing consciousness and purposeful activity to the body. Sir John Eccles, the great neuroscientist, spent his life searching for the seat of the psyche in the brain, but neither he nor many others in neuroscience have located the neuronal center where the personality, soul, or spirit is located.

Hindus believe spirit—consciousness—permeates the universe and resides in every living thing, the lowest form being a clod of dirt, with millions of micro-organisms, and the highest form being human. Buddhists stress deep meditation, communion with the divine source of consciousness, and kindness towards all sentient creatures. A sentient creature goes through innumerable lives, advancing to higher levels of awareness with good thoughts and behavior until the attainment of Nirvana, complete peace with God, a state achieved by the Buddha, which in Sanskrit means the Awakened One.

If consciousness is a transmission, the Buddha had a true insight. With death, the signal is lost at the receiving brain, but since the source of consciousness in the cosmic sender is immortal, the message is safe and can be preserved or sent out again to another capable receiver.

The lion snaps her jaws at the zebra's throat, cutting off the zebra's carotid arteries; the zebra loses consciousness and collapses into a meal for the lion pride. Where did the zebra's consciousness go? The lions are aware, enjoying their meal of flesh, and the zebra's body is completely defenseless. Is this the work of a compassionate God?

We can keep the brain and consciousness going with nutrients in a liquid solution. Sever the carotid arteries and connect to a glucose pump; remove the skull along natural fissures, and remove the face, skin, etc. You end up with consciousness in a jar but without sensations of any sort. Not a desirable way to continue consciousness, but it works.

Is there another way consciousness may continue after death and the brain's dissolution? Life is like a candle string in space-time, and consciousness is the flame beginning to burn along the string and eventually coming to the end of it or blowing out in a puff of wind. We know that the universe runs in opposite pairs, such as matter and anti-matter, or positive and negative magnetic poles. It also runs in cycles, like night following day and day following night. Death is paired with life: death following life and life following death. Eventually the universe will be gone and be created again with another Big Bang, the beginning of time. Your day of birth will come again; your personality and consciousness will return. Déjà vu.

Possibly, your personality and consciousness translate to another body, a transmigration of the soul. Or God transmits your soul to a new body. Or God salvages your spirit after your body has perished and preserves it in a special place, such as Heaven. Such are the possible ways of defeating death.

Yet, we grieve at the death of a loved one. Is the grief for the dead person or for ourselves who remain on Earth without the one we have lost? Some people go to funerals joyfully with jazz processions and parades; others honor their dead ancestors at el Día de los Muertos with sugar skulls and dressed skeletons with offerings of golden marigolds and foods.

A child asks, "What happened to my fish, Mom? It's floating upside-down. What's the matter with it?" Mom says, "Your little fish is dead; it went to Heaven because it was a good little fish." "Will I die too, Mom?" "Yes, but not for a long, long time. You're young, strong, smart, and careful about dangers." "What is Heaven, Mom?"

Christianity teaches that Jesus defeated death and rose from the cenotaph to greet again his disciples and give them his last instructions before ascending to Heaven. Jesus gave us life beyond the grave if we can believe in Him. So, the priests promise to the faithful at funerals and comfort relatives of the dead. Be faithful, be obedient to the commands of God's prophet, and you shall never die, even as your body ages, falls apart, rots, and turns to dust onto dust. Thus, religion gives us solace in the face of death, but religion is not about what is; it is about what we feel.

A childrens prayer:

Now I lay me down to sleep
Pray the Lord my soul to keep.
If I die before I wake
I pray for God my soul to take.

Ben Franklin wrote, "Fear not death, for the sooner we die, the longer shall we be immortal."[3]

John Donne wrote, "Death be not proud, though some have called thee mighty and dreadful, for thou are not so."[4]

And in another of Donne's meditations: "Now this bell tolling softly for another, says to me, thou must die; any man's death diminishes me because I am involved in mankind; and therefore, never send to know for whom the bell tolls; it tolls for thee."[5]

---

3. Benjamin Franklin, *Poor Richard's Almanack* (Mount Vernon: Peter Pauper Press, 2003), 50.
4. John Donne, *The Complete English Poems*, ed. A. J. Smith (London: Penguin Books, 1996), 293.
5. John Donne, *Devotions upon Emergent Occasions and Death's Duel*, ed. John Carey (New York: Oxford University Press, 1999), 108.

Robert Louis Stevenson, author of *Dr. Jekyll and Mr. Hyde*:

Under the wide and starry sky
Dig the grave and let me die
And I laid me down with a will
This be the verse you gave me;
Here he lies where he longed to be;
Home is the sailor, home from the sea
And the hunter home from the hill.[6]

St. Paul, 1 Corinthians 15:55: "O death, where is thy sting? O grave, where is thy victory?"

Walt Whitman in "Song of Myself" from *Leaves of Grass*:

Has anyone supposed it lucky to be born?
I hasten to inform him or her it is just as lucky to die, and I know it...
I am the mate and companion of people, all just as immortal and fathomless as myself,
(They do not know how immortal, but I know)

The two old, simple problems, ever intertwined, present, baffled, grappled,
By each successive age insolvable, pass'd on
To ours today and we pass on the same...

I know I am deathless...

I laugh at what you call dissolution
And I know the amplitude of time.

---

6. Robert Louis Stevenson, *The Collected Poems of Robert Louis Stevenson*, ed. Janet Adam Smith (New York: Penguin Books, 2004), 178.

I pass death with the dying, and birth with the new-washed babe...and am not contained between my hat and boots.[7]

From Taps, played at military funerals:

Day is done, gone the sun
From the lake, from the hills, from the sky;
All is well, safely rest, God is nigh.[8]

We light a candle to honor a saint or a departed loved one because we associate the light of the candle with life. The Japanese put candles in little boats and let them drift in a stream as a remembrance of the spirits of the dead. As a child, I had nightmares about my mother dying. She adored me and I her. In my dreams, I would cry and, shedding bitter tears, say over and over, "I will light a candle for you, Mother. I will never forget you." She died when she was ninety-two years old. I will never forget her for as long as I live. May she rest in eternal peace and joy in the arms of Mary, mother of God.

All the above are fine sentiments and speculations, but they don't answer the fundamental question of how we can avoid death in the real world.

The probability of dying increases with each passing year of life after the age of ten. It is said that the life span of a human is three score and ten—the design life of a human body. After the age of seventy years, your survivability statistic comes to a precipice, and from that, you fall to your destruction after a few more years. At seventy-eight, I'm living on borrowed time. At my last Athens College prep school reunion in Greece at graduation, the oldest graduates walk down first the grand entrance stairway to the grounds, and the new graduates

---

7. Walt Whitman, "Song of Myself," *Leaves of Grass* (New York: Penguin Books, 2005), 77.
8. "Day is Done" a.k.a. "Taps," United States Armed Forces bugle call.

walk down last. It was a shock to me four years ago to see only a few old graduates ahead of me on the stairs. Death is as certain as that the sun will rise tomorrow. No living thing has an unlimited life span, not even olive and redwood trees, which may live for thousands of years.

Each biography has a year of birth and a year of death unless a person is still living; then, you get the year of birth and a dash, waiting to be filled in by historians. If the year or birth or death is not known, the writer places a question mark, but not that there is a question about whether the subject had a birth or a death. It is said that two things are certain in life: death and taxes. I say taxes you can avoid; join a tax-exempt religious commune. Or pool your resources and buy a homestead in a place with no property tax; produce most of what you consume and barter for whatever else you need. As to attaining immortality, forget it, but you will be defeating death in a way if you can overcome your fear of it, as I have done.

Francis Bacon again:

> Certainly, the contemplation of death, as the wages of sin, and passage to another world is holy and religious; but the fear of it, as a tribute due unto nature is weak . . . It is as natural to die, as to be born; and to a little infant, perhaps, the one is as painful as the other. He that dies in earnest pursuit is like one that is wounded in hot blood; who, for the time scarce feels the hurt; and therefore, a mind fixed and bent upon somewhat that is good, doth avert the dolors of death.[9]

Marcus Aurelius, Roman emperor and stoic philosopher, also proclaims death as a natural thing to be accepted with equanimity in his "Meditations." Natural also is the poisonous fang of a snake. I will not accept something simply because it's natural. Disease, poverty, cruelty, and war are natural too, but we are trying to cure these with all our might.

Let us, however, give death its due; without death, there would be

---

9. Francis Bacon, *The Essays*, ed. John Pitcher (London: Penguin Books, 1985), 92.

no evolution in living things, and we would not exist today as humans with all our marvelous faculties for reasoning, art, and creativity. Animals die to be replaced by more complex and adaptable species. New life forms replace the old as a newer generation of organisms replaces the old and tries new things and lifestyles. The soil itself that we prize for our crops was created by dying organisms. Without death, we would have on Earth living fossils piled high, instead of fossil fuels, fossils perpetually going through the same movements until the end of time. So, death is natural and necessary.

When death becomes necessary for me, how should I behave? Facing death, should I cry, panic, despair, quit doing what I usually do, such as my work, bow down, pray, wear a blinder, and deny the moment? No, it's best to go in style, with a smile, even laughter, because death should be laughed at; it's easily the biggest practical joke nature pulls on us.

Laughing while dying? That's a good death. A good death follows a good life: working well, adding something of value to the world without regrets or fear, and leaving this world to make room for new people.

What about the pain, perhaps the agony that often accompanies dying? A hospice service will make you comfortable with morphine. I like to think that I may be able to stay fully aware and alert near death, putting my last moment to good use for my work or for my family.

Still, I hate death because I love life and the world dearly. But I am not afraid of dying. I lost my fear of death when I became sixty-eight years old, that was ten years ago, and when I lost my mother at ninety-two and my father at one hundred years and seventeen days. I saw how quick and simple death really is; nothing about which to make a big fuss if you can avoid the heroic actions of physicians trying to extend your life further than its natural span. After my parents died in my care (I had looked after them for their last twenty years), I delved into all the major religions and engaged in deep meditation. I even wrote and published an earlier version of this book, but I did not become a true believer of any faith. I did acquire, however, a measure of inner peace and stability, which survived subsequent upheavals and disappointments in my life. Moreover, I got rid of all the fears I had experienced in my previous life: fear of flying, of crowds, of heights, of failure, and of death.

Animals fear death—for a good reason. They would not survive for long without this fear when predators approach, becoming easy prey. They run away instinctively from danger with all the energy and speed they can muster. One exception is the occasional curious cat. Only humans often place other values above their personal survival: freedom, honor, loved ones, friends, country, or their faith in God.

In 1999, the Egyptian pilot who terrifically crashed the EgyptAir plane near the coast of Massachusetts with 217 people on board kept calmly repeating (as he sent the plane into a nosedive): "Tawkalt: I rely on Allah."

Jesus, according to Luke 23:46, said upon dying for his faith on the cross: "Father, into thy hands I commit my Spirit."[10]

Patrick Henry declared at the Virginia Convention in 1775: "Is life so dear, a place so sweet, as to be purchased at the price of chains and slavery? Forbid it, Almighty God. I know not what course others may take, but as for me, give me liberty or give me death!"[11]

A soldier may throw himself on a grenade to save his buddies in a foxhole. Men and women have been known to fall in battle to do their duty and save their honor. A few soldiers, having misplaced their red badge of courage, turn their backs to the enemy and run. An old Greek poem says, "What an honor it is for a young man to die, first in the fire of battle for his country, sword in hand."[12]

Is my own lack of any fears a danger to my life? I think not. I still have concerns about dangers: disease, accident, loss of life and limb, and I reason my way out of predicaments, as a human being should be doing. Recently, I read in the news about a woman who had been fearful of many things, but after an injury to her brain, she lost all fear.

---

10. Luke 23:46 (NIV).
11. Patrick Henry, "Give Me Liberty or Give Me Death," *The Essential Writings and Speeches of Patrick Henry*, ed. Robert L. Heninger (New York: Penguin Books, 2007), 110-112.
12. Tyrtaeus, *The Fragments of Tyrtaeus: Text and Translation with an Introduction*, trans. Douglas E. Gerber (Leiden: Brill, 1999), 35.

Defeating Death

I wondered if that's what happened to me, but I have not suffered any brain injury or disease. I must have come to my fearlessness naturally or through my philosophy.

Some people are loath to face death without fear because their life's work is not done. I have accomplished much of what I set out to do in my life. What remains is to get the original ideas and ideals in my writings better known in the world beyond my family and friends. I am not contained between my hat and boots. I am not my body because, more than anything else, I am my ideas and ideals—and for as long as these continue to be cherished by some of my fellow humans, I continue to live. "My mind fixed and bent on something good, I avert the dolors of death."[13]

December 2010

On board the cruise ship Rotterdam,
    pursuing the Dean Ornish therapy for coronary blockage

---

13. Francis Bacon, *The Essays*, 92.

18

ON NON-REDUCTIVE PHYSICALISM

Physicalism is like the old school of materialism: all that exists is matter and energy as revealed to us by modern physics, known as monism—as opposed to dualism, which allows for the existence of mind or spirit. Non-reductive physicalism allows for properties that cannot be reduced to physical properties, properties such as mental states. Science is a powerful method that allows us to discover truths outside our minds in nature through observation, experiment, quantification, measurement, hypothesis testing, and duplication of results by peers. Science has led to a myriad of modern technological advances, which expand and preserve our lives. We experience, however, many individual instances of internal and subjective sense perceptions, known as qualia, which are different from the patterns we sense, such as the pixels in an image and the physical input to our minds. Such qualia or mental states form a class of objects that exist separately from material objects, leading us to non-reductive physicalism, a philosophy that is true, desirable, and beneficial to humans (humanistic) without denying the immense value of science.

Qualia have to do with consciousness, which cannot be explained reductively (with physical referents), using the scientific method. Yet we must deal with consciousness because it's part of living, and we cannot escape living except by dying. We should examine here the issue of consciousness without regard to the Freudian division of the mind into "conscious" and "subconscious" parts (the latter being by far the larger part of the mind). We want to consider all of living as consciousness, that part of which we're normally aware and that part which is usually below awareness.

To function effectively as thinking beings, we employ complex mental structures or concepts, such as the human will, which can have irreducibly non-physical properties and which enable us to act with volition and intentionality to achieve desired but not immediately obtainable results.

In such a process of thinking, introspection can reveal truths outside the realm of physical science. Sigmund Freud made important discoveries about the human mind through introspection of his own mind and the introspections of his patients. The discoveries of Eastern philosophers and those discoveries of mystics both in the East and West were also derived from introspection, looking inward. Mathematical objects, for example, the exponential, were discovered by pure thinking, not from observation, but they sometimes match observed phenomena. The Fibonacci series describes well many processes in nature, but it's a mental object. Mathematical objects sometimes are closely related to physical reality and become very useful. The Fourier series was a discovery that had no use until the development of electronics one hundred years after its formulation. Today, many physicists are working on the mental objects of strings to explain the nature of all material things, which strings may or may not exist physically because they have not so far been detected.

Another argument against strict physicalism is the case of the human artifact of an intelligent robot. If the robot talks to us just like a human being behind a screen, is it sentient, or is it a zombie? Robert Kirk argues that such a robot is a zombie without human feelings, simply imitating human speech to deceive us. The robot lacks intentionality or will, like an actor simply reciting a script. The robot has no concept of justice, what we consider fair, as we do.

The ancient Greeks believed that the world was imbued with

justice. In other words, it was ruled by laws that mortals and gods also had to obey. In our courts, we try to administer justice, to punish those who disobey the laws of the State. Justice is a mental construct, nowhere to be found in today's physics.

I am, however, deeply grateful to modern scientists who have dispelled harmful fantasies about nature. We no longer fear lightning, thanks to the lightning rod. Disease is not caused by evil spirits but by germs. A mentally ill person is not possessed by demons and punished (unless that person is found guilty of a crime and to be sane somehow). We don't ordinarily sacrifice our daughter to propitiate Poseidon for favorable winds. Our judicial systems still lag behind scientific knowledge. Any person committing a horrid crime out of anger, greed, jealousy, or religiosity is sick in the head, not possessed by an evil spirit, and should be given a sentence of treatment and isolation from society.

Unfortunately, science does not provide us with ethical guidelines; ethics has no part in the scientific method. We're told by science what works in nature and what does not, but we're not told what to do and how to do it.

We cannot forget also that science has limitations imposed by our cranial capacity and much more remains to be discovered about nature than we have discovered so far. "There are more things under heaven, Horatio, that have ever been dreamed of in your philosophy."[1] We cannot exclude the possibility that spiritual things exist, although these things may be different from the way they were imagined to be in the past. We cannot conclude that monism is valid based on what we have learned so far. Moreover, we cannot exclude the dualism of René Descartes or the triadism of Sir John Eccles, expecting that future science will uphold that view because we don't know the shape of future science.

With a sufficiently high intelligence and training in all sciences and mathematics, I can read the writings of any human, even Einstein's, and understand these writings to apply them in my life.

---

1. William Shakespeare, *Hamlet*, ed. Barbara A. Mowat and Paul Werstine (New York: Simon & Schuster, 2012), 1:5:167-168.

If an alien being, however, approaches me from outer space and communicates with me in English or mathematics, I'm probably not going to understand that being because it's likely far more complex and intelligent than I am. I would be like a dog listening to the master. We should be ready, then, to listen to other voices and obey, even if we don't completely get their meaning.

The arts are such voices: poetry, painting, dance, and music; their melodies are not measurable, not quantifiable, not physical, although the media are physical.

Similarly, some people say God is an experience outside of direct observation, but we can see signs of the unseen, the effects of something out there, like dark energy and dark matter.

Moreover, very rare events—call them miracles if you like—cannot be investigated with the scientific method because they're not controllable, and we cannot isolate them and observe them in the laboratory. The phenomenon of life itself may be one of these rare occurrences that we cannot duplicate, but it happened on Earth four billion years ago.

Non-reductive physicalism, in conclusion, is a philosophy that makes us human with all our feelings and intuitions, modest in the estimation of our capabilities, and hopeful. We may even indulge in a belief in spirits if they are benign. The placebo effect is well recognized in medical science, although it's not well understood. The placebo effect is, on average, 20 percent of the result in medical treatments, and a drug is discounted as impotent if that is all that it achieves. The placebo effect can be as high as 80 percent under certain circumstances, such as if the patient's belief is powerful and the doctor or nurse also believes in the efficacy of the treatment. Belief in the goodness of things is beneficial, just as it is harmful to believe in the evil of things, an effect known as the nocebo.

Now, I'll go so far as to say that faith in a compassionate and caring God and other benign spirits can be a lifesaver in some circumstances. Strong faith in God is the ultimate placebo, effective in the sense that it brings to the fore internal forces in us that can overcome disease, injury, and other ills and provide us with a miraculous cure, though that may be rare. We see these effects in AA meetings, drug rehabilitation centers, and other faith-healing groups.

It may be that the mind extends beyond our individual brain to other humans, as proposed by Rupert Sheldrake in his New-Age message, and that human beings possess more than physical attributes; they possess a vital force, elan vital, or the zoticon particle and wave, which connects us to other beings and to a Cosmic Mind.

19

THE FIFTH FORCE

Modern physics claims that four forces control everything that happens in our universe. These four forces are: first, gravitation, weak but extending to the end of space, pulling matter together; second, electromagnetism pushing objects around, strong but limited in range; third, the weak nuclear force binding electrons to the nucleus, forming the atom; fourth, the strong nuclear force, tightly bonding quarks into protons and neutrons, forming the nucleus. As a fifth force, some astrophysicists have postulated a mysterious "dark force," or "hypercharge," which accelerates the galaxies away from each other as the universe expands. I think that galaxies are dropping towards the origin of the universe under the force of gravity because space is curved. (If astronomers can measure the acceleration of expansion, they may find this acceleration is the gravitational constant g.) The fifth force in the universe is not hypercharge; it is life, more specifically, the source of all life, the light of mystics.

Why Call Life a Force?

What is life when we call it a force? In freezing weather, when water drops from the sky, the water turns to crystals of snow with magical designs, but lifeless. Using mostly carbon chains with other materials on Earth and electromagnetism, life forms DNA crystal structures—stable structures, growing, replicating, and defying entropy. Entropy is the tendency of physical systems towards greater disorder or chaos if left alone; it is the cause of failure, decay, and death of stars and atoms, known as the second law of thermodynamics in physics.

In thermodynamics, the change in entropy has a mathematical expression, which is the heat change in an isolated system from hotter to cooler divided by the absolute temperature of the system. The units of entropy are joules/Kelvin, the same as in Boltzmann's constant. Entropy itself can be expressed as Boltzmann's constant times the logarithm of the number of microstates observed in the system. Thus, entropy is a physical entity. On the other hand, communication theory defines entropy as a mental entity, the quantity of information in a message or system, calculated from state probabilities. We compute the entropy by adding the products of the probability of each state times the logarithm of the same probability over the space of all possible states. Taking the negative of this entropy, we get negentropy, in which the force of life tends to increase, according to Irwin Schrödinger, Nobel prize-winning physicist, in his little book *What Is Life?*

What is life, really? I respond, what is gravitation, really? We cannot know what is out there, really. We can only observe events with our limited senses, using the best instruments devised, dreaming up models to match our data, predicting the course of events, and sometimes controlling their outcome. As a force of nature, life acts on objects in certain ways, ways we can observe; can we quantify the effects of life acting and express the effects with mathematical equations? I think that will be exceedingly difficult, but it's worth trying to do as best as we can with mathematical tools already invented and to be invented. As Isaac Newton devised calculus to deal with what were in his time the mysteries of motion and gravity, we may think up new mathematics to explain the enigmas of life and mind.

An unimpeded apple drops towards the Earth when placed in the planet's gravitational field. A plane flies through the atmosphere, propelled by the electromagnetic field of jet engines. An embryo grows

The Fifth Force

and flourishes in the field of the life force. I have placed two apparently identical plants side by side in the same ground and given them equal care; sometimes, one thrives while the other dies. One was in life's field, the other not. I wish I could understand the life force well enough to save a plant or a child from dying prematurely.

Gravitation emanates from a massive object; how do we locate the source of life's field of force? If we can locate this source, we can place a living thing in the field and see it thrive with negentropy.

Thinking of life as a field of force causing negative entropy changes our search for causes and effects in nature. Scientists generally believe that living things are the result of the four forces of physics acting together at the microscopic and macroscopic levels to produce the rare event of a living thing on a planet with a suitable environment. That way of thinking may be at a dead end. In laboratories for many decades now, researchers have been duplicating the conditions on earth when life first emerged about three to billion years ago; they have succeeded in making complex amino acids, the precursors of life, but have not yet come close to producing a living organism of the simplest sort that grows and duplicates.

Also, for many decades, computer scientists have been designing increasingly complex programs for robots to simulate thought and other behaviors of living things, such as pattern recognition, planning, and deciding. Such computer behaviors are still mechanical, not displaying the adaptability of even simple animals. We are still a long way from getting HAL of Arthur C. Clark's 2001 epic. Something is missing from our calculations.

When we observe even tiny organisms under the microscope, we notice they behave differently from non-living systems. They behave with purpose, which is to absorb nutrients, grow, survive, replicate, and enjoy. The behavior of organisms can be predicted to some degree, but they never fail to surprise us, doing the unpredictable in pursuing their purpose.

Physics, chemistry, and computer science explain much about living things, but not all we need to know to understand how they work; some unknown element is missing; if you like, call it spirit. Biology, psychology, anthropology, sociology, economics, and political science all deal with organisms involving the mysterious life force; that is why all these sciences are less able to predict events than the sciences dealing with non-biological phenomena.

Yet, let us not become too mystical. When we observe a phenomenon that we cannot explain with our existing knowledge, we tend to imagine mysterious and divine forces at work. Ancient people thought lightning, thunder, droughts, and flooding were all the acts of gods. The gods, not poor hygiene, punished the ancients for their sins with plagues. Evil spirits took up residence in people, driving them insane, not chemical imbalances in the brains of the sick. A proper cure was exorcism, which Jesus used with the man called Legion.

I prefer a rational approach to problems; therefore, I imagine the existence of a life force.

Is Life Beyond Our Understanding?

The *Star Wars* epic of George Lucas often refers to "The Force" and "The Dark Side of the Force." I tend to think there is no dark side to the life force; objectively, it is the same thing. Speaking of life, Walt Whitman wrote, "I and this mystery here we stand."[1] Indeed, life is a mystery because we do not yet understand how it works. I like to solve mysteries, not to perpetuate them. No doubt, some things are beyond human understanding, but it is more profitable to focus on what we can figure out rather than on what we cannot. The process of living is something we are getting to understand and control with modern science. Once we know what causes life, we can answer other big questions, such as whether the spirit continues and has a place to inhabit after the body's dissolution.

If life is a force, it must accelerate something, changing the energy of a system. The kinetic energy of an object with mass is in the mass

---

1. Walt Whitman, "Song of Myself," *Leaves of Grass and Other Writings: A Norton Critical Edition*, ed. Sculley Bradley and Harold W. Blodgett (New York: W. W. Norton & Company, 1973), 51.

The Fifth Force

times the square of the velocity divided by two. When the kinetic energy stays level, the object is running with its momentum, but when the object accelerates, slows down, speeds up, or changes direction, we suppose that a force, such as electromagnetism, caused it to do so. Similarly, a change in the heat flow energy into or out of a system may decrease entropy; we say the life force caused this change. Alternately, the life force accelerates the flow of information into or out of a system. When we observe that information or negentropy accelerates in a system, we can conclude that the system is in life's field of force.

In plain words, when you throw a stick into a well and, after a minute or so, you hear a smack, you have witnessed the force of gravity at work. If what you hear is a yelp, however, and an angry digger emerges, you have seen an effect from the life force.

If we are monitoring the state of a living system, measuring the change in entropy at intervals, we may observe an acceleration of the entropy and note that the organism is dying because the life force is being withdrawn; similarly, when negentropy is accelerating, we note that the life force is being applied to the organism, causing it to grow and multiply. In matters of the mind, forgetting implies loss of information or negentropy, while learning indicates adaptation and growth, leading to a longer life of the brain because of the application of the life force.

Instinctual or conscious learning transforms the organism, enabling it to survive more effectively. Evolution is a form of learning that spans many generations. Birds learn to build better nests for their young in safer places, not as individuals but as a species. Social insects, such as bees and termites, evolved the institutions of the queen, drones, workers, and warriors over millions of years.

How We Feel Life

Subjectively, when the life force floods our mind, we experience joy, energy, and creativity; when the life force decreases in us, we become sluggish and sometimes depressed intellectually and emotionally. Religious people believe that God's grace shines upon them when they do well; His grace is not with them when they fail. But God shines on all of us all the time; therefore, when the divine light is not warming us, something in the way is impeding it. We don't know what this light is, but occasionally, we experience it and know its effect on growth and joy.

But the life force is not partial to us humans; with the force, we are on an equal footing as worms or mosquitoes, deserving no special dispensations. We are smarter, and if that is enough, our species will continue, perhaps for as long as four hundred million years, like the shark and the cockroach.

The Zoticon Particle

The life force is mediated by the zoticon, as electromagnetism is mediated by the photon. A photon behaves as a particle in some observations and as a wave in others. Larger particles have shorter wavelengths. It would be helpful to locate the zoticon and measure its wavelength, as it would be helpful to detect the graviton, which mediates gravity. We would understand better how the life force operates on materials, building organisms on Earth and on other planets, when conditions allow life, with the presence of water, right temperatures, pressures, soils, and atmospheres.

As a particle, the zoticon sets up a field of force, which promotes the acceleration of entropy in a system, such as an organism. A living thing is suspended in the force field of the zoticon, the field collapsing when the organism's end is near. When the organism dies, the zoticon escapes the body, going out to space at the speed of light to the origin of the universe. In religious terms, the organism's spirit returns to the Godhead. Nothing is lost; it just changes form. When the lion kills the zebra and consumes it, energy transfers to the predator, but the zoticon of the zebra escapes, eventually returning to animate another living form.

You may be saying, Now, this is all remarkably interesting, but how do I use the zoticon to do what I want? We know how to use photons to power our cars, planes, and aircraft, to produce electricity for thousands of different appliances and tools, and even to send rockets to the moon. We can even strip the electrons from atoms and hurtle the protons around the Large Hadron Collider to explore the subatomic world. But the zoticon is more like the graviton, also still undetected by physicists. The graviton builds up a field to infinity, strong close to a mass, rapidly becoming weaker away from the mass as the square of the distance. We can navigate with gravitation, put objects in the gravitational field to fall, and push objects up against the field to build up potential energy, but we cannot change it, neutralize it, or produce it.

Similarly, we cannot change, neutralize, or produce the zoticon field of force; we can only navigate through the field using our creative talents, designing, building, and disseminating worthwhile works. Hold on to your obsession of helping others; preserve the rain forests, defend endangered species, recycle everything, and don't pollute. We exist in a web of zoticons. When our zoticon spirit inhabits our bodies, we can contribute to the information available in the world, spreading knowledge, supporting life on the planet, and promoting the well-being of all spiritual beings.

Death and Transfiguration

Religious people believe that spirits cannot be destroyed, that they are immortal. Certainly, something in living things animates them. When your mother and father meet with death, their bodies quickly change into something quite different from the living persons they were. Something vital has been withdrawn from the bodies. Immediately after a plant or animal has died, it looks drastically different from a live one. A stabilizing force has left it as if a supporting column has failed, the body crashing, falling apart. This is as obvious an observation as of old when people saw Earth's curved horizon from a height but did not conceive that the planet was spherical. The stabilizing force is that of life.

The life force permeates nature, the same as gravity, acting in theory to infinite distances, spreading its effects far and wide in the universe. (God is immanent in the universe.) Art, beauty, and joy are all expressions of the life force. Plants pump water up to their stems, leaves, and flowers, greening the Earth with the energy of sunlight or geothermal sources because of the life force. Animals bounce around, charming us with their fluid motions as they forage, hunt, or run away from predators. Their bodies quickly decay when the life force has moved out of them.

Life is a spiritual force of immense but subtle power, directing the actions of plants and animals, spreading its wings from the dense jungles to the vast tundra and into the wide deserts. Matter and energy are absorbed and converted to living tissue. With the evolution of intelligence, organisms may spread throughout the universe, incorporating everything in one unified living whole, preventing the Big Crunch. In the meantime, when a plant or animal dies, life withdraws to a central source, from whence it beams out again to a different entity being born.

Life is an Organizing Force

Life moves things in all directions: up, down, and sideways. It fashions designs, reducing entropy or increasing information. A highly organized system holds more information and less entropy; it's self-organizing. Life is also an organizing force. Living systems build structures, reducing entropy in the world. We find these structures, these patterns of organization, in nature and in the arts of humans. Life is the essence of all fine arts, literature, painting, sculpture, dance, music, cooking, perfumery, architecture, and drama. We are thrilled to our life's core when we enjoy such arts or the splendors of nature. Even a painting made with a can dripping colors embodies design with order and organization, although it appears to be chaotic.

We prize new artistic expressions and innovations in design patterns because an unexpected event, an improbable event, carries more information, according to Claude Shannon's entropy formula. Profuse as it is now, life on this planet was an improbable event, and it is so in other parts of the universe. No other sphere in our solar system appears to allow for life, conditions for organisms on the surface of planets or satellites being anywhere from inhospitably cold as on Mars to hellishly hot as on Venus. Blue-white Earth is a rare jewel in space, harboring our kind of life and all its wonders.

No human can create such a jewel of fine art as the Earth, no matter how great the artist's talent or love for creation.

Talent and love are potent channels for the expression of the life force. Love is what we feel in life's field of force. Place living things (plants, animals, or people) in this field of love, and they thrive. We have seen the expression of the life force in the flowering of artistic geniuses like Wolfgang Amadeus Mozart, Vincent van Gogh, and Michelangelo. The life force creates order, yet artists often live and work in a messy environment; their private lives are often messy, too, with divorces, affairs, and mental instabilities. Why do we have this paradox of order within disorder with artists, creators of designs, melodies, harmonies, and symmetries? Artists crave chaos because chaotic situations stimulate them to create order in their chosen medium of expression. Artists ignore the messes they are in because they are possessed by love and lust in their inner world.

In all of us, love for mates, children, family, community, work, play, and the world drives the will to greater effort in designing, building, growing, and thriving. Love, our mammalian heritage, is the springboard for the life force.

Love and Hatred

But what can we say about hatred and anger? Are these the expressions of a death force? What rational explanation can we provide for what people call evil? Hatred and anger powerfully drive the will to destroy rather than build, thus increasing entropy in the world, at least for a while. But sometimes, the destruction of old structures is necessary to create new and improved forms. The dilapidated and unsafe building must be demolished for a shiny, new glass and steel skyscraper to go up. Forest fires are sometimes beneficial to the land, clearing old trees, controlling insects, and fertilizing the soil, so new and different growth may spring up. Thus, evil serves a good end. To be objective, we refrain from postulating the existence of a death force to explain unpleasant events. The withdrawal of life energy from organisms is the explanation for death and decay; these release materials to the world like fertilizers, which feed the next growth cycle to a finer bloom.

Death makes evolution possible; it allows for new orders of living things to emerge, organisms with superior equipment for survival. The death of the dinosaurs was necessary for the rise of mammals and humans.

When we contemplate the acts of vicious people, like the Mafiosi, pirates, serial killers, terrorists, and bloody dictators, we may think they are driven by the opposite of God, that is, Satan. Dualism is everywhere in nature: we have matter and antimatter, protons and antiprotons, electrons and positrons, night and day, summer and winter, health and illness, birth and death, creation and destruction, and good and evil. There is no anti-graviton, however, and there is no anti-zoticon.

Death is the absence of the life force; evil is the absence of goodness, as darkness is the absence of light. In an era of suicidal-homicidal maniacs, holding on to such beliefs is difficult but vital. As an enlightened person, reject fear, hatred, and anger. You can do better controlling such emotions using your intellect; of the emotions, The Beatles sang in the nineteen sixties, all you need is love.

20

WHAT TO DO ABOUT GAIA?

We have seen Earth from space, photos from satellites and from the moon, a blue-white marble of a living planet in the black background. A new consciousness of our planetary home has emerged in humankind, which some thinkers consider an integrated living system, striving for homeostasis, for stability, and for survival like any one of the tiny creatures that inhabit the soil, the sea, and the skies. Is such a conception of the entire Earth as a living creature valid? Does the whole Earth possess a form of consciousness and the will to live? People speak of the earth mother, Gaia, whom the Greeks imagined as a goddess dressed in magnificent clothing, the goddess of fertility, a caring mother for all living things, providing food for us, her children, grains, vegetables, and fruits. A nice image; not true, but appealing to those who love the Earth as I do.

As a child growing up in my lovely native land of Greece, I was fond of pastoral scenes and landscapes: the blue skies and seas, the green valleys and purple mountains, the golden sunrises and sunsets, and the wind swirling white clouds above. I loved the wild animals running or flying about, the fishes in the water I could see, and the domesticated animals in the fields grazing; they filled me with peace and contentment. As I continued life in America, I developed the same love for the wilderness and the countryside with its farms and pastures. I finally acquired a sizable piece of land for country living together with my brother, and we spent eighteen years on this land, planting an orchard, growing vegetable gardens, and keeping chickens, turkeys, and goats among the native gophers, snakes, cottontail rabbits, squirrels, and occasional visiting coyotes trying to get into the chicken coop and sometimes succeeding. That piece of land and comfortable home is now only a memory, sold after the passing of my brother, but a wonderful memory to hold on to, like my memory of Greece, my idyllic Arcadia.

Over the years in America, I transferred my love for Greece and my California farm to the planet as a home. I accepted the Earth as my mother when my human mother passed on, and I have become concerned about Earth's well-being as if it's a living entity. I am concerned about the destruction we humans are wreaking on our home planet (we have no other home at present). Planetary warming or climate change is well documented by earth scientists and widely ignored or disputed by many people. The many among the people, as Plato pointed out, don't tend to be well-informed or to possess critical thinking. I seek the opinions of the few who are smart and expert.

I don't need expert opinion, however, to see the damage we're doing with our constantly growing population and machines to the air we take into our lungs, the water we drink, and the soils where we grow our foods. I can see the trash we produce constantly accumulating in our dumps, the plastic in the seas, the smog and poisons in the air and waters. I witness the forest fires raging in my California and my Greece when I visit my country of birth in the summer.

During the decades of my life, I have seen in the US and in Greece with my own eyes, the destruction of animal habitats, rampant exploitation of land and forests, fisheries, and waters, the spoiling of such resources for ourselves and for our fellow creatures to satisfy our greed for more goods, many of these goods having little real value.

Still, much beauty and splendor remain on Earth in remote locations from the poles to the equator on land and sea, where humans have not settled in large numbers. I enjoy documentaries about such locations and the wildlife thriving but endangered, such as *Planet Earth*. In my imagination, I see myself surviving as a spirit after my passing and flying like an eagle from peak to peak on Earth, over green valleys and rivers, one with the Earth until its end.

Such imaginings are romantic nonsense, perhaps, as may be the notion known as the Gaia Hypothesis by James Lovelock and Lynn Margulis, scientists who in the 1970s proposed the hypothesis of Earth as a living entity comprising all living things on it, interacting with and controlling the inorganic parts of the globe. Gaia maintains the homeostasis or equilibrium of the planet with all organisms, large and small, so that life may thrive.

For example, early photosynthetic bacteria and plants absorbed much of the carbon dioxide from the early atmosphere and released oxygen which gave rise to the complex multicellular eukaryotic organisms, such as animals and humans. Other organisms in the oceans absorb minerals and maintain the salinity of water at a tolerable level.

An objection to the Gaia hypothesis is that it's an exaggerated teleological argument, endowing the planet with purpose, and thus it's not scientific. Yet the planet has gone through periods of extreme heat from volcanic eruptions and periods of global glaciation when it was frozen over, but life continued in sheltered areas of the ocean and land.

In case the Earth is looking after all living things, however, can we expect a homeostatic response to the planetary warming and other damage we're inflicting? Will Gaia seek revenge and subdue us humans who are disturbing her well-being? Gaia may not be conscious, but the ecological challenges will inevitably confront us if we continue in our destructive ways. We humans and our machines are too numerous for the Earth to sustain us in good health and we're overusing the resources of the planet to exhaustion. We're like lemmings marching to our demise.

As our pollution of the air, soil, and waters continues, we're increasingly unable to maintain a healthy environment for our children, and we succumb more easily to pathogens, viruses, and harmful bacteria, which are adapting to our antibiotics and other medicines. Eventually, a pandemic of infection is likely to emerge, which will thoroughly decimate our kind and limit our capacity to continue causing damage to the planet. Or we can elect to mend our ways and stop our destructive ways and live in harmony with Gaia and all her creatures for the balance of Gaia's days around the sun.

21

THE UNIVERSE OF PERFECTION

In his *Meditations*, Marcus Aurelius wrote, "Everything is but what your opinion makes it; and that opinion lies within yourself."[1]

I hold certain opinions about matter and spirit, which opinions shape my life profitably. I begin by imagining a universe where everything is perfect: all matter in it has taken the form of a tightly ordered crystal, which never changes. Being a crystal, such a universe would not be subject to the second law of thermodynamics: it would not move towards greater disorder. Energies flow inside the crystal structure in never-ending cycles sustaining the existence of vast numbers of spiritual beings, garnered from living planets everywhere. This is a universe of peace, tranquility, total security, and bliss.

The souls in such a heaven are linked together in a master mind, which sees to all their needs, immaterial as these needs are. Spirits in Heaven exist in perfect harmony with each other. Yet, sometimes, a soul will pine for living in a material world, with all its vibrant sensations, the risks and thrills of adventure. Then it is sent out to a planet outside the heavenly orb to experience material life once again and procreate

---

1. Marcus Aurelius, *Meditations*, trans. Gregory Hays (New York: Modern Library, 2002), 52.

new bodies into which spirits may enter. The connection of the soul to Heaven is never lost; after the death of the body, the soul returns to Heaven to enrich it with new experiences and bring new growth to the universal mind.

I choose to think I am such a soul. I am not my body but an imperishable spirit making its home in my body; my body is a possession, like my clothes, house, or car, to be discarded when worn out and not useful anymore and replaced by a new body—or no material body upon my return to Heaven. I can provide no scientific evidence for the existence of the crystal universe of Heaven or even for the existence of an immortal soul in me inhabiting my material body; I find it helpful in my life to think and feel it is so. I choose to feel I'm always tethered to Heaven, no matter what dangers threaten my body. I'm like a deep-sea diver or a space-walking astronaut with my lifeline to Heaven and companions above. I am a surveyor craft landed on this planet to collect data and sensations, transmitting these to my home in the crystal universe for my fellows there to experience.

I am confronting dangers in my adventures here, yet my soul is always safe from harm; if my body is destroyed, or when it dies of old age, God will withdraw my spirit through the umbilical cord connecting me to Heaven. I can experience my body aging, suffering injury, disease, and damage; if I cannot prevent these ills, I am not concerned. I seek help from above and continue my life on Earth as best as I can.

As I pass from moment to moment, I keep in mind that my spirit is priceless, being the immortal and important part of me, but my body, having evolved over billions of years through innumerable struggles and dangers, this body is also very valuable, deserving the best of care to survive long and well in order to serve the goals of my spirit.

Even when walking through the dark valley of death, I will not be afraid; my spirit is safe with God. If my body perishes, it will be a small loss compared to the safety of my spirit. Not that my spirit can be lost, but it may be barred from Heaven and go to a different place, a place of oppressive power, anger, and cruelty.

I remember in my daily efforts that my mission on Earth is justice, peace, compassion, knowledge, and wisdom. I focus on my mission: to experience many sensations, adventures, learning, arts, actions, and helping my own spiritual growth and that of family, friends, and community. To continue doing so, I also want to make my body as strong, healthy, and versatile as it can be for my age and constitution so I can cope with life's mountains and pitfalls.

How do these ideas of mine differ from religious teachings? They differ because I take them as conscious choices, assumptions, or definitions; no one can argue with definitions. The test of a definition is not its truth, because a definition is arbitrary, but its usefulness in solving a problem. I define spirit, God, and heaven as I choose because my definitions help me solve the problem of my existence and continued survival on Earth, even beyond this Earth.

Should I discover that one of my notions is a detriment rather than an aid in my life, I am ready to reject it, replacing it with a more effective notion. So does a physician when a particular medicine does not heal a patient; the physician tries a different prescription that may help, not harm the patient. This approach of mine is also very different from the various religious doctrines, which sometimes do harm, but are not erased from the scriptures by the patriarchs, except rarely. In this respect, my approach to spiritual matters is more scientific than religious, evolving when I meet with new facts and experiences and not becoming petrified.

The commandments to myself are not carved in stone; I prefer to change, adapting to new trials. I visualize my move before taking it, seeing the result in perfection, sensing that I am guided by a beam of light from above. I become keenly aware of my surroundings, my body and mind acting deliberately to do what is right, what is proper, what brings forth good fruit, and what is beautiful.

Beauty is indeed immortal, such as we find in great works of art. And my spirit is immortal, but can it change as artistic expression changes? Can my soul get better or worse? Yes, it can, just as character changes. The spirit aims towards perfection, which is not possible on

Earth or any other material planet, yet that goal of perfection is clear to me. I see that goal in what I think, feel, and do. I clearly visualize the perfect moves I need to make in any game I play. When I achieve that perfection occasionally, then I am in "the zone," as athletes say. I cannot fail in that state of mind but can only do what is right and successful.

Otherwise, what happens if my spirit changes for the worse? Can it go back to Heaven? I think admission back to Heaven would be barred; Heaven cannot allow an infected spirit to come back. That sick spirit needs to go through lives of purification, penance, and cleansing on other planets before being re-admitted to the crystal orb of perfection. Sometimes a soul goes so far astray that it cannot hope to enter Heaven anymore and is sucked into a sphere of evil, known as Hell, a place of grief, agony, and slavery.

My main effort in life is to avoid the whirlpool of Hell, to seek the updraft of Heaven, not just to prolong the use of my body or to enjoy the pleasures of the flesh. Yes, I want to prolong life to get the maximum mileage I can from this body in order to learn more things, experience fascinating adventures, and do good work for myself and my fellows. But when the time comes to go away from this sphere, I will leave without fear or regret, having done the best I could have done with the gift of life given to me.

I will have no regret upon dying but joy instead, looking forward to joining my beloved parents and friends who passed on before me. I will be eager to arrive in Heaven and be in the company of people who share my feelings and beliefs, congenial souls, those of Socrates, Plato, Aristotle, Jesus, the Buddha, Mohammad, Laotse, Descartes, Bacon, Shakespeare, Tolstoy, Gandhi, and Whitman, the souls which are brothers of my own. It will be great indeed to be talking to these people, remembering together our lives on Earth, discussing the ideas that intrigued us all during our lifetimes and the opinions laid down in our writings and talks.

Yet, what if I'm mistaken in hoping for the immortality of my spirit? In that case, my consciousness will dissipate in Earth's air upon my death as my body goes still and begins to decompose. There will be no harm done to me or to anyone else because I imagined a great existence in an afterlife. In the meantime, I enjoy romancing the soul; transcendent hope sustains me, filling me with meaning and purpose, moving me to good feelings, deeds, and accomplishments.

AFTERWORD
TREAD WATER ON PONTOONS

Ever since Jesus walked on water according to the gospel writers, people have been trying to imitate this feat with or without devices. Leonardo da Vinci designed pontoons for this purpose on paper, as he did for his flying machine, and Yoav Rosen holds US Patent #3783532 for water shoes he is proud to demonstrate on video. Water shoes are like ski shoes, which prevent sinking in soft snow. Some insects can sit or walk on water with the aid of surface tension, but the water strider has the advantage of a small body mass held up by tiny air bubbles trapped in its leg hairs.

We can only speculate on how Jesus walked on water. He's mentioned hardly at all by historians of his period, unlike Caesar Augustus—Jesus being, you see, unimportant. Josephus, the Jewish historian who turned to a Roman coat to survive, refers to Jesus and his followers in two brief passages. The "historical Jesus" are those events in the gospels we find credible. Followers of the prophet memorized events and speeches, as did the followers of Socrates, Buddha, and Mohammed; later, the gospel writers wrote these memories down, hardly following the example of Thucydides in *The History of the Peloponnesian War*, whose language they used.

The accuracy of memories is doubtful, especially when collected

Afterword

under the influence. Some scholars argue that Jesus never existed, and critics in this club also say Homer and Shakespeare were conjured by other writers. The same will be said about me someday, but now I want to show you how to tread water on pontoons, to delve into intuition and mysticism to advantage, without soaking or drowning.

On religion, I possess the faith of the water strider. In his essay "Mysticism and Logic," Bertrand Russell paraded the evils of mysticism and the virtues of logic. Also, in "Why I Am Not a Christian," Russell selected instances of Christian defects, such as the cursing of the fig tree by Jesus, to castigate the Christian faith. More recently, in *The God Delusion,* a bestselling book, Richard Dawkins, a noted British biologist and atheist, argued against religion of any sort, condemning religion because of its evolutionary faux pas.

Only a fool in delusion denies evolution shaped our bodies, but a bigger fool denies the existence of our spirits, which evolved more recently since civilization began ten thousand years or so ago. This book, *The God Connection,* may, for now, be ignored by the larger public, just as the observations of Galileo, the paintings of van Gogh, and the poems of Shelley or Whitman languished in obscurity for a time. It follows, logically, that my writings, since they have not, so far, been widely recognized for their eminence, will be much admired posthumously—lucky me.

Religion is neither bad nor good; its practice may be faulty, as the practice of any art or science. My bend is scientific rather than poetic. Formalized science is logical, organized, systematic, objective, and factual, as it should be. Science and technology in the making are none of these things. When we explore for new things in science and technology, we delve into mysticism: the unreal, the romantic, the realm of dreams.

Children are naturally good at exploring—becoming creative, playful, adventurous, and daring—having recently arrived from another universe. As we grow in our abilities and learn facts and theories discovered by others, we are at risk of losing our creative impulse and becoming scholars—experts in canned knowledge. On a journey to discovery, throw away your clothes, shed your skin, and even tread water on pontoons. Oh yes, you also face the risk of drowning, most unpleasant.

With my views on religion, I would find myself in a most unpleasant situation in another time or place, burned at the stake or mercifully locked up in an asylum. Arguing about the existence of God is amusing. God exists if you or I declare so, and we project our image of God to the world. If we deny God, we do away with the ideals associated with divinity. I have a God delusion; if I forget, God springs from within me, and I confuse the outer universe with my inner one. Most insanities are caused by such a confusion of feelings and thoughts with the material world outside.

It's insanity to argue about the substance of God once we have accepted that He exists. Is God a triad: the Father, the Son, and the Holy Spirit? I get belly laughs reading about wars waged in old Europe over this issue and whether the whole of religious truth lies only in the Bible or also in the writings of the Holy Fathers, the early bishops of the Christian Church. Muslims in Asia these days wage battles, one sect of Islam against another, Sunni against Shia, Shia and Sunni against Sufi and Sikh, derivatives of Islam and Hinduism, like the derivatives in financial markets, created instruments of faith. I have faith in what I think; otherwise, I might as well hang my head out to dry, but you will not find me amongst my enemies, those of different opinions, strapped with explosives other than my words.

I hold the opinion that God is good, that Allah is compassionate and merciful, that Zeus is powerful indeed, Athena wise, Aphrodite beautiful, Hephaestus industrious, Hermes fast, and Apollo gracious, such ideal beings possessing all the qualities I desire for myself and my fellow humans. What you believe is the Holy Truth; what I believe is a myth. Give me the power of the myth, anytime, but do not expect me to submit myself for martyrdom to defend my myth.

Chester Carlson believed in the myth of success and money, that they would give him happiness and fulfillment. An admirer of Thomas Edison, he believed as a young man that a major invention, like xerography, would benefit himself and others. A child of poor and sickly parents, he worked his way through school and earned a California

Afterword

Institute of Technology BS in physics in 1930. At work in Bell Labs, he found his job dull and was laid off in one year, so he studied law and became a patent attorney.

On the side, Carlson labored for years to develop xerography in his apartment and for more years to have it accepted for further refinement and marketing by a small maker of camera film, Haloid Corporation (many major corporations turned him down). Haloid became Xerox, making billions for investors and a large fortune for Carlson and his wife, Doris. This inventor dealt with myths as much as with science. He would not have achieved what he did, burdened with adversity, without the power of faith. Carlson, sickly with arthritis and overwork, died in a movie theater in 1968; he was sixty-two.

Before his death, Chester and Doris waded deep into the occult, sinking under dark waters; they also embraced Eastern religions with the enticing lure of reincarnation. Carlson endowed a chair for Ian Stevenson, psychiatrist MD at the University of Virginia for research in reincarnation. Stevenson worked on past life memories (regression), not with adults in hypnosis, but with children between ages two and four in a normal state of consciousness. What is a better source of evidence for past lives, babbling babies or dopey adults? Another source of information about the survival of the human personality comes from the memories of people who were clinically dead for a while and revived, memories reported as near-death experiences. That is evidence we can rely on, right? Give me a break.

Chester and Doris Carlson left their fortune to the Vedanta Center in Chicago, the Rochester Zen Center, and other charities.

I'm no Chester Carlson, endangering my health and longevity for money and success to leave my fortune to charity. I feel for the poor and unfortunate, but let them emulate Carlson a little and do for themselves what is necessary, for starters, by limiting the size of their families. Those among us who have been unfortunate do not need more money, but more training in the can-do attitudes of their fellow Americans, such as we have seen in some African American and Hispanic communities: pride is the key. Those escaping poverty will then become less apt to meet with misfortune in the future.

Afterword

The poor would get less poor if they worked harder, spent less money, saved, and quit smoking, liquor, junk food, and other vices. They will not move to do these things if they have enough help given to them by the rest of us. We need to leave the poor with a little less than enough help, as I do with my grown children.

As to Chester Carlson's belief in reincarnation, that was a delusion because he took the notion of a rebirth of the spirit too seriously. George Patton, the great American general of WWII fame, in his poem "Through a Glass, Darkly," depicts himself as the reincarnation of soldiers from the past, dying in battle and becoming reborn to die again in the future. Yes, we have many indications of something like reincarnation going on in the world, but I do not take the idea seriously until we have proof of the matter. I try not to take anything too seriously.

As a teenager, I became ambitious and serious, largely losing my childish playfulness. I was solemn until late in life when I decided that nothing in the universe is worthy of a totally serious look: neither taxes nor death, neither illness nor aging, neither poverty nor riches, neither disasters nor calm. The universe is indifferent to us, so I would be indifferent to it, no matter what it threw at me. Better still, I would try to poke fun at the world, its chanciness, caprice, idiocy, nonsense, and inevitable doom.

Scientists and prophets agree on doom. Your body and mine, our families, nation, planet, sun, and even the stars like diamonds in the sky, are all destined for the cosmic garbage dump. Scientists say nothing is left after the destruction of our bodies except chemical elements because scientists are well-trained in materialism. Prophets (and I) say that some things of inestimable value are spirited away to an ideal world without time or end because we are well-trained in optimism.

We can find more than doom, nonsense, and indifference in the world if we imagine virtue, beauty, and goodness and project these ideals outward with words and actions. Yes, Virginia, there is a Santa Claus. There is a God because divinity springs from our hearts out to the world and changes the world into becoming Heaven. I am not an atheist or a theist in the sense of any religion. Jehovah rules. Krishna is the fountain of life. Allah is Great, and Mohammed is His Prophet. Jesus is the Son of God. We are all of us children of God. All these beliefs are fine, but what we say and do next is the key to enlightenment.

Late in my life, I found enlightenment, illumination, epiphany—in my own way. Follow me. I have growing inside of me a bit of Heaven, the size of a mustard seed, barely sprouting but keeping me in peace and joy nearly all the time and nearly under all circumstances. I do not attach myself to any dogma about the afterlife because I have no fear of death or anything else. Fear does approach my house sometimes, but I do not allow fear inside. If fear has sneaked in, I pick up such a big stick, fear is out in no time. I do not, it follows, assume religion because of fear. I subscribe to no specific religion; I pick and choose those moral teachings in the expressions of all major philosophies, arts, literature, and religions that make sense to me.

Islam (maligned these days because of al-Qaeda), Judaism, Christianity, and Hinduism all have much in common because the source is the same: tribalism, perhaps, or a Supreme Being. Religions say their truths are revealed, not discovered. I accept revelation, wary of its limitations. The prophets were inspired, but there was much noise and interference in the transmission channel. Judging from what I read in the scriptures, ours and theirs, a message of a sort came to the prophets, but the static was bad. "Thou shalt not kill—whz, bzz, crck." "Love thy neighbor as thyself—st, wt, rp."

If you are a prophet, it's hard to make out the message, so you commit poetry. The Quran, great Arabic poetry, has no more offensive language and stories than the Bible I was taught. Offense lies in taking up arms against good people of a different religion and butchering them in the name of a compassionate and merciful God. Christians have shown no more mercy towards Muslims than Muslims toward Christians. Hindus (and Buddhists) are more to my liking, unless in India, they attack mosques, burning and killing their Indian brothers who pray to Allah.

Goethe said Mozart proved the existence of God. Mendelssohn, Gauss, Beethoven, van Gogh, and every great genius we have produced as a species supports the same thesis. Some musical passages, certain paintings, or a few scenes in nature are like glimpses into Heaven.

Atheists say these geniuses are simply the outcome of a rare and fortuitous combination of genes and influences. Think again, my friend, how rare genius would be that way, rarer than a dozen chimps pounding on keyboards and producing the works of Shakespeare—given sufficient time. Indications are that genius (a household deity to the Romans) enters some people when young and receptive to the source of it, whatever you want to call the source: God, Universal Intelligence, or Fountainhead, dear Ayn Rand.

Atheists argue against theists and the reverse, one side never persuading the other to change opinions. Theists were persuaded by parents, godparents, teachers, or members of the cloth that God exists and God is good; they stick to what they have been taught. Atheists almost invariably revolted against such persuasion when young and naturally rebellious after seeing the mistakes of the doctrine being stuffed into them or the errors of their organized religion, such as priests sexually molesting children. Bertrand Russell, as a young orphan, writes in his *Autobiography* about being raised by his pious grandparents in so heavy a religious atmosphere, such that he could not endure it. I argue against atheists and against theists, but mostly against idiocy and cruelty, whatever the source.

I approach my terminal station hopeful but rational; I reach the other shore, treading water on pontoons.

I preach and practice benevolence towards all who would do no harm to me or mine. I even forgive those who have damaged me but who cease and desist after I have forgiven them. If they do not, I turn my other side to them. God help them save their souls; their asses belong to me (as Warden Norton said to his prisoners in *The Shawshank Redemption*). I believe in self-defense, a universal right under the self-evident truth of justice.

I believe that freedom of body, mind, and spirit is more precious than life itself for me and my innocent fellow humans, an ideal worth fighting for.

Afterword

I believe, with Plato, that our worthy ideas, our ideals, are imperishable, remaining after us to guide others on the path of virtue.

I believe it is possible that everything in the universe is spiritual, nothing material. After all, matter is not that solid; particles are waves, and the opposite, as photons are electromagnetic waves, including light. The world we experience and know is Mind more than Matter, but as I'm not a Christian Scientist, put me down for a blood transfusion if I need it.

I believe nothing is lost in the universe; only recycled. Pollute not, but recycle everything as God recycles our spirits. Recycle everything we use on Earth, and Earth will be Paradise again.

BIBLIOGRAPHY

Anderson, Sherwood. *Winesburg, Ohio*. New York: Modern Library, 1947.

Augustine. *Confessions*. Translated by Henry Chadwick. Oxford: Oxford University Press, 1991.

Aurelius, Marcus. *Meditations*. Translated by Gregory Hays. New York: Modern Library, 2002.

Bhaktivedanta Swami Prabhupada, A. C. *Bhagavad-Gita As It Is*. Los Angeles: Bhaktivedanta Book Trust, 1983.

Benson, Herbert. *The Relaxation Response*. New York: Avon Books, 1975.

Blake, William. *The Complete Poetry and Prose of William Blake*. Edited by David V. Erdman. New York: Anchor Books, 1988.

Bodhidharma. *The Zen Teaching of Bodhidharma*. Translated by Red Pine. Port Townsend, WA: Empty Bowl, 1987.

Capra, Fritjof. *The Tao of Physics*. New York: Bantam Books, 1977.

Castaneda, Carlos. *Journey to Ixtlan*. New York: Washington Square Press, 1972.

Churchill, Winston S. *The Second World War: Volume 1: The Gathering Storm*. Boston: Houghton Mifflin, 1948.

Confucius. *The Analects*. Translated by D. C. Lau. London: Penguin Books, 1979.

Dass, Ram. *Journey of Awakening*. New York: Bantam Books, 1978.

Davies, Paul. *The Mind of God*. New York: Simon and Schuster, 1992.

Dawood, N. J., trans. *Quran*. London: Penguin Books, 1956.

Descartes, René. *Meditations on First Philosophy*. Translated by John Cottingham. Cambridge: Cambridge University Press, 1986.

Easwaran, Eknath, ed. *The Dhammapada*. Tomales: Nilgiri Press, 1995.

Eckhart, Meister. *Selected Writings*. Translated by Oliver Davies. London: Penguin Books, 1994.

Eckhart, Meister. *The Essential Sermons*. Translated and edited by Bernard McGinn. Mahwah, NJ: Paulist Press, 1981.

Eckhart, Meister. *The Complete Mystical Works of Meister Eckhart*. Translated and edited by Maurice O'C. Walshe. New York: Crossroad Publishing Company, 2009.

Emerson, Ralph Waldo. *Essays: Second Series*. New York: AMS Press, 1968.

Englebert, Omer. *St. Francis of Assisi: A Biography*. Ann Arbor: Servant Books, 1965.

Frankl, Viktor E. *Man's Search for Meaning*. New York: Washington Square Press, 1959.

Franklin, Benjamin. *Poor Richard's Almanack*. Mount Vernon: Peter Pauper Press, 2003.

Freud, Sigmund. *A General Introduction to Psychoanalysis*. Garden City: Garden City Publishing, 1943.

Frost, Robert. *Selected Poems of Robert Frost*. New York: Barnes and Noble Books, 1993.

Frost, Robert. *The Road Not Taken: A Selection of Robert Frost's Poems*. Edited by Louis Untermeyer. New York: Henry Holt and Company, 2019.

Bibliography

Gascoigne, Bamber. *The Christians*. New York: William Morrow & Co. 1977.
Gardner, Gerald. *High Magic's Aid*. Godolphin House, 1949.
Gawain, Shakti. *Creative Visualization: Use the Power of Your Imagination to Create What You Want in Your Life*. Novato, CA: New World Library, 2002.
Goethe, Johann Wolfgang von. *Selected Poems*. Translated by David Luke. New York: Penguin Classics, 2005.
Greeley, Horace. "Go West Young Man." Editorial. *New York Tribune*, 1865.
Hawking, Stephen. *A Brief History of Time*. New York: Bantam Books, 1988.
Hesse, Hermann. *Siddhartha*. New York: New Directions, 1951.
Hill, Napoleon. *Outwitting the Devil: The Secret to Freedom and Success*. Edited by Sharon Lechter. New York: Sterling, 2011.
Hubbard, L. Ron. *Dianetics*. Los Angeles: Bridge Publications, 1992.
Hull, William. *Memoirs of the American Revolution: So Far as It Related to the States of North and South Carolina and Georgia*. New York: Samuel Campbell, 1811.
James, William. *The Varieties of Religious Experience*. New York: Longmans, Green & Co., 1935.
Keats, John. *The Letters of John Keats*. Edited by Maurice Buxton Forman. Oxford: Oxford University Press, 2011.
Kershaw, Ian. *The End: The Defiance and Destruction of Hitler's Germany, 1944-1945*. New York: Penguin Press, 2011.
Khayyam, Omar. *The Rubaiyat of Omar Khayyam*. Translated by Edward FitzGerald. 1979 Reprint Collins Sherriffs Edition. London and Glasgow: Collins Clear-Type Press, 1979.
Khayyam, Omar. *The Rubáiyát of Omar Khayyám: A Critical Edition*. Translated by Edward FitzGerald, edited by Christopher Decker. Charlottesville: University of Virginia Press, 2008.
Kopp, Sheldon, B. *Guru: Metaphors from a Psychotherapist*. New York: Bantam Books, 1976.
Krishnamurti, Jiddu. *The Book of Life*. San Francisco: HarperCollins, 1995.
LeShan, Lawrence. *How to Meditate: A Guide to Self-Discovery*. New York: Bantam Books, 1974.
Laotse. *Tao Te Ching*. Translated by Gia-fu Feng and Jane English. New York: Vintage Books, 1972.
Laotse. *Tao Te Ching*. Translated by James Legge. New York: Dover Publications, 1997.
Laotse. *Tao Te Ching*. Translated by Stephen Mitchell. New York: Harper & Row, 1988.
Laotse. *Tao Te Ching*. Translated by Jonathan Star. New York: TarcherPerigee, 2001.
Laotse. *The Wisdom of Laotse*. Translated by Lin Yutang. New York: Modern Library, 1949.
LaVey, Anton Szandor. *The Satanic Bible*. New York: Avon Books, 1969.
Leary, Timothy. *Flashbacks: A Personal and Cultural History of an Era*. New York: G.P. Putnam's Sons, 1983.
Lewis, C. S. *The Screwtape Letters*. New York: MacMillan Publishing, 1974.
Lubrecht, Peter T. *Carl Schurz: German-American Statesman: My Country Right or Wrong*. Mount Pleasant, SC: Arcadia Publishing, 2019.

Bibliography

Maltz, Maxwell. *Psycho-Cybernetics*. Englewood Cliffs: Prentice-Hall, 1960.

Masters, Robert, and Jean Houston. *The Varieties of Psychedelic Experience: The Classic Guide to the Effects of LSD on the Human Psyche*. New York: Dell Publishing, 1966.

Nietzsche, Friedrich. *Twilight of the Idols*. Translated by Duncan Large. Oxford: Oxford University Press, 1998.

Plato. *Apology*. Translated by G. M. A. Grube. Indianapolis: Hackett Publishing Company, 2000.

Plato. *Apology*. Translated by Benjamin Jowett. New York: Dover Publications, 2002.

Plato. *Phaedo*. Translated by Eva Brann, Peter Kalkavage, and Eric Salem. Newburyport, MA: Focus Philosophical Library, 1998.

Plato. *Phaedo*. Translated by G.M.A. Grube. Indianapolis: Hackett Publishing Company, 2002.

Plato. *Phaedo*. Translated by Benjamin Jowett. Oxford: Clarendon Press, 1892.

Pliny the Younger. *The Letters of the Younger Pliny*. Translated by Betty Radice. London: Penguin Classics, 1969.

Robbins, Rossell H. *The Encyclopedia of Witchcraft and Demonology*. New York: Crown Publishers, 1959.

Roosevelt, Franklin D. *The Public Papers and Addresses of Franklin D. Roosevelt: Vol. 2, The Year of Crisis 1933*. Edited by Samuel I. Rosenman. New York: Random House, 1938.

Rumi, Jalaluddin. *Signs of the Unseen: The Discourses of Jalaluddin Rumi*. Translated by W. M. Thackston. Putney: Threshold Books, 1994.

Russell, Bertrand. *An Outline of Philosophy*. New York: Routledge, 2009.

Schrödinger, Erwin. *What is Life?* Cambridge: Cambridge University Press, 1967.

Scott, William Anderson. *Daniel a Model for Young Men*. New York: Carlton & Phillips, 1854.

Selye, Hans. *The Stress of Life*. New York: McGraw-Hill, 1956.

Shakespeare, William. *As You Like It*. Edited by Barbara A. Mowat and Paul Werstine. Folger Shakespeare Library. New York: Simon & Schuster, 2004.

Shakespeare, William. *Hamlet*. Edited by Barbara A. Mowat and Paul Werstine. New York: Simon & Schuster, 2012.

Shakespeare, William. *Julius Caesar*. Edited by Barbara A. Mowat and Paul Werstine. New York: Simon & Schuster, 2009.

Shakespeare, William. *The Tempest*. Edited by Barbara A. Mowat and Paul Werstine. New York: Simon & Schuster, 2009.

Shannon, C. E. "The Mathematical Theory of Communication." Bell System Technical Journal 27, no. 3 (1948): 623-56.

Shelley, Percy Bysshe. *Shelley's Poetry and Prose*. Edited by Donald H. Reiman and Neil Fraistat. New York: Norton, 2002.

Smith, Huston. *The World's Religions: Our Great Wisdom Traditions*. San Francisco: HarperOne, 1991.

Soule, John Babsone Lane. "Go West Young Man." Editorial. *Terre Haute Express*, 1851.

Suzuki, Shunryu. *Zen Mind, Beginner's Mind*. New York: Weatherhill, 1970.

Tacitus. *The Annals*. Translated by A. J. Woodman. Indianapolis: Hackett Publishing Company, 2004.

Bibliography

Thoreau, Henry David. *Walden*. Edited by Bill McKibben. Boston: Beacon Press, 2004.

Viereck, George Sylvester. "What Life Means to Einstein: An Interview by George Sylvester Viereck." *Saturday Evening Post*, October 26, 1929.

Voltaire. *Candide*. Translated by Theo Cuffe. Oxford: Oxford University Press, 2008.

Watts, Alan. *The Way of Zen*. New York: Pantheon, 1957.

Wilson, A. N. *Paul: The Mind of the Apostle*. New York: W.W. Norton Company, 1997.

Whitehead, Alfred North. *Process and Reality: An Essay in Cosmology*. Corrected Edition. Edited by David Ray Griffin and Donald W. Sherburne. New York: Free Press, 1978.

Whitman, Walt. *Leaves of Grass*. New York: Penguin Books, 1959.

Whitman, Walt. *Leaves of Grass: The Death-Bed Edition*. New York: Modern Library, 2005.

Whitman, Walt. *Leaves of Grass*. Edited by Sculley Bradley and Harold W. Blodgett. New York: W.W. Norton & Company, 1980.

Zilbergeld, Bernie, and Arnold Lazarus. *Mind Power: Getting What You Want Through Mental Training*. New York: Ivy Books, 1987.

Zhuangzi. *The Complete Works of Zhuangzi*. Translated by Burton Watson. New York: Columbia University Press, 1968.

ABOUT THE AUTHOR

Basil E. Gala was born in Corfu, Greece, and educated at Athens College, a Greek-American preparatory school. At Athens College, he was an honor student and winner of the Delta prize for public speaking; also he edited the school newspaper and magazine. Upon graduation, he immigrated to the United States and earned a master's degree in engineering science from the California Institute of Technology and a PhD in electrical engineering from the University of Southern California.

He worked as an aerospace engineer and university professor until his retirement.

Holden-Day published Dr. Gala's computer text *The Computation of Probability* in 1973. In 2002, New Vistas Media published the first edition of *The God Connection*.

Dr. Gala has two grown daughters and lives in rural San Diego County, California.

INDEX

A

Acropolis, 197, 262, 330
Alexander the Great, 4, 68, 98, 113, 121, 228, 259, 263
Ali Pasha, 133
alien intelligence, 307
Allah, 4, 47, 77-79, 92, 117, 126, 130, 152, 395, 430, 459, 462
angels, 5, 30, 40, 47-49, 52, 72, 77-78, 125, 129-130, 155, 170, 295, 345-346
Aphrodite, 65, 68, 192, 459
Archangel Gabriel, 47-48, 77, 130, 263, 379
Archimedes, 34, 64, 97, 265, 323-324, 339
art, 142, 378, 394, 413, 443
Asahara, Shoko, 4, 134-135
atheist, 13, 14, 16, 252, 412, 458, 461
Aum Shinri Kyo, 4, 134
Aztec priests, 145, 153

B

Bacchanalia, 143, 155, 193
Bacon, Francis, 6, 22, 55, 331, 428, 431, 454
Berkowitz, David, 150
Bible, 21, 73, 83, 173, 188, 195, 211, 336, 459
Big Bang, 63, 116, 176, 293, 295, 424
Bodhidharma, 86, 110, 113
Bonaparte, Napoleon, 4, 16, 113, 122, 167, 228-229, 259, 263, 282
Bosch, Hieronymus, 162
Brahma, 56, 80, 235, 288
Branch Davidians, 133
Brief History of Time, 175-176, 293
Buddha, 4, 19, 42, 54, 62, 74, 80-81, 89-90, 100, 128-129, 145, 160, 175, 183, 195, 199-200, 202, 203, 227, 232, 234-236, 245, 253, 270, 281-282, 291, 294, 317, 321, 332, 374, 408, 414, 423, 454, 457
Buddhism, 53, 54, 83, 86, 89-91, 110, 113, 134, 235, 268, 334, 353
Byzantine Empire, 111, 136, 334

C

Calvin, John, 141-142
Carnegie, Andrew, 230, 246-247, 297, 311
central processing unit, 8, 44, 264
Castaneda, Carlos, 46, 104, 274-276, 413
Chamberlain, Neville, 148
Chopra, Deepak, 88, 361
Christ, Jesus, 3-5, 19, 26, 34, 38-40, 42, 45, 48, 54, 55, 59, 60-62, 67, 71, 72-77, 80-81, 83, 85, 90, 93, 95, 101, 104-108, 109, 110, 118-119, 120-121, 123-124, 126-127, 130, 139-141, 143, 145, 149, 153-155, 161, 164-165, 170, 175, 183, 186, 195-197, 200, 203, 210-211, 219, 227, 232-36, 241-243, 248, 251, 253, 262-264, 267, 269, 270, 281-282, 284, 293, 296, 300, 311, 313, 317, 321-322, 332, 349, 364, 374, 379, 380, 386-387, 408, 425, 430, 440, 454, 457-458, 462
Christianity, 11-12, 14, 53, 54, 71, 73, 76, 79, 85, 88, 106, 112, 118, 137-138, 140-141, 214, 228, 284, 300, 311, 342, 425, 462
Churchill, Winston, 55, 68, 164, 183, 230
computer, 6, 29, 33, 41, 44, 68, 184-185, 298, 372, 419, 420, 439
computer program, 6, 29, 63, 102, 118, 122, 159, 162
Confucius, 21-22, 83, 234, 321
Constantine, 19, 71, 76, 111, 118, 138, 284
Constantinople, 92, 111, 136, 334
cosmic, 6-7, 9-10, 56, 63, 84, 91, 170, 172, 201, 229, 284, 286-287, 335, 387, 410-411, 424, 461
cosmic connection, 10, 284
cosmic consciousness, 167, 169
Cosmic Mind, 6-7, 9-10, 22, 56, 89, 103, 117, 145, 204, 227, 230, 415, 436
cosmos, 30, 56, 103, 156, 184, 286, 288-290, 294
creation, 64, 80, 85, 89, 97, 155, 183, 187, 189, 197, 246, 270, 280, 286, 288, 322, 380, 445, 446
creator, 17, 18, 23, 34, 61, 63, 77-78, 111, 128, 169, 175, 177, 219, 282, 288, 322, 336, 393
Cronus, 65
crucifixion, 71, 75, 123-124, 236, 364
Crusades, 125, 135-137
crystal universe, 162-163, 177, 452
cult, 17, 91, 118, 132, 133-135, 150, 154

D

Darwin, Charles, 31, 54, 128
DeLorean, 57
demagogue, 111, 260, 410
Demiurge, 288
Democritus, 339, 409
demons, 40, 149, 151, 155, 243, 253, 346, 434
Descartes, René, 2, 6-7, 9, 22-23, 54, 115, 252, 317, 322, 331, 385, 400, 416, 434, 454
Dewey, John 25-26

Index

dharma, 30, 81-82, 230
Di Mambro, Joseph, 134
diaspora, 70
Divine Comedy, 157
divine order, 171
divine source, 32, 71, 75, 82, 163, 259, 272, 298, 380, 423
Dome of the Rock, 136
Donne, John, 169, 373-374, 417, 425
dreams, 5, 8, 39, 43-46, 114, 169, 255, 265-266, 277, 305, 396, 414, 421, 458
dryads, 35

E

Earth, 3, 6, 8, 20, 29, 31, 35-38, 40, 45, 49, 56, 62-63, 65, 67, 70-71, 78, 83, 103, 107, 109, 125, 127, 148, 161, 165, 170-177, 184-185, 190-192, 195, 197-198, 202, 219, 225, 241, 245-246, 249-250, 279, 283, 287, 289, 295-297, 303-305, 313-314, 319-320, 323-324, 383-384, 402-403, 435, 438, 442, 445, 447-449, 453-454, 464
Ecclesiastes, 246
Eckhart, Meister, 117, 120-121, 280-281
Eddy, Mary Baker, 161, 212, 244
Einstein, Albert, 34, 45, 48, 54, 68, 97, 103, 219, 232, 294-295, 318, 327, 329, 339-340, 356, 404, 409
Emerson, Ralph Waldo, 24-25, 68, 85, 410, 416,
evil empire, 153, 157, 174

F

Final Judgment, 173,
Fox, George, 12, 129
Fourier, 116-117, 290, 433
Franciscans, 120, 140-141
Freud, Sigmund, 2, 8-9, 14, 16-17, 44, 54, 150, 253-254, 268, 280, 412, 433

G

Gaia, 36, 447-450
Gautama, Siddhartha, 54, 80-81, 129, 160, 170, 199-200, 353
Grand Army, 167, 229
Great Depression, 165, 381
great spirit, 5, 32, 61, 67, 143, 175, 224, 317
gulag, 135, 138
Guyana, 4, 132-133

H

hallucinations, 16, 72, 129, 145, 203, 267, 277-278
Hamlet, 39, 246, 414
Heaven's Gate, 133-134, 154
higher reality, 160, 282
Hill, Napoleon, 55, 172, 297, 299, 390
Holy Ghost, 33, 38-39, 108, 126, 301,
Holy Spirit, 39, 48, 58-59, 74, 91, 108, 113, 143, 195, 210, 219, 296, 459
Holy Synod, 112
hypertension, 257
hypnosis, 16, 158, 180-182, 254, 258-262, 350, 460
hypometabolic state, 258

I

intellectual property, 240
Islam, 47, 54, 61, 66, 69, 71, 76-79, 112, 126, 136, 138, 145, 155, 210, 312, 332, 459, 462

J

Jack the Ripper, 173
Jehovah, 5, 70-72, 222, 395, 461
Jerusalem, 45, 75, 108, 124, 136
Jesus Christ. *See* Christ, Jesus
Joan of Arc, 130
Judaism, 54, 71, 79, 118, 138, 155, 462
Judgment Day, 5, 25, 78, 171-173

K

Kashmir, 135
Khomeini, Ruhollah, 138, 156
King Jr., Martin Luther, 237, 296
koan, 88
Koresh, David, 4, 133, 282
Krishna, 4, 128, 155, 203, 248, 461

L

Laotse, 83-86, 99, 145, 170, 189, 233-234, 282, 317, 354, 454
Leary, Timothy, 144, 274
Lecter, Hannibal, 150
Leda, 48

Index

Lourdes, 130
Luther, Martin, 141

M

Maharishi Mahesh Yogi, 256
marijuana, 143-144
masochism, 128
Mendelssohn, Felix, 9, 45, 232, 263, 462
messiah, 5, 11, 45, 48, 57, 62, 74, 93, 100-101, 121-123, 133, 137-139
Mohammad, 4, 19, 42, 47, 54, 61-62, 67, 71, 76-81, 107, 110, 130, 145, 161, 164, 170, 175, 183, 196, 267, 281-282, 294, 296, 301, 317, 320-321, 332, 336, 374, 379, 408, 454, 457, 462
Moses, 4-5, 45, 54, 61-62, 70-73, 77, 81, 95, 107-108, 123, 139, 145, 147, 164, 222, 229, 240, 278, 281-282, 296, 310, 332, 374
Mount Sinai, 72, 81, 95, 139, 147, 222, 374
mystics, 13, 25, 50-51, 69-70, 79, 83, 117, 120-121, 123, 131, 167, 171, 177-178, 207, 246, 267, 270, 273, 279, 281-282, 286, 290, 296, 303, 307, 319, 321, 387, 433, 437

N

nuclear holocaust, 148
Nuremberg, 137

O

Order of the Solar Temple, 134
Ottoman Empire, 112, 133

P

Parthenon, 197, 248, 330
Patton, George, 263, 461
People's Temple, 132
peyote, 143, 145, 275
philanthropy, 247
Pilate, Pontius, 140
Pliny the Younger, 140
Pritikin, Nathan, 243
psychoactive, 17, 142-145, 275-276, 321, 413
psychotherapy, 17, 150, 253-256, 260
Purgatory, 38, 141, 175, 178, 293
purification, 164, 454

Q

quantum mechanics, 116, 289, 303, 327-328, 339, 405
quantum physics, 40, 329

R

religiosity, 129, 131, 434
resurrection of the spirit, 165
roshi, 88, 96
Rumi, Jalaluddin, 69, 79, 281

S

Sabbath, 155, 222, 224
Saladin, 136
Satan, 47, 69, 73, 115, 125, 133, 141, 149-157, 163, 181, 184-186, 203, 227, 244, 267, 279, 289-290, 307, 320, 446
satanic universe, 156
satori, 62, 88, 268, 282
Shelley, Percy Bysshe, 9, 68, 91, 246, 263, 458
Shinto, 30
Solomon, 73, 240
Souli, 133
St. Dominic, 141
St. Francis of Assisi, 117, 119-120, 129, 140-141, 164, 238
Stalin, Joseph, 3, 137-138, 173, 230, 237, 346
Stalingrad, 138
Sufis, 69, 79, 160, 272, 281, 459
swami, 99, 101
swastika, 137, 261

T

Tchaikovsky, Pyotr, 130-131
Theodosius I, 140
theologian, 120, 138, 141
Third Reich, 108, 137, 156, 229
Tiberius, 140

U

universe of evil, 163
Upanishads, 53, 58-59, 157, 168, 228, 266, 277, 347, 417

Index

V

Varieties of Psychedelic Experience, 144
Viet Nam, 146, 300

W

Whitman, Walt, 5, 24-25, 68, 85, 91, 168, 189, 191, 208-209, 211, 410, 415, 426-427, 440, 454, 458

Y

yang, 83, 189, 192, 197
yin, 83, 189, 192, 197
Young, Brigham, 107

Z

Zen, 86-91, 99, 110, 113-114, 120, 145, 207-210, 268, 270, 277-278, 353-354, 460
Zhuangzi, 83-84, 234

Milton Keynes UK
Ingram Content Group UK Ltd.
UKHW031618231124
451036UK00004B/60